"*The Rise and Triumph of the Modern Self* is perhaps the most significant analysis and evaluation of Western culture written by a Protestant during the past fifty years. If you want to understand the social, cultural, and political convulsions we are now experiencing, buy this book, and read it for all it is worth. Highly recommended."

    Bruce Riley Ashford, Professor of Theology and Culture, Southeastern Baptist
    Theological Seminary; coauthor, *The Gospel of Our King*

"Carl Trueman has a rare gift for fusing the deep social insights of a Philip Rieff, a Christopher Lasch, or an Augusto Del Noce with a vital Christian faith and marvelously engaging style. Psalm 8 names the central question of every age, including our own: 'What is man?' In explaining the development of the modern self and the challenges it poses to human identity and happiness, Trueman makes sense of a fragmenting world. This book is essential reading for anyone concerned for sustaining the Christian faith in a rapidly changing culture."

    Charles J. Chaput, Archbishop Emeritus of Philadelphia

"This is a characteristically brilliant book by Carl Trueman, helping the church understand why people believe that sexual difference is a matter of psychological choice. Indeed, Trueman shows how the story we tell ourselves about normalized LGBTQ+ values is false and foolish. With wisdom and clarity, Trueman guides readers through the work of Charles Taylor, Philip Rieff, British Romantic poets, and Continental philosophers to trace the history of expressive individualism from the eighteenth century to the present. The rejection of *mimesis* (finding excellence by imitating something greater than yourself) for *poiesis* (finding authenticity by inventing yourself on your own terms), in addition to the Romantic movement's welding of sexual expression as a building block of political liberation, ushers in the modern LGBTQ+ movement as if on cue. This book reveals how important it is for thinking Christians to distinguish virtue from virtue signaling. The former makes you brave; the latter renders you a man pleaser, which is a hard line to toe in a world where there are so few real men left to please."

    Rosaria Butterfield, Former Professor of English, Syracuse University; author,
    The Gospel Comes with a House Key

"Moderns, especially Christian moderns, wonder how our society arrived at this strange moment when nearly everything about the self and sexuality that our grandparents believed is ridiculed. This genealogy of culture, clearly and elegantly written, will help all of us understand how we got to where we are, so that we can plot our own futures with more clarity and confidence. This book is a must-read for Christians and all others who are disturbed by the dictatorship of relativism that surrounds us."

    Gerald R. McDermott, Former Anglican Chair of Divinity, Beeson Divinity School

"Carl Trueman is a superb teacher. Sharp, perceptive, and lucid, this book is the worthy fruit of learnedness and insight. But more than a teacher, Trueman also has the voice of a prophet. He speaks truth masterfully, with power. In bringing clarity on how we got to our present desert wilderness as a culture, Trueman helps us understand our crooked ways—and situates us to make straight the way of the Lord."

    Adeline A. Allen, Associate Professor of Law, Trinity Law School

"This is an amazing piece of work. Blending social commentary with an insightful history of ideas as well as keen philosophical and theological analyses, Carl Trueman has given us what is undoubtedly the most accessible and informed account of the modern self and how it has shaped and informed the cultural battles of the first quarter of the twenty-first century. It is a fair-minded, carefully wrought diagnosis of what ails our present age. This book is essential reading for all serious religious believers who rightly sense that the ground is shifting underneath their feet, that the missionaries for the modern self are not content with simply allowing believers to practice their faith in peace but see these believers and their institutions as targets for colonization and involuntary assimilation. For this reason, every president of a faith-based college or university should read *The Rise and Triumph of the Modern Self* more than once."

Francis J. Beckwith, Professor of Philosophy and Church-State Studies and Associate Director of the Graduate Program in Philosophy, Baylor University

"Those looking for a light read that provides escape from the cares of the world will not find *The Rise and Triumph of the Modern Self* their book of choice. But this volume will richly reward readers who don't mind thinking hard about important (though sometimes unpleasant) topics. Christians have been taken off guard by how rapidly cultural mores have changed around them, but Carl Trueman demonstrates that radical thinkers have long been laying a foundation for these developments. Readers should press on to the end—the final paragraphs are among the best."

David VanDrunen, Robert B. Strimple Professor of Systematic Theology and Christian Ethics, Westminster Seminary California

"Carl Trueman's gifts as an intellectual historian shine in this profound and lucid book. *The Rise and Triumph of the Modern Self* needs to be read by anyone who wants to understand our current cultural distempers."

R. R. Reno, Editor, *First Things*

"Carl Trueman has written an excellent book: ambitious in its scope yet circumspect in its claims and temperate, even gentlemanly, in its tone. *The Rise and Triumph of the Modern Self* will prove indispensable in moving beyond the superficiality of moralistic and liberationist interpretations to a deeper understanding and should be required reading for all who truly wish to understand the times we live in or are concerned about the human future. I very much hope it receives the wide readership it deserves."

Michael Hanby, Associate Professor of Religion and Philosophy of Science, Pontifical John Paul II Institute for Studies on Marriage and Family at the Catholic University of America

Our culture did not simply wake up one morning and decide to reject sexual mores that have held civilization together for millennia. The sexual revolution that has overthrown basic human and teleological assumptions over the past sixty years has a history. With the adroit skill of an intellectual historian, the patience and humility of a master teacher, and the charity and conviction of a Christian pastor, Carl Trueman offers us this necessary book. We cannot respond appropriately to our times unless we understand how and why our times are defined such as they are. Trueman's work is a great gift to us in our continuing struggle to live in the world but be not of the world."

John D. Wilsey, Associate Professor of Church History and Philosophy, The Southern Baptist Theological Seminary; author, *God's Cold Warrior* and *American Exceptionalism and Civil Religion*

The Rise and Triumph of the Modern Self

Other Crossway Books by Carl R. Trueman

The Creedal Imperative

Histories and Fallacies: Problems Faced in the Writing of History

Luther on the Christian Life: Cross and Freedom

The Rise and Triumph
of the Modern Self

Cultural Amnesia, Expressive Individualism,
and the Road to Sexual Revolution

CARL R. TRUEMAN

Foreword by Rod Dreher

WHEATON, ILLINOIS

The Rise and Triumph of the Modern Self: Cultural Amnesia, Expressive Individualism, and the Road to Sexual Revolution

Copyright © 2020 by Carl R. Trueman

Published by Crossway
       1300 Crescent Street
       Wheaton, Illinois 60187

Cover design: Spencer Fuller, Faceout Studios

Cover image: Stocksy Image #1264340, 1825354, 2007929, Shutterstock Image #430366777

First printing 2020

Printed in the United States of America

Scripture quotations are from the ESV® Bible (The Holy Bible, English Standard Version®), copyright © 2001 by Crossway, a publishing ministry of Good News Publishers. Used by permission. All rights reserved.

Hardcover ISBN: 978-1-4335-5633-3
ePub ISBN: 978-1-4335-5636-4
PDF ISBN: 978-1-4335-5634-0
Mobipocket ISBN: 978-1-4335-5635-7

Library of Congress Cataloging-in-Publication Data

Names: Trueman, Carl R., author.
Title: The rise and triumph of the modern self : cultural amnesia, expressive individualism, and the road to sexual revolution / Carl R. Trueman ; foreword by Rod Dreher.
Description: Wheaton, Illinois : Crossway, 2020. | Includes bibliographical references and index.
Identifiers: LCCN 2019041970 (print) | LCCN 2019041971 (ebook) | ISBN 9781433556333 (hardcover) | ISBN 9781433556340 (pdf) | ISBN 9781433556357 (mobi) | ISBN 9781433556364 (epub)
Subjects: LCSH: Sexual freedom—History. | Sex. | Self. | Civilization, Modern.
Classification: LCC HQ32 .T78 2020 (print) | LCC HQ32 (ebook) | DDC 306.709—dc23
LC record available at https://lccn.loc.gov/2019041970
LC ebook record available at https://lccn.loc.gov/2019041971

Crossway is a publishing ministry of Good News Publishers.

LB		29	28	27	26	25	24	23	22	21	20
15	14	13	12	11	10	9	8	7	6	5	4	3	2

To
Matt and Gwen Franck
and
Fran and Suann Maier

*There is nothing on this earth to be
more prized than true friendship.*

THOMAS AQUINAS

Contents

Foreword

Rod Dreher

In his 1983 Templeton Prize address, Aleksandr Solzhenitsyn offered this summary explanation for why all the horrors of Soviet communism came to pass: "Men have forgotten God; that's why all this has happened."[1]

This answer is also a valid explanation for the crises enveloping the West today, including the widespread falling away from faith, the disintegration of the family, a loss of communal purpose, erotomania, erasing the boundaries between male and female, and a general spirit of demonic destruction that denies the sacredness of human life. Because men have forgotten God, they have also forgotten man; that's why all this has happened.

We have to go deeper. The *ways* in which men have forgotten God matter. We have to understand *how* and *why* they have forgotten God if we are to diagnose this sickness and to produce a vaccination, even a cure. Unfortunately, the gaze of most Christians cannot seem to penetrate the surface of postmodernity. Many regard the collapse moralistically, as if the tide could be turned back with a robust reassertion of Christian doctrine and ethical rigor.

Three cheers for robust reassertions of doctrinal orthodoxy and ethical rigor! But it's not enough. Ordinary Christians need—desperately need—

---

1. Aleksandr Solzhenitsyn, "'Men Have Forgotten God': Aleksandr Solzhenitsyn's 1983 Templeton Address," *National Review*, December 11, 2018, https://www.nationalreview.com/2018/12/aleksandr-solzhenitsyn-men-have-forgotten-god-speech/.

a more profound and holistic grasp of the modern and postmodern condition. It is the water in which we swim, the air that we breathe. There is no escaping it, but we can figure out how to live in it and through it without losing our faith. Yet any proposed Christian solution to the crisis of modernity will fail if it does not address the core causes of the Great Forgetting.

Some secular thinkers have produced analyses that are an unappreciated gift to the church in this post-Christian era. The late sociologist and critic Philip Rieff (1922–2006) was an agnostic Jew who understood with unusual perceptiveness how the psychologization of modern life, and its manifestation in the sexual revolution, was the poison pill that was killing our religion and therefore our civilization. Rieff's prose, though, is not easy to read. Some years ago, as I worked on my book *The Benedict Option*, I asked my friend Carl Trueman, who shares my view of Rieff's importance and who is a thinker and writer of impressive lucidity, to write a book about Rieff that explains to the laity why we need his insights to build a defense.

Trueman has written that book—you're holding it in your hands— but he has given us something much more valuable than a layman's handbook on Philip Rieff. Indeed, *The Rise and Triumph of the Modern Self* is an indispensable guide to how and why men have forgotten God. Trueman's tour de force analyzes the roots of the crisis in the thought and writing of men like Jean-Jacques Rousseau, Karl Marx, Friedrich Nietzsche, and Sigmund Freud—the usual suspects, you might say—but he also factors in figures like nineteenth-century English poets, who taught elites how to think and feel in radically different ways.

By the time the reader arrives at the book's conclusion, which explains why transgenderism is not simply a quirky offshoot of identity politics but rather the ultimate expression of the spirit of modernity, the reader will grasp why the trans phenomenon has been so readily accepted by contemporaries—and why the church's efforts to resist it and the sexual revolution of which it is a part have been so feeble and ineffective.

Trueman's book is in no way a standard conservative Christian polemic against modernity. Those are a dime a dozen. Nor is it a pietistic exhortation to prayer, study, and sober living, of which we have countless examples. Rather, it is a sophisticated survey and analysis of cultural history by a brilliant teacher who is not only an orthodox Christian but also a pastor who understands the actual needs of the flock—and who, unlike so many intellectuals, can write like a dream. I can't emphasize strongly enough how *practical* this book is and how useful it will be to pastors, priests, and intellectually engaged Christians of all denominations.

So many Christian books seek to explain the church to the modern world. But in these pages, Carl Trueman explains modernity to the church, with depth, clarity, and force. The significance of *The Rise and Triumph of the Modern Self*, arriving at this late hour, is hard to overstate. In his 1983 Templeton Prize address, Solzhenitsyn also said,

> Today's world has reached a state which, if it had been described to preceding centuries, would have called forth the cry: "This is the Apocalypse!"
>
> Yet we have grown used to this kind of world; we even feel at home in it.[2]

Yes, even Christians. Carl Trueman's prophetic role is to reveal to the church today how that happened, so that even now, we might repent and, in so doing, find ways to keep the true light of faith burning in this present darkness, which comprehends it not.

---

2. Solzhenitsyn, "'Men Have Forgotten God.'"

Preface

Every book I have written has involved incurring significant debts to numerous people, and none more so than this one. Rod Dreher floated the idea in his column at the *American Conservative* that someone should write an introduction to the thought of Philip Rieff, and Justin Taylor at Crossway picked up on this and asked if I would be willing to do so. Rod's enthusiasm that I say yes closed the deal. What started as an idea for a modest introductory book has morphed into something much more ambitious, but without Rod and Justin, this work would never have been written. I am, of course, honored that Rod agreed to write the foreword.

This is the fourth book I have published with Crossway, and once again, the experience has been a delightful one for me. All the team deserves thanks, and especially David Barshinger, Darcy Ryan, Lauren Susanto, and Amy Kruis.

I did much of the research for the book during a yearlong sojourn at Princeton University during 2017–2018, where I was the William E. Simon Fellow in Religion and Public Life in the James Madison Program. It was without doubt the high point of my academic life, and I will be forever grateful to Professors Robert P. George and Bradford P. Wilson for granting me such a privilege and to Debra Parker, Ch'nel Duke, Evelyn Behling, and Duanyi Wang, whose hard work made the year so pleasant. I am also indebted to all the 2017–2018 Madison fellows. I always felt that I was by far the stupidest person in the room at the Tuesday coffee discussions over which Robby and Brad presided, but I like to think that at the end I left a little less stupid than when I first arrived. The presentation of chapter 3 to the fellows and of a synopsis of the book to an undergraduate seminar, chaired by my dear friend and fellow Madisonian John Wilsey, were also very important to forming my opinions on the relevant topics.

Numerous friends have offered thoughtful critiques of sections of the book: Nathan Pinkoski gave of his time when we were both at Princeton to help me better understand Alasdair MacIntyre and then kindly read and commented on the MacIntyre section of the manuscript. Matt Franck and Adeline Allen both generously shared their expertise in constitutional law. Any flaws in the final product are, of course, my fault.

I am also thankful to Archbishop Charles Chaput and Fran Maier not only for their personal kindness and friendship toward me but also for introducing me to the work of Augusto Del Noce via a seminar given by Carlo Lancelotti at the Archdiocese of Philadelphia.

A number of the ideas that appear in the book were first tested in lectures and discussions. I am thankful to Patrick Berch, David Hall, Todd Pruitt, Mike Allen, Scott Swain, Scott Redd, Chad Vegas, Reformed Theological Seminary, Southwestern Baptist Theological Seminary, Princeton University, and Grove City College for providing venues for testing out some of my arguments. Aimee Byrd brought my attention to some important literature. Rosaria Butterfield provided fascinating insights into what it was like to be in the LGBTQ+ community. In addition, I am also grateful to Rusty Reno, Matt Schmitz, Julia Yost, and Ramona Tausz for allowing me to engage with the kind of cultural topics at the core of this book via the *First Things* website and magazine. Julia and Ramona deserve particular thanks for consistently proving that I have never been edited without improvement. Ryan T. Anderson, Serena Sigilitto, and R. J. Snell have also been very kind in allowing me to publish at *Public Discourse*, another wonderful venue for refining arguments and floating theories. I should also thank Ryan and Serena for permission to reuse material on Rieff for chapters 1 and 2 that first appeared in *Public Discourse*.

At the end of my Princeton fellowship, I had the great pleasure of taking a position at Grove City College. I am thankful to President Paul J.

McNulty for encouraging my work and to Paul Kengor, Jeff Trimbath, and Robert Rider, of the Institute for Faith and Freedom, for providing me with research assistants. Lorenzo Carrazana did great work during the 2018–2019 academic year. Then, in the summer of 2019, Kirsten Holmberg took over and provided truly outstanding feedback, corrections, and commentary on a number of central chapters. It is good to have a student assistant who is unafraid to offer probing criticism of her professor's work.

As always, Catriona provided a wonderful home environment and tolerated my academic daydreaming far beyond the call of duty. It is a blessed man indeed who has such a life partner.

Finally, I dedicate this book, with gratitude, to four dear friends: Matt and Gwen Franck and Fran and Suann Maier.

Carl R. Trueman
Grove City College
Pennsylvania
August 2019

Introduction

And worse I may be yet; the worst is not
So long as we can say "This is the worst."

WILLIAM SHAKESPEARE, *KING LEAR*

Why This Book?

The origins of this book lie in my curiosity about how and why a particular statement has come to be regarded as coherent and meaningful:
"I am a woman trapped in a man's body." My grandfather died in 1994,
less than thirty years ago, and yet, had he ever heard that sentence uttered in his presence, I have little doubt that he would have burst out
laughing and considered it a piece of incoherent gibberish. And yet
today it is a sentence that many in our society regard as not only meaningful but so significant that to deny it or question it in some way is to
reveal oneself as stupid, immoral, or subject to yet another irrational
phobia. And those who think of it as meaningful are not restricted to
the veterans of college seminars on queer theory or French poststructuralism. They are ordinary people with little or no direct knowledge
of the critical postmodern philosophies whose advocates swagger along
the corridors of our most hallowed centers of learning.

And yet that sentence carries with it a world of metaphysical assumptions. It touches on the connection between the mind and the
body, given the priority it grants to inner conviction over biological

reality. It separates gender from sex, given that it drives a wedge between chromosomes and how society defines being a man or a woman. And in its political connection to homosexuality and lesbianism via the LGBTQ+ movement, it rests on notions of civil rights and of individual liberty. In short, to move from the commonplace thinking of my grandfather's world to that of today demands a host of key shifts in popular beliefs in these and other areas. It is the story of those shifts—or, perhaps better, of the background to those shifts—that I seek to address in subsequent chapters.

At the heart of this book lies a basic conviction: the so-called sexual revolution of the last sixty years, culminating in its latest triumph—the normalization of transgenderism—cannot be properly understood until it is set within the context of a much broader transformation in how society understands the nature of human selfhood.[1] The sexual revolution is as much a symptom as it is a cause of the culture that now surrounds us everywhere we look, from sitcoms to Congress. In short, the sexual revolution is simply one manifestation of the larger revolution of the self that has taken place in the West. And it is only as we come to understand that wider context that we can truly understand the dynamics of the sexual politics that now dominate our culture.

Such a claim needs not only justification—that is the task of the rest of this book—but also clarification as to the meaning of the terms employed in making it. While many readers probably have some understanding of what is meant by *sexual revolution*, the idea of the *self* may prove somewhat more elusive. Yes, we have probably all heard of the

---

1. I am aware that LGBTQ+ people object to the term *transgenderism* as indicating a denial of the reality of transgender people and therefore as a pejorative term. Nonetheless, I use it in this book to point to the underlying philosophical assumptions that must be regarded as correct if a person's claim to be transgender is to be seen as coherent. If it is legitimate for LGBTQ+ theorists and advocates to use terms such as *cisgenderism* to refer to the ideology that underlies opposition to the transgender movement, then it is also legitimate to use *transgenderism* to refer to the ideology that underpins it. For the meaning and use of *cisgenderism* as a term, see Erica Lennon and Brian J. Mistler, "Cisgenderism," *Transgender Studies Quarterly* 1, nos. 1–2 (2014): 63–64, https://doi.org/10.1215/23289252-2399623. It is also worth noting that the term *transgenderism* was itself used by transgender groups in the 1970s: see Cristan Williams, "Transgender," *Transgender Studies Quarterly* 1, nos. 1–2 (2014): 232–34, https://doi .org/10.1215/23289252-2400136. The anathematizing of the term is a good example of how one group uses language to privilege its own position and delegitimize that of its critics, an accusation usually aimed at conservatives but clearly no monopoly of one particular side.

sexual revolution, and we no doubt consider ourselves to be *selves*. But what exactly do I mean by these terms?

The Sexual Revolution

When I use the term *sexual revolution*, I am referring to the radical and ongoing transformation of sexual attitudes and behaviors that has occurred in the West since the early 1960s. Various factors have contributed to this shift, from the advent of the pill to the anonymity of the internet.

The behaviors that characterize the sexual revolution are not unprecedented: homosexuality, pornography, and sex outside the bounds of marriage, for example, have been hardy perennials throughout human history. What marks the modern sexual revolution out as distinctive is the way it has normalized these and other sexual phenomena. It is not therefore the fact that modern people look at sexually explicit material while earlier generations did not that constitutes the revolutionary nature of our times. It is that the use of pornography no longer carries the connotations of shame and social stigma it once did and has even come to be regarded as a normal part of mainstream culture. The sexual revolution does not simply represent a growth in the routine transgression of traditional sexual codes or even a modest expansion of the boundaries of what is and is not acceptable sexual behavior; rather, it involves the abolition of such codes in their entirety. More than that, it has come in certain areas, such as that of homosexuality, to require the positive repudiation of traditional sexual mores to the point where belief in, or maintenance of, such traditional views has come to be seen as ridiculous and even a sign of serious mental or moral deficiency.

The most obvious evidence of this change is the way language has been transformed to serve the purpose of rendering illegitimate any dissent from the current political consensus on sexuality. Criticism of homosexuality is now *homophobia*; that of transgenderism is *transphobia*. The use of the term *phobia* is deliberate and effectively places such criticism of the new sexual culture into the realm of the irrational and points toward an underlying bigotry on the part of those who hold such views.

As I highlight in chapter 9, this kind of thinking underlies even decisions in the Supreme Court. It is also evident in the artifacts of popular culture: no one today needs to be told that a movie with the title *The 40-Year-Old Virgin* is a comedy. The very idea of someone reaching the age of forty with no experience of sexual intercourse is inherently comic because of the value society now places on sex. To be sexually inactive is to be a less-than-whole person, to be obviously unfulfilled or weird. The old sexual codes of celibacy outside marriage and chastity within it are considered ridiculous and oppressive, and their advocates wicked or stupid or both. The sexual revolution is truly a revolution in that it has turned the moral world upside down.

The Nature of the Self

The second term that needs clarification is that of the self. We all have a consciousness of being a *self*. At base, this connects to our sense of individuality. I am aware that I am me and not, say, George Clooney or Donald Trump. But in this book I use the term to mean more than simply a basic level of self-consciousness. For me to be a self in the sense I am using the term here involves an understanding of what the purpose of my life is, of what constitutes the good life, of how I understand myself—my *self*—in relation to others and to the world around me.

In this context—and as will become very clear in subsequent chapters—I am deeply indebted to the work of the Canadian philosopher Charles Taylor, particularly as found in his book *Sources of the Self: The Making of the Modern Identity*.[2] In that work, Taylor highlights three points of significance in the modern development of what it means to be a self: a focus on inwardness, or the inner psychological life, as decisive for who we think we are; the affirmation of ordinary life that develops in the modern era; and the notion that nature provides us with an inner moral source.[3] These developments manifest

---

2. Charles Taylor, *Sources of the Self: The Making of the Modern Identity* (Cambridge, MA: Harvard University Press, 1989).

3. Taylor, *Sources of the Self*, x.

themselves in numerous ways. Most significant for my argument in this book, they lead to a prioritization of the individual's inner psychology—we might even say "feelings" or "intuitions"—for our sense of who we are and what the purpose of our lives is. To leap ahead, transgenderism provides an excellent example: people who think they are a woman trapped in a man's body are really making their inner psychological convictions absolutely decisive for who they are; and to the extent that, prior to "coming out," they have publicly denied this inner reality, to that extent they have had an inauthentic existence. This is why the language of "living a lie" often appears in the testimonies of transgender people.

Another way of approaching the matter of the self is to ask what it is that makes a person happy. Is happiness found in directing oneself outward or inward? For example, is job satisfaction to be found in the fact that it enables me to feed and clothe my family? Or is it to be found in the fact that the very actions involved in my work bring me a sense of inner psychological well-being? The answer I give speaks eloquently of what I consider the purpose of life and the meaning of happiness. In sum, it is indicative of how I think of my *self.*

To return to my earlier statement, that the sexual revolution is a manifestation of a much deeper and wider revolution in what it means to be a self, my basic point should now be clear: the changes we have witnessed in the content and significance of sexual codes since the 1960s are symptomatic of deeper changes in how we think of the purpose of life, the meaning of happiness, and what actually constitutes people's sense of who they are and what they are for. The sexual revolution did not cause the sexual revolution, nor did technology such as the pill or the internet. Those things may have facilitated it, but its causes lie much deeper, in the changes in what it meant to be an authentic, fulfilled human self. And those changes stretch back well before the Swinging Sixties.

Thinking Clearly about the Sexual Revolution

Having defined the basic terms of discussion, I want to highlight a couple of typical mistakes that individuals, particularly those who are committed to strong religious views, can make in approaching a subject like the sexual revolution. Given the contentious nature of such subjects, and often the deeply personal convictions that they involve, there is a tendency to do one of two things. First, one can so emphasize a universal, metaphysical principle to which one is committed that one fails to understand the particulars of what one is analyzing. Second, one can become so preoccupied with the particulars that one fails to see the significance of the more general context.

To illustrate the former point, in teaching history I often begin my courses by asking students the following question: "Is the statement 'The Twin Towers fell down on 9/11 because of gravity' true or false?" The correct response, of course, is that it is true—but as my students quickly realize, that answer actually explains nothing of any significance about the tragic events of that day. To do that with any degree of adequacy, one needs to address other factors, from American foreign policy to the rise of militant Islam. The point I am making in asking the question is simple: the universal law of gravity explains why everything in general falls toward the earth, but it explains no specific incident of such a fall with any degree of adequacy.

Those who hold to grand schemes of reality can all tend this way. The Christian might be tempted to declare that the reason for the sexual revolution was sin. People are sinful; therefore, they will inevitably reject God's laws regarding sexuality. The Marxist might declare that the reason for the Russian Revolution was class struggle. Rich people exploit the poor; therefore, the poor will inevitably rise up in rebellion. Within the framework of each belief system, the answer is true, but in neither case are such blunt statements capable of explaining the particulars of the events in question—why the sexual revolution has thus far legitimated homosexuality but not incest, for example, or why the workers' revolution happened in Russia and not in Germany. To answer those questions, one needs to address specific matters of context.

This approach also manifests itself in more subtle and nuanced ways. There is a tendency among social conservatives to blame expressive individualism for the problems that they regard as currently putting strain on the liberal Western order, particularly as it manifests itself in the chaos of identity politics. The difficulty with this claim is that expressive individualism is something that affects us all. It is the very essence of the culture of which we are all a part. To put it bluntly: we are all expressive individuals now. Just as some choose to identify themselves by their sexual orientation, so the religious person chooses to be a Christian or a Muslim. And this raises the question of why society finds some choices to be legitimate and others to be irrelevant or even unacceptable. The answer to that is to be found not by simply repeating the phrase "expressive individualism" but by looking at the historical development of the relationship between society at large and individual identity.

But there is an opposite problem to the temptation presented by overgeneralized explanatory schemes that one must also avoid. That is the tendency to treat symptoms in isolation. This is harder to articulate, but the speed of the transformation of sexual mores over the last two decades provides a good example. Many Christians were amazed at how swiftly society moved from a position where in the early 2000s a majority of people were broadly opposed to gay marriage to one where, by 2020, transgenderism is well on its way to becoming more or less normalized. The mistake such Christians made was failing to realize that broader, underlying social and cultural conditions made both gay marriage and then transgender ideology first plausible and then normative and that these conditions have been developing over hundreds of years. They are therefore by now very deep seated and themselves an intuitive part of life. Acceptance of gay marriage and transgenderism are simply the latest outworking, the most recent symptoms, of deep and long-established cultural pathologies.

The basic principle is this: no individual historical phenomenon is its own cause. The French Revolution did not cause the French Revolution. The First World War did not cause the First World War. Every historical phenomenon is the result of a wide variety of factors that can vary from the technological to the political to the philosophical. Without the development of atomic technology, there could have been no bomb dropped on Hiroshima. Without the Second World War, there would have been no reason to drop a bomb on Hiroshima. And without a certain philosophy of war, there would have been no justification for dropping a bomb on Hiroshima.

It is the same with the sexual revolution. It has a context—a broader revolution in how the self is understood—and emerges from a specific historical matrix. Developments in technology, in philosophy, and in politics are just three of the factors that serve to make it possible, plausible, and finally actual. They also serve to give it decisive shape and help explain why it has taken the form that it currently has. I cannot give an exhaustive account of this causal context, but what I offer in this book is an account of the intellectual shifts, and their popular impact, that have facilitated the revolution in sexual practices and thinking that now dominates key aspects of the public square.

The Argument

Part 1 of this book sets forth in two chapters some of the basic concepts that I subsequently use for exploring the historical narrative. Of particular importance here are the ideas of three philosophers of the modern condition: Philip Rieff, Charles Taylor, and Alasdair MacIntyre. Rieff developed some very useful concepts—the triumph of the therapeutic, psychological man, the anticulture, and deathworks—which I use at various points throughout parts 2 and 3. Taylor is extremely helpful both in understanding how the modern notion of the expressive self has emerged and also how this connects to the wider politics of society. His contributions on the dialogical nature of selfhood, on the nature of what he calls "the social imaginary," and on the politics of recognition allow for answers to the question of why certain identities (e.g., LGBTQ+) enjoy great cachet today while others (e.g., religious conservatives) are increasingly marginalized. Finally, MacIntyre is useful because in a series of books starting in the early 1980s, he has repeatedly argued that modern ethical discourse has broken down because it rests ultimately on incommensurable narratives and that claims to moral truth are really expressions of emotional preference. These insights are extremely helpful in understanding both the fruitless nature and the extreme polarizing rhetoric of many of the great moral debates of our time, not least those surrounding matters of sex and identity.

Part 2 of the book looks at some important developments in the eighteenth and nineteenth centuries, starting with the thought of Jean-Jacques Rousseau, examining the contribution of a number of figures associated with Romanticism, and ending with discussion of the ideas of Friedrich Nietzsche, Karl Marx, and Charles Darwin. The central point here is that with the era of Rousseau and Romanticism a new understanding of human selfhood emerged, one focused on the inner life of the individual. This thinking finds its significant critical corollary in a view of society/culture as oppressive. In Percy Bysshe Shelley and William Blake in particular, this aspect of culture is identified above all with society's Christian sexual codes and particularly with the normative status of lifelong, monogamous marriage.

This suspicion about society/culture receives added power and philosophical depth in the work of Nietzsche and Marx, who in different ways argue that the history of society is a history of power and oppression and that even notions such as human nature are constructs designed to reinforce and perpetuate this subjugation. Indeed, along with Darwin, they deal lethal blows, philosophically and scientifically, to the ideas that nature has an intrinsic meaning and that human beings have special significance or an essence that determines how they should behave. In the hands of Nietzsche, Marx, and Darwin, the world loses its innate teleology. These three effectively strip away the metaphysical foundations for both human identity and for morality, leaving the latter, as Nietzsche is happy to point out, a matter of mere taste and manipulative power games. The Romantics grounded ethics in aesthetics, in the cultivation of empathy and sympathy, confident that a universal, shared human nature provided a firm foundation for such. Nietzsche sees such arguments from taste as a manipulative means by which the weak subjugate the strong, and Marx sees them as a means of oppression by the dominant class. The groundwork for rejecting traditional morality, both philosophical and scientific, is therefore in place by the end of the nineteenth century. With Nietzsche's genealogical approach to morality and Marx's dialectical materialism, the foundations have also been laid for an icono-clastic view of the past—for seeing history as a tale of oppression and for making its victims into the real heroes of the narrative.

If part 2 deals with the psychologizing of the self, part 3 deals with the sexualizing of psychology and the politicizing of sex. The central figure here is that of Sigmund Freud. It is Freud, more than any other figure, who made plausible the idea that humans, from infancy onward, are at core sexual beings. It is our sexual desires that are ultimately decisive for who we are. And this belief shaped Freud's own theory of civilization: society/culture is the result of a trade-off between the anarchic sexual drives of human beings and the necessity for them to live together in commu-nities. When Freud's thought is then appropriated by certain Marxist thinkers, most notably Wilhelm Reich and Herbert Marcuse, the result is a heady mix of sex and politics. The New Left that emerges from this synthesis sees oppression as a fundamentally psychological category and sexual codes as its primary instruments. The theoretical—and the rhetori-cal—background to the sexual revolution is therefore established.

Part 4 engages with a number of different areas of contemporary so-ciety in order to demonstrate how deeply the conceptual developments of parts 2 and 3 have come to transform modern Western culture. In chapter 8, I outline the rise to prominence of the erotic with examples from both high culture, in the form of surrealism, and pop culture, in the form of pornography. My conclusion is that the triumph of the erotic does not simply involve an expansion of the boundaries of accept-able sexual behavior or of notions of modesty but actually requires the abolition of such in their entirety. In chapter 9, I address three particular areas of relevance, the Supreme Court judgment on gay marriage, the ethics of Peter Singer, and the culture of protest on college campuses. I argue that each is a function of the broader revolution of the self that I describe in parts 2 and 3. Then, in chapter 10, I address the history of the LGBTQ+ movement, arguing that it is not the result of intrinsic affinities shared by its component parties but an alliance of historical and political convenience rooted in a shared sexual iconoclasm. I also make the case that it increasingly reveals the inherent instability of the broader project of the sexual revolution, as is clear from the current conflict that transgenderism has precipitated among feminists.

In conclusion, I offer some reflections on possible futures that we might have to face, from the difficulties posed by transgenderism and the prospects for religious freedom to ways in which the church should prepare for the challenges that are coming.

What This Book Is Not

Before moving to the main body of the argument, three further comments are necessary to clarify my purpose in writing. First, this book is not intended as an exhaustive account of how the present normative understanding of the self has emerged and come to dominate public discourse. As with all historical accounts, the narrative and analysis that I present here are both limited and provisional. I indicate in the conclusion that other factors play into the shaping of modern selfhood and the sexual revolution, not least those associated with developments in technology. Such things are beyond the scope of this book but still relevant to the phenomena that I seek to describe. My task here is limited: to demonstrate how many of the ideas now informing both the conscious thinking and the instinctive intuitions of Western men and women have deep historical roots and a coherent genealogy that helps explain why society thinks and behaves the way it does. I want to help the reader see that the debates about sexuality that increasingly dominate our public square need to be set in a much broader and deeper context than we typically acknowledge—and that all of us are to some extent implicated. It is therefore primarily a history that reveals the intellectual background of the modern revolution in selfhood with a view to showing *that* the ideas of key figures stretching back centuries have come to permeate our culture at all levels, from the halls of academe to the intuitions of ordinary men and women; it is not an exhaustive account of *how* those ideas came to do so.

Second, this book is not a lament for a lost golden age or even for the parlous state of culture as we now face it. Lamentation is popular in many conservative and Christian circles, and I have indulged in it a few times myself. No doubt the Ciceronian cry "O tempora! O mores!" has its therapeutic appeal in a therapeutic time like ours, whether as a form of Pharisaic reassurance that we are not like others, such as those in the LGBTQ+ movement, or as a means of convincing ourselves that we have the special knowledge that allows us to stand above the petty enchantments and superficial pleasures of this present age. But in terms of positive action, lamentation offers little and delivers less. As for the notion of some lost golden age, it is truly very hard for any competent historian to be nostalgic. What past times were better than the present? An era before antibiotics when childbirth or even minor cuts might lead to septicemia and death? The great days of the nineteenth century when the church was culturally powerful and marriage was between one man and one woman for life but little children worked in factories and swept chimneys? Perhaps the Great Depression? The Second World War? The era of Vietnam? Every age has had its darkness and its dangers. The task of the Christian is not to whine about the moment in which he or she lives but to understand its problems and respond appropriately to them.

Third, I have written this book with the same principle in mind that I have tried to embody in the classroom for well over a quarter century: my task as a historian is first to explain an action, an idea, or an event in context. Only when that hard work has been done can the teacher move to any kind of critique. While I cannot claim to have always attained this ideal in everything I have said or written, it seems to me that giving an accurate account of one's opponents' views, however obnoxious one may consider them to be, is vital, and never more so than in our age of cheap Twitter insults and casual slanders. There is nothing to be gained from refuting a straw man. In the accounts I give of, among others, Rousseau, the Romantics, Nietzsche, Marx, Darwin, Freud, the New Left, surrealism, Hugh Hefner, Anthony Kennedy, Peter Singer, Adrienne Rich, Judith Butler, and LGBTQ+ activism, I have therefore tried to be as careful and dispassionate as possible. Some readers might find this odd, given my personal dissent from much of what they each represent. But truthfulness is not optional. My hope is that I have represented the views of these groups and individuals in such a manner that, were they to read this book, they might demur to my conclusions but at least recognize themselves in my account of their thought. All historians owe that much to the subjects of their inquiries.

What I offer here is essentially a prolegomenon to the many discussions that Christians and others need to have about the most pressing issues of our day, particularly as they manifest themselves in the variety of ways in which the sexual revolution affects us—personally, culturally, legally, theologically, ecclesiastically. My aim is to explain how and why a certain notion of the self has come to dominate the culture of the West, why this self finds its most obvious manifestation in the transformation of sexual mores, and what the wider implications of this transformation are and may well be in the future. Understanding the times is a precondition of responding appropriately to the times. And understanding the times requires a knowledge of the history that has led up to the present. This book is intended as a small contribution to that vital task.

Part 1

ARCHITECTURE OF THE REVOLUTION

1

Reimagining the Self

You see, but you do not observe.

SHERLOCK HOLMES, *A SCANDAL IN BOHEMIA*

I noted in the introduction that the underlying argument of this book is that the sexual revolution, and its various manifestations in modern society, cannot be treated in isolation but must rather be interpreted as the specific and perhaps most obvious social manifestation of a much deeper and wider revolution in the understanding of what it means to be a self. While sex may be presented today as little more than a recreational activity, sexuality is presented as that which lies at the very heart of what it means to be an authentic person. That is a profound claim that is arguably unprecedented in history. How that situation comes to be is a long and complicated story, and I can address only a few of the most salient aspects of the relevant narrative in a single volume. And even before I attempt to do so, it is first necessary to set forth a number of basic theoretical concepts that provide a framework, a set of what we might describe as architectural principles, for structuring and analyzing the personalities, events, and ideas that play into the rise of the modern self.

In this task, the writings of three analysts of modernity are particularly useful: Charles Taylor, the philosopher; Philip Rieff, the psychological sociologist; and Alasdair MacIntyre, the ethicist.[1] While all three have different emphases and concerns, they offer accounts of the modern world that share certain important affinities and also provide helpful insights into understanding not simply how modern Western society thinks but how and why it has come to think the way that it does. In this chapter and the next, therefore, I want to offer an outline of some of their key ideas that help set the scene for the interpretation of our contemporary world offered in the subsequent account of how the concept of the modern psychologized and sexualized self has emerged.

The Social Imaginary

To return to the questions I posed in the introduction: How has the current highly individualistic, iconoclastic, sexually obsessed, and materialistic mindset come to triumph in the West? Or, to put the question in a more pressing and specific fashion, as I did earlier, Why does the sentence "I am a woman trapped in a man's body" make sense not simply to those who have sat in poststructuralist and queer-theory seminars but to my neighbors, to people I pass on the street, to coworkers who have no particular political ax to grind and who are blissfully unaware of the rebarbative jargon and arcane concepts of Michel Foucault and his myriad epigones and incomprehensible imitators? The statement is, after all, emblematic of a view of personhood that has almost completely dispensed with the idea of any authority beyond that of personal, psychological conviction, an oddly Cartesian notion: I think I am a woman, therefore I am a woman. How did such a strange idea become the common orthodox currency of our culture?

To make some attempt at addressing the issue, it is useful to take note of a helpful concept deployed by Canadian philosopher Charles Taylor in his analysis of how societies think, that of the *social imaginary*. Taylor is interesting because he is a philosopher whose work also engages with

---

1. MacIntyre is discussed in chap. 2.

broader historical and sociological themes. In *A Secular Age*, he offers a major analysis of the way modern society in general, and not just the intellectual classes, has moved away from being permeated by Christianity and religious faith to the point that such are no longer the default for the majority of people but actually are rather exceptional. In the course of his argument, he introduces the idea of the social imaginary to address the question of how theories developed by social elites might be related to the way ordinary people think and act, even when such people have never read these elites or spent any time self-consciously reflecting on the implications of their theories. Here is how he defines the concept:

> I want to speak of "social imaginary" here, rather than social theory, because there are important differences between the two. There are, in fact, several differences. I speak of "imaginary" (i) because I'm talking about the way ordinary people "imagine" their social surroundings, and this is often not expressed in theoretical terms, it is carried in images, stories, legends, etc. But it is also the case that (ii) theory is often the possession of a small minority, whereas what is interesting in the social imaginary is that it is shared by large groups of people, if not the whole society. Which leads to a third difference: (iii) the social imaginary is that common understanding which makes possible common practices, and a widely shared sense of legitimacy.[2]

As Taylor describes it here, the social imaginary is a somewhat amorphous concept precisely because it refers to the myriad beliefs, practices, normative expectations, and even implicit assumptions that members of a society share and that shape their daily lives. It is not so much a conscious philosophy of life as a set of intuitions and practices. In sum, the social imaginary is the way people think about the world, how they imagine it to be, how they act intuitively in relation to it—though that is emphatically not to make the social imaginary simply into a set of identifiable ideas.[3]

---

2. Charles Taylor, *A Secular Age* (Cambridge, MA: Belknap Press of Harvard University Press, 2007), 171–72. Taylor has devoted an entire book to discussing the concept: *Modern Social Imaginaries* (Durham, NC: Duke University Press, 2004).

3. "The social imaginary is not a set of ideas; rather, it is what enables, through making sense of, the practices of a society." Taylor, *Modern Social Imaginaries*, 2.

It is the totality of the way we look at our world, to make sense of it and to make sense of our behavior within it.

This is a very helpful concept precisely because it takes account of the fact that the way we think about many things is not grounded in a self-conscious belief in a particular theory of the world to which we have committed ourselves. We live our lives in a more intuitive fashion than that. The fact that "I am a woman trapped in a man's body" makes sense to Joe Smith probably has far less to do with him being committed to an elaborate understanding of the nature of gender and its relationship to biological sex than to the fact that it seems intuitively correct to affirm someone in his or her chosen identity and hurtful not to do so, however strange the particulars of that self-identification might have seemed to previous generations. We might perhaps say that, looked at from this angle, the social imaginary is a matter of intuitive social taste. And the question of how the tastes and intuitions of the general public are formed is the question of how the social imaginary comes to take the shape that it does.

Sometimes, as Taylor notes, the theories of the elite do infiltrate these imaginaries.[4] For example, the ideas of Luther on church authority came to grip the popular imagination in sixteenth-century Saxony and beyond through myriad popular pamphlets and woodcuts designed to have an impact on everyday people. And one might add that sometimes the theories of the elite have an affinity with elements of the existing social imaginary that reinforces them, that provides them with an idiom by which they might be expressed or justified, or that transforms them. Sexual identity politics might be a good example, whereby sex outside the ideal of monogamous heterosexual marriage has always occurred but has only recently become much easier to transact (with the advent of cheap and efficient contraception). It has also moved from being primarily personal in significance to also being political, given the debates that swirl around abortion, birth control, and LGBTQ+ matters. The way this occurred is fairly simple to discern:

---

4. Taylor, *A Secular Age*, 172.

first, there was the promiscuous behavior; then there was the technology to facilitate it, in the form of contraception and antibiotics; and, as technology enabled the sexually promiscuous to avoid the natural consequences of their actions (unwanted pregnancies, disease), so those rationales that justified the behavior became more plausible (and arguments against it became less so), and therefore the behavior itself became more acceptable.

Any account of the sexual revolution and of the underlying revolution in the understanding of the self, of which the sexual revolution is simply the latest iteration, must therefore not simply take into account the ideas of the cultural elite but must also look at how the intuitions of society at large have been formed. Ideas in themselves are only part of the story. The notion of the self that makes transgenderism plausible certainly has its theoretical and philosophical rationales. But it is also the product of much wider cultural phenomena that have shaped the intuitions of those who are blissfully unaware of its various intellectual origins and metaphysical assumptions.

Mimesis and Poiesis

A second useful element in Taylor's work that connects to the social imaginary and to which we will have recourse is the relationship between *mimesis* and *poiesis*. Put simply, these terms refer to two different ways of thinking about the world. A mimetic view regards the world as having a given order and a given meaning and thus sees human beings as required to discover that meaning and conform themselves to it. Poiesis, by way of contrast, sees the world as so much raw material out of which meaning and purpose can be created by the individual.

Both of Taylor's major works—*Sources of the Self* and *A Secular Age*—are narratives that tell the story of the move in Western culture from a predominantly mimetic view of the world to one that is primarily poietic. Various matters characterize this shift. As society moves from a view of the world as possessing intrinsic meaning, so it also moves away from a view of humanity as having a specific, given end. Teleology is thereby attenuated, whether it is that of Aristotle, with his view of man as a political animal and his understanding of ethics as an important function of that, or that of Christianity, with its notion that human life in this earthly sphere is to be regulated by the fact that humanity's ultimate destiny is eternal communion with God.

Again, the story of this shift is not simply one that can be told in terms of great thinkers and their ideas. It is true that individuals such as René Descartes and Francis Bacon served to weaken the significance of the connection between the divine and the created, and therefore of a teleological understanding of human nature, which one finds in the thought of a thinker such as Thomas Aquinas.[5] But for a poietic view of reality to eclipse the mimetic in the social imaginary, other factors must be at play.

To make this point more clearly, one might reflect on the nature of life in medieval Europe, a predominantly agrarian society. Given that agricultural technology was then, by today's standards, relatively primitive, farming was utterly dependent on geography and the seasons. These were givens; while the farmer would plough up the ground and scatter the seed, he had no control over the weather, minimal control over the soil, and thus comparatively little control over whether his endeavors would succeed. That might well have meant for many that they had no control over life or death: they were entirely at the mercy of the environment.

In such a world, the authority of the created order was obvious and unavoidable. The world was what it was, and the individual needed to conform to it. Sowing seed in December or harvesting crops in March was doomed to failure. Yet with the advent of more-advanced agricultural technology, this given authority of the environment became increasingly attenuated. The development of irrigation meant that water could be moved or stored and then used when necessary. Increased knowledge of soil science and fertilizers and pesticides meant that the land could be manipulated to yield more and better crops. More controversially, the recent development of genetics has allowed for the production of foods

---

5. Taylor, *A Secular Age*, 97–99.

that are immune to certain conditions or parasites. I could go on, but the point is clear: whether we consider certain innovations to be good or bad, technology affects in profound ways how we think about the world and imagine our place in it. Today's world is not the objectively authoritative place that it was eight hundred years ago; we think of it much more as a case of raw material that we can manipulate by our own power to our own purposes.

This has much broader significance than matters such as agriculture. The development of the automobile and then the aircraft served to shatter the previous authority of geographical space. If distance is ultimately a matter of time, then the distance from Philadelphia to London today is now less than that from Philadelphia to Chicago was a mere two hundred years ago. And once modern telecommunications and information technology entered the picture, the situation was even more radically altered—and that by human inventions. Had I immigrated to the United States in 1850, I might well have said goodbye forever to my relatives and friends left in England. Today, I can not only speak to them whenever I wish, I can even see them on my phone or computer whenever the fancy takes me.

To this, one should add the developments in medical technology. Again, old authorities have been challenged and found wanting. Diseases that were in past ages untreatable are now no longer death sentences. What were once deadly infections can be dispatched as so much trivia because of antibiotics. Childbirth no longer poses the serious risk to women's health that was routine in earlier ages. And all these developments have served to weaken the authority of the natural world and persuade human beings of their power.

In saying this, I am not making an evaluation of technology as good or bad. It can clearly be both. The point I am making is that we all live in a world in which it is increasingly easy to imagine that reality is something we can manipulate according to our own wills and desires, and not something that we necessarily need to conform ourselves to or passively accept. And this broader context makes intuitive, for example, those philosophical claims of Friedrich Nietzsche, in which human beings are called to transcend themselves, to make their lives into works of art, to take the place of God as self-creators and the inventors, not the discoverers, of meaning. Few people have read Nietzsche, but many intuitively think in Nietzschean ways about their relationship to the natural world precisely because the highly technological world in which we now live— a world in which *virtual* reality *is* a reality—makes it so easy to do so. Self-creation is a routine part of our modern social imaginary.

And that is simply another way of saying that this is also a significant component of how we imagine our personal identities, our *selves*. Again, to return to that statement I highlighted in the introduction—"I am a woman trapped in a man's body"—such a statement is plausible only in a world in which the predominant way of thinking is poietic rather than mimetic. And a poietic world is one in which transcendent purpose collapses into the immanent and in which given purpose collapses into any purpose I choose to create or decide for myself. Human nature, one might say, becomes something individuals or societies invent for themselves.

Philip Rieff and the Nature of Culture

Philip Rieff, the late professor of sociology at the University of Pennsylvania, is significant for this study because of his application of psychology to the patterns and pathologies of cultural change in the last one hundred years. In his book *The Triumph of the Therapeutic* (1966), Rieff used Sigmund Freud as his starting point for a theory of culture that he then proceeded to explicate by examining the work of subsequent thinkers, such as Carl Jung, D. H. Lawrence, and Wilhelm Reich. Rieff took as basic Freud's argument that civilization was the result of sublimating sexual desire in a manner that left human beings perennially discontented but remarkably creative, and he developed this notion into a broad theory of culture and a means of critiquing the shifts that he saw developing at a rapid rate in the mid-twentieth century.[6] To read Rieff's book today is a fascinating experience, mainly because the claims that he

---

6. Freud's most famous expression of this argument is his monograph *Civilization and Its Discontents*, trans. James Strachey (New York: W. W. Norton, 1989). For further discussion of Freud's theory, see chap. 6.

makes about the direction of society, and the implications these would have for how people would come to think of themselves, are so startlingly prescient that it is very hard to dismiss his underlying analytical framework. The work has a prophetic quality to it that is likely to impress any reader who is willing to persevere through his rather opaque prose style.[7]

Rieff's approach to culture is characterized by a number of ideas. Foremost is his notion that cultures are primarily defined by what they forbid. This is a basically Freudian concept: if sexual taboos drive civilization, then civilization is really defined at its base by a negative idea, by that behavior that it denounces and renounces as unacceptable. This in turn has institutional implications: a culture's vitality depends on the authority of those institutions that enforce or inculcate these renunciations and thus communicate them from one generation to the next. As Rieff expresses it,

> A culture survives principally . . . by the power of its institutions to bind and loose men in the conduct of their affairs with reasons which sink so deep into the self that they become commonly and implicitly understood.[8]

This connects to the second important aspect of culture for Rieff: culture, at least historically, directs the individual outward. It is in communal activities that individuals find their true selves; the true self in traditional cultures is therefore something that is given and learned, not something that the individual creates for himself. This insight allows us to connect the thinking of Rieff to that of Charles Taylor in a constructive manner, via the affinity that exists between Rieff's concept of psychological man and Taylor's concept of the expressive individual.

---

7. Rieff was not unique in criticizing modern society as therapeutic. Leszek Kołakowski also saw essentially the same pathology as distinguishing the contemporary era, although he labeled it "the culture of analgesics." See his *The Presence of Myth*, trans. Adam Czerniawski (Chicago: University of Chicago Press, 1989), 83–109.

8. Philip Rieff, *The Triumph of the Therapeutic: Uses of Faith after Freud*, 40th anniversary ed. (1966; repr., Wilmington: ISI Books, 2006), 2. While discussion of institutions is beyond the scope of this book, it is worth noting here that the world in which we now live is characterized by what sociologist Zygmunt Bauman has called "liquidity," a state of constant change and flux. Given this liquidity, Rieff's statement here points to a significant problem that contemporary societies now face: if cultures depend on strong institutions, then when those institutions are weakened or thrown into chaos, those cultures, too, are weakened or thrown into chaos. See Zygmunt Bauman, *Liquid Modernity* (Cambridge: Polity, 2000); also Zygmunt Bauman and Carlo Bordoni, *State of Crisis* (Cambridge: Polity, 2014).

Psychological Man and Expressive Individualism

Rieff describes the outward direction of traditional culture as follows: "Culture is another name for a design of motives directing the self outward, toward those communal purposes in which alone the self can be realized and satisfied."[9] This is an important point: culture directs individuals outward. It is greater than, prior to, and formative of the individual. We learn who we are by learning how to conform ourselves to the purposes of the larger community to which we belong. This is of great significance for understanding Rieff, since it is this emphasis on culture as that which directs the individual outward toward communal purposes that underlies his schematization of human history in terms of representative types, figures whom he regards as embodying the spirit of their age. It also allows us to understand why Rieff was convinced that his (and now our) age represented something dramatic and innovative in cultural history.[10]

First, Rieff argues, there was the culture of political man, of the sort set forth as an ideal in the thought of Plato and Aristotle. In contrast to the idiotic man (literally, the private man), the political man is the one who finds his identity in the activities in which he engages in the public life of the *polis*. Aristotle, in his *Politics* and *Nicomachean Ethics*, offers perhaps the classic description of political man. He attends the assembly, frequents the Areopagus, is deeply immersed in what one might call civic community life. That is where he is who he is; the outwardly directed activity of political life is where he finds his sense of self.

Eventually, political man gave way to the second major type, that of religious man. The man of the Middle Ages was precisely such a person, someone who found his primary sense of self in his involvement in religious activities: attending mass, celebrating feast days, taking part in religious processions, going on pilgrimages. Chaucer's *Canterbury Tales* is a classic representation of this type of culture. Who are the characters in the book? Each obviously has his or her own individual existence

---

9. Rieff, *Triumph of the Therapeutic*, 3.

10. Rieff first develops the following scheme in *Freud: The Mind of the Moralist* (New York: Viking, 1959). A helpful summary is provided in his essay "Reflections on Psychological Man in America," in Rieff, *The Feeling Intellect: Selected Writings*, ed. Jonathan B. Imber (Chicago: University of Chicago Press, 1990), 3–10.

and profession, but above all, they are pilgrims who find their sense of identity in a communal context as they participate in a religiously motivated journey to Canterbury. I might also add that so much of the way medieval society is structured—from the dominance of its church buildings to the liturgical calendar, which marks time itself in religious terms—points toward religion as the key to culture during this time.

In Rieff's historical scheme, religious man was eventually displaced by a third type, what he calls economic man. Economic man is the individual who finds his sense of self in his economic activity: trade, production, the making of money. Rieff himself saw economic man as an unstable and temporary category, and given Karl Marx's perceptive observations on the dramatic way that capitalism constantly revolutionizes society's means of production, this would seem to be a reasonable assumption. And economic man thus gives way to the latest player on the historical stage, that which Rieff dubs "psychological man"—a type characterized not so much by finding identity in outward directed activities as was true for the previous types but rather in the inward quest for personal psychological happiness.

As a historical framework, Rieff's scheme is far too simplistic. The idea that one can chart human history through the rise and fall of these four distinct types of human being is far fetched at best. For a start, the apostle Paul's development of the concept of the will is what facilitates the rise of inner psychological narrative as a means of reflecting on the self. In the fourth century, Paul's intellectual heir Augustine produced the *Confessions*, the first great Western work of psychological autobiography, which indicates the existence of life understood in terms of inner mental space long before Freud. And one can scarcely look at the Middle Ages or the early modern era and neatly abstract the religious from the political or, indeed, the psychological: Martin Luther is only the most obvious example of this complexity. He was an Augustinian friar whose life would have revolved around religious observances and yet whose introspective angst played a key role in the birth of the modern age. Nevertheless, if the historical scheme is greatly oversimplified, the significance of the rise of psychological categories as the dominant factor in how Westerners think of themselves and who they consider themselves to be is surely a persuasive insight. One does not need to agree with Rieff on how society came to be dominated by the therapeutic to agree with him that such domination did emerge in the latter part of the twentieth century and currently shows no signs of abating.

Indeed, in characterizing the modern age as that of psychological man, Rieff makes a point very similar to that of Charles Taylor in his understanding of the human self: that psychological categories and an inward focus are the hallmarks of being a modern person. This is what Taylor refers to as *expressive individualism*, that each of us finds our meaning by giving expression to our own feelings and desires. For Taylor, this kind of self exists in what he describes as a *culture of authenticity*, which he defines as follows:

> The understanding of life which emerges with the Romantic expressivism of the late eighteenth century, that each of us has his/her own way of realizing our humanity, and that it is important to find and live out one's own, as against surrendering to conformity with a model imposed on us from outside, by society, or the previous generation, or religious or political authority.[11]

This shift to psychological man and to expressive individualism is far reaching in its implications, as I argue in future chapters. Taylor, for example, rightly sees it as underpinning the consumer revolution that took place after the Second World War.[12] At this point, it is simply worth noting that it involves a very different way of thinking about and relating to the world around us.[13]

---

11. Taylor, *A Secular Age*, 475.

12. Taylor, *A Secular Age*, 474.

13. Roger Scruton notes the shift in the understanding of selfhood relative to forms of dance. Commenting on earlier forms of dancing, he observes that such typically assumed live music, formal steps that needed to be learned, and a meaning or pleasure derived from the individual being part of a coordinated whole, a social group. Such dancing was thus deeply social, and the ways in which the individual expressed his or her identity was communal. He contrasts this with modern nightclub-style dancing, in which the individual simply—to use the colloquial phrase—does his or her own thing. The former, he says, involves dancing *with* others, the latter *at* others (which, incidentally, has also involved a sexualizing of dancing's purpose consonant with the sexualizing of society). "Dancing Properly," in *Confessions of a Heretic: Selected Essays* (Widworthy, UK: Notting Hill Editions, 2016), 50–64.

Take, for example, the issue of job satisfaction, something that is significant for most adults. My grandfather left school at fifteen and spent the rest of his working life as a sheet metal worker in a factory in Birmingham, the industrial heartland of England. If he had been asked if he found satisfaction in his work, there is a distinct possibility he would not even have understood the question, given that it really reflects the concerns of psychological man's world, to which he did not belong. But if he did understand, he would probably have answered in terms of whether his work gave him the money to put food on his family's table and shoes on his children's feet. If it did so, then yes, he would have affirmed that his job satisfied him. His needs were those of his family, and in enabling him to meet them, his work gave him satisfaction. My grandfather was, if anything, a Rieffian economic man whose economic production and the results of that for others (i.e., his family) were key to his sense of self. If I am asked the same question, my instinct is to talk about the pleasure that teaching gives me, about the sense of personal fulfillment I feel when a student learns a new idea or becomes excited about some concept as a result of my classes. The difference is stark: for my grandfather, job satisfaction was empirical, outwardly directed, and unrelated to his psychological state; for members of mine and subsequent generations, the issue of *feeling* is central.

Rieff sees two historic reversals underlying this new world of psychological man. The first is a transformation of the understanding of therapy. Traditionally, the role of the therapist in any given culture was to enable the patient to grasp the nature of the community to which he belonged. So in a religious world, the task of the religious therapist, the priest, was to train individuals in the rituals, the language, the doctrines, and the symbols of the church by which they might then participate in the community. These are the things that promote commitment to the community, which is prior to, and more important than, any particular individual.[14]

---

14. See, for example, Rieff's comments on the medieval church: "In the Middle Ages, this tradition [of therapy] was institutionalized in a church civilization, with the therapeutic functions reserved to functionaries of the churches. . . . Ultimately, it is the community that cures. The function of the classical therapist is to commit the patient to the symbol system of the community, as best he can and by whatever techniques are sanctioned (e.g., ritual or dialectical, magical or rational)." *Triumph of the Therapeutic*, 57.

This view depends on an understanding of the wider community as a positive good for those individuals who constitute it. That, as I note in parts 2 and 3, is an idea that has come under vigorous criticism, beginning in the eighteenth century with Jean-Jacques Rousseau, who regarded the community as a hindrance to the full expression of the authentic individual, a point picked up and given artistic expression by the Romantics. In Freud, Rieff's intellectual source and himself an admirer of Rousseau (albeit supplementing Rousseau with the much darker view of nature found in the Marquis de Sade), the notion of the community as a good is also placed under pressure and significantly qualified. A charitable reading of his cultural theory allows that the repressed community we have is at best merely preferable to the bloodthirsty chaos that the alternative offers. For Marx and for Nietzsche (though for very different reasons), the present community is one that needs to be overthrown in order for humanity to reach its full potential. And once we have the fusion of the thought of Marx and Freud in figures such as Wilhelm Reich and Herbert Marcuse, the community as it now exists becomes not simply repressive but oppressive and in need of revolutionary change specifically in terms of its sexual codes. In short, the basic thrust of much modern thinking serves to shatter the idea of the individual as one whose best interests are served by being educated to conform to the canons and protocols of society. And that is the intellectual foundation for the first reversal, whereby therapy ceases to serve the purpose of socializing an individual. Instead, it seeks to protect the individual from the kind of harmful neuroses that society itself creates through its smothering of the individual's ability simply to be herself.

This then leads to the second reversal. In the worlds of political, religious, and economic man, commitment was outwardly directed to those communal beliefs, practices, and institutions that were bigger than the individual and in which the individual, to the degree that he or she conformed to or cooperated with them, found meaning. The ancient Athenian was committed to the assembly, the medieval Christian to his church, and the twentieth-century factory worker to his trade union and working man's club. All of them found their purpose and well-being by being committed to something outside themselves. In the world of psychological man, however, the commitment is first and foremost to the self and is inwardly directed. Thus, the order is reversed. Outward institutions become in effect the servants of the individual and her sense of inner well-being.

In fact, I might press this point further: institutions cease to be places for the formation of individuals via their schooling in the various practices and disciplines that allow them to take their place in society. Instead, they become platforms for performance, where individuals are allowed to be their authentic selves precisely because they are able to give expression to who they are "inside." Rieff characterizes the values of modern society and the person in such terms:

> Reticence, secrecy, concealment of self have been transformed into social problems; once they were aspects of civility, when the great Western formulary summed up in the creedal phrase "Know thyself" encouraged obedience to communal purposes rather than suspicion of them.[15]

For such selves in such a world, institutions such as schools and churches are places where one goes to perform, not to be formed—or, perhaps better, where one goes to be formed by performing.[16]

This helps explain in part the concern in recent years over making the classroom a "safe place"—that is, a place where students go not to be exposed to ideas that may challenge their deepest beliefs and commitments (part of what was traditionally considered to be the role of education) but to be affirmed and reassured. While hostile commentators berate this tendency as that caused by the hypersensitivity of a generation of "snowflakes," it is actually the result of the slow but steady psychologizing of the self and the triumph of inward-directed therapeutic categories over traditional outward-directed educational philosophies. That which hinders my outward expression of my inner

---

15. Rieff, *Triumph of the Therapeutic*, 17.

16. This point has recently been made by Yuval Levin: "We have moved, roughly speaking, from thinking of institutions as molds that shape people's character and habits toward seeing them as platforms that allow people to be themselves and to display themselves before a wider world." *A Time to Build: From Family and Community to Congress and the Campus: How Recommitting to Our Institutions Can Revive the American Dream* (New York: Basic Books, 2020), 33–34.

feelings—that which challenges or attempts to falsify my psychological beliefs about myself and thus to disturb my sense of inner well-being—is by definition harmful and to be rejected. And that means that traditional institutions must be transformed to conform to the psychological self, not vice versa.

This could also be described, using Taylor's terminology, as the triumph of expressive individualism and of poiesis over mimesis. If education is to allow the individual simply to be himself, unhindered by outward pressure to conform to any greater reality, then the individual is king. He can be whoever he wants to be. And rejecting the notion of any external authority or meaning to which education is to conform, the individual simply makes himself the creator of any meaning that there might be. So-called "external" or "objective" truths are then simply constructs designed by the powerful to intimidate and to harm the weak. Overthrowing them—and thus overthrowing the notion that there is a great reality to which we are all accountable, whether that of the *polis*, of some religion, or of the economy—becomes the central purpose of educational institutions. They are not to be places to form or to transform but rather places where students can perform. The triumph of the therapeutic represents the advent of the expressive individual as the normative type of human being and of the relativizing of all meaning and truth to personal taste.

Two Key Questions

If, as I argue in future chapters, it is true that we now live in a world in which the therapeutic needs of Rieff's psychological man stand at the center of life, it would then perhaps be possible to offer an explanation as to why human identity has become so plastic and statements such as "I am a man trapped in a woman's body" come to make sense. If the inner psychological life of the individual is sovereign, then identity becomes as potentially unlimited as the human imagination. Yet this would still leave some questions unresolved, questions that have a particular urgency in our current political climate. Why, for example, have the politics of sexual identity become so ferocious that any dissent from the latest orthodoxy is greeted with scorn and sometimes even legal action? A moment's reflection would seem to suggest that this is, on the surface at least, a rather odd phenomenon. What does it matter, to borrow a phrase oft used in the gay marriage debate surrounding the Supreme Court case of *Obergefell v. Hodges*, 576 US ___ (2015), what people do in private? Why should my agreement or disagreement with what consenting adults do behind closed doors be of any great public importance? If two men have a sexual relationship in the privacy of their bedroom, my disagreement with such behavior neither picks their pockets nor breaks their legs, as Thomas Jefferson would say. So why should disagreement with current sexual mores be regarded as somehow immoral and intolerable in the wider public sphere?

Such questions miss an important point. If it were just sexual activity that were at issue, passions would likely not run so deep. But far more than codes of behavior are at stake here. In addressing the behavior that has come to prominence through the sexual revolution, we are actually not so much speaking of practices as we are speaking of identities. And when we are speaking of identities, the public, political stakes are incredibly high and raise a whole different set of issues.

To anticipate the argument of later chapters, for the sexual revolutionaries who follow the line of Wilhelm Reich and Herbert Marcuse—for example, the feminist thinker Shulamith Firestone—the answer as to why dissent from the sexual revolution is to be eradicated is a simple one of political liberation. The oppressive nature of bourgeois society is built on repressive sexual codes that maintain the patriarchal nuclear family as the norm. As long as this state of affairs holds, there can be no true liberation, political or economic. Shattering sexual codes is therefore one of the principal emancipatory tasks of the political revolutionary. But few people have read Reich or Marcuse or Firestone. Fewer still perhaps accept the Marxist-Freudian metanarrative on which their politicized view of sex rests. But some of the ideas of these thinkers and philosophies are now part of the broader social imaginary of the West and have become the intuitive orthodoxy of much of society (for example, that oppression is primarily a psychological category enforced through sex and gender codes). That is part of the world of psychological man or expressive individualism, where personal authenticity is found through public performance of inward desires. And as the most powerful inward desires of most people are sexual in nature, so identity itself has come to be thought of as strongly sexual in nature.

Yet here I come to an important phenomenon requiring that I qualify the notion of the modern self simply as psychological man or the expressive individual: even now in our sexually libertarian world, certain sexual taboos remain in place, pedophilia being perhaps the most obvious. Not all expressions of individuality, not all behaviors that bring about a sense of inner psychological happiness for the agent, are regarded as legitimate. Whether any given individual notices it or not, society still imposes itself on its members and shapes and corrals their behavior.[17]

Now, while we might hope and pray that things such as pedophilia and incest remain taboo, we cannot be sure that such will be the case because sexual codes have changed so dramatically over the last few decades, and as I argue in chapter 9, the grounds on which one might mount a compelling argument against them have already been conceded by our culture. Nevertheless, even if the current sexual taboos rest on very shaky legal and philosophical foundations, they do reveal something important that must be taken into account when we are talking about psychologically constructed identity: not all psychological identities are considered to be legitimate, because society will not allow for the expression of every particular form of sexual desire, and therefore, not all sexual minorities enjoy the protection either of the law or of the general cultural ethos.

And so I arrive at two key questions that need to be answered: Why is it important that identity is publicly acknowledged? And why is it that the public acknowledgment of some identities is compulsory and of others is forbidden? There are two parts to this answer, one drawn from

---

17. There is some evidence that attitudes toward pedophilia might be changing: see Dorothy Cummings McLean, "TEDx Speaker: 'Pedophilia Is an Unchangeable Sexual Orientation,' 'Anyone' Could Be Born That Way," July 18, 2018, https://www.lifesitenews.com/news/ted-speaker-pedophilia-is-an-unchangeable-sexual-orientation-anyone-could-b.

Rieff (the analytic attitude) and one drawn from Taylor (the importance and nature of recognition).

The Analytic Attitude

At first glance, the concepts of psychological man or expressive individualism would not seem in themselves to offer an answer to the question of why public acknowledgment of the validity of particular identities is important or of why certain identities become respectable and others do not. For example, one could easily argue that expressive individualism really only requires freedom for me to be who I think I am, as long as that does not interfere with the lives of others. If I declare myself to be gay, it would seem that as long as that does not prevent me from holding a job, voting, receiving an education, or availing myself of the necessities of life, there is little reason for me to want anything more. Why would I need my neighbors to affirm my homosexuality as a good thing? To use the matter of cake baking: Mr. Bun, the Christian cake baker, may not be willing to make a cake for my gay wedding, but he will sell me his baked goods in general and will even recommend to me a baker who will fulfill my wedding requirements. His policy on wedding cakes is not going to cause me to starve or even require that I travel great distances to avail myself of baked goods. Why should such amicable tolerance of my homosexuality not suffice? Surely a situation whereby my identity is tolerated by others in a manner that allows me to go about my daily business would seem to be a reasonable state of affairs?

Yet the history of the sexual—or perhaps better, identity—revolution has clearly not played out in quite such a fashion. In fact, precisely such a scenario as that outlined above led to one of the most contentious and divisive Supreme Court cases of recent years.[18] It is clearly indisputable that mere tolerance of sexual identities that break with the heterosexual norm has not proved an acceptable option to the sexual revolutionaries. Nothing short of full equality under the law and full recognition of the legitimacy of certain nontraditional sexual identities by wider society has

---

18. Masterpiece Cakeshop v. Colorado Civil Rights Commission, 584 U.S. ___ (2018).

emerged as the ambition of the LGBTQ+ movement. It is not enough that I can buy a wedding cake somewhere in town. I must be able to buy a wedding cake from each and every baker in town who ever caters for weddings. Why is this the case?[19]

One could build an answer to this question on one aspect of Philip Rieff's definition of traditional culture—that it normally directs the self outward to communal purposes in which it can find satisfaction but that this direction has clearly been reversed in the era of psychological man. Satisfaction and meaning—authenticity—are now found by an inward turn, and the culture is reconfigured to this end. Indeed, it must now serve the purpose of meeting my psychological needs; I must not tailor my psychological needs to the nature of society, for that would create anxiety and make me inauthentic. The refusal to bake me a wedding cake, therefore, is not an act consistent with the therapeutic ideal; in fact, it is the opposite—an act causing me psychological harm.

There is therefore an outward, social dimension to my psychological well-being that demands others acknowledge my inward, psychological identity. We all as individuals still inhabit the same social spaces, still interact with other individuals, and so these other individuals must be coerced to be part of our therapeutic world. The era of psychological man therefore requires changes in the culture and its institutions, practices, and beliefs that affect everyone. They all need to adapt to reflect a therapeutic mentality that focuses on the psychological well-being of the individual. Rieff calls this societal characteristic *the analytic attitude.*

Once society starts to manifest the analytic attitude, there is, to borrow a phrase from Nietzsche, a transvaluation of values.[20] That which was

---

19. For an analysis of how the LGBTQ+ movement has progressed from demands for tolerance to demands for equality, see Darel E. Paul, *From Tolerance to Equality: How Elites Brought America to Same-Sex Marriage* (Waco, TX: Baylor University Press, 2018).

20. Nietzsche planned four books under the general title of "A Transvaluation of Values," although only one, *The Anti-Christ*, was completed. In this book, he attacks the morality of Christianity (and its expression in the work of Immanuel Kant), demanding that the metaphysical death of God requires a thoroughgoing revision (rejection) of traditional morality. As he declares in chap. 47, "What sets us apart is not that we recognize no God, either in history or in nature or behind nature—but that we find that which has been reverenced as God not 'godlike' but pitiable, absurd, harmful, not merely an error but a *crime against life*. . . . We deny God as God." *Twilight of the Idols and The Anti-Christ*, trans. R. J. Hollingdale (London: Penguin, 2003), 174–75. Nietzsche's point is that claims to transcendent moral codes are oppressive of the individual and deny true life.

previously deemed good comes to be regarded as bad; that which was previously regarded as healthy comes to be deemed sickness. The turn to the psychological self is fundamentally iconoclastic with regard to traditional moral codes as they are now seen to be part of the problem rather than the solution. Emphasis on what we might call the "right to psychological happiness" of the individual will also have some obvious practical effects. For example, language will become much more contested than in the past, because words that cause "psychological harm" will become problematic and will need to be policed and suppressed. To use pejorative racial or sexual epithets ceases to be a trivial matter. Instead, it becomes an extremely serious act of oppression. This explains why so much outrage in the public square is now directed at what one might call speech crimes. Even the neologism *hate speech* speaks to this. While earlier generations might have seen damage to body or property as the most serious categories of crime, a highly psychologized era will accord increasing importance to words as means of oppression. And this represents a serious challenge to one of the foundations of liberal democracy: freedom of speech. Once harm and oppression are regarded as being primarily psychological categories, freedom of speech then becomes part of the problem, not the solution, because words become potential weapons. Rieff's understanding of the current situation thus stands very close to that offered by Reich and Marcuse, who saw oppression as a primarily psychological phenomenon and the demolition of sexual codes and the dispatching of freedom of speech as necessary elements of the political revolution, even as (unlike them) Rieff laments these realities as signifying the death of culture rather than the birth pangs of the coming liberated utopia.

Yet Rieff's approach still leaves open the pressing question of why some identities are acceptable and their acceptance compulsory and enforced, and other identities do not enjoy such privilege. The foot fetishist, too, surely suffers psychological harm when he is denied the right to proclaim his proclivities in public and receive acclamation and even legal protection for so doing. Yet few if any care to take up his cause. Why not? He would seem to have just as much a claim to being a marginalized sexual minority as anyone in the LGBTQ+ movement. And no cake baker is being sued for refusing to bake cakes that glorify incest or the Ku Klux Klan. Again, why not? Rieff certainly offers a plausible framework for understanding the psychological nature of oppression in the therapeutic world, but he does not allow us to discern why some marginal identities gain mainstream acceptance and others remain (at least for the present) beyond the pale.

Charles Taylor and the Politics of Recognition

The question of why some identities find acceptance and others do not is simply a version of the question of how identity is formed in the first place. Much of this book focuses on the rise of the psychological self. The turn to epistemology in the Enlightenment and the work of men such as Rousseau led to an emphasis on the inner life as characterizing the authentic person. Yet before I address the historical narrative of the rise of the modern plastic, psychological, expressive self, it is necessary to note that for all psychological man's inward turn, individual personal identity is not ultimately an internal monologue conducted in isolation by an individual self-consciousness. On the contrary, it is a dialogue between self-conscious beings. We each know ourselves as we know other people.

A simple example of why this is important to understand is provided by Descartes's famous idea that in the act of doubting my own existence, I have to acknowledge that I do exist on the grounds that there has to be an "I" that doubts.[21] As plausible as that sounds, a key question that Descartes fails to ask is, What exactly is this "I" that is doing the doubting? Whatever the "I" might be, it is clearly something that has a facility with language, and language itself is something that typically involves interaction with other linguistic beings. I cannot therefore necessarily grant the "I" the privilege of self-consciousness prior to its engagement with others. The "I" is necessarily a social being.[22]

---

21. See René Descartes, *Discourse on Method; and, Meditations on First Philosophy*, trans. Donald A. Cress (Indianapolis: Hackett, 1993).

22. This is the argument of Charles Taylor in *The Language Animal* (Cambridge, MA: Belknap Press of Harvard University Press, 2016). For Taylor's criticism of Descartes, with particular attention to the essentially monological nature of the self his philosophy assumes, see esp. 64–65.

Building on this basic insight in his analyses of the rise of the modern self, Charles Taylor has done much to show that expressive individualism is a social phenomenon that emerges through the dialogical nature of what it means to be a person. As he expresses it,

> One is a self only among other selves. A self can never be described without reference to those who surround it.[23]

Elsewhere, he offers a more elaborate, though still succinct, summary of his position:

> The general feature of human life that I want to evoke is its fundamentally dialogical character. We become full human agents, capable of understanding ourselves, and hence of defining an identity, through our acquisition of rich human languages of expression. . . . I want to take "language" in a broad sense, covering not only the words we speak but also other modes of expression whereby we define ourselves, including the "languages" of art, of gesture, of love and the like. But we are inducted into these in exchange with others. No one acquires the languages needed for self-definition on their own. We are introduced to them through exchanges with others who matter to us.[24]

Taylor is here pointing to the fact that who we think we are is intimately connected to those to whom we relate—family, friends, coworkers. When asked who I am, for example, I do not respond by pointing the inquirer to my DNA code or to such generalities as my gender. I would typically define myself in relation to other people and other things—the child of John, the husband of Catriona, a professor at Grove City College, the author of a particular book. Circumstances would influence the specific content, but the reply would likely touch on my relationship with others.

This also connects to another point: the human need to belong. If our identities are shaped by our connection to and interaction with significant others, then identity also arises in the context of belonging. To have an identity means that I am being acknowledged by others.

---

23. Charles Taylor, *Sources of the Self: The Making of the Modern Identity* (Cambridge, MA: Harvard University Press, 1989), 35.

24. Charles Taylor, *The Malaise of Modernity* (Concord, ON: Anansi, 1991), 32–33.

To wander through a town and to be ignored by everyone I encounter would understandably lead me to question whether they considered me to be a nonperson or at least a person unworthy of acknowledgment. If I am treated by everyone I encounter as if I am worthless, I will probably end up feeling that I am worthless.

The Amish practice of shunning provides an example of this. When someone has committed some act that dramatically contradicts or defies the practices of the community, he can then be shunned. In extreme cases, this can mean that he is completely ignored by the Amish community. In this way, community identity is maintained by denying practical membership to the transgressor. The person ceases to be recognized as Amish by other Amish. While that individual continues to exist, his identity within the Amish community is effectively erased.[25]

Individual identity is thus truly a dialogue: how a person thinks of himself is the result of learning the language of the community so that he can be a part of the community. It also explains the basic human need to belong: the idea of the isolated Rousseauesque man of nature, living all by himself and for himself, may be superficially attractive, but a moment's reflection would indicate how strange, if not completely absurd, it would be.[26] In fact, to conduct such a thought experiment is likely to induce a kind of intellectual vertigo precisely because so much of who we are and how we think of ourselves is tied up with the people with whom we interact. To remove them from the picture is in a sense to remove ourselves, at least ourselves as we know ourselves. Again, if I ask what it would be like to be me if I had been born not in Dudley, England, to English parents but rather in Delhi to an Indian mother and father, the question is really impossible to answer for a very simple reason: I would then have been not me but someone completely different.

This dialogical dimension of identity also points to another aspect of modern selfhood. There is, for sure, a deep desire in the modern West

25. See "Why Do the Amish Practice Shunning?," Amish America, accessed February 14, 2019, http://amishamerica.com/why-do-the-amish-practice-shunning/.

26. On Rousseau, see chap. 3.

for self-expression, to perform in public in a manner consistent with that which one feels or thinks one is on the inside. That is the essence of authenticity as I will note in the thought of Rousseau in chapter 3. It is also the idea of authenticity that dominates the contemporary cultural imagination. Yet the desire to belong to some larger whole, to find unity with others, is also characteristic of modern selfhood. One might note a comparatively trivial example of this: the teenager who dresses in a particular way to express her individuality and yet at the same time ends up wearing more or less the same clothes as every other member of her peer group. Her clothing is both a means of self-expression and a means of finding unity with a larger group at one and the same time.

Taylor's own attitude to this issue is rooted in his appropriation of the thought of the nineteenth-century German philosopher G. W. F. Hegel. Frederick Neuhouser summarizes Taylor's approach to Hegel in terms that make the latter's relevance obvious:

> [Taylor's argument is] that Hegel's social philosophy attempted to satisfy two aspirations bequeathed to us by the Enlightenment and its Romantic successors: aspiration to radical autonomy and to expressive unity with nature and society.[27]

In short, Hegel is useful because he is the key philosopher who wrestled with the quintessential problem of identity in the modern era: how to connect the aspiration to express oneself as an individual and to be free with the desire for being at one with (or belonging to) society as a whole. How can I simultaneously be myself and belong to a larger social group? This is where Hegel's thought is of great contemporary relevance.

Hegel begins the most famous section of his *Phenomenology of Spirit*, on the relationship between master and slave, with the following statement: "Self-consciousness exists in and for itself when, and by the fact that, it so exists for another; that is, it exists only in being acknowledged."[28] What Hegel means by this is that self-consciousness is found only in a

---

27. Frederick Neuhouser, preface to Charles Taylor, *Hegel and Modern Society* (Cambridge: Cambridge University Press, 2015), vii.
28. G. W. F. Hegel, *Phenomenology of Spirit*, trans. A. V. Miller (Oxford: Oxford University Press, 1977), 111.

fully developed form where two such self-consciousnesses recognize each other as mutually recognizing each other. That is a rather convoluted and inelegant way of saying that a human being is most self-conscious when she knows that other people are acknowledging her as a self-conscious being.

A trivial example might help elucidate this idea further. Children often play improvised team sports in the schoolyard during recess. Typically team captains—normally a couple of the stronger leadership types in the playground pecking order—take it in turns to select players for their team. The moment of being selected often gives the one chosen a thrill, a feeling of excitement, of satisfaction, and, perhaps more negatively, of superiority relative to those who have not yet been picked. That is a moment of being *recognized*, of being acknowledged as valuable, by another—and, crucially, of knowing oneself that one has been so acknowledged. One imagines that this experience is somewhat different from that of, say, a Jack Russell terrier whose master comes home after work and calls him to sit on his lap. The Jack Russell may well be thrilled by the return of his master and by the fact that he has been acknowledged or recognized in such a way, but unlike the child picked for the playground team, he will lack the self-consciousness necessary to reflect on the fact that he has been so acknowledged. One might describe the Jack Russell's reaction as simply instinctive.

This idea—that identity requires recognition by another—is a vital insight into the subject I am exploring in this book. It also points toward the way identity can thus become contentious. Hegel himself points to this conflict in his chapter on the master-slave dialectic.[29] In a meeting of two primitive self-consciousnesses, recognition or acknowledgment of another self-consciousness requires a setting aside or a denial of oneself. The ultimate form of this dynamic is that the one self-consciousness comes to dominate the other totally, to negate it entirely. That is, if I meet someone else, the greatest way that my existence can be recognized by him is for me to fight and kill him. Recognition thus becomes a life-and-death struggle. But because death is also somewhat self-defeating

---

29. Hegel, *Phenomenology of Spirit*, 111–19.

from the victor's standpoint—once the other person is dead, he cannot give me the recognition I desire—real life means that a compromise situation holds, whereby the one person comes to hold a superior position to the other who yet remains alive. A hierarchy of master and slave is thereby established, whereby the stronger receives from the weaker the recognition he desires.

To return to the playground example, one sees this hierarchical form of recognition at play in the action of team selection. The fact that the teams are picked by leaders indicates that a number of the children are recognized as such by the rest. The captains are captains because the other children acknowledge them as their superiors in some way. Recognition thus always stands in potential relationship to hierarchy and therefore to potential struggle and conflict. Again, playgrounds provide a good example, that of the school bully. The bully is one who establishes his dominant role in a particular hierarchy by the use of power to subjugate those who are weaker. The recognition they grant him is vital to his own self-consciousness but is extracted from others in a way that negates them to some significant degree, such that they know themselves to be below him in the hierarchy of power, to be somehow "less" than him.

Clearly, the dialogical nature of identity creates the possibility for tension not simply between individuals but also between the desires of the individual and the concerns of the community and, of course, between one community and another. Hegel was aware of this, and it forms an important part of his understanding of the political culture of the modern state.[30] And this is where the issue becomes complicated. It is also where one can begin to construct an answer to the question as to why only certain identities appear to enjoy legitimacy and widespread social privilege. To put the matter another way, it helps explain why some identities find recognition in society while others do not.

---

30. "Fully developed self-consciousness, according to Hegel, is to be found only where such recognition is mutual, indeed, where two (or more) self-consciousnesses '*recognise* themselves as *mutually recognising* one another,' as, for example, in the modern constitutional state." Stephen Houlgate, *An Introduction to Hegel: Freedom, Truth and History*, 2nd ed. (Oxford: Blackwell, 2005), 68.

Here it is helpful to note a concept that Taylor draws from Hegel, that of *Sittlichkeit*. This term cannot be captured by a single English word, and so Taylor retains the original German in his work but offers this explanation of its precise meaning:

> *Sittlichkeit* refers to the moral obligations I have to an ongoing community of which I am part. These obligations are based on established norms and uses, and that is why the etymological root in *Sitten* is important for Hegel's use. The crucial characteristic of *Sittlichkeit* is that it enjoins us to bring about what already is. This is a paradoxical way of putting it, but in fact the common life which is the basis of my *sittlich* obligation is already there in existence. It is in virtue of its being an ongoing affair that I have these obligations; and my fulfilment of these obligations is what sustains it and keeps it in being. Hence in *Sittlichkeit* there is no gap between what ought to be and what is, between *Sollen* and *Sein*.[31]

What this means is that society itself is an ethical community. What it implies is that the individual finds her self-consciousness in being recognized by that society, and this occurs because she is behaving according to the conventions of that society. In short, there is a need for the expressive individual to be at one with the expressive community.

One can rephrase this idea using an analogy with language. For people to be self-conscious and to express themselves to others, they need to be able to speak the language of the community to which they belong or to which they wish to speak, to use its vocabulary and to follow its grammatical and syntactical rules. Of course, it is individuals who use the language, but the language is not something they invent for themselves. If that were the case, it would not be a language in the commonly understood sense of the word. Rather, it is something prior to them and that they have to learn. Further, it is as individuals use language that both the language has reality and its existence is sustained.

Again, a trivial example makes this point clear. Anyone who has ever traveled in a country where they could not speak the native language

---

31. Taylor, *Hegel and Modern Society*, 81. See also the discussion in Craig Browne and Andrew P. Lynch, *Taylor and Politics: A Critical Introduction* (Edinburgh: Edinburgh University Press, 2018), 70–72.

and the local population could not speak that of the traveler will know the personal frustration this involves. Such a person is alienated from the society in which she happens to find herself and is not able to be a proper part of the community. It is only as the traveler acquires the local language that she is able to give expression to her personal identity in a way that is recognized by the locals and that allows her in some sense to belong.

What is vital to notice is that recognition is therefore a social phenomenon. It is important to me to have my identity recognized, but the framework and conventions both for expressing my identity and for that identity being recognized are socially constructed, specific to the context in which I find myself. The Roman soldier dresses in a certain way and is recognized by the populace as who and what he is because he dons a particular uniform. To wear that uniform today might indicate nothing more than the fact that one is going to a fancy dress party. At worst it might be a sign of insanity. It will certainly not mean that one is recognized as the brave member of a military unit. And so it is with other forms of dress and behavior. We might wish to express ourselves, but we typically do so in ways that are sanctioned by the modern society in which we happen to live.

When applied to the question of identity, specifically the kind of identities that the sexual revolution has brought in its wake, one can conclude that those that are considered legitimate—summed up by the LGBTQ+ acronym—are legitimate because they are recognized by the wider moral structure, the *Sittlichkeit*, of our society. The intuitive moral structure of our modern social imaginary prioritizes victimhood, sees selfhood in psychological terms, regards traditional sexual codes as oppressive and life denying, and places a premium on the individual's right to define his or her own existence. All these things play into legitimizing and strengthening those groups that can define themselves in such terms. They capture, one might say, the spirit of the age. This helps explain why these identities are recognized and others are not. Pedophiles, for example, are currently unpersuasive as a victimized class, given the fact that they appear more as victimizers, however iconoclastic they are with regard to traditional sexual codes. Gay men, however, as consenting adults, are not seen as victimizers and can call on a long history of social marginalization and victimhood. They can thus claim a right to recognition, a recognition that is connected to a further aspect of the modern moral imagination, that of dignity.

The Question of Dignity

One of the underlying themes of this book, following Rieff, Taylor, and MacIntyre, is that psychological man and expressive individualism shape the dominant understanding of what it means to be a human self in this present age. Yet given the argument of the previous section, for these to be the controlling notions of the self demands that society itself embody certain assumptions. For the expressive individual to receive recognition means that the assumptions of expressive individualism must be the assumptions of society as a whole. For the individual to be king, society must recognize the supreme value of the individual.

Taylor argues that central to this thinking is the shift from a society based on the notion of honor to that based on the notion of dignity.[32] The former is built on the idea of a given social hierarchy. The medieval feudal lord was owed honor by his vassals simply by virtue of his birth. The world in which he lived considered him to be intrinsically superior to those below him. The same applied to the samurai in Japan. Their position in the social hierarchy meant that they were automatically considered superior to those who sat below them in the hierarchy. The English class system retains vestiges of this idea, and the Hindu caste system is perhaps its most obvious embodiment in the modern age.

This framework for recognition has been effectively demolished by two dramatic developments. First, technological and economic changes have over the centuries broken down the old hierarchical structures of society. To give an exhaustive account of this process is beyond the scope of this study, but it is worth briefly noting a number of factors that have

---

32. See Charles Taylor, "The Politics of Recognition," in *Philosophical Arguments* (Cambridge, MA: Harvard University Press, 1997), 225–56.

fostered this shift. Second, certain intellectual developments have proved lethal to traditional, hierarchical ways of thinking.

The rise of technology is clearly important to the demolition of old hierarchies, changing the relationship of human beings to their environment and transforming economic relationships between individuals. The rise of industrialism and the importance of capital in nineteenth-century England, for example, meant that the traditional nobility ceased to be as socially and politically important as it once had been. Power came to reside not so much in the ownership of traditional landed estates but in money, in capital, in that which could be invested in factories, and in the production and distribution of goods. This shift also fueled the growth of cities and in many places transformed local populations through both emigration and immigration in a manner that subverted traditional local hierarchies. I might also add that the kind of skills technology demanded—and still demands—came to favor the young, who were able to learn and adapt more easily. One has only to look at how the current IT industry is often dominated by young, free-thinking, entrepreneurial types to see how even the former (but still relatively recent) hierarchies of the business world have been attenuated and even rendered superfluous. Rigid social hierarchies that embodied and enforced honor codes have been made impractical and implausible in modern capitalist society, as Karl Marx and Friedrich Engels observed long ago in *The Communist Manifesto*.[33]

As noted above, the assault on hierarchies was not simply the result of changing technological and economic conditions. Intellectual developments in the seventeenth and eighteenth centuries also proved lethal to old hierarchical ways of thinking. For example, while the epistemology of Descartes might not at first glance appear to have great political significance, it effectively moved the individual knowing subject to the center. And this move surely found its most eloquent psychological expression in the work of Rousseau, for whom society and culture were the problems, the things that corrupted the individual and prevented

---

33. For Marx and Engels, see chap. 5.

him from being truly authentic. Given that the hierarchies of honor-based societies would be examples of precisely the kind of corrupting conventions that the egalitarian Rousseau would have regarded with disdain, the clear notion is that all human beings are created intrinsically equal. As Rousseau famously expressed it at the start of *The Social Contract*, "Man is born free and everywhere is in chains." And the implication of this thinking is that all human beings therefore possess equal dignity.[34]

Rousseau's key ideas were picked up and reinforced by the subsequent Romantics: the individual is at his most authentic before he is shaped (and corrupted) by the need to conform to social conventions. Thus, in the seventeenth and eighteenth centuries, identity turns inward, a move that is fundamentally antihierarchical in its implications. Society's structure is no longer regarded as reflecting the intrinsic superiority or inferiority of particular individuals and particular groups. Indeed, to make the claim that society's actual structure does reflect the intrinsic superiority or inferiority of individuals represents a very significant moral problem, one that needs to be overcome in some way. And if such hierarchies seek to manifest themselves by the granting or withholding of recognition, then that particular issue needs urgently to be addressed. Equal dignity relativizes the importance of the external circumstances. As noted above, hierarchies are the product of society and are therefore corrupting. They are what make the individual inauthentic.

This confluence of changing material conditions, social and economic practices, and intellectual developments served to shatter the old hierarchies of medieval and early modern Europe and paved the way for a more egalitarian view of humanity. And this is a critically important development because it goes to the very heart of the issue of recognition since it fundamentally changes the terms of the dialogical nature of personal identity. In the past, a person's identity came from

---

34. Jean-Jacques Rousseau, *The Social Contract and Other Later Political Writings*, ed. and trans. Victor Gourevitch, Cambridge Texts in the History of Political Thought (Cambridge: Cambridge University Press, 1997), 41.

without, the result of being set within a fixed social hierarchy. One might perhaps say that belonging, or being recognized, was therefore a question of understanding one's place in that preexisting social hierarchy into which one had been born. One simply had to learn to think and to act in accordance with one's position within that hierarchy. For example, the peasant had to understand his place in relation to the lord. Failure to do so would make the peasant a rebel against the social order, and this would call forth punitive measures against him from the lord. The lord had to act in order to reassert the importance of the given hierarchical order. This was exactly what the notion of honor represented.

The net result of the collapse of traditional hierarchies is that notions of honor no longer shape the pattern of social engagement and, therefore, of recognition in today's society. That role is now played by the notion of dignity, which each and every human being possesses not by virtue of their social status but simply by being human. This egalitarian concept changes everything in theory, and as it therefore comes to change everything in practice, it almost inevitably involves conflict, for it brings us back to that important point concerning the *Sittlichkeit* of society: How does society understand identity, and what range of identities does it consider to be legitimate? If I am to be recognized and if I am to belong, then there needs to be conformity between that social reality and my personal reality. And sometimes that conformity needs to be realized through conflict, whereby the ethics of one group or era are consciously defeated by those of another.

To take one example, in 1954 the Supreme Court of the United States ruled in the case of *Brown v. Board of Education of Topeka*, 347 US 483 (1954), that the segregation of white and African American children in public schools was unconstitutional. The language of the ruling offers insights into the importance of recognition:

> To separate [African American children] from others of similar age and qualifications solely because of their race generates a feeling of

inferiority as to their status in the community that may affect their hearts and minds in a way unlikely ever to be undone.[35]

Two things are worthy of note here. First, there is the psychological language: school segregation generates *feelings* of inferiority in African American children. The judgment is clearly operating within a world in which the psychological turn regarding selfhood has struck deep roots. This is emphatically not a criticism at this point, merely an observation. One of the big problems with "separate but equal" as regarded by the Supreme Court is the deleterious psychological effects that it has. And the Supreme Court clearly views this as a legitimate criterion for a legal ruling—a point that offers insights into the kind of culture in which the justices are operating.

Second, there is in this judgment the nature of the recognition (or lack thereof) that segregation represents: it generates feelings of *inferiority*. And it is surely obvious as to why this should be the case. For all the rhetoric of "separate but equal" that the proponents of segregation had used, it is quite clear that the white denial of integration to African Americans represented a refusal to recognize them as possessing equal dignity. This denial of recognition constituted a declaration in terms of social practices that the African American community was inferior to that of the whites, that it did not measure up to the criteria necessary for being recognized. The only way to rectify this situation was therefore to legislate integration and thereby to require that educational institutions did accord the African American community the recognition necessary for full equality, not simply before the law but via the law in the *Sittlichkeit* of modern America.

This observation is important in enabling us to understand why, for example, in a society where sexuality is foundational to personal identity, mere tolerance of homosexuality is bound to become unacceptable. The issue is not one of simply decriminalizing behavior; that would certainly mean that homosexual acts were tolerated by society,

---

35. Text available at "Brown v. Board of Education of Topeka, 347 U.S. 483 (1954)," Justia, accessed February 22, 2019, https://supreme.justia.com/cases/federal/us/347/483/.

but the acts are only a part of the overall problem. The real issue is one of recognition, of recognizing the legitimacy of who the person thinks he actually is. That requires more than mere tolerance; it requires equality before the law and recognition by the law and in society. And that means that those who refuse to grant such recognition will be the ones who find themselves on the wrong side of both the law and emerging social attitudes.

The person who objects to homosexual practice is, in contemporary society, actually objecting to homosexual identity. And the refusal by any individual to recognize an identity that society at large recognizes as legitimate is a moral offense, not simply a matter of indifference. The question of identity in the modern world is a question of dignity. For this reason, the various court cases in America concerning the provision of cakes and flowers for gay weddings are not ultimately about the flowers or the cakes. They are about the recognition of gay identity and, according to members of the LGBTQ+ community, the recognition that they need in order to feel that they are equal members of society.

For this reason, the appropriation by the LGBTQ+ community of the civil rights language of the 1950s and 1960s cannot be understood as a simple, cynical move to appropriate the history of the suffering of one community in order to advance the political ambitions of another. It is certainly the case that calling on the language of "Jim Crow" and segregation provides powerful rhetorical ammunition for the LGBTQ+ cause and indeed makes public criticism of its political demands very, very difficult. Yet the civil rights movement of the 1950s and the sexual identity rights movement of the present day, in fact, rest on different, even antithetical, premises, the former grounded in a notion of dignity based on a universal human nature, the latter on the sovereign right of individual self-determination. But they do share this in common: they represent demands for society to recognize the dignity of particular individuals, particular identities, and particular communities in social practices, cultural attitudes, and, therefore, legislation.

Concluding Reflections

The various concepts outlined in this chapter present facets of the overall narrative that will occupy the historical section of this book. Central to understanding the world in which we live is the idea of the social imaginary. This concept highlights that the tremendous changes we are witnessing can be interpreted through a variety of lenses. First, it is important to understand that most of us do not think about the world in the way we do because we have reasoned from first principles to a comprehensive understanding of the cosmos. Rather, we generally operate on the basis of intuitions that we have often unconsciously absorbed from the culture around us. Second, we need to understand that our sense of selfhood, of who we are, is both intuitive and deeply intertwined with the expectations, ethical and otherwise, of the society in which we are placed. The desire to be recognized, to be accepted, to belong is a deep and perennial human need, and no individual sets the terms of that recognition or belonging all by himself. To be a self is to be in a dialogical relationship with other selves and thus with the wider social context.

That observation then raises the question of the nature and origin of the expectations and intuitions that constitute the social imaginary. Here of great importance are both the emergence of a picture of the world as lacking intrinsic meaning and authority and the notion that what meaning it possesses must therefore first be put there by us as creative human agents. While it might seem far fetched to connect, say, Descartes's grounding of certainty in his consciousness of his own doubting to the claims of a contemporary transgender activist that sex and gender are separable, in fact both represent a psychological approach to reality. How the world moves from one to the other is a long, complicated story, but the two are connected. And one does not have to have read Descartes—or Judith Butler—to think intuitively about the world in terms for which they provide the theoretical rationale.

Rieff and Taylor are both correct in seeing psychological man and the expressive individual as the result of a long historical process and as the normative types in this present age. The psychologized, expressive individual that is the social norm today is unique, unprecedented, and singularly significant. The emergence of such selves is a matter of central importance in the history of the West as it is both a symptom and a cause of the many social, ethical, and political questions we now face. To use another of the concepts outlined above, this new view of the self also reflects and facilitates a distinct move away from a mimetic view of the world as possessing intrinsic meaning to a poietic one, where the onus for meaning lies with the human self as constructive agent. But before we turn to the narrative of how this new understanding of selfhood emerged, and why it tilts so strongly in a sexual direction, we need to outline some of the other pathologies that shape our contemporary culture. Indeed, we need to understand why Rieff describes our current situation not as a culture but rather as an anticulture.

2

Reimagining Our Culture

"What are you rebelling against?" "Whatcha got?"

MARLON BRANDO, *THE WILD ONE*

In the last chapter, we introduced a number of concepts that are of help in thinking about the current state of Western culture. The idea of the social imaginary is useful in highlighting the fact that most of us do not self-consciously reflect on life and the world as we live in it but instead think and act intuitively in accordance with the way we instinctively imagine the world to be. That view is shaped by the environment in which we live, and that environment also sets the terms by which human beings can be recognized by others—the way we each come to meet that deep human need of belonging. Each individual self is constituted in dialogue with other selves and with the overall expectations of the culture in which they live.

This still leaves open a number of significant questions. Why, for example, does our culture have the particular ethical shape it does? We might be more specific: Why does our social imaginary make sex such a basic marker of identity, and attitudes to sex such a fundamental test for recognition? Why does the public apparently need to know the sexual orientation of movie stars or their attitude to gay marriage, when neither are particularly relevant to their technical competence to pursue their profession? Why is it so important to educate even elementary school children in the taxonomy of sexual preferences? It has not always been that way.

These specific questions are addressed in later chapters. But the argument of those chapters is best set within the context of a prior answer to another question: What are the broader pathologies of our cultural moment that have provided the context for such acrimonious culture wars over sex and identity? Again, Philip Rieff and Charles Taylor are helpful here, as is the Catholic moral philosopher Alasdair MacIntyre.

The Modern West as a Third-World Culture

Despite the broad and somewhat simplistic nature of his account of the historical evolution of human beings from political man onward, Philip Rieff has proved most prescient in his analysis of psychological man and the therapeutic society to which he belongs. But his contribution to understanding modern culture does not end there. Indeed, it is arguable that the therapeutic society is simply the specific manifestation of a more general type of culture that he describes in his later trilogy *Sacred Order / Social Order*.[1] Here he introduces the terms *first*, *second*, and *third* worlds, although he does not use this terminology to express what is typically intended by third world—developing countries in Africa, Asia, and South America. His interest is neither geographic nor economic. Rather, he uses this language to refer to the type of culture that societies embody.

As we will see in chapter 6, Sigmund Freud believed that culture/civilization was the result of prohibitions. The essential culture of a society is determined by the things that it forbids and how it forbids them. Those interdicts (to use Rieff's favored term) repress human instincts, instincts that are sublimated in other pursuits—art, politics, and so on.[2] It is also important to note that Freud regarded religion as playing a

---

1. The three volumes in Philip Rieff's *Sacred Order / Social Order* (Charlottesville: University of Virginia Press, 2006–2008) are vol. 1, *My Life among the Deathworks: Illustrations of the Aesthetics of Authority*, ed. Kenneth S. Piver; vol. 2, *The Crisis of the Officer Class: The Decline of the Tragic Sensibility*, ed. Alan Woolfolk; and vol. 3, *The Jew of Culture: Freud, Moses, and Modernity*, ed. Arnold M. Eisen and Gideon Lewis-Kraus.

2. Freud's classic statement of this idea is his essay *Civilization and Its Discontents*, trans. James Strachey (New York: W. W. Norton, 1989).

significant role in justifying and enforcing this system of repression. For him, religion was an illusion, something whose purpose lay not so much in its actual truth value as in its social function in providing a transcendent, supernatural authoritative rationale, one that stood beyond and behind this natural world as we know it, for these interdicts.[3]

Rieff, picking up on these twin points, regards the social order—that which embodies society's moral values, the essence of civilization—as ultimately grounded in a sacred order. Or at least he sees this as having been the case until recently. It is the loss of this extrinsic justification for moral codes that is so catastrophic for society at large, the narrative of which loss (at least at the level of intellectual discourse) is the subject of parts 2 and 3 of this book.

According to Rieff, first and second worlds justify their morality by appeal to something transcendent, beyond the material world.[4] First worlds are pagan, but that does not mean they lack moral codes rooted in something greater than themselves. Their moral codes are based in myths. We might think of Lycurgus, legendary ruler of Sparta, whose laws were given authority by receiving the approval of the oracle at Delphi. However intrinsically wise or pragmatically beneficial his laws might have been, it was the sacred myth, the stamp of supernatural approval, that gave them their real authority. To any Spartan who questioned why the laws stipulated the things they did, Lycurgus's answer would not have been a simple "Because I say so." Rather, it would have been "Because the oracle at Delphi has sanctioned them." The appeal is to an order, a sacred order, beyond the social arrangements and pragmatic conveniences of Spartan society. Rieff characterizes such a world as one where fate is the controlling idea. It is not God as some transcendent being who is in charge, but it is still a force prior to the natural order and beyond the control of mere men and women.[5]

Second worlds are those worlds that are characterized not so much by fate as by faith. The obvious example here is Christianity.[6] The Christian

---

3. Freud's argument on this point can be found in his book *The Future of an Illusion*, trans. James Strachey (New York: W. W. Norton, 1989).

4. Rieff, *Deathworks*, 4, 12.

5. Rieff, *Deathworks*, 49.

6. Rieff, *Deathworks*, 5, 12.

faith shaped the cultures of the West in an incalculably deep way. Law codes were rooted in the will of God revealed in the Bible. Aquinas's theory of law builds his entire moral edifice on the character of God himself. Concepts of justice and mercy were shaped by the Bible's teaching. Our law courts still reflect that thinking to some degree: witnesses on the stand are traditionally required to place their hands on a sacred text (typically the Bible) and swear to tell the truth. The idea that they—and indeed, the entire proceedings—are in some sense accountable to the sacred is thus dramatically displayed in the very actions that surround the business of the courtroom.

First and second worlds thus have a moral, and therefore cultural, stability because their foundations lie in something beyond themselves. To put it another way, they do not have to justify themselves on the basis of themselves. Third worlds, by way of stark contrast to the first and second worlds, do not root their cultures, their social orders, their moral imperatives in anything sacred. They do have to justify themselves, but they cannot do so on the basis of something sacred or transcendent. Instead, they have to do so on the basis of themselves. The inherent instability of this approach should be obvious. Children who ask their parents why they have to eat their vegetables before they can enjoy the ice cream dessert may well be persuaded by the response "Because I say so" simply because of the accepted hierarchy to which they belong. But when they reach a certain age and start querying the validity of the hierarchy, then that answer will no longer carry significant weight. The command ceases to have authority when the hierarchy it presupposes ceases to have authority. Rieff's point is that third worlds have abandoned the notion of a sacred order, and so the interdicts of first and second worlds cease to have any plausibility because they lack any justification beyond themselves. Rieff expresses this thinking as follows:

> Culture and sacred order are inseparable, the former the registration of the latter as a systemic expression of the practical relation between humans and the shadow aspect of reality as it is lived. No culture has ever preserved itself where it is not a registration of sacred order. There, cultures have not survived. The third culture notion of a culture that

persists independent of all sacred orders is unprecedented in human history.[7]

Rieff's central point here is that the abandonment of a sacred order leaves cultures without any foundation.[8] The culture with no sacred order therefore has the task—for Rieff, the impossible task—of justifying itself only by reference to itself. Morality will thus tend toward a matter of simple consequentialist pragmatism, with the notion of what are and are not desirable outcomes being shaped by the distinct cultural pathologies of the day.

Charles Taylor has a parallel concept to the third world in what he calls the *immanent frame*. Prior ages were characterized by a transcendent frame, a belief that this world stood under the authority of a reality that transcended its mere material existence. Rieff's third worlds are the worlds of Taylor's immanent frame, where *this world* is all that there is, and so moral discourse cannot find its justification or root its authority in anything that lies beyond it.

Taylor matter-of-factly describes the cultural significance of the shift from a transcendent to an immanent frame of reference:

> At first, the social order is seen as offering us a blueprint for how things, in the human realm, can hang together to our mutual benefit, and this is identified with the plan of Providence, what God asks us to realize. But it is in the nature of a self-sufficient immanent order that it can be envisaged without reference to God; and very soon the proper blueprint is attributed to Nature.[9]

Taylor thus sees the move from Rieff's second to third world as a somewhat gradual one, whereby the idea of God slowly becomes an unnecessary hypothesis. And Rieff sees this move as one of catastrophic cultural significance and as embodying, or leading to, distinct and damaging

---

7. Rieff, *Deathworks*, 13.

8. Leszek Kołakowski makes a similar observation on the importance of the concept of the sacred in maintaining the moral stability of society; see his "The Revenge of the Sacred in Secular Culture," in *Modernity on Endless Trial* (Chicago: University of Chicago Press, 1990), 63–74.

9. Charles Taylor, *A Secular Age* (Cambridge, MA: Belknap Press of Harvard University Press, 2007), 543.

cultural pathologies. As noted, the shift from first to second worlds does not disrupt the fundamental logic of culture: ethical codes are rooted in some kind of sacred order, and cultures are still defined by that which they forbid. But the fact that third worlds do not build their moral codes on a sacred order renders their cultures profoundly volatile, subject to confusion, and liable to collapse.

We can perhaps see this point more clearly by taking a specific example: abortion. A prohibition on abortion really depends on the notion of personhood. Is an embryo a person with potential or a potential person? When personhood is seen as something connected to the sacred and transcending the merely material—say, as the possession of a soul or of the image of God—then the embryo is a person of potential and protected in, say, the Christian sacred order because she possesses the image of God from the moment of conception. That at six weeks she cannot fend for herself or even be parted from her mother's body and survive is irrelevant, because such material factors are really incidental to the core notion of personhood and need to be set in the context of a metaphysics grounded in a sacred order.

Once one removes the sacred order, however, the question of the embryo's status is much more contested. To say that an embryo is a person becomes an arbitrary claim when the things we typically associate with personhood through our everyday experience of it—a degree of independent existence, the capacity for self-reflection, the ability to act with intention toward the future, and so on—are apparently absent. What a person is or is not is, in the third world, now a matter for debate, as the work of Peter Singer has demonstrated—attempts to argue from natural law detached from sacred order notwithstanding, since such arguments themselves depend on a prior metaphysics of nature and cannot simply be justified on the basis of nature.[10]

Now if personhood has become a contested matter on which there is no agreement, other criteria for determining the legitimacy of abortion come into play. In the therapeutic culture, these tend to resolve themselves

---

10. For more on Peter Singer, see "Ivy League Ethics," p. 315, in chap. 9.

into the simple question of whether giving birth to the child will be conducive to the mother's mental well-being—itself a highly subjective concept for which no real objective criteria can be supplied. Who is to naysay the pregnant woman who claims that she will have a breakdown if she gives birth, and on what grounds would they do so? Hence that which was once considered anathema in the second world becomes a matter of moral indifference in the third. Or we might go even further: given the priority of the mother's health, perhaps abortion in many cases becomes a moral imperative.[11]

What is true about abortion can be extrapolated into other areas. In our contemporary society, sexual morality has become largely a matter of pragmatic considerations—"Will this make me happy? How can I attenuate the risks? Does it harm someone else's psychological well-being?"—and because these measures are always changing and are frequently subjective, they provide no stable framework for ethics. Contraception minimizes the risk of unwanted pregnancy, thus facilitating sex as recreation without the need for the context of a long-term stable relationship. Condoms curtail the spread of sexually transmitted diseases and therefore enable "safe sex" in the gay community. Mutual consent moves to the center of discussions about what is and is not acceptable sexual behavior. And this, in its turn, places huge pressure on even the most deeply rooted of sexual taboos. Why should incest be prohibited if it is between consenting adults and there is no risk of conception?

To tie two strands of Rieff's thought together, these third-world cultures are really just therapeutic cultures, the cultures of psychological man: the only moral criterion that can be applied to behavior is whether it conduces to the feeling of well-being in the individuals concerned. Ethics, therefore, becomes a function of feeling. Again, we can also draw connections to the expressive individualism of Charles

---

11. It is also worth noting in this context the confusion that exists in law relative to the child in the womb. In California in 2004, Scott Peterson was convicted of the murders of both his wife, Laci, and their unborn son in 2002. That such cases can be successfully prosecuted is interesting in a nation where abortion is legal and, therefore, the child in the womb does not enjoy absolute protection should the mother wish to terminate the pregnancy.

Taylor: cultures of the third world / immanent frame are preoccupied with the self-actualization and fulfillment of the individual because there is no greater purpose that can be justified in any ultimately authoritative sense.

One important point to note is that all three cultures—first, second, and third—can exist simultaneously in the same society. This is the reason why society now often feels like a cultural battle zone: it consists of groups of people who simply think about the moral structure of the world in utterly incompatible ways. Third-world cultures operate with a narrative framework that is incommensurable with the other two. The Southern Baptist who believes marriage is defined by the Bible to reflect the relationship of Christ to his church is inevitably going to be in conflict with the secularist who thinks that marriage is a fluid social arrangement designed for the convenience and happiness of the contracting parties and to last no longer than it is conducive to those ends. More significantly, the Southern Baptist is not going to have any basis on which he can argue his case with a denizen of a third world on which the two of them can agree. Put simply, there is no common ground on which the denizens of third worlds can engage in meaningful dialogue with those of the first or second. They acknowledge no transcendent authority by which morals and behavior can be justified or judged. More than that, third worlds are characterized by total opposition to any kind of sacred order and to those verticals in authority (religious institutions and authorities) that typically mediate that sacred order.[12]

Such a position leads to a complete breakdown of communication. To return to the matter of abortion, it is possible to envisage a debate in a second-world culture between pro-life and pro-choice individuals in which real communication takes place. This is because the basic terms of debate would be matters of mutual agreement. In a Christian second world, that is a question of when the embryo comes to bear the image

---

12. Commenting on Rieff's concept of third-world culture, James Davison Hunter writes, "What makes the contemporary war distinctive is that it is a movement of negation against *all* sacred orders and directed, in its particulars, against the verticals in authority that mediate sacred order to social order." Introduction to Rieff, *Deathworks*, xxiii.

of God or have a soul. There might well still be disagreements on that point—Thomas Aquinas, for example, standing in a well-established tradition rooted in the thought of Aristotle, believed that the child in the womb did not receive a soul until forty or ninety days after conception, depending on whether it was a boy or a girl.[13] Yet both sides would agree that the matter is not to be resolved with reference to purely pragmatic or subjective criteria but must be addressed with reference to an authority grounded in the sacred.

When a representative of a second world, however, clashes with a representative of a third world, there is no real argument taking place. There is no common authority on which they might agree to the terms of debate in order to determine exactly what it is they are debating. The one looks to a sacred order, the other to matters that do not rise above the concerns of the immanent order. In short, the bases on which these representatives of different cultures make their judgments are entirely antithetical to each other. Indeed, the very notion of what constitutes a *person* becomes a matter of nothing more than subjective preference.[14]

Of course, reality renders Rieff's taxonomy a little more complicated than he appears to concede. The multicultural nature of most Western societies today, combined with the rise of awareness of global diversity, places second cultures in potential conflict with each other and not just first and third worlds. Thus, a sacred order that looks to the image of God as foundational for understanding what it means to be a human person stands in contrast to an alternative sacred order— say, a Buddhist or a Confucian one. And history bears witness to the fact that Christian sacred orders have spilled a lot of blood in inter-necine civil wars, as witness, for example, the Thirty Years War of the seventeenth century. And so, second worlds are themselves frequently arenas of conflict and not to be regarded as representing some kind of utopian ideal or golden age, past or future. But Rieff's basic point, that we now live in an age in the West where the dominant culture is

---

13. See Aquinas's discussion of the matter in his commentary on the *Sentences* of Peter Lombard: *Scriptum Super Libros Sententiarum* 3.3.5.2, responsio.

14. See further the discussion of Peter Singer, "Ivy League Ethics," p. 315, in chap. 9.

one that rejects any transcendent sacred order and is thus foundationally different from that which preceded it is essentially correct. And that places us in the midst of a world in which moral instability and volatility are the order of the day. This is where the work of Alasdair MacIntyre becomes significant for our story.

Alasdair MacIntyre and Emotivism

Before exploring more aspects of Rieff's idea of third-world culture, it is worth noting the similarity of some of his conclusions about modern ethical discourse with those of Alasdair MacIntyre, the third of the three figures who have analyzed the malaise of modernity with whom we are concerned.

MacIntyre is best known for his influential work *After Virtue* (1981), which helped revive serious academic interest in virtue ethics.[15] In this book, he was wrestling with the problem created by the collapse of Marxism, an ideology to which he himself had previously subscribed. Marxism is a comprehensive account of social reality, and its decline in the second half of the twentieth century had a profound effect on those who had seen in it the secret of a socialist utopia. MacIntyre therefore found himself searching for an alternative grounding for morality. In doing so, he drew deeply on both the thought of Aristotle and the subsequent tradition that built on his work.

What MacIntyre finds to be helpful in the Aristotelian-Thomist approach to the world is the commitment to a teleological view of human nature and moral action. Actions can be morally assessed only in terms of their ends. This is not merely a consequentialist or pragmatic ethics, whereby the good of an action is judged simply by the good of its effect. MacIntyre's commitment to teleology involves two further elements of great importance. First, he insists that teleology enables individuals to distinguish between what they are and what they should be. Second, he argues that the process by which we evaluate the end of human actions needs to be understood as one that is

---

15. Alasdair MacIntyre, *After Virtue: A Study in Moral Theory* (London: Duckworth, 1981).

socially embedded. In short, individuals do not exist in isolation; they exist in society, in specific communities; and understanding their ends requires understanding that they are constituted by that society or those specific communities.

This latter point is one with which Karl Marx would have agreed. For Marx, the individual needs to be conceived of not as an isolated figure but rather as she is connected to society as a whole and thus in terms of her social relationships. MacIntyre's teleological construction of ethics is therefore a point of continuity between his Marxist phase and his later Aristotelian-Thomist arguments.[16] This also pushes him to develop a further point of great significance: ethics can exist only within a tradition. The idea of a neutral standpoint from which some absolute ethical principles can be deduced is for MacIntyre a myth. Therefore, we might add, the study of a society's ethics takes you to the very heart of how a society thinks about itself, how it constructs social relations, and why the people it contains think the way they do. As MacIntyre himself expresses it, a "moral philosophy . . . characteristically presupposes a sociology."[17] This means that ethical discourse arises out of, and assumes, a set of beliefs about the nature of the society in which it occurs. This has obvious affinities with the Freud-Rieff notion that cultures are defined by their interdicts and taboos. In both cases, ethics takes one to the very heart of what a culture or society is.

This insight offers MacIntyre a basis for understanding the chaotic nature of modern ethical discourse. Put simply, modern ethical discourse is chaotic because there is no longer a strong community consensus on the nature of the proper ends of human existence. If morality is a function of the social conventions of the community and yet the community lacks consensus on those social conventions, or those social conventions are hotly contested, ethical chaos is the result. We should be clear that making ethics a matter of community conventions does not necessarily

---

16. This point is noted by Christopher Stephen Lutz, *Reading Alasdair MacIntyre's "After Virtue"* (London: Continuum, 2012), 33.

17. Alasdair MacIntyre, *After Virtue: A Study in Moral Theory*, 2nd ed. (London: Duckworth, 1985), 23.

demand moral relativism—those community conventions could in theory be rooted in universal realities, such as natural law—but it does point to the need for the community to agree on its conventions in order for meaningful moral discussion and decision making to take place. Thus, MacIntyre's ethics has two overriding and related concerns: the nature of ends and the nature of communities.

We might apply MacIntyre's insight to an issue that was not in his purview at the time of *After Virtue* but that became one of the major points of political contention in the United States in the twenty-first century: the nature of marriage. Marriage as a lifelong and exclusive bond between two people of the opposite sex is a social convention, the understanding of which is deeply embedded within the tradition of Western society. Yet the traditional understanding of marriage has been overthrown in recent decades, and therefore the matter provides a fine test case for MacIntyre's theory.

In Christian tradition, embodied, for example, in the liturgy of the Book of Common Prayer, marriage has a threefold purpose: lifelong companionship, mutual sexual satisfaction, and procreation. By such a traditional definition, it is necessarily an institution that requires a partnership between people of the opposite sex, that is, a man and a woman. And this position—now a matter of acrimonious contention in the West—was the basic social consensus, the tradition, on the matter for many centuries.

Given this prior consensus on the ends of marriage, the advent of calls for gay marriage are clearly far more significant than simply being demands for the expansion of the category of who the legitimate contracting parties might be. Gay marriage actually demands a fundamental revision of the ends of marriage and therefore of the essence of marriage. The arguments for gay marriage rest on a view that ascribes a different end, a different telos, to marriage because it requires the rejection of the notion that marriage must be the proper context—and indeed, the necessary moral prerequisite—for conception.[18] Individuals who disagree

---

18. This point is made with pungency by Sherif Girgis, Ryan T. Anderson, and Robert P. George in *What Is Marriage? Man and Woman: A Defense* (New York: Encounter Books, 2012), 30: "Marriage is

about gay marriage might think they are disagreeing merely about the limits of the legitimate identity of the contracting parties, but their actual differences go much deeper than that. They disagree on nothing less than the very definition of marriage relative to its ends.[19]

If, as MacIntyre claims, every set of moral values presupposes a set of social assumptions, then what are the major social assumptions that he sees as dominant in the West? The key one for MacIntyre is what he calls *emotivism*, which he defines as follows:

> Emotivism is the doctrine that all evaluative judgments and more specifically all moral judgments are *nothing but* expressions of preference, expressions of attitude or feeling, insofar as they are moral or evaluative in character.[20]

In other words, the language of morality as now used is really nothing more than the language of personal preference based on nothing more rational or objective than sentiments or feelings. This is MacIntyre's key observation: emotivism is a theory not of meaning but of use; it is about how we use moral concepts and moral language. Stated most negatively, it is a way of granting those attitudes or values that we happen to prefer a kind of transcendent, objective authority. Essentially, emotivism presents preferences as if they were truth claims. Thus, the statement *Homosexuality is wrong* should be understood as *I personally disapprove of homosexuality, and you should do likewise.* The plausibility of this position rests on the failure of other attempts to find objective grounding for

---

ordered to family life because the act by which spouses make love also makes new life; one and the same act both seals a marriage and brings forth children. That is why marriage alone is the loving union of mind and body fulfilled by the procreation—and rearing—of whole new human beings."

19. Lest this argument be seen as merely an expression of homophobia, it is worth noting that the same would apply to a disagreement between a traditional Christian advocate of marriage and someone who believes in no-fault divorce. The former might well accept that divorce is legitimate in some circumstances—say, in the case of adultery or desertion by one of the parties—but would yet maintain that, short of such morally culpable circumstances, marriage is a lifelong bond, dissolved only at death. The advocate of no-fault divorce, however, regards marriage as a bond that holds only as long as the contracting parties find it convenient to maintain. Again, the difference is over the ends—and therefore over the very essence—of marriage. It is thus the advent of no-fault divorce, signed into law by the governor of California, Ronald Reagan, in 1970 that represents the moment at which marriage was truly "redefined." For a thorough statement of this argument, see Girgis, Anderson, and George, *What Is Marriage?*.

20. MacIntyre, *After Virtue*, 2nd ed., 11–12; emphasis original.

moral claims. Emotivism is therefore a function of the failed history of ethical theory.[21]

MacIntyre is aware that emotivism is not an entirely new phenomenon in the twentieth century. He notes that elements were present in the thought of David Hume, and we might add that much of what I note in part 2 of this book regarding Jean-Jacques Rousseau and the Romantic poets is consistent with a view that correlates moral evaluation with personal aesthetics, sentiments, and tastes.[22] Where MacIntyre sees the twentieth century marking a significant development is in the conscious elaboration of emotivism as a specific ethical theory. For this he holds the Cambridge philosopher and leading member of the Bloomsbury Group G. E. Moore responsible.[23]

In his *Ethics in the Conflicts of Modernity* (2016), it is noteworthy that MacIntyre moves from using the language of emotivism to that of expressivism, a point that is useful for bringing his insights into fruitful relation to those of Charles Taylor by making the connection between ethics and Taylor's normative type of self. The expressive individual can be a normative type only within a certain kind of sociological context, and therefore the expressive individual embodies a certain kind of ethics. The expressive individual is the same as the emotivist, the one who (mistakenly) grants his own personal preferences the status of universal moral imperatives.

What MacIntyre finds most disturbing is precisely the normative nature of this expressivism in modern society. Emotivist/expressivist theory is one thing; what is striking (and what was not foreseen by the theorists) is what happens when emotivism actually comes to enjoy widespread, perhaps even universal, currency. It is, after all, one thing

---

21. MacIntyre, *After Virtue*, 2nd ed., 19.

22. MacIntyre, *After Virtue*, 2nd ed., 14.

23. MacIntyre, *After Virtue*, 2nd ed., 14–17. MacIntyre regards Moore's student Charles L. Stevenson as providing the definitive theoretical account of emotivism in his work *Ethics and Language* (New Haven, CT: Yale University Press, 1945). See MacIntyre, *After Virtue*, 2nd ed., 17–18; MacIntyre, *Ethics in the Conflicts of Modernity: An Essay on Desire, Practical Reasoning, and Narrative* (Cambridge: Cambridge University Press, 2016), 17. An earlier example of emotivism as a theory of ethics can be found in Bazarov, the nihilist antihero of Ivan Turgenev's novel *Fathers and Sons* (1862), as in this exchange with his friend Arkady: "'In general there are no principles . . . but there are feelings. Everything depends on them. . . . Why do I like chemistry? Why do you like apples? It's on the strength of your feelings too. People'll never get deeper than that. . . .' 'What d'you mean? Is honesty just a feeling?' 'Of course!'" Turgenev, *Fathers and Sons*, trans. Richard Freeborn (Oxford: Oxford University Press, 1991), 128.

for a member of the Bloomsbury Group in the early twentieth century to use the idea as a means of critiquing popular understandings of morality in order to justify the leisurely indulgences of their club of smug Cambridge elite; it is quite another to see it gain widespread hold in society at a practical level.

It is important to distinguish here between emotivism as a moral theory and emotivism as a social theory. The former is very flimsy. Few, if any of us, are likely to argue that our own moral views are simply based on our emotional preferences. But the latter seems today to offer a good way of understanding how most people actually live their lives. "It just feels right," "I know in my heart it is a good thing," and other similar stock phrases are familiar to us all, and all point to the subjective, emotional foundation of so much ethical discussion today. And as MacIntyre makes clear, once the basis for such discussion lacks any agreed-on metaphysical or metanarratival framework, it is doomed to degenerate into nothing more than the assertion of incommensurable opinions and preferences.

It is also worth noting how emotivism is useful as a rhetorical strategy. When it comes to moral arguments, the tendency of the present age is to assert *our* moral convictions as normative and correct by rejecting those with which we disagree as irrational prejudice rooted in personal, emotional preference. That is precisely what underlies the ever-increasing number of words ending in *-phobia* by which society automatically assigns moral positions out of accord with the dominant *Sittlichkeit* to the category of neurotic bigotry. This is even evident in the thinking of such an august institution as the Supreme Court, as is clear in the case of *United States v. Windsor*, 570 U.S. 744 (2013), which struck down the Defense of Marriage Act and characterized religious objections to homosexuality as rooted in animus.[24]

MacIntyre's view of emotivism as social theory has clear affinities with Taylor and Rieff. What MacIntyre identifies as a loss of an agreed-on metanarrative within which meaningful ethical discussion (and even disagreement) can take place connects to Taylor's claims

---

24. See "*United States v. Windsor* (2013)," p. 308, in chap. 9.

regarding the move to an immanent frame and a culture of expressive individualism, and to Rieff's explanation of modern culture in psychological terms with the rise of the therapeutic self, whereby the good is identified with what makes me feel happy. All three would argue that an overriding desire for inner personal happiness and a sense of psychological well-being lie at the heart of the modern age and make ethics at root a subjective discourse. Human beings may still like to think they believe in good and bad, but these concepts are unhitched from any transcendent framework and merely reflect personal, emotional, and psychological preferences. In practice, it is we who decide our own preferred ends and shape our ethics to that purpose. Any greater sense of purpose, any transcendent teleology, is now dead and buried. More negatively, we are all then tempted to use the rhetoric of emotivism to dismiss views with which we disagree as arbitrary prejudices. Emotivism as a theory is that which explains why those with whom we disagree think the way they do, but it is not something we care to apply to ourselves. It is in reality a social theory that explains all our inability to have meaningful ethical discussion today, but each side in any debate tends to use it polemically as if it were the moral theory to which their opponents are committed.

Third Worlds as Anticultures

If chaotic moral discourse is one characteristic of third-world cultures, because they have lost any agreement on those assumptions that order them to particular ends, then other cultural phenomena stand in close relation to this chaos. Perhaps one of the most obvious is the way the cultural elites in third worlds are committed to cultural iconoclasm and to the overthrow of the beliefs, values, and behaviors of the past—that attitude C. S. Lewis called "chronological snobbery" raised to the level of a basic cultural instinct. Whereas in the first and second worlds, intellectuals and institutions such as universities were the conduits for the transmission and preservation of culture, now the intellectual class is devoted to the opposite—to the subversion, destabilization, and destruction of the culture's traditions. In fact, so radical and disruptive is this phenomenon that Rieff argues that what these third-world elites are promoting does not even deserve the name of "culture." Culture is, after all, the name given to those traditions, institutions, and patterns of behavior that transmit the values of one generation to the next. But that is not the way of elites in third worlds. Rather, they are attempting to abolish such transmission and the means by which it would typically take place. They are, in the words of Rieff, creating not a culture but an anticulture, called such because of its iconoclastic, purely destructive attitude toward all that the first and second worlds hold dear:

> Whether our third worlds, as inventions of radically remissive late second world elites, can be called "cultures" takes the answer, I believe, that our thirds should be called "anti-cultures." Anti-cultures translate no sacred order into social. Recycling fantasy firsts, thirds exist only as negations of sacred orders in seconds.[25]

What Rieff is saying here is that the hallmark of those cultures that have abandoned the sacred orders of second worlds is their repudiation of the interdicts of the latter.[26] Remissions—the occasional permission to break the rules that second worlds allow—become the norm in third worlds. For example, the tradition of allowing the best man at a British wedding to tell a rude joke or two about the bridegroom might be deemed acceptable behavior in a second world because it happens only on the occasion of a marriage. But in the third world, crudity becomes the norm because the general interdict against such is seen as a tyrannical hangover from an outdated way of viewing the world. The casual use of expletives by public figures such as politicians as a means of demonstrating their authenticity provides a good example. Another

---

25. Rieff, *Deathworks*, 6. Speaking of the attitude of the cultural elites ("the officer classes"), Rieff makes the following contrast between first, second, and third worlds: "The officer class in all sacred orders, first worlds or seconds, are remembrancers. The officer classes of third world anti-cultures are conveyancers. The conveyancer's gift lies in the hostility to culture in any of its first or second forms." *Deathworks*, 189.

26. Chantal Delsol describes this cultural pathology as "the ideology of the apostate," which is summarized by the fact that "contemporary thought is structured around a rejection of the former morality." See her *Icarus Fallen: The Search for Meaning in an Uncertain World*, trans. Robin Dick (Wilmington, DE: ISI Books, 2003), 87.

might be the relentless cynicism and violence that is now the typical fare in movies and sitcoms.[27]

As with Rieff's taxonomy of the changing nature of the human self, this claim about third worlds and their elites needs a little nuancing, both to pursue historical accuracy and to allow for the fact that change, even dramatic change, does not necessarily indicate the shift from second to third worlds. Failure to make this latter point would open the way for an uncritical nostalgia (at best) or a reactionary justification of each and every status quo (at worst).

For example, if we think of the Reformation of the sixteenth century, there is a clear sense in which the cultural elites in the key centers of the movement for church reform were not simply preserving and transmitting the culture of the previous era. This is true both intellectually and institutionally. Intellectually, men such as Luther and Calvin were repudiating significant parts of the theology that had shaped medieval Europe. They rejected the understanding of the mass in terms of transubstantiation and sacrifice, and they replaced the sacramental focus of the church with one centered on the preaching of God's word. In addition, they launched an assault on the institution of the church, rejecting the claims of its hierarchy on numerous points, not least the supremacy of the pope, and redefining both the basis and the scope of its authority.

All this is true. But a more careful look at the Reformation indicates that the Protestant elites were not committed so much to cultural iconoclasm as to what they considered to be cultural retrieval. Protestants and Roman Catholics may well disagree as to how well this retrieval was executed—indeed, they may disagree as to whether it was retrieval at all—but the Reformation was really a debate within a second world about the precise nature and implications of the Christian sacred order for society, not about its intentional repudiation. One of the hallmarks of this reality is that the Bible as a sacred text lay at the heart of the sixteenth-century church reforms for both sides of the Reformation debate. Further, history

---

27. See Thomas S. Hibbs, *Shows about Nothing: Nihilism in Popular Culture*, 2nd ed. (Waco, TX: Baylor University Press, 2012).

as an authoritative source of wisdom plays a significant role for both Catholics and Protestants in the sixteenth century. The Reformers themselves constantly made the point that they were not rejecting tradition so much as clarifying and reforming it in light of their understanding of God's word. Sacred text and ecclesiastical history were agreed-on authorities for both. The question was not whether they were to be rejected but how they were to be understood.

This is in stark contrast with what Rieff identifies as the destructive approach of third-world elites to the past. He claims that what they offer is not a revised or corrected history, a history reformed in light of new insights. Rather, it is the destruction of history and its replacement with nothing of any significant substance. Moral iconoclasm is not so much a positive philosophy as a cultural mood. And it affects everything.[28]

Given this reality, a more pointed and difficult example in our current political climate might be that of slavery in the Southern United States in the nineteenth century. Any view of culture that regards the rejection of previously held beliefs and practices as a sign of the advent of third-world instability and even nihilism is vulnerable to the accusation that it would have nothing to say by which an institution such as slavery might be addressed.

In fact, the debate over slavery in the United States is an interesting example of the type of conflict that can take place within a second world. As Mark Noll has persuasively argued, the issue of slavery was one that both sides saw as a matter to be justified or rejected on the basis of the Bible.[29] There is no need for second worlds to be static and to preserve social and cultural institutions and structures unchanged from one generation to the next. Social orders based on sacred orders are quite capable of internal debate and reform based on the working out in practice of their underlying

---

28. Leszek Kołakowski makes a similar observation about modern culture: "When I try . . . to point out the most dangerous characteristic of modernity, I tend to sum up my fear in one phrase: the disappearance of taboos. There is no way to distinguish between 'good' taboos and 'bad' taboos, artificially to support the former and remove the latter; the abrogation of one, on the pretext of its irrationality, results in a domino effect that brings the withering away of others." And at the heart of this Kołakowski sees, like Rieff, the destruction of traditional sexual codes. *Modernity on Endless Trial*, 13.

29. See Mark A. Noll, *The Civil War as a Theological Crisis* (Chapel Hill: University of North Carolina Press, 2006).

beliefs; the key is that such changes take place on the basis of accepted sacred authorities. What marks the debates of the present day is that there are no such accepted authorities, and so the cultural game is marked by a continual subversion of stability rather than the establishment of greater stability through clarification of the social order in light of the sacred order.

Yet we can also at points see the beginnings of third worlds within second worlds themselves. Again, debates over slavery provide a good example. Commenting on the growing concern in the European Enlightenment with the evils of slavery and other issues of oppression and man-made suffering, historian Margaret Jacob makes the following observation:

> Rather than embrace inferiority as explanatory, the Scottish philosophers saw stages of human progress; English reformers proclaimed the abolition of slavery, while French philosophes like Rousseau became dreamers of democracy. Not all of these reformers were materialists. Yet none of them invoked divine providence or the hand of God to explain the effects of imperialism, or the nature of monarchical authority, or the equality and human rights demanded now for all the peoples of the world.[30]

What Jacob is describing here is, in Rieff's taxonomy, the shift from second to third worlds: these thinkers are critiquing their world and making moral judgments without any reference to God or to divine providence or to anything that transcends the natural order. They do not see theology as necessary for their arguments. They may represent a variety of philosophical positions—some may profess pure materialism, while others might be theists of varying degrees of orthodoxy—but what they share in common is the fact that any kind of sacred order is irrelevant to the cogency of their arguments for the social order. It is not divine revelation that makes them think slavery is immoral or democracy desirable. Rather, it is the fact that a new understanding of humanity, based on the individual and on the individual's dignity, is

---

30. Margaret C. Jacob, *The Secular Enlightenment* (Princeton, NJ: Princeton University Press, 2019), 31.

coming to the fore. This is not to say that the positions they are advocating are not morally admirable; it is simply to make a comment on the significance of the way they make their arguments. There is no reference to God, no appeal to any kind of sacred order. These philosophers lived in a predominantly second world, but they had already detached their discourse from that which provided its foundation. The elites, we might say, were already on the move toward third-world culture. The inward turn at the Enlightenment may not initially have killed God, but it did make him in practice an increasingly unnecessary hypothesis. This inward turn, the turn to the individual, gave the individual a value—a dignity—that eventually came to stand as independent of any sacred order or set of divine commands.[31]

Third Worlds as Antihistorical

This rejection of second-world practices and beliefs is epitomized by third-world rejection of the past as worthy of respect and as a source of significant wisdom for the present. And while this antihistorical tendency started as the preserve of a comparatively small section of society, it has grown to be the representative mindset of Western society at large.[32]

This antihistorical tendency has numerous causes. In terms of the broad social imaginary, it is clear that technology plays a role in cultivating an attitude that sees the past as inferior to the present and the present as inferior to that which is to come. After all, who wants to return to a world with no proper sewage systems in place and no anesthetics? This attitude also connects to the destabilizing effects of consumerism and capitalism. Marx and Engels noted in *The Communist Manifesto* that the capitalism of the Industrial Revolution depended on the constant

---

31. See "The Question of Dignity," p. 64, in chap. 1.

32. "The guiding elites of our third world are virtuosi of decreation, of fictions where once commanding truths were. Third world elites are characterized by their relentless promotion of the clean sweep. At the end of the nineteenth century, those promoters were a few literary men recondite as Baudelaire. At the beginning of the twenty-first century, the occupations and names of the promoters are legion." Rieff, *Deathworks*, 4. He also observes that "the higher you go on the social and educational ladder, the greater the resistance to and negation of second world truth." *Deathworks*, 10. Third worlds are very much the result of revolutions led by the elites.

re-creation of markets, and today we witness the continuation of that in, say, the strategies of a company such as Apple, with their clever production of new iPhone models and their nurturing of dissatisfaction with the old and desire for the new on which their marketing depends. Fashion, too, plays a similar role to technology: the creation of aesthetic trends in clothing, for example, is also designed to create future markets. The present is only momentarily satisfying; the future will bring new and better delights. All this is predicated on the creation and exploitation of future-oriented desires and therefore serves quietly and perhaps imperceptibly to downgrade the value of the past.

This antihistorical tendency also has more self-conscious, philosophical roots. It is arguably an implication of that program of turning inward that finds one of its first major modern expressions in the philosophy of Descartes and, as we will observe in part 2, emerges as a comprehensive cultural program at the hands of Rousseau and then the Romantics, whereby society—and therefore the history that has made society the way it is—becomes problematic, a hindrance to individual authenticity. We will see this in William Wordsworth but also in a more pointed form in the work of Percy Bysshe Shelley and William Blake. All point to culture as corrupting and as inhibiting of the individual's authenticity.[33]

Perhaps pride of place in the intellectual pantheon of those who helped give a rationale for the rejection of history goes to Karl Marx. That might strike the reader as rather strange, given that Marx was himself steeped in history. His materialist philosophy was based on his reading of history, how societies change, and how the means of production in each age are critical to understanding the human condition in that age. Yet Marx's subversion of history is the result of the way he regards the dynamic of the historical process: it is essentially the story of oppression, specifically the oppression represented by the domination of one class by another. The memorable first lines of part 1 of the *Communist Manifesto* capture this thinking succinctly:

---

33. On Rousseau, see chap. 3; on the Romantics, see chap. 4.

The history of all hitherto existing society is the history of class struggles. Freeman and slave, patrician and plebeian, lord and serf, guild-
master and journeyman, in a word, oppressor and oppressed, stood
in constant opposition to one another, carried on an uninterrupted
now hidden, now open fight, a fight that each time ended, either in
a revolutionary re-constitution of society at large, or in the common
ruin of the contending classes.[34]

The point is simple: history is one long story of oppression. And when
one holds such a view, the usefulness of history is not so much that it is
a source of positive wisdom for the present as that it provides warnings
about how people are exploited.

For those who see history through this lens, historians will thus fall into
one of two camps: reactionaries who use history to justify exploitation and
radicals who use history to unmask the exploitation it embodies. As I argue
later, it is the latter model that has come to dominate history as an academic
discipline. Suffice it here to note that this idea is now deeply embedded in
our cultural imaginary, where phrases such as "being on the right side of history" are typically deployed (as they were in the debates over gay marriage)
to argue for the repudiation of established historical norms.

Further, a relatively simple taxonomy comes into play: history is
about victimizers and victims, with the former being the villains and
the latter the heroes. Older narratives that, say, exalted the achievements
of great individuals or nations come to be viewed as the propaganda
of the powerful, and victimhood takes on a special status. Not only is
history rejected, but the history of history itself is also consigned to the
trash bin.[35] In this regard, we can see the modern turn to the weak and the
marginalized in the academic discipline of history to be a scholarly manifestation of the wider victimhood culture that now has great significance in

---

34. Karl Marx and Friedrich Engels, *The Communist Manifesto*, in *The Marx-Engels Reader*, ed.
Robert C. Tucker, 2nd ed. (London: W. W. Norton, 1978), 473–74.

35. Delsol sees this attitude as part of the ideology of the apostate: "The contemporary ideology of
the apostate works tirelessly to rehabilitate the victims of the previous dominant morality: the former
subjects of the colonial powers, women, and various deviants from the former consensus. . . . We are
witness to an immense trial of our ancestors, complete with judges, lawyers, and awarded damages."
Icarus Fallen, 87.

public debates and popular attitudes about rights and dignity.[36] Expressive individualism, the psychologizing of human identity, and the antihistorical tendencies of the anticulture would appear to be very closely connected.

Death by Art: The Role of Deathworks

We noted earlier the comment by Margaret Jacob that Enlightenment opponents of slavery did not necessarily deny the existence of God but that their arguments did not need him as a hypothesis. This is interesting, but the group that she is describing was a small intellectual elite. In fact, to call it a "group" implies a level of self-conscious organization that the thinkers of the Enlightenment did not really possess in any significant way. Of course, in the eighteenth century, intellectuals from Edinburgh to Vienna and beyond read each other's books. We might even say that they were part of a broad cultural mood that was coming to grip the imagination of the intellectual class. But how did the intellectual iconoclasm of those such as Voltaire, Rousseau, and Hume come to be the cultural taste of people at large? The answer for Rieff comes via what he calls "deathworks." He defines this concept as

> an all-out assault upon something vital to the established culture. Every deathwork represents an admiring final assault on the objects of its admiration: the sacred orders of which their arts are some expression in the repressive mode.[37]

To understand exactly what Rieff is saying here, it is important to remember his basic agreement with Freud on the nature of culture/ civilization: culture is constituted by those things that it forbids; the frustration that such rules create finds an outlet in art; thus, works of art are also constitutive of the culture, reflecting in some way the interdicts that are in place. A deathwork, by contrast, represents an attack on established cultural art forms in a manner designed to undo the deeper moral structure of society. We might add that deathworks

---

36. On the issue of victimhood culture in general, see Bradley Campbell and Jason Manning, *The Rise of Victimhood Culture: Microaggressions, Safe Spaces, and the New Culture Wars* (New York: Palgrave Macmillan, 2018).

37. Rieff, *Deathworks*, 7.

are powerful because they are an important factor in changing the ethos of society, of altering that social imaginary with which, and according to which, we live our lives. Deathworks make the old values look ridiculous. They represent not so much arguments against the old order as subversions of it. They aim at changing the aesthetic tastes and sympathies of society so as to undermine the commands on which that society was based.

One of the key examples Rieff gives is that of Andres Serrano's infamous work *Piss Christ*, in which a crucifix is shown submerged in the artist's urine. In many ways, this is a quintessential example of that to which Rieff is pointing: a symbol of something deeply sacred to the second world being presented in a form that degrades it and makes it utterly repulsive. Serrano is not simply mocking the sacred order in this work of art; he has turned it into something dirty, disgusting, and vile. The highest authority of the second world, God, is literally cast into the sewer, the lowest of the low. The sacramental is made into the excremental.[38] And just to be clear—this is not simply an assault on the private religious sensibilities of Roman Catholics; it is an assault on the very authority, the sacred order, by which second worlds are legitimated. Its power lies not in any argument it proposes but rather in the way the clean is subverted by the vile. Religion is not rendered untrue. It is made distasteful and disgusting.[39]

Yet Rieff also notes that deathworks are not all as obvious in their assault on authority as *Piss Christ*, nor can they be restricted exclusively to the category of works of art. A deathwork can be anything that sets itself in opposition to the second-world culture.[40] We might take cynicism and irony, for example. These have a tendency to subvert the kind of traditional, vertical structures of authority that characterize second worlds. Rieff himself cites James Joyce's *Finnegans Wake* as an example of a work of art that does just this through its subversive use of language to mock

---

38. Rieff, *Deathworks*, 98–99.

39. Serrano has himself defended *Piss Christ* as "an act of devotion," claiming that he has always been a Christian and Catholic and that the work was designed to provoke people into thinking more deeply about the horrors of Christ's crucifixion. See Andres Serrano, "Protecting Freedom of Expression, from Piss Christ to Charlie Hebdo," *Creative Time Reports*, January 30, 2015, http://creativetimereports.org /2015/01/30/free-speech-piss-christ-charlie-hebdo-andres-serrano/.

40. Rieff, *Deathworks*, 8.

those things that Christians hold dear. It may not be the aesthetically repellent approach of Serrano and his *Piss Christ*, but it is nonetheless corrosive of the sacred order.[41] Satire could also be considered a deathwork. The subtle mockery of established authority that characterizes a satirical TV show or a humorous column in a newspaper could be categorized as a deathwork, slowly but surely undermining the established order of things.

Take, for example, the opening lines of T. S. Eliot's poem "The Love Song of J. Alfred Prufrock":

> Let us go then, you and I,
> When the evening is spread out against the sky
> Like a patient etherized upon a table.[42]

The first two lines would lead the reader to believe that this is the start of some great Romantic poem, worthy perhaps of William Wordsworth or John Keats. Then the shift in the third line to the prosaic present, with its cold, clinical connotations, renders the opening couplet not simply misleading but ridiculous. Romantic sensibilities are made to look silly or at best forlorn. The modern age has come; the quest for beauty and transcendence in nature is now implausible and even somewhat childish. This is the work of the deathwork.

Perhaps the quintessential deathwork of our time, and one that has really become far more widespread since Rieff's death in 2006, is pornography. Of course, as soon as pornography is mentioned, the question of how to define it comes to the fore. A good working definition is provided by the Catechism of the Catholic Church, section 2354:

> *Pornography* consists in removing real or simulated sexual acts from the intimacy of the partners, in order to display them deliberately to third parties. It offends against chastity because it perverts the conjugal act, the intimate giving of spouses to each other. It does grave injury to

---

41. Rieff, *Deathworks*, 94–96.
42. T. S. Eliot, "The Love Song of J. Alfred Prufrock," Poetry Foundation, accessed June 14, 2019, https://www.poetryfoundation.org/poetrymagazine/poems/44212/the-love-song-of-j-alfred-prufrock.

the dignity of its participants (actors, vendors, the public), since each one becomes an object of base pleasure and illicit profit for others. It immerses all who are involved in the illusion of a fantasy world. It is a grave offense. Civil authorities should prevent the production and distribution of pornographic materials.[43]

This definition brings out neatly the deathwork aspect of pornography. It is a cultural artifact that takes human sexual activity and divorces it from any moral content. We might add that it also divorces it from any larger narrative or historical context. The sex in pornography is presented as an end in itself. Yet sexual activity in a second world has a sacred significance as part of a relationship, as part of a personal history, as something that—given its connection to reproduction—links past to future, and as the necessary precondition for culture. Supremely, in Christian thought it becomes an analogue for the relationship between Christ and his church. Like *Piss Christ*, pornography might therefore be described as blasphemous in the manner in which it desecrates the holy and tramples on sacred authority. In short, the major problem with pornography is not what many religious conservatives might understand it to be—its promotion of lust and its objectifying of the participants. It certainly does both of those things, but the problem is also much deeper: it repudiates any notion that sex has significance beyond the act itself, and therefore it rejects any notion that it is emblematic of a sacred order.

The important thing about deathworks is that they subvert and destroy the sacred order without really having anything with which to replace it. If Nietzsche's madman unchains the earth from the sun, then we might say that deathworks are instrumental in this exercise, communicating the message of the death of God via aesthetic forms that come to shape the popular imagination—or, to put it in Taylor's language, to shape the social imaginary.[44]

---

43. "Catechism of the Catholic Church," Vatican, Libreria Editrice Vaticana, 1993, accessed January 30, 2020, https://www.vatican.va/archive/ENG0015/_INDEX.HTM.

44. For the significance of Nietzsche's madman, see "Friedrich Nietzsche: Unchaining the Earth from the Sun," p. 166, in chap. 5.

Forgetfulness

Underlying the notion of the deathwork is, as we noted, a basic repudiation of history as a source of authority and wisdom. This in turn means that what Rieff calls "forgetfulness" is one of the hallmarks of third worlds and a dominant trait of modern education. It is not simply that society just happens to be antihistorical in the way it approaches history. It has a vested interest in the actual erasure of history, of those things that conjure up unpleasant ideas that might disrupt happiness in the present. Recent years have seen good, if controversial, examples of this in both the United States and Europe, as campaigns on university campuses and beyond have pushed for such things as the renaming of buildings and the removal of statues that commemorate individuals who may not have conformed in their own day to the specific morality demanded in the twenty-first century.

But the antihistorical tendency of modern society manifests itself in other, even more pointed and controversial ways. For Rieff, it is no surprise to find a third world characterized by the widespread acceptance—even promotion—of abortion. Indeed, abortion functions as emblematic of precisely the deep antihistorical pathology of our third world:

> Forgetfulness is now the curricular form of our higher education. This form guarantees that we, of the transition from second to third worlds, will become the first barbarians. Barbarism is not an expression of simple technologies or of mysterious taboos; at least there were taboos and, moreover, in all first worlds, the immense authority of the past. By contrast, the coming barbarism, much of it here and now, not least to be found among our most cultivated classes, is our ruthless forgetting of the authority of the past. Sacred history, which never repeats itself, is thus profaned in an unprecedented way by transgression so deep that it is unacknowledged. The transgression of forgetfulness makes the cruelty of abortion absolutely sacrilegious; more precisely, antireligious. According to the unspoken doxology of our *abolitionist/abortionist* movements, identities are to be flushed as far away down the memory hole as our flush-away technologies of repression permit.[45]

---

45. Rieff, *Deathworks*, 106.

This passage contains numerous points of note. There is Rieff's use of the term *barbarism*. We might typically associate this word with the kind of destruction related to rioting or vandalism. Rieff would not disagree—but his understanding of such vandalism is more far reaching than, say, physical damage done to a neighborhood. For him, it is the vandalism that seeks to erase the past, or at least the significance of that past. It is a barbarism that finds its expression both physically, in the destruction of the artifacts of the past, and metaphysically, in its annihilation of the ideas, customs, and practices of the past. This is true barbarism, and it is manifested in things as apparently diverse as art, architecture, technology, consumerism, and the sophisticated ideologies promoted in university seminars.

Then there is the graphic image of human identities being flushed away like aborted fetuses. This is a clever connection that Rieff makes. Debates about abortion today are typically not focused on the question of when life starts. Rather, they are debates about when personhood begins, a point used by Peter Singer to argue for the legitimacy of postnatal infanticide.[46] In other words, the abortion debate is really about human identity, about who and what human beings are. And the fact that babies can be aborted and then disposed of like so much excrement is a telltale sign for Rieff that we live in a third world. Abortion, too, is a deathwork—not simply because it works the death of the unborn child but because it profanes that which the second world regarded as sacred: human life made in the image of God from the moment of conception. It revises the definition of what it means to be a person and also makes that which was once thought to be a person into something akin to a piece of garbage or excrement. It is therefore antireligious because it takes that which is most sacred in the social order, life itself, and flushes it down the toilet without a second thought. And it is antihistorical because it erases the physical consequences of the sexual act between a man and a woman. In short, it is an act that can be deemed routinely acceptable only in a world that has repudiated any transcendent framework in

---

46. On Singer and infanticide, see "Ivy League Ethics," p. 315, in chap. 9.

favor of the individual preferences of the immediate present. Abortion presupposes a metaphysics, or, perhaps better, an antimetaphysics.

Conclusion

The works of Rieff, Taylor, and MacIntyre provide us with very helpful categories for analyzing the pathologies of this present age and for avoiding a common mistake. There is always a temptation in social criticism either to attenuate the differences between past and present in a manner that misses new developments and distinctives in social practices and thought, or to emphasize the alleged uniqueness of today so much that the roots of current ideas and behaviors are sidelined and ignored. In this context, the conceptual categories offered by these three thinkers provide us with different perspectives on modernity that allow for reflecting on the present in a manner that acknowledges both continuities with and differences from the past.

What is clear from their writings is this: questions connected to notions of human identity, of which those raised by the LGBTQ+ movement are only the most obvious contemporary example, cannot be abstracted from broader questions of how the self is understood, how ethical discourse operates, how history and tradition are valued (if at all), and how cultural elites understand the content and purpose of art. In the following chapters, these various aspects of the modern age and the analytical categories developed by Rieff, Taylor, and MacIntyre form the framework for understanding exactly what is at stake in the contemporary manifestation of the revolution of the self, of which the sexual revolution is only the most obvious part.

Part 2

FOUNDATIONS OF THE REVOLUTION

3

The Other Genevan

Jean-Jacques Rousseau and
the Foundations of Modern Selfhood

Such, such were the joys.
When we all girls & boys,
In our youth-time were seen,
On the Ecchoing Green.

WILLIAM BLAKE

The world in which we live is increasingly dominated by psychological
categories. Indeed, the big political questions of our time are those of
identity, and modern identities have a distinctly psychological aspect. As
we noted in part 1, Philip Rieff described the dominant understanding
of the self of this present age as that of psychological man, the successor
to the political man, religious man, and economic man of previous eras.
Charles Taylor, too, sees the expressive individual as now the normative
type of self in our society and as the basic presupposition of much of
what happens in our world, from attitudes toward the sexual revolution
to judgments in law courts and protests on campuses. Yet psychological man and expressive individualism did not emerge in the twentieth

century from a vacuum, nor were they self-caused. Like all historical phenomena, they have a genealogy, a story that stretches back in time and makes their emergence and their cultural dominance comprehensible.

To understand their emergence, therefore, it is necessary to examine their origins. Of course, this presents us with an immediate problem, the perennial difficulty faced by anyone trying to construct a historical narrative, that of the historical starting point. To the question Where should the starting point be? there is really only one answer—and that is itself a question: How far back do you wish to go? While the advent of psychological man in his present form, with all the political and cultural potency that he possesses, is a relatively recent phenomenon, the various factors that led to this moment of cultural dominance are extremely diffuse, long-standing, and complicated. Indeed, there is a sense that, as soon as the mind or the will was recognized as separable from the body or as a separate constitutive element of the person, psychological man became a very real conceptual possibility. From this perspective, the apostle Paul and Augustine are central figures. There was only at best a very vague concept of the will in classical philosophy; it is only when Paul offers his psychological account of the Christian's inner struggle in his first-century New Testament letters, which was then picked up and developed in a deeply personal and elaborate way by Augustine in his *Confessions* at the end of the fourth century, that we find the basic tools for conceptualizing humans as primarily psychological beings.

The psychological man of Rieff would therefore require a genealogy stretching back at least to the ancient church, and our historical narrative would become so vast and ungainly as to be next to useless. To avoid such an unhelpful outcome, it is necessary to focus on a few key individuals and movements that offer particularly clear and important articulations of stages in the grand narrative we are trying to establish. For that purpose, in this chapter special attention is given to the work of one thinker: the eighteenth-century philosopher Jean-Jacques Rousseau. The choice is not arbitrary. While Christians may instinctively think of John Calvin, for good or for ill, as the most influential figure to be associated with Geneva, it is actually Rousseau who is far closer to the sensibilities of our present age. As one of the key intellectual progenitors of both the French Revolution and Romanticism, he exerted considerable influence on the ideological formation of the modern world. As one of Sigmund Freud's heroes, his fingerprints can be found even on the rise of the psychoanalytic movement of the late nineteenth century. And as the man whose autobiography sought to find reality by looking within himself, he is in many ways the aboriginal paradigm for psychological man.

Rousseau's *Confessions*

Jean-Jacques Rousseau is one of the strangest geniuses in the history of Western philosophy, a self-taught individual whose writings articulated key ideas that are now assumed as basic in much political thinking.[1] Given the role his thought played in later Western thought, specifically in shaping the notion of what it means to be a self, he is arguably one of the most practically influential thinkers in history. My interest in him here is specifically in the role that his views of psychology and culture play in his understanding of what it means to be human and how it shapes his conceptualization of the relationship between the individual and society.[2]

That the psychological inner life is of vital importance to Rousseau is clear from his autobiography, the *Confessions*, which he starts with a famous opening statement of purpose:

---

1. The standard scholarly biography of Rousseau in English is that by Maurice Cranston, in three volumes: vol. 1, *Jean-Jacques: The Early Life and Work of Jean-Jacques Rousseau, 1712–1754*; vol. 2, *The Noble Savage: Jean-Jacques Rousseau, 1754–1762*; vol. 3, *The Solitary Self: Jean-Jacques Rousseau in Exile and Adversity* (Chicago: University of Chicago Press, 1991–1999). The most accessible English biography is Leo Damrosch, *Jean-Jacques Rousseau: Restless Genius* (New York: Mariner Books, 2005). Damrosch's admiration for Rousseau makes him a sympathetic interpreter of his life but also at times somewhat uncritical. Thus, Rousseau's appalling treatment of his children (he had all five sent, at birth, to orphanages) is glossed with little comment. An excellent overview of contemporary perspectives on Rousseau is Patrick Riley, ed., *The Cambridge Companion to Rousseau* (Cambridge: Cambridge University Press, 2001).

2. Charles Taylor identifies Rousseau as a "crucial influence" in the development of modern understandings of the self: *Sources of the Self: The Making of the Modern Identity* (Cambridge, MA: Harvard University Press, 1989), 356. Cf. his comment on 362: "Rousseau is at the origin point of a great deal of contemporary culture, of the philosophies of self-exploration, as well as of creeds which make self-determining freedom the key to virtue."

I am resolved on an undertaking that has no model and will have no imitator. I want to show my fellow-men a man in all the truth of nature; and this man is to be myself.[3]

He explains this purpose in more detail later on:

The particular object of my confessions is to make known my inner self, exactly as it was in every circumstance of my life. It is the history of my soul that I promised, and to relate it faithfully I require no other memorandum; all I need do, as I have done up until now, is to look inside myself.[4]

Thus, the purpose of autobiography, the delineation of the story of one particular self by that self, is to be psychological in its orientation, for that is where the real person is to be found. Obviously, lives are marked by the interaction of the individual with the world around—people, places, and so on. But the real drama, that which takes one to the heart of what constitutes the essence of a person, is the inner psychological life that is shaped by these outward circumstances and contingencies.

That the work was unprecedented in its inner psychological pre-occupations is clearly a piece of hyperbolic self-promotion on Rousseau's part. He acknowledges elsewhere that several precedents inspired him, including the writings of the essayist Michel de Montaigne. Further, though he nowhere in the *Confessions* explicitly acknowledges his influence, it is obvious that Augustine's own autobiography, with its psychological concerns, was a precedent to which this work was to be an implicitly polemical counterpoint.[5] As Ann Hartle notes in her

---

3. Jean-Jacques Rousseau, *Confessions*, ed. Patrick Coleman, trans. Angela Scholar (Oxford: Oxford University Press, 2000), 5.

4. Rousseau, *Confessions*, 270. In the Neuchâtel preface to his *Confessions*, Rousseau comments, "No one can write a man's life except himself. His inner mode of being, his true life, is known only to himself; and yet he disguises it; under the cover of his life's story, he offers an apology; he presents himself as he wants to be seen, not at all as he is." *Confessions*, 644.

5. In the Neuchâtel preface, Rousseau acknowledges both Montaigne and the historian Girolamo Cardano as precedents, though he criticizes them for their dishonesty in presenting themselves, and even their faults, in the most favorable light. *Confessions*, 644. The same criticism might be made of Rousseau himself for the way he explains his decision to place his children in the orphanage as being in their best interest. *Confessions*, 347–48. On Rousseau's precedents, see Christopher Kelly, "Rousseau's *Confessions*,"

comparative study of Rousseau and Augustine, Rousseau's *Confessions* is in a significant sense his answer to Augustine on the question of what it means to be human and have a human nature.[6]

What the *Confessions* provides is Rousseau's mature understanding of the self in narrative form such that it is an example to its readership. It is, in Hartle's memorable phrase, a "philosophical work of art."[7] He may well present the book as a naive, facile account of his inner life, but it is in reality a very carefully constructed work with a definite philosophical and didactic purpose.

Three Key Moments

Three incidents in Rousseau's *Confessions* merit detailed comment before we turn to the systematic statements of the ideas contained in his major philosophical treatises. These passages clearly delineate important elements of his understanding of what it means to be human and how that connects to broader social realities.

The first occurs in book 1, where a local man, M. Verrat, persuades the young Rousseau to steal some of Verrat's mother's asparagus for him so that he might sell it and make some money. Rousseau's account of his act of theft allows him to reflect in some detail on the psychology of what he was doing, and two things stand out in his analysis. First, he emphasizes that the motivation for the crime was not greed but "only to oblige the person who was making me do it."[8] Thus, the act was driven not by some inward impulse that was intrinsically sinful but by a good desire that led him to perform a sinful act. He stole the asparagus to help Verrat. The desire was a basically good one; it was only the manner in which he fulfilled it that was morally problematic. This is important for understanding Rousseau's view of the nature of human corruption as something that is created and fostered by social conditions and not something to be considered innate.

---

in Riley, *Cambridge Companion to Rousseau*, 303. Kelly even suggests that reading Augustine was the direct inspiration for Rousseau's autobiographical project (305).

6. Ann Hartle, *The Modern Self in Rousseau's "Confessions": A Reply to St. Augustine* (Notre Dame, IN: University of Notre Dame Press, 1983), 11.

7. Hartle, *Modern Self*, 9.

8. Rousseau, *Confessions*, 32.

This is obvious in a second aspect of the narrative, which underlines that the crime is the result of social pressure, not some internal tendency to depravity—in this case, the cajoling by M. Verrat. It does not arise spontaneously within Rousseau himself but derives from his relationship with Verrat. Indeed, in the context of the *Confessions* as a whole, this story comes immediately after Rousseau's acquisition of numerous vices that were each the result of the social conditions in which he found himself: his master treated him badly, hence he started lying and became lazy; his father punished him rather too harshly, and this made him both manipulative and covetous. Society, or at least the society in which he found himself, is to blame for the young Rousseau's delinquency. His corruption is essentially the result of his reaction to corrupting circumstances.[9]

The incident with the asparagus bears obvious comparison with the precedent in Augustine's *Confessions*, the famous theft of pears in book 2, which serves as the literary representation of Augustine's fall into sin. The plot in Augustine's work is simple: Augustine and a group of friends raid a neighbor's garden late one night and steal pears. These pears are neither attractive to look at nor tasty to eat. In fact, Augustine had more and better pears in his own garden. So the youths throw their ill-gotten gains to some pigs and carry on their way with much laughter.[10]

The account has both points of similarity and a fundamental point of difference with Rousseau's tale of stealing the asparagus. Like Rousseau, Augustine acknowledges that there is a strong social dimension to his behavior at this point. Had he been alone, he notes, he would not have engaged in the theft. It was the fact that he was with a group of youths who encouraged each other in their escapade that brought him to act in the way he did. Laughter, he comments, is a social activity and was also a key element in cultivating the pleasure that drove the gang on to their act of theft. Stealing in this instance is facilitated by the delight the thieves received from doing it together.

---

9. Rousseau, *Confessions*, 31–32.

10. The original account is found in Augustine, *Confessions* 2.9. A good recent translation is Augustine, *Confessions: A New Translation*, trans. Sarah Ruden (New York: Modern Library, 2017).

A further similarity can be seen in what does not motivate the crime. Augustine, like Rousseau, denies that his crime was motivated by greed. He is explicit that he had better pears in his own garden, to which he had easy and legitimate access. It is not the possession of better and more attractive pears, nor even the mere possession of further pears of any quality, that lies behind the act, any more than it was Rousseau's desire for asparagus that drove him to crime. Personal gain is not a motive. Yet this does not mean that Augustine shares the same positive motivation with Rousseau. For Augustine, the theft is not the result of a good desire misdirected (as it is for Rousseau) but rather of the sheer sinful delight to be had in breaking the law.

The difference between the two is instructive. For Augustine, the moral flaw is ultimately intrinsic to him. He is by nature wicked, a sinner. Circumstances merely provide an opportunity for a particular action to reveal the immorality of his innate inner disposition. And he is answerable to an external law—indeed, a law grounded in the being of God—which his sinful will takes a strange, perverse delight in breaking. For Rousseau, by way of contrast, his natural humanity is fundamentally sound, and the sinful act comes from social pressures and conditioning. He becomes depraved by the pressures society places on him. We might therefore summarize the basic difference between the two men as follows: Augustine blames himself for his sin because he is basically wicked from birth; Rousseau blames society for his sin because he is basically good at birth and then perverted by external forces.

What the account of the asparagus does is point to the fact that, for Rousseau, the social order is a source of falsehood or, to use the modern term, inauthenticity. Men and women are born good and corrupted by the society that surrounds them. As Charles Taylor expresses Rousseau's thinking, "The original impulse of nature is right, but the effect of a depraved culture is that we lose contact with it."[11]

The second incident makes this point very clear. It is Rousseau's description and analysis of an encounter he had in Venice with a prostitute

---

11. Taylor, *Sources of the Self*, 357.

called Zulietta. In fact, so important is this incident to Rousseau that he claims it as the "one incident in my life which portrays my nature in its true colours."[12]

The events of the encounter are easy to relate. Rousseau visits Zulietta and is struck by her beauty and charm. Immediately, he starts to experience feelings of inferiority and unworthiness in her presence. Why should he have such a wonderful creature at his disposal, to do with as he wished? Agitated to the point of tears, Rousseau suddenly notices that one of her nipples is malformed, and this observation, trivial as it is, immediately changes everything. Now he surmises that this defect is a sign of some natural vice, and the woman who one moment had been to him like a goddess is suddenly a vicious monster.[13]

The question as to why Rousseau regards this encounter as so critical for enabling the reader to understand him does not actually emerge in the story itself but is revealed at the start of book 8, our third incident. It is then that Rousseau recounts a momentous journey from Paris to Vincennes to visit his friend Denis Diderot. On the way, he comes across a copy of the newspaper *Mercure de France* and reads therein about an essay competition being held by the Academy of Dijon. The question on which contestants are asked to write is this: "Whether the restoration of the Sciences and Arts has contributed to the purification of morals." Rousseau decides to submit an entry, and, as he describes in the *Confessions*, the basic framework of his mature system comes to him as he walks toward Vincennes such that he arrives there in a state of great excitement and agitation.[14] It is in reflecting on this question that Rousseau later sees himself as making his breakthrough—his equivalent of Augustine's conversion to Christianity.[15]

The essay he writes for this competition is his famous *Discourse on the Sciences and the Arts* (the *First Discourse*), which sets forth in an admittedly

---

12. Rousseau, *Confessions*, 311.
13. Rousseau, *Confessions*, 311–12.
14. "What I remember quite distinctly about this occasion is that when I arrived in Vincennes I was in a state of agitation bordering on delirium." Rousseau, *Confessions*, 342.
15. The language Rousseau uses about his moment is akin to that used in evangelical conversion stories: "The moment I read these words [the title of the proposed essay] I saw another universe and I became another man." *Confessions*, 342.

rather confused manner the essential principles of his later thinking. The connection to the Venice incident with the prostitute is this: Rousseau has come to understand that people are not monsters by nature but by virtue of their social conditioning, and it is the imagination that mystifies and thereby hides the real causes of corruption. Zulietta was neither goddess nor monster. Her deformed nipple was not the result of some moral judgment, divine or otherwise metaphysical, on her life, or the physical manifestation of her inner depravity. Her prostitution was the result of social circumstances, not some intrinsic flaw. And this realization was what set Rousseau on his path to demonstrate that it is social institutions that breed corruption and wickedness, a point that was to have huge repercussions for his later thinking about society, ethics, and the individual.

The Hypothetical and Primeval State of Nature

The essay that Rousseau submitted to the *Mercure de France* has come down to us as his *First Discourse*. This work is remarkable not so much for its careful and cogent argument (it is arguably neither careful nor cogent) but for its bracing rhetoric. Ever the contrarian, Rousseau addressed the prize topic by arguing the precise opposite of what might be expected. Rather than affirming the inherently civilizing power of the arts and sciences, Rousseau accuses them of lying at the root of modern vices. Consistent with his account of Verrat and Zulietta, he presents the case for civilization, not individuals, being the source of social ills.

Thus, in part 1, he expresses the problem as follows:

> How sweet it would be to live among us if the outward countenance were always the image of the heart's dispositions; if decency were virtue; if our maxims were our rules: if genuine Philosophy were inseparable from the title of Philosopher! . . . Before Art had fashioned our manners and taught our passions to speak in ready-made term, our morals were rustic but natural; and differences in conduct conveyed differences of character at first glance.[16]

---

16. Jean-Jacques Rousseau, *The Discourses and Other Early Political Writings*, ed. and trans. Victor Gourevitch, Cambridge Texts in the History of Political Thought (Cambridge: Cambridge University Press, 1997), 7.

This is one of Rousseau's earliest expressions of what he imagined it must have been like for humans to live in the state of nature, before the advent of social institutions. In such a time human beings had simple desires connected to simple needs that were simply satisfied. There was no discontinuity or disconnect between what individuals thought or wanted and how they behaved. It was a world in which, to use the modern term, what you see is what you get where people are concerned. It is therefore the socializing of the human condition that has created the various problems that now afflict human existence.

This pleasant innocence of the state of nature is an important theme in Rousseau's thinking but must be qualified in a significant way to avoid misunderstanding. The state of nature for Rousseau is not a historical epoch. He is not attempting to describe actual history so much as engage in a thought experiment. Rousseau's *Discourse* does not set forth a historical narrative that, if discredited, thereby proves fatal to his philosophy. If there never was an era of noble savagery, then the basic point of his argument would still be sound. He is offering here not an insight into the past but a theoretical construct for the purpose of making possible a distinction between nature and culture and thereby laying the foundation for a critique of culture and its effects on the individual. This hypothetical state of nature essentially provides a basic measure by which the role of social conventions and institutions can be assessed in terms of their role in shaping human morals and behavior.

Lest we be in any doubt about the unfortunate impact of the sciences and the arts, Rousseau makes himself clear by moving straight from the words quoted above to comments on contemporary society:

> Today, when subtler inquiries and a more refined taste have reduced the Art of pleasing to principles, a vile and deceiving uniformity prevails in our morals and all minds seem to have been cast in the same mold: constantly politeness demands, propriety commands: constantly one follows custom, never one's own genius. One no longer dares to appear what one is; and under this perpetual constraint, the men who make up the herd that is called society will, when placed in similar

circumstances, all act in similar ways unless more powerful motives incline them differently.[17]

And this bleak description leads to even bleaker moral outcomes for human relationships and for society as a whole:

> What a train of vices must attend upon such uncertainty. No more sincere friendships; no more real esteem; no more well-founded trust. Suspicions, offenses, fears, coolness, reserve, hatred, betrayal, will constantly hide beneath this even and deceitful veil of politeness, beneath this so much vaunted urbanity which we owe to the enlightenment of our century.[18]

In short, while education in the arts and sciences might be expected to enhance humanity and improve life, Rousseau sees a real danger of exactly the opposite: it will in reality foster hypocrisy and wickedness because it creates a society where the need to belong and to conform requires individuals to be false to who they really are. Society creates the rules by which the individual must play in order to be accepted, and those rules are contrary to the simple economy of easily met innate desires created by basic physical needs found in the state of nature.

This claim is of great significance for understanding many of the pathologies of our current cultural moment. We might say that Rousseau is arguing, at a basic level, that it is society and the relations and conditions that society embodies that decisively shape and, in the description above, decisively corrupt individuals. That is a point so basic to much of modern liberal thought that it verges on the platitudinous.

In chapter 1 we noted the Hegelian concept of *Sittlichkeit*, picked up by Charles Taylor, as a useful means of highlighting the dialogical nature of how one constructs a sense of self. *Sittlichkeit* is the term used to refer to the ethical structure of society at large, embodying the code of behavior to which one must conform in order to belong and to be accepted. Now, human beings are self-conscious, but their self-consciousness develops through interaction with the world outside the self, particularly with other

---

17. Rousseau, *Discourses*, 8.
18. Rousseau, *Discourses*, 8.

similar self-consciousnesses, the grammar and syntax of which interaction is connected to the ethical expectations of society as a whole. And this interactive development connects to another basic human desire, that of being recognized, of being accepted by others, in a manner that acknowledges one's identity. If we apply this dynamic to what Rousseau is claiming, his point seems to be that it is this desire to be recognized set within a society whose *Sittlichkeit*, or ethical framework, inherently oppresses individual desires that then proves so problematic. It is this tension that fosters ambition, a competitive and even destructive attitude to others, and that thereby, by introducing refinements and personal ambition, disrupts the balance that would exist in some primeval state. Authentic self-expression of the kind available to the hypothetical savage, unencumbered by the expectations of culture, is therefore impossible to the one born in a civilized society because that society will not allow such behavior and is likely, in fact, to punish it. The authentic human being is regarded with contempt by cultivated society, perhaps even as a criminal. To be a member of such society, one must therefore suppress these personal, natural desires and instincts and conform to socially normative canons of behavior. And in the process, one becomes inauthentic, untrue to one's inner (real) self. To use the modern phrase, one ends up living a lie.

The Two Loves

This is where an important distinction in Rousseau's thought is significant, that between *amour de soi-même* ("self-love") and *amour propre*. In the hypothetical state of nature, human beings simply possess the first, self-love, a point Rousseau makes in part 1 of the *Second Discourse*. This is basically the desire for self-preservation. Human beings in the hypothetical state of nature desire to survive, to continue their own existence, and that is basic to who they are.[19]

In his notes to the *Second Discourse* (note 15), Rousseau defines *amour propre*, in contrast to self-love, as follows:

---

19. Rousseau, *Discourses*, 150.

Amour propre is only a relative sentiment, factitious, and born in society, which inclines every individual to set greater store by himself than by anyone else, inspires men with all the evils they do one another, and is the genuine source of honor.[20]

In sum, self-love in the natural state is a good, leading individuals to seek self-preservation. *Amour propre*, however, is the result of the rivalries and interpersonal competitions and conflicts that society generates. This is what renders men and women corrupt, disingenuous, and false to themselves.

There is some debate within scholarly circles as to whether *amour propre* in Rousseau is an intrinsically negative concept or whether it is in itself morally neutral but typically manifested in immoral ways.[21] In its negative "inflamed" form, however, *amour propre* unequivocally consists in the pride, competitiveness, and desire for superiority and mastery over others that typifies society. As he narrates a hypothetical history of society in the *Second Discourse*, Rousseau imagines how rivalries, envy, and discontent might develop in a social context as primitive people gathered at a tree or outside a hut:

Everyone began to look at everyone else and to wish to be looked at himself, and public esteem acquired a price. The one who sang or danced best, the handsomest, the strongest, the most skillful, or the most eloquent came to be the most highly regarded, and this was the first step at once toward inequality and vice: from these first preferences arose vanity and contempt on the one hand, shame and envy on the other; and the fermentation caused by these new leavens eventually produced compounds fatal to happiness and innocence.[22]

Gone is the innocence of the natural man whose desires and needs were simple and matched each other perfectly. Now a competitive social sphere has been introduced that creates needs—to be the best, to be the

---

20. Rousseau, *Discourses*, 218.
21. For the former view, see Grace G. Roosevelt, *Reading Rousseau in the Nuclear Age* (Philadelphia: Temple University Press, 1990), 30; for the latter, see N. J. H. Dent, *Rousseau: An Introduction to His Psychological, Social and Political Theory* (Oxford: Blackwell, 1988), 21.
22. Rousseau, *Discourses*, 166.

most highly regarded, to be the master—which by definition cannot be satisfied for all people all the time. Thus comes inequality and the strife and struggles that mark human existence.

All these problematic aspects of human behavior come not as a result of some innate perversion that corrupts men and women from birth but rather as that of existing in a social environment with others. It is the alien demands of that environment—to be better than this other person, to be more beautiful than that one—that corrupt individuals and alienate them from who they really are. In this context, conscience (as we will see) acts as a means of reminding the individual of the fact that his best interests are served by empathizing with others and treating them as he would wish to be treated himself.

In contrast to *amour propre*, we should note that when Rousseau speaks of "self-love" as applied to the natural state, it is not a form of untrammeled selfishness, as the English translation might suggest. Further, the idea of self-preservation might also tend to imply that selfishness lies at the core of what it means to be human. One could easily imagine a world in which self-love might indeed be conceived of in such a way, given that any individual committed to an unqualified notion of self-preservation could well act in a manner hostile to all other individuals as potential threats to his own existence. But Rousseau does not think that this is the case; he would regard such a love as the very *amour propre* that is so problematic. Rather, he regards self-love in the natural state as coordinated with pity as an intrinsic part of natural human virtue.

Rousseau defines pity as an innate repugnance to the idea of others who belong to the same species suffering. The natural man does not like to see one of his fellows in pain or difficulty and will, if he can, act to alleviate such. All the other social virtues, such as generosity and mercy, flow from this one basic source:

> There is, besides, another Principle . . . which, having been given to man in order under certain circumstances to soften the ferociousness of his amour propre or of the desire for self-preservation prior to the birth of amour propre tempers his ardor for well-being with an innate repugnance to see his kind suffer. . . . I do not believe I need fear any

contradiction in granting man the only Natural virtue which the most extreme Detractor of human virtues [Thomas Hobbes] was forced to acknowledge. I speak of Pity, a disposition suited to beings as weak and as subject to so many ills as we are; a virtue all the more universal and useful to man as it precedes the exercise of all reflection in him, and so Natural that even the beasts sometimes show evident signs of it.[23]

This is a noteworthy passage because it makes clear that Rousseau, in addition to setting up a contrast between the innocence of the natural state and the corruption of society, roots his understanding of ethics in personal sentiment. It is empathy that shapes self-love in a manner that makes human beings moral. As he argues in the *Second Discourse*, pity or empathy in the natural state takes the place of laws, morals, and virtue because it naturally moves us toward alleviating the suffering of others.[24] We empathize with those in pain and therefore are motivated to relieve their suffering. Moral imperatives may well present themselves as having an intrinsic authority and status, but they find their origin and foundation in a personal sentiment, an emotional reaction to circumstances—that of the empathy and pity that someone naturally feels in the natural state for some other one of their kind who is in pain or difficulty.[25] Human ethical action thus arises out of psychological sentiment. It is the fact that we are naturally empathetic that makes us moral.

---

23. Rousseau, *Discourses*, 152. The background to Rousseau's comments here is the view of Thomas Hobbes, that *pity* is the word given to the feeling that one person has toward another who is suffering some misfortune. Hobbes allows that pity is basic to the human condition, but he roots it in an essential selfishness: one feels pity for the person who is suffering because of the fear that such a thing might also happen to oneself. See Thomas Hobbes, *Leviathan*, ed. J. C. A. Gaskin (Oxford: Oxford University Press, 1996), 39. Rousseau views pity far less cynically, as an instinctive, prereflective response to the suffering of other members of one's species.

24. Rousseau, *Discourses*, 154.

25. Rousseau is not alone in the eighteenth century in seeing sentiment as key to understanding the ethical behavior of human beings. See, for example, David Hume, *Enquiries concerning Human Understanding and concerning the Principles of Morals*, ed. L. A. Selby-Bigge, rev. P. H. Nidditch (Oxford: Oxford University Press, 1975), 272 (§221): "The notion of morals implies some sentiment common to all mankind, which recommends the same object to general approbation, and makes every man, or most men, agree in the same opinion or decision concerning it. It also implies some sentiment, so universal and comprehensive as to extend to all mankind, and render the actions and conduct, even of the persons the most remote, an object of applause or censure, according as they agree or disagree with that rule of right which is established."

Rousseau makes this thinking clear in *Emile*, his treatise on education, when discussing the terminology of public morality:

> I would show that *justice* and *goodness* are not merely abstract words—
> pure moral beings formed by the understanding—but are true affections
> of the soul enlightened by reason, are hence only an ordered develop-
> ment of our primitive affections; that by reason alone, independent of
> conscience, no natural law can be established; and that the entire right
> of nature is only a chimera if it is not founded on a natural need in the
> human heart.[26]

In an important footnote to this passage, Rousseau uses as an example of that most basic of ethical principles the maxim that you should do unto others as you would wish them to do to you. Even this code, he argues, is rooted in a prior sentimental capacity, for it depends on the ability to identify with others in their condition and therefore to desire for them what you would desire for yourself.

Pity as a foundation for ethics therefore points toward two important elements of Rousseau's thought. The first is the social dimension of human beings even in their hypothetical natural state, for pity is always directed toward another. It cannot exist in perfect isolation as a solipsistic virtue. As noted above, self-love is not a matter of untrammeled self-interest at the expense of all others, nor is it exemplified in a kind of splendid isolation. The key to appropriate self-love is that the individual's desires are connected to basic needs and do not exceed them: enough food to eat, a mate for companionship and procreation, and sufficient rest to keep the body healthy. As to the fears of the man in the state of nature, those fears are simple: merely pain and hunger. Other desires and other fears, and the concomitant disturbance that they bring to individuals, are the fruit of *amour propre* and thus of the society that is its necessary precondition.[27] The key to basic social ethics is therefore the ability to empathize with others and apply to them the same principles as you apply to yourself. Each individual is to relate to every other individual

---

26. Jean-Jacques Rousseau, *Emile; or, On Education*, trans. Allan Bloom (New York: Basic Books, 1979), 235.

27. Roosevelt, *Reading Rousseau*, 29; Dent, *Rousseau*, 20.

in a way that respects his or her own personal integrity and sovereignty. Problems emerge only when one person tries to dominate another.

The second important element of Rousseau's thought that emerges in the discussion of pity and the foundation of ethics in sentiment is that he sees aesthetics as key to morality. The virtuous person is the one whose instincts, whose sentimental or emotional responses to particular situations, are correctly attuned. No law can make men or women moral if their sentiments are not properly ordered.

This is an extremely significant notion. It has obvious implications for education: if human beings in the state of nature have naturally correct sentiments, then the purpose of education in the real, actual world in which we live becomes not what it was traditionally conceived as being: the training of individuals in the intellectual, social, and moral competencies necessary for being a member of society. On the contrary, education is about allowing the person to mature in a manner that protects her from precisely those cultural influences that traditional schooling is designed to cultivate and that merely inflame *amour propre*. These serve only to alienate her from who she really is, making her inauthentic.

By rooting ethics in sentiment, Rousseau also provides an obvious and instructive point of comparison with the emotivism that Alasdair MacIntyre sees as characterizing the way ethical discourse is to be understood today. In the latter scheme, to say that something is good is in reality merely to express a personal emotional preference. For Rousseau, ethical discourse is about personal sentiments—which amounts to the same thing, although he would reject moral relativism as a necessary implication.

In dealing with the issue of sentiment or emotional response, we should of course acknowledge that ethics typically does involve something along the lines of what Rousseau suggests. If I see an old man being attacked by muggers in the street and I need to google "Is mugging old men a good or a bad thing?" before acting, most people would say that I am behaving in a manner that shows a level of moral inadequacy on my part. Responding to something like a mugging should be intuitive: either I run to help, or I take immediate steps to fetch help, without really engaging in any discursive reasoning based on first principles. We might say that to be a moral person, my instincts or my sentiments need to be properly attuned to the situation, and that it is those instincts, and not any heteronomous law, that motivate me to act. Sentiments, emotions, and aesthetic considerations form an important part of ethical activity.

Nevertheless, between Rousseau and our day, there has clearly been a significant change, as witnessed by the rampant ethical subjectivism of our modern culture of anarchic emotive morality and expressive individualism. There is now no consensus about what it is that should evoke our empathy and sympathy: the baby in the womb or the pregnant teenager whose life will be utterly disrupted by having a child? The transgender teen who wants to become a woman or his parents who fear he is making a terrible mistake? The ethic Rousseau articulates may be rooted in sentiment, but it is not quite the same as the emotionally driven ethical subjectivism we have today. On the contrary, Rousseau sees empathy as having a universal stability because it is grounded in his confident assertion of a universal human nature possessing a conscience that is the same for everyone. Indeed, in *Emile* he has the Savoyard Vicar of book 4 define conscience as follows:

> There is in the depths of souls, then, an innate principle of justice and virtue according to which, in spite of our own maxims, we judge our actions and those of others as good or bad. It is to this principle that I give the name conscience.[28]

So important is this understanding of conscience to Rousseau that he then places the following eulogy to conscience in the mouth of the Savoyard Vicar:

> Conscience, conscience! Divine instinct, immortal and celestial voice, certain guide of a being that is ignorant and limited but intelligent and free; infallible judge of good and bad which makes man like unto God; it is you who make the excellence of his nature and the morality of his actions. Without you I sense nothing in me that raises me above the beasts, other than the sad privilege of leading myself astray from error

---

28. Rousseau, *Emile*, 289.

to error with the aid of an understanding without rule and a reason without principle.[29]

There is a sense in which Rousseau here says nothing that many orthodox Christians of his day, especially Protestants, would not have affirmed. There is an internal, intuitive moral compass that guides and directs the individual in right behavior toward others. As in the example of the mugging above, instinct plays a significant role in how we behave in the moral sphere.

There are, however, significant differences between the views of Rousseau and those of traditional Protestantism that are decisive for his construction of conscience. Unlike the Augustinian stream of Christian thought, of which orthodox Protestantism is one development, Rousseau does not regard human beings as innately perverted. For Augustine, it is precisely the fact that human beings are born depraved and subject to internal moral conflict and confusion that renders sentiment and instinct unreliable, even positively deceptive, guides to moral action. For Rousseau, however, individuals are intrinsically good, with sentiments that are properly ordered and attuned to ethical ends, until they are corrupted by the forces of society. Thus there is no tension, in his thinking, between conscience and will other than that generated by being a member of society and thus being made vulnerable to the perverted ambitions of an inflamed *amour propre*.[30]

For Rousseau, the individual is at his best—he is most truly himself as he should be—when he acts in accordance with his nature. This is the deep principle of Rousseau's understanding of authentic personhood and of ethics. And conscience is the internal, pristine, and, for Rousseau, God-given voice that points each one in this direction. It is society, with its temptations and its corruptions, that prevents conscience from being the omnipotent governor of human action. Here we have the conceptual framework for understanding the incidents with the theft of the

29. Rousseau, *Emile*, 290.
30. "Inflamed" is Dent's term to describe *amour propre* in its negative form. It is an adjective he uses to make it clear that, in his view, *amour propre* in itself is not necessarily a bad thing. Rather, it is its perversion that is the problem. Dent, *Rousseau*, 56–58.

asparagus and the encounter with Zulietta. In both cases, Rousseau's sin, if we can call it such, was the result of the perversion of his natural sentiments by the demands and expectations of society. Had he been at one with his nature, then he would not have behaved or thought as he did.

Again, this notion finds expression in another powerfully phrased passage where Rousseau praises the nature of true moral freedom:

> But the eternal laws of nature and order do exist. For the wise man, they take the place of positive law. They are written in the depth of his heart by conscience and reason. It is to these that he ought to enslave himself in order to be free. The only slave is the man who does evil, for he always does it in spite of himself. Freedom is found in no form of government; it is in the heart of the free man. He takes it with him everywhere. The vile man takes his servitude everywhere. The latter would be a slave in Geneva, the former a free man in Paris.[31]

The one who is truly free is the one who is free to be himself. We might recast this and say that the one who is shaped by society and not by his own conscience and reason is truly a slave. Alienated from his true self and in bondage to the demands of the society in which he lives, he is consequently less human, less authentic, than the one who acts in accordance with his own nature. It does not matter in what social or political context the evil man finds himself. He is always less than free, always less than he should be, because he is never walking in obedience to that inner voice that should guide him. It is following that inner voice that makes one truly free, truly authentic. Our access to the true order of the world and our place in it is thus primarily inward.[32]

Conclusion: The Significance of Rousseau

While Rousseau may well be little read, or even unknown, to the majority of the West's inhabitants today, it should be clear from the above that many of his ideas have become the commonplace assumptions of Western culture.

---

31. Rousseau, *Emile*, 473.
32. According to Taylor, this is the key move that Rousseau makes and that thus paves the way for later psychological constructions of the self. *Sources of the Self*, 369.

The most obvious is his focus on inward psychological life as that which offers the most profound account of personal identity. His *Confessions* is predicated on such an idea and provides not only an early example of the literary genre of psychological autobiography but also a rationale for seeing the inner life of each person as the most important or distinctive thing about him or her. Indeed, it is that inner life that truly constitutes unique personal identity. If Rieff is correct in seeing the modern age as the age of psychological man, we can see that the trajectory toward that aspect of our times is already present in the work of Rousseau.

A further point of contact between Rousseau and our age, and one that stands in positive connection to his psychologizing of selfhood, is the notion that it is society or culture that is the problem. This idea is perhaps one of the most dominant social and political assumptions today. That society, or nurture, is to blame for the problems individuals have in this world, not the individuals themselves considered in abstraction from their social environment, is virtually an unquestioned orthodoxy, and it influences everything, from philosophies of education to debates about crime and punishment.

This contrast between nature and society/culture that Rousseau draws also lies at the heart of the rise of two phenomena that, as noted earlier, Charles Taylor sees as critical to understanding the modern age: expressive individualism and the concept of dignity. As to the first, Rousseau lays the foundation for expressive individualism through his notion that the individual is most authentic when acting out in public those desires and feelings that characterize his inner psychological life. While he would not have anticipated how this would later manifest itself, this construction of selfhood and human authenticity is the necessary philosophical precondition for modern identity politics, particularly as it manifests itself in the sexual politics of our day.

It should, for example, be clear that some such construction of freedom and selfhood as that offered by Rousseau is at work in the modern transgender movement. That it is the inner voice, freed from any and all external influences—even from chromosomes and the primary sexual characteristics of the physical body—that shapes identity for the transgender person is a position consistent with Rousseau's idea that personal authenticity is rooted in the notion that nature, free from heteronomous cultural constraints, and selfhood, conceived of as inner psychological conviction, are the real guides to true identity. Rousseau would no doubt have been surprised at the latest results of his conception of nature and freedom, but the affinities are clear.

Of course, it is more complicated than that, and Rousseau's notion of *amour propre* acknowledges this. Human beings are social animals, and the behaviors and beliefs that validate them or give them a sense of personal worth or authenticity are socially determined. We noted this point earlier in the discussion of the dialogical nature of selfhood with reference to Charles Taylor's use of G. W. F. Hegel. Rousseau predates Hegel, but he is aware of how selfhood in practice is a dialogue, even if he sees this dialogue as problematic and potentially militating against personal authenticity. That is the problem that he pinpoints in the *Second Discourse* when he discusses the need for public esteem as a root cause of evil. Yet the moral neutrality of *amour propre* considered in the abstract—that it can be either evil or, given the right social conditions, shaped for good—underlines Rousseau's acknowledgment that there is a perennial human need for social recognition of some kind. He knows that society sets the terms by which individual identity is established and recognized. The key question is how to arrange society in such a way that it sets those terms in a manner consonant with self-love or in a way that does not lead to an alienated, inauthentic selfhood. This is a point to which I will return. For now, it is sufficient simply to note it.[33]

To the second point, that of dignity, Rousseau regards individuals as having an integrity and a value that derives from their inward self-consciousness and not from the society in which they exist (such a society being, by definition, something that is liable to make the individual

---

33. In his *Considerations on the Government of Poland and on Its Projected Reformation*, Rousseau notes the role of social gatherings in constituting and preserving the identity of ancient peoples, the examples being the Jews under Moses, the Spartans under Lycurgus, and Rome under Numa. The involvement of all the people in the public festivals of these societies was crucial both to individual and corporate identity, with no tension or opposition between the two. See Jean-Jacques Rousseau, *The Social Contract and Other Later Political Writings*, ed. and trans. Victor Gourevitch, Cambridge Texts in the History of Political Thought (Cambridge: Cambridge University Press, 1997), 179–82.

inauthentic), so all individuals have a value in themselves and not derived from their extrinsic position in the social hierarchy. As with expressive individualism, this egalitarian impulse we note here in Rousseau will prove a critical precondition for the rise of modern identity movements and their contemporary political manifestations, such as the campaign for LGBTQ+ rights.

There are other implications of Rousseau's thought that have clear affinities with the pathologies of our own age. The idea of the innate innocence of the hypothetical state of nature presses toward a cult of childhood and youth. Whereas in a society based on, say, Confucian ideals, age is to be respected because age brings with it wisdom, the Western world of today generally credits youth with wisdom and sees old age as corrupt, myopic, or behind the times. For example, we have in recent years been treated to children and teenagers lecturing the older generation on everything from healthcare to the environment to matters such as Brexit and Donald Trump. Opining on each of these topics in any useful way actually requires some level of experience and knowledge of the kind that only comes when significant time has been spent studying the subjects at hand and observing how the world works. But that has not stopped serious newspapers and pundits taking the voice of youth seriously. Why? In part, it is surely because Rousseau's basic point about nature, society, and the authenticity of youthful innocence has become one of the unacknowledged assumptions of this present age. It is part of the social imaginary.

Further, Rousseau's points about the state of nature and the effects of society also carry with them a certain antihistorical tendency. If the state of nature is the ideal, and if society corrupts, then the history of society becomes the history of the corruption and oppression of human nature. It ceases to be a source of wisdom and becomes rather a tale of woe. That is a tendency that will become a hallmark of the modern age, from Marx's notion of history as class struggle to Freud's concept of civilization to the recent claims that "being on the right side of history" actually (and somewhat ironically) requires the overthrow of historical definitions of social practices such as marriage.

Finally, in accenting the role of sentiment/empathy in ethics, Rousseau also points us to the critical importance of the concept of human nature to the stability of ethical discourse. When read in light of the anarchic moral relativism and ethical emotivism of our present age, it is clear that Rousseau is saved from such only by his commitment to the divine origin of conscience and thus to the foundational stability and consistency of a human nature that is separately instantiated in every individual. Deny that, and what you have is a world in which the subjective sentiments of each person determine their own selfhood. Taylor refers to Rousseau's thinking here as "self-determining freedom," which he defines as follows:

> It is the idea that I am free when I decide for myself what concerns me, rather than being shaped by external influences. It is a standard of freedom that obviously goes beyond what has been called negative liberty, where I am free to do what I want without interference by others because that is compatible with my being shaped by society and its laws of conformity. Self-determining freedom demands that I break the hold of all such external impositions, and decide for myself.[34]

Take away the idea of universal human nature, and ethics descends into the subjective emotivism that MacIntyre sees as characterizing our present age. Empathy on its own is liable not just to be a sentiment but to degenerate into a sentimentalism that simply wants other people to be happy in their own way on their own terms. It is the collapse of this metaconcept of human nature that will prove so critical to our discussion.

---

34. Charles Taylor, *The Ethics of Authenticity* (Cambridge, MA: Harvard University Press, 1991), 27.

4

Unacknowledged Legislators

Wordsworth, Shelley, and Blake

Man is a poetical animal.

WILLIAM HAZLITT

In Jean-Jacques Rousseau's emphasis on self-love, sentiment/empathy, conscience, and the contrast between the hypothetical state of nature and the manner in which society can (and typically does) lead to inflamed *amour propre*, we can see emerging the basic outlines of modern expressive individualism. The real identity of an individual is to be found in the inner psychological autobiography. The authentic individual is one who behaves outwardly in accordance with this inner psychological nature. Society and its conventions are the enemy, suppressing desire and perverting the individual in a way that prevents the real, authentic self from being able to express itself. The essential dynamics of the modern understanding of the self are therefore already in place in the thought of Rousseau by the late eighteenth century.

The question with which I started, however, remains: How did such ideas—ideas originally floated in elite intellectual circles—become not simply the common currency of our society but so deeply embedded in

such that most people never reflect on them in any critical or self-conscious way and are apparently convinced that they are simply a natural part of our existence? To understand that, we need to see how ideas akin to those of Rousseau served to reshape culture more generally. And that brings us to the artistic movement known as Romanticism.[1]

The question of the definition of Romanticism, as with so many *-isms*, is a vexed one but need not detain us here.[2] My interest is not in establishing the essence (or not) of a putatively unified movement or describing family resemblances with a view to connecting disparate figures and movements in a constructed unity. Rather, mine is the more narrow aim of noting how certain cultural dispositions were manifested, communicated, and reinforced in the period after Rousseau. Thus, it is one particular strand of Romanticism—that of expressivism, and that as manifested in the poetry of the time—that is of interest here. It is in poetry, both in the theoretical reflection on its tasks and in its actual practice, that we find a number of key ideas emerging that prove of immense importance in the long story of the rise of sexual identity politics. First, there is the notion of poetry putting the listeners or readers in touch with an authentic reality that strips away the constructed corruptions of society and connects them to some more universal and authentic nature. Second, there is the related issue of the importance ascribed to aesthetics, or the idea that poetry (and therefore the poet) fulfills a profoundly ethical task in ennobling humanity by cultivating the correct sentiments through the medium of art. Third, there is the connection that emerges from this thinking, of seeing poetry as a political, even revolutionary, exercise and poets as, in Shelley's phrase, "the unacknowledged legislators of the World."[3] And finally, there are the specific connections we see emerging in the poetry and prose of men such as Percy Bysshe Shelley

---

1. Charles Taylor sees the connection between Rousseau and Romanticism as a key part of what he calls "the expressivist turn": "The picture of nature as a source was a crucial part of the conceptual armoury in which Romanticism arose and conquered European culture and sensibility." *Sources of the Self: The Making of the Modern Identity* (Cambridge, MA: Harvard University Press, 1989), 368.

2. A recent survey of definitions is found in the introduction to Carmen Casaliggi and Porscha Fermanis, *Romanticism: A Literary and Cultural History* (London: Routledge, 2016), 1–18.

3. Percy Bysshe Shelley, *Shelley's Poetry and Prose*, ed. Donald H. Reiman and Neil Fraistat, 2nd ed., Norton Critical Edition (New York: W. W. Norton, 2002), 535.

and William Blake between attacks on organized Christianity, notions of political liberation, and the idea of sexual freedom. With radical poets such as Shelley and Blake, we begin to see the emergence of the important emphasis on sex as the central element of individual authenticity.

William Wordsworth: Poetry, Nature, and Authenticity

In the preface to the 1802 (second) edition of *Lyrical Ballads*, the collection of poems that William Wordsworth and Samuel Taylor Coleridge first published in 1800, Wordsworth offered what was to become the most famous manifesto for expressivist poetry. Two aspects of the preface are of particular importance: first, the emphasis on inward emotion, and second, the priority given to the ordinary and the nondescript, even the rural, as subject matter.[4]

As to the first, the text is suffused with the language of emotions, pleasure, and aesthetics. The purpose of his poems is "to illustrate the manner in which our feelings and ideas are associated in a state of excitement."[5] He distinguishes his poetry from the conventional poetry of the day by stating that it is the feelings that it arouses that make significant the actions they describe, not vice versa.[6] This, he argues, gives the poet a creative freedom unknown by, say, the historian or the biographer, whose tasks impose on them a canon of historical exactitude. For the historian, it is the events and the actions that are intrinsically important. The poet, by contrast,

> writes under one restriction only, namely, that of the necessity of giving immediate pleasure to a human Being possessed of that information which may be expected from him, not as a lawyer, physician, a mariner, an astronomer or a natural philosopher, but as a Man.[7]

---

4. Describing the preface to the second edition, Malcolm Guite notes that it was "something of a manifesto of the new poetry with which both men were now associated: free, natural, lucid, unforced, drawn to discover the beautiful in what is close and everyday as well as what is remote, but equally committed to finding in folktale, superstition, and myth, emblems of our own inner nature and deeper truths about the human heart." *Mariner: A Theological Voyage with Samuel Taylor Coleridge*, Studies in Theology and the Arts (Downers Grove, IL: IVP Academic, 2018), 185.

5. William Wordsworth, *The Major Works*, ed. Stephen Gill (Oxford: Oxford University Press, 2000), 598.

6. Wordsworth, *Major Works*, 599.

7. Wordsworth, *Major Works*, 605.

It is, therefore, the *experience* of poetry that is the important element. The phenomena the poem describes are of value only to the extent that the poet is able to present them in a form that calls forth the desired emotional response from the audience. In fact, what makes a poet a poet is the ability to recall the powerful emotions caused by the external stimuli of nature and then to express these in a form that enables others to have the same experience. To use Wordsworth's own phrase, poetry "is the spontaneous overflow of powerful feelings" and that reproduced in the audience by the poet representing his own recollection of such in a form suited to that end.[8] The poet is essentially one who has the gift of recalling powerful emotional engagement with nature and articulating it in a form that stimulates an analogous response in an audience for whom the original stimuli are absent.[9]

The experience of poetry is not, however, a matter of mere entertainment. It has a much more profound purpose: it connects human beings to that which truly makes them human:

> [The Poet] is the rock of defence of human nature; an upholder and preserver, carrying every where with him relationship and love. In spite of difference of soil and climate, of language and manners, of laws and customs, in spite of things silently gone out of mind and things violently destroyed, the Poet binds together by passion and knowledge the vast empire of human society, as it is spread over the whole earth, and over all time.[10]

There is therefore an ethical purpose to poetic aesthetics: it is to reconnect the individual with human nature in general, to make people truly human again by taking them to that which is universal.

This is the same kind of note that Rousseau strikes in his reflection on the hypothetical state of nature and the need for individuals somehow to recapture that innocence in order to have the appropriate sentiments, that self-love shaped by and correctly ordered by empathy. In the aftermath of the French Revolution, with the disastrous blood-

---

8. Wordsworth, *Major Works*, 611.
9. Wordsworth, *Major Works*, 607.
10. Wordsworth, *Major Works*, 606.

shed that resulted from the attempt to build a just society on the basis of reason alone, this argument for an aesthetic approach to making men and women moral surely had a renewed urgency. And here we find Wordsworth arguing that this aim can be achieved through poetry and the genius of the poet.

This optimistic view of poetry leads to the second element of Wordsworth's poetic sensibility, one that again has affinities with the earlier arguments of Rousseau: his preference for the ordinary and, indeed, for the rural as choice for his poetic subjects. The reason for this proclivity lay in his belief that urbanization had a deleterious effect on human nature. This was scarcely a view unique to him. It is clearly consistent with Rousseau's general criticism of the influence of organized society on moral thinking. And it was articulated by a number of Wordsworth's contemporaries, such as William Blake and William Hazlitt. In his famous essay "On Poetry in General," Hazlitt, the artist and literary critic, summed up what he saw as the disenchanting impact of the modern world on the state of humanity, an impact he seemed to see as tragically inevitable. Above all, it engendered a spirit alien to that of poetry:

> It is not only the progress of mechanical knowledge, but the necessary advances of civilization that are unfavourable to the spirit of poetry. We not only stand in less awe of the preternatural world, but we can calculate more surely, and look with more indifference, upon the regular routine of this.[11]

And, Hazlitt argued, it was precisely because of the advent of this society of rationalized calculation and scientific precision that poetry was necessary as never before, noting with irony that prose is perfectly suited as a medium for the prosaic existence that industrial society promotes.[12] There was something about the form and matter of poetry that went beyond anything mere prose could achieve. Wordsworth and Coleridge stand on this same ground.

---

11. William Hazlitt, *Selected Writings*, ed. Jon Cook (Oxford: Oxford University Press, 1998), 319.

12. "Society, by degrees, is constructed into a machine that carries us safely and insipidly from one end of life to the other, in a very comfortable prose style." Hazlitt, *Selected Writings*, 319.

Wordsworth thought that the monotonous grind of city life, particularly the dehumanizing effect of industrial labor, had both blunted human sensibilities and left individuals vulnerable to a craving for the sensational and spectacular in order to enliven their humdrum existence. This he considered to be unprecedented in human history. The fall of humanity into the inauthenticity that Rousseau posits with the rise of inauthentic social existence is for Wordsworth that which takes place with the dramatic rise of urban life in the late eighteenth century. Against this, Wordsworth posits a return to rural life, to simple country practices, and to the joys and pains of ordinary country existence.[13] Rustic life, rooted as it is in more elementary feelings that are not yet shaped by the confected habits and conventions of polite society, provides better material for the expression of what it means to be authentically human. The inward turn is therefore for Wordsworth simultaneously the rural turn, as it is there, in simple country life and simple country folk, that one can find human nature in a less corrupt state.[14]

Wordsworth's decision to focus on the ordinary experiences of simple rural life was not without its critics. One of the more thoughtful examples occurred in 1802, when he received a letter from a student, John Wilson, who found particularly distasteful Wordsworth's decision to write about a young simpleton in a poem titled "The Idiot Boy." Responding to Wilson's reasoned criticism gave Wordsworth a chance to elaborate more fully on his reason for choosing poor rural folk as the material for his poems. He wishes, he says, to write poetry that probes authentic human nature, which decision then raises an important question:

> But where are we to find the best measure of this? I answer, from with[in] by stripping our own hearts naked, and by looking out of ourselves to[ward me]n who lead the simplest lives most according to nature men who [ha]ve never known false refinements, wayward and artificial desires, false criti[ci]sms, effeminate habits of thinking and feeling, or who, having known these [t]hings, have outgrown them. This latter class is the most to be depended upon, but it is very small in

---

13. Wordsworth, *Major Works*, 599.
14. Wordsworth, *Major Works*, 596–97.

number. People in our rank in life are perpetually falling into one sad mistake, namely, that of supposing that human nature and the persons they associate with are one and the same thing. Whom do we generally associate with? Gentlemen, persons of fortune, professional men, ladies persons who can afford to buy or can easily procure books of half a guinea price, hot-pressed, and printed upon superfine paper. These persons are, it is true, a part of human nature, but we err lamentably if we suppose them to be fair representatives of the vast mass of human existence.[15]

This passage is both fascinating and revealing. To find genuine, authentic human nature, Wordsworth declares that we must turn inward. That is where we can find that which is universal, because the so-called sophisticated lives of the educated elites are confected and actually offer no normative insights into that which is common to us all and which binds humanity together. They offer a picture not of real, authentic human nature but rather of a thin and unrepresentative strand of human life that conforms to the artificially constructed canons of social acceptability. They are fakes, inauthentic examples of humanity, because they are not true to themselves but rather true to the customs and conventions of the phony world to which they belong. Yet merely turning inward might itself be a problem precisely because of the power of these cultural canons and conventions in shaping who we are. The power of the civilized elite is such that it makes us believe that, as fake as it is, it is genuine, the real thing. To use later Marxist idiom, we might say that sophisticated urban life cultivates a false consciousness. But as Wordsworth's juxtaposition of rural life and city sophistication indicates, "civilization" really serves to corrupt and to hide that which is truly universal in our nature and thus cuts us off from what it means to be authentically human.

The reference to "false refinements, wayward and artificial desires, false criticisms," and so on could easily have been written by Rousseau. As with Rousseau's *Discourses*, Wordsworth's poetic manifesto assumes a basic antithesis between nature and culture, with the latter

---

15. Wordsworth, *Major Works*, 622.

having a deleterious effect on the former. Sophisticated society particularizes people and alienates them from that which all human beings have in common. As such, it provides the context for the strife and conflict, the pride and the competition, that have generated such problems for society. If one therefore wishes to see what it is to be truly human, if one wishes to move toward the improvement of the human condition, one must rid oneself of these false habits of thought and behavior that are the result of such artificial society and that foster such problematic divisions.

How does one do this? Wordsworth believes that this is done via poetry, or rather, by poetry that focuses on that which is uncorrupted and real. By reflecting on rural life, untouched and unspoiled by the artificiality of urban sophistication, and by representing it in a poetic form designed to arouse the appropriate emotional response, the poet is key to this process whereby people are enabled to grasp once again that which is true, authentic, and universal in human existence. Human nature as it exists in civilized society is a corrupt construct. Only by going back before the effects of "civilization" can one hope to find that which is truly human, and enabling people to do this is the task of the poet.

In his autobiographical epic, *The Prelude*, Wordsworth presents this thinking in a deeply personal way, pressing the role of rural life and the untamed countryside in his own education and upbringing, placing the emphasis not so much on simple country folk as on the direct exposure this environment gave him to the power of nature itself. In a dramatic couplet in book 1, he summarizes neatly how he grew up in an unspoiled and untamed natural environment and how this was the means by which he received his most significant education, that of his spirit:

> Fair seed time had my soul, and I grew up
> Fostered alike by beauty and by fear.[16]

Nature thus provides the important experience of both the beautiful and the sublime, both of which have an impact on him that occupies him

---

16. William Wordsworth, *The Prelude*, ed. James Engell and Michael D. Raymond (Oxford: Oxford University Press, 2016), 1.279–80.

for much of books 1 and 2 and for significant other passages throughout the poem. As the poem progresses, however, Wordsworth recounts how he himself becomes more enamored of human reason and seeks to find truth through rationalism and logic. This he finds epitomized in the triumph and then the tragedy of the French Revolution, an event that first inspired joy in his heart and later great disillusionment. What is interesting is how, in the latter stages of the work, particularly books 12 and 13, he returns to the idea that nature provides the basic unity to existence, which neither reason nor the refinements of sophisticated society can do. Here, in a climactic passage in book 12, he declares that love can hardly thrive

> In cities, where the human heart is sick,
> And the eye feeds it not, and cannot feed:
> Thus far, no further, is that inference good.
> Yes, in those wanderings deeply did I feel
> How we mislead each other; above all
> How Books mislead us, looking for their fame
> To judgments of the wealthy Few who see
> By artificial lights, how they debase
> The Many for the pleasure of those Few;
> Effeminately level down the truth
> To certain general notions for the sake
> Of being understood at once, or else
> Through want of better knowledge in the men
> Who frame them, flattering thus our self-conceit
> With pictures that ambitiously set forth
> The differences, the outward marks by which
> Society has parted man from man,
> Neglectful of the universal heart.[17]

Of significance here is both the criticism of city life and of books. Books present ideas, rational ideas, which militate against the deeper unity of the human race. It is the cult of reason, playing to the artificiality of sophisticated urban life, that has alienated men and women from each

---

17. Wordsworth, *The Prelude*, 12.202–19.

other. The answer, then, is to return to that experience of rural life and of the natural world to which it is so close. That takes us to the heart of who and what we really are, and that is also a turn inward, from the false sophistication of outward society to the unalloyed and uncorrupted movements of the unspoiled heart.

Percy Bysshe Shelley and the Poetic Truths of Nature

Wordsworth's younger contemporary Percy Bysshe Shelley also articulates a view of the poet's task as enabling the audience to move from the particulars of existence to the universal truths of human nature via the aesthetic experience that poetry gives the reader. This experience also involves an inward movement, as it did for Wordsworth. But for Shelley the focus is not so much rural life, unspoiled by urban sophistication, as it is the innate, raw power of nature considered in itself and manifested in the beauty and the sublimity of the natural world. And with Shelley this turn takes on a much more explicitly political tenor.

Shelley explained and defended his philosophy of poetry in an essay, *A Defence of Poetry*, which was a response to an article by his friend the satirist Thomas Love Peacock titled "The Four Ages of Poetry." This latter essay had appeared in *Ollier's Literary Miscellany* in 1820. Peacock therein identified his own (and thus Shelley's) poetic time as the "Age of Bronze," in which poetry had become pretentious and pointless in its pseudosimplicity. He therefore urged intelligent people to abandon it and study the sciences instead. Shelley's response was thus an attempt to defend the public usefulness of the poetic task.[18]

There are two aspects of fundamental importance to Shelley's philosophy of poetry, which he sets forth in *A Defence*. The first correlates to the emotional expressivism of Wordsworth and is tied closely to nature. For Shelley, nature in itself has the power—indeed, an "unseen Power"— to move and shape the poet, and poetry (which, for Shelley, is a term of wide reference, covering both literary and representative arts) is the

---

18. See *Shelley's Poetry and Prose*, 509–10.

inevitable result of this movement.[19] In a famous passage from *A Defence of Poetry*, Shelley describes the process or experience of this power as follows:

> Poetry, in a general sense, may be defined to be "the expression of the Imagination": and poetry is connate with the origin of man. Man is an instrument over which a series of external and internal impressions are driven, like the alternations of an ever-changing wind over an Aeolian lyre, which move it by their motion to ever-changing melody.[20]

The image of the Aeolian lyre is significant. This is a musical instrument played by the wind, not by any human hand. Essentially, the force of nature in the form of wind strikes the harp's chimes and causes it to create music, to give expression to what would otherwise be an inexpressible force, in accordance with the harp's own construction. The point of the analogy is clear: poetry is the result of the forces of nature moving the poet to give them literary or artistic expression. The poet is inspired by nature, not simply by way of his own emotional reaction to it but by forces that are innate within nature itself, and therefore external to him, and that move him in his works of artistic creation.

This is not unique to Shelley: Hazlitt articulates a very similar view, without using the lyre analogy, in "On Poetry in General."[21] In short, poetry for Shelley and Hazlitt is artistic creation dynamically inspired by nature, reflecting nature, illuminating nature, communicating the power of nature, and also, through its specifically human form, revealing something of the nature of human beings themselves.[22] What distinguishes

---

19. The opening stanza of his "Hymn to Intellectual Beauty" expresses this idea with eloquence, particularly its opening lines: "The awful shadow of some unseen Power / Floats though unseen amongst us." *Shelley's Poetry and Prose*, 93.

20. Shelley wrote this essay in 1821, but it was first published by his widow in 1840 in Percy Bysshe Shelley, *Essays, Letters from Abroad, Translations and Fragments*, ed. Mary Shelley, 2 vols. (London: Edward Moxon, 1840), although this text is no longer considered to be based on the most accurate manuscript. I am therefore using the edition in *Shelley's Poetry and Prose*, 509–35, quotation on 511.

21. Hazlitt states, "The best general notion which I can give of poetry is, that it is the natural impression of any object or event, by its vividness exciting an involuntary movement of imagination and passion, and producing, by sympathy, a certain modulation of the voice, of sounds, expressing it." *Selected Writings*, 308–9.

22. As Hazlitt puts it, "Neither a mere description of natural objects, nor a mere delineation of natural feelings, however distinct or forcible, constitutes the ultimate end and aim of poetry, without the heightenings of the imagination. The light of poetry is not only a direct but also a reflected light,

poets from the mass of humankind is their exceptional ability to give lyrical expression to this force through poetry in a manner that allows others who lack such talents to experience the same.[23] And it also means that poetry cannot simply be produced on a whim or made to order: it is inspired by nature, not only in the sense that nature provokes a reaction but also because the power of nature itself causes the poetic response.[24]

The other aspect of Shelley's thinking about poetry is the nature of the truth or truths to which poetry presses its audience. If Wordsworth saw the artificiality of polite and sophisticated society and the alienation caused by industrialization as cutting men and women off from authentic life, then Shelley exhibits a tendency to see the particulars of all forms of life in general as obscuring real, changeless truths.[25] Thus the poet has not only an origin point—the impact of the forces of nature on his soul—but also a purpose: to reveal the universal truths that are obscured by the particulars of day-to-day existence. For Shelley the poet therefore has a priestlike status in the way that he helps put members of society back in touch with reality. The poet does not simply describe the world in a metrical form of language with a view to stirring up the same emotional response in his audience that he himself has experienced. He does something

that while it shews us the object, throws a sparkling radiance on all around it: the flame of the passions, communicated to the imagination, reveals to us, as with a flash of lightning, the inmost recesses of thought, and penetrates our whole being." *Selected Writings*, 311.

23. *Shelley's Poetry and Prose*, 512. Later in *A Defence*, Shelley describes the poet using a memorable image: "A Poet is a nightingale who sits in darkness, and sings to cheer its own solitude with sweet sounds; his auditors are as men entranced by the melody of an unseen musician, who feel that they are moved and softened, yet know not whence or why." *Shelley's Poetry and Prose*, 516.

24. Shelley states, "A man cannot say 'I will compose poetry.' The greatest poet even cannot say it: for the mind in creation is as a fading coal which some invisible influence, like an inconstant wind, awakens to transitory brightness: this power arises from within, like the colour of a flower which fades and changes as it is developed, and the conscious portions of our natures are unprophetic either of its approach or its departure." *Shelley's Poetry and Prose*, 531.

25. This idea has typically been characterized as a Platonic aspect to Shelley's philosophy; see the influential study of Romantic thought by M. H. Abrams, *The Mirror and the Lamp: Romantic Theory and the Critical Traditions* (Oxford: Oxford University Press, 1953). The problem is that "Platonism" is a term so flexible and expansive in application as to be almost meaningless. Further, there are also strong materialist and future-oriented dimensions to Shelley's political thought that stand at odds with traditional characterizations of Platonism; see Paul Hamilton, "Literature and Philosophy," in *The Cambridge Companion to Shelley*, ed. Timothy Morton (Cambridge: Cambridge University Press, 2006), 166–84.

much more significant: he enables the audience to see beyond the ephemeral particulars of life to a much deeper reality, a deeper unity. As he himself expresses it,

> A Poem is the very image of life expressed in its eternal truth. There is this difference between a story and a poem, that a story is a catalogue of detached facts, which have no other bond of connexion than time, place, circumstance, cause and effect; the other is the creation of actions according to the unchangeable forms of human nature, as existing in the mind of the creator, which is itself the image of all other minds. The one is partial, and applies only to a definite period of time, and a certain combination of events which can never again recur; the other is universal, and contains within itself the germ of a relation to whatever motives or actions have place in the possible varieties of human nature. . . . The story of particular facts is as a mirror which obscures and distorts that which should be beautiful: Poetry is a mirror which makes beautiful that which is distorted.[26]

The point is clear: poetry enables the audience to see beyond the everyday experience of the world—experience that often seems chaotic and in conflict with itself—to the underlying eternal harmony that truly exists. Poetry is, he says elsewhere, a mimetic art.[27] We can all experience nature as real, as having its own objective reality. But the poet transfigures that experience, that reality, through the medium of poetic expression, which "purges from our inward sight the film of familiarity which obscures from us the wonder of our being."[28] Poetry harmonizes and finds unity in those things that have been torn apart by setting them in true relationship to each other and in this way confronts us with the sheer wonder of what it means to exist. And this has an aesthetic purpose: "It compels us to feel that which we perceive, and to imagine that which we know."[29]

---

26. *Shelley's Poetry and Prose*, 515.
27. *Shelley's Poetry and Prose*, 208.
28. *Shelley's Poetry and Prose*, 533.
29. *Shelley's Poetry and Prose*, 533.

Poetry, Ethics, and Aesthetics

Both Wordsworth and Shelley articulate views of poetry that press a clear connection between poetic aesthetics and ethics. For Wordsworth, the creation of empathy with ordinary, rural people facing the typical joys and hardships of life reconnects the person who lives in artificial high society or is alienated by industrialized labor to a common, universal human nature. Put bluntly, it makes them into better people. This improvement is achieved aesthetically and not by rational argumentation. As Rousseau considered correctly formed and ordered sentiments to be essential to making a person moral, so Wordsworth sees the instrument for doing that to be poetry preoccupied with rural life that is close to nature.

Shelley also makes the connection between ethical improvement and aesthetics. Again echoing Rousseau, Shelley states that for people to be truly good, they must be able to place themselves in the position of other human beings, to experience their pleasures and pains as if they were their own. And the key to this experience is not reason but rather the imagination, that human facility that is peculiarly susceptible to the influence of poetry. This is why poetry is so vital to the moral well-being of society.[30]

Shelley's argument for poetry is therefore, in a sense, utilitarian in that its purpose is not simply the moment of pleasure that reading a good poem brings or the contemplation of nature that it might induce. The pleasure is not an end in itself. The purpose of poetry and the pleasure it involves is nothing less than the moral improvement of the audience. And this leads to a further aspect of Shelley's theory of poetry: the very form of poetry plays an important role in achieving its effect. In fact, Shelley believes that when poetic productions become directly didactic, they immediately cease to be great. The prioritizing of the message over the aesthetic is a sign of decadence. Such productions become either cheap pastiches or simply the hectoring, moralizing voice of the vested interests of the powerful, as were exemplified, he claims, in the dramas that marked the court of Charles II.[31]

---

30. Shelley states, "A man, to be greatly good, must imagine intensely and comprehensively; he must put himself in the place of another and of many others; the pains and pleasures of his species must become his own. The great instrument of moral good is the imagination; and poetry administers to the effect by acting upon the cause." *Shelley's Poetry and Prose*, 517.

31. *Shelley's Poetry and Prose*, 520–21.

Didactic poetry is for Shelley a virtual contradiction in terms. As he says in the preface to *Prometheus Unbound*, he abhors direct poetic didacticism because if something can be adequately expressed in prose, then it is inevitably going to be "tedious and supererogatory" in verse.[32] The deepest truths about existence cannot, by their very definition, be conveyed without the use of poetry because the imagination plays the key role in enabling empathy between the audience and the subject of the poem. Therefore the aesthetic nature of poetry is vital. Content and form cannot be separated but are bound together by their common purpose.

Again, as with Rousseau, Shelley sees correct sentiments as foundational for the reception of moral reasoning. He asserts that human beings are unprepared for reasoned arguments until such time as sentiments like love and trust have first been cultivated. And the truly important virtues can be formed only through forms of art such as poetry. Therefore, art must have a central role in the moral reformation of humanity. Poetry, by presenting the audience with "beautiful idealisms of moral excellence," elevates the individual morally in such a way that reason can then (at best) act as a kind of supplement, providing argument and support for what has already been grasped at an emotional level.[33] It is therefore not surprising when Shelley comments in the main text of *A Defence* that many of those thinkers whom he most admires for their writings in the cause of the liberation of humanity—John Locke, David Hume, Edward Gibbon, Voltaire, Rousseau, and their followers—made almost no real impact on the world. Of these, he only really has time for Rousseau, and he gives an interesting explanation for this in a footnote: only Rousseau was a poet, the rest (including, he says, Voltaire) were "mere reasoners."[34] Mere reason does not stir the sentiments or emotions as is necessary for true moral transformation. True morality is always built on a foundation of sentimental morality.[35]

---

32. *Shelley's Poetry and Prose*, 209.
33. *Shelley's Poetry and Prose*, 209.
34. *Shelley's Poetry and Prose*, 530.
35. Shelley explains, "[I am] aware that until the mind can love, and admire, and trust and hope, and endure, reasoned principles of moral conduct are seeds cast upon the highway of life which the unconscious passenger tramples into dust, although they would bear the harvest of his happiness." *Shelley's Poetry and Prose*, 209.

Shelley makes this point about the moral vitality cultivated by the impact of poetry on the sentiments most powerfully in a passage in which he declares that a society's greatest poetry coincides with the period of its greatest moral and intellectual culture. He uses Athens as an example:

> The drama at Athens or wheresoever else it may have approached to its perfection, coexisted with the moral and intellectual greatness of the age. The tragedies of the Athenian poets are as mirrors in which the spectator beholds himself, under a thin disguise of circumstance, stript of all but that ideal perfection and energy which every one feels to be the internal type of all that he loves, admires, and would become. The imagination is enlarged by a sympathy with pains and passions so mighty that they distend in their conception the capacity of that by which they are conceived; the good affections are strengthened by pity, indignation, terror and sorrow; and an exalted calm is prolonged from the satiety of this high exercise of them into the tumult of familiar life.[36]

In a manner reminiscent of Aristotle, Shelley sees the importance of Greek tragedy as lying in the emotional experience it cultivates within the audience by drawing it into the dramatic experiences of the characters on the stage. The audience is thereby improved by the stimulation and strengthening of good affections. We might perhaps say that the poet is therefore both the creation of his age and the creator of his age. Bad ages produce bad poets and have their decadence and moral decline reinforced thereby. Virtuous ages produce virtuous poets and have their greatness and moral superiority strengthened thereby. And this in turn means that the poet is someone of great political significance: both a sign of the moral strength of the times and a means for maintaining the same.

Poetry and Politics

More than Wordsworth, whose early political ardor was cooled somewhat by the disappointment of the French Revolution and who (unlike Shelley) lived long enough to become something of a political reactionary,

---

36. *Shelley's Poetry and Prose*, 520.

Shelley was a political radical until the day he died. Art for Shelley thus serves an overtly political cause; or, perhaps better, art for Shelley is a political cause precisely because it is that which makes people truly human. It allows them to see beyond the way the world around them is to the way that it really should be. It is future oriented. Poetry is the means to transform the individual member of the audience, and so it also brings about a new consciousness with clear political implications. Poetically radicalized sentiments drive radical politics.

In the preface to *The Revolt of Islam*, Shelley again makes it clear that the aesthetics of poetry is crucial to its moralizing and politicizing impact and that this is designed with the purpose of cultivating an aspirational political radicalism:

> [*The Revolt of Islam*] is an experiment on the temper of the Public mind, as to how far a thirst for a happier condition of moral and political mind survives, among the enlightened and refined, the tempests which have shaken the age in which we live. I have sought to enlist the harmony of metrical language, the ethereal combinations of the fancy, the rapid and subtle transitions of human passion, all those elements which essentially compose a Poem, in the cause of a liberal and comprehensive morality; and in the view of kindling within the bosoms of my readers a virtuous enthusiasm for those doctrines of liberty and justice, that faith and hope in something good, which neither violence nor misrepresentation nor prejudice can ever totally extinguish among mankind.[37]

Language, harmony, meter, imagination, emotional transitions—all these serve to achieve the effect at which Shelley aims, namely, the arousing of feelings or sentiments that will make human beings better people and thus serve the cause of freedom. The audience will have its collective emotional consciousness expanded by poetry in such a way that it will long for—indeed, strive for—liberation from the constraints and the corruption that mark the present. And the poet is the midwife of this political transformation through his poetry, a point that (as we noted with regard to moral transformation) must shape not just the

---

37. Percy Bysshe Shelley, *Poetical Works*, ed. Thomas Hutchinson, corr. G. M. Matthews (Oxford: Oxford University Press, 1971), 32.

content but also the aesthetics, the form, of his compositions. Poetic language has the power to cultivate sentiments in the audience that lie deep within the human breast and to which mere prose or rational argument cannot gain access. In fact, as noted above, it is only as the heart is awakened by poetry that it is then able to understand rational arguments regarding morality. The ethical and thus the political are built on the foundation of the aesthetic and are both, therefore, dependent on poetry.

Underlying Shelley's poetry is, of course, a personal political radicalism that is far more overt and intentional than what we typically find in Wordsworth. For Shelley poetry is revolutionary because it exposes political oppression for what it is. It moves the audience by summoning up images of freedom and its possibilities and drives the imagination to see visions of potential liberation. Experiencing such visions, people will then themselves desire to see them realized in actuality. Revolutionary themes therefore permeate his poetry. At times, the political impulse actually leads him to use a more popular, easily accessible style so that a poem might have a more immediate impact on his target audience. Thus, "The Mask of Anarchy," written after hearing the news of the Peterloo Massacre of 1819, has a simpler poetic form in terms of rhyme and meter. It is written, so Shelley claims, more in the style of a popular song with an intentionally more direct and immediate appeal to the simple working people whose political consciousness he was trying to raise.[38]

The early poem *Queen Mab* is an excellent example of Shelley's political art. In it, he presents his readers with a picture of both past and present, highlighting the oppressed and enslaved position of human beings. But then he moves in cantos 8–9 to describe an idyllic future when all the conflicts of the present age are resolved and all nature comes to exist in harmonious relationship. The poem is thus a superb marriage of content

---

38. See the introduction to the poem in *Shelley's Poetry and Prose*, 315. This is a fascinating move on his part and foreshadows the rather more crass aesthetics of modern forms of entertainment, such as reality TV, which have a social and political impact by evoking emotional and sentimental responses through the use of highly demotic forms. The sitcom *Will and Grace* may have been ephemeral and intellectually very light fare as far as the history of Western culture is concerned, but its presentation of a gay couple as likable, humorous, and kind was a means of humanizing homosexuals and normalizing/domesticating homosexuality at a key point in the cultural debates over gay rights.

and form: its content is a history of the world that culminates in a future utopia, and its form, poetry, is precisely what Shelley believes will bring about this result through its ennobling impact on the audience.

Queen Mab makes it clear that for Shelley, poetry is in no sense an attempt to create mere nostalgia for a certain way of life now long passed or to pacify the audience with entertaining fantasies of unobtainable utopias. His vision is not for the return to some mythical rural childhood of humanity such as might be discerned in some of Wordsworth's poems. Quite the opposite. Its purpose is to inspire individuals with a desire for liberty and to encourage them to move toward the future, to usher in a revolutionary age when oppressors will be no more and freedom will be truly realized.

Of course, Shelley is acutely aware that the violent path to freedom as exemplified in the French Revolution proved to be a road to nowhere and culminated not in the liberation of humanity but in bloodshed and then the rise of a new tyrant, Napoleon Bonaparte, to replace the old.[39] Poetry is for him the alternative to such violence. Its impact will be inherently ennobling. It will enable people to find the harmony in nature behind the chaos of the present, and it will raise political consciousness in such a way that the ends of social revolution will be achieved peaceably and more perfectly than any process of direct violent activism could achieve. The eschatological utopia depicted in *Queen Mab* is brought about gradually by evil slowly exhausting itself through its own contradictions and thereby leaving human beings free to live according to reason, which is itself rooted in an instinctive and unfettered passion that delights in love to others.[40]

The poet for Shelley is therefore a person of singular revolutionary political importance. Indeed, to use the phrase with which Shelley closes *A Defence of Poetry*, "Poets are the unacknowledged legislators of the World" because they are the ones who transform people, and therefore

---

39. As for Beethoven, so for Shelley, Napoleon had been a devastating disappointment, the betrayer of liberty and a bloodthirsty tyrant, as is clear from his poem "Written on Hearing the News of the Death of Napoleon." *Shelley's Poetry and Prose*, 465–66.

40. Shelley, *Queen Mab*, Canto 9.38–56, in *Shelley's Poetry and Prose*, 67.

the world, through their artistic creations. They bring visions of possible futures into the present, they give hope, they inspire, they create desires for something better; and though they themselves do not necessarily understand the full significance and power of the words that they have been inspired to write, they yet move their audience toward a world of universal love and freedom.[41] Man, as Hazlitt says, is "a poetical animal"; Shelley would agree.[42]

Freedom from Religion, Freedom for Love

It should be clear by now that poets such as Wordsworth and Shelley represent cultural tendencies that stand in positive relation to some of the pathologies that are of great significance today. We see in their work and their understanding of the poet's task the artistic expression of the new way of conceptualizing human selfhood that we noted in Rousseau: a selfhood rooted in a belief that human authenticity is to be found by freeing oneself from, or transcending, the alien demands of civilization; by returning to the impulses of nature; and by rooting what it means to be truly human in feeling prior to any consideration of reason.

Both men share an emphasis on the corrupting nature of society that has alienated human beings from their own authentic identity and thus an emphasis on an inward, psychological turn in order to find one's true self. Then there is the related priority placed on sympathy and empathy, emotional responses to suffering and to identifying with others, as the foundations of ethical thinking. This in turn finds its corollary in an emphasis on aesthetics rather than rational argument as being the most powerful means of exerting influence and changing people for the better. And we might also note the consequent importance of the poet or the artist as the means of transforming society. Credit where credit is due: Percy Bysshe Shelley made the case for cultural figures as the key to political revolution over a century before Antonio Gramsci and then the New Left.

---

41. *Shelley's Poetry and Prose*, 535.

42. The quotation is seen here in its larger context: "Fear is poetry, hope is poetry, love is poetry, hatred is poetry; contempt, jealousy, remorse, admiration, wonder, pity, despair, or madness, are all poetry. Poetry is that fine particle within us, that expands, rarefies, refines, raises our whole being: without it 'man's life is poor as beast's.' Man is a poetical animal." Hazlitt, *Selected Writings*, 309–10.

Yet two further elements are particularly prominent in Shelley that are harbingers of much of the politicized cultural discourse of our own day: his attack on institutional religion and his understanding that sexual liberation is central to political liberation. And for Shelley, as for many in our own day, these two concerns are closely linked because one of the most obvious ways in which religion has historically exerted its power is in the policing of sexual behavior and sexual relationships.

Shelley's disdain for religion, or, more specifically, Christianity and Judaism, is evident from his earliest writings, indeed, from the moment when, as an undergraduate, he and his friend Thomas Jefferson Hogg authored the pamphlet *The Necessity of Atheism* and were expelled from Oxford for their pains. Then, in the early poem *Queen Mab*, the fairy guide launches a powerful attack on the Jews as they howl "hideous praises to their Demon-God"—which is in effect an attack on Christianity expressed in the then more socially acceptable idiom of anti-Jewish polemic.[43]

For Shelley, religion is a means of manipulation by which the powerful keep others subjugated and which is perpetuated primarily by the self-interest of those who have used it to gain the power they enjoy.[44] God himself is the very prototype of human tyranny, a willful, arbitrary, unaccountable despot.[45] But most important for our purposes is that there is a clear connection in Shelley's mind between religion, political oppression, and restrictions on sexual activity (i.e., the maintenance of chastity as an ideal and the promotion of monogamy as a binding and normative institution). In one of the visions of the future in *Queen Mab*, the fairy sees a world in which men and women return to a state of nature. The happy denizens of this poetic Eden behave in a manner that he characterizes as follows:

Unchecked by dull and selfish chastity,
That virtue of the cheaply virtuous,
Who pride themselves in senselessness and frost.[46]

43. Shelley, *Queen Mab*, Canto 2.150, in *Shelley's Poetry and Prose*, 27.
44. Shelley, *Queen Mab*, Canto 4.203–26, in *Shelley's Poetry and Prose*, 40–41.
45. Shelley, *Queen Mab*, Canto 6.103–10, in *Shelley's Poetry and Prose*, 50.
46. Shelley, *Queen Mab*, Canto 9.84–86, in *Shelley's Poetry and Prose*, 68.

The contempt for traditional sexual mores is obvious. And it is here that we see an expression of the connection between authenticity and sexual freedom that will become so important in the late twentieth century. As we noted in the introduction, expressive individualism may be the necessary precondition for the sexual revolution and modern identity politics, but it cannot in itself explain why it has taken the sexual form that it has. And here we see that that connection between individual authenticity and sexual liberation is not of recent vintage but has a clear precedent in Shelley some two hundred years ago.

Yet far from being unique in this, Shelley is somewhat representative of radical thought at the start of the nineteenth century. Traditional moral thought and practice in the area of sex had undergone dramatic transformation in the previous decades in a number of ways. In his history of sex, Faramerz Dabhoiwala summarizes this shift by pointing to three significant and closely related developments in the 1700s: (1) the increasing importance ascribed to conscience (basically understood as natural instinct) as a reliable guide to moral behavior, (2) a growing public distaste for judicial punishment of consenting heterosexual transgressors (such as adulterers) of standard moral codes, and (3) the rising view that the moral laws based on external authorities such as the Bible might in fact be social constructs and actually stand problematically over against the natural laws governing human nature.[47] The first and third of these tendencies are obviously important for our narrative as they bring together two elements in a way that remains influential today. When healthy sexual activity is considered a matter to be judged by instinct, then inevitably those institutions that disagree with such will be seen as problematic and as hindering human authenticity and freedom. And when the primary culprit historically is religion, this means that religion will be the target of the sexual reformers. In the West, this specifically meant Christianity.

This latter point is very clear from the way the critique of traditional sexual mores manifested itself. In its most radical forms, this cultural shift on sex involved a vigorous attack on the institution of marriage and

---

47. Faramerz Dabhoiwala, *The Origins of Sex: A History of the First Sexual Revolution* (Oxford: Oxford University Press, 2012), 87–110.

thus on that which constructed and maintained it, that is, Christianity and the church. Shelley's father-in-law, William Godwin, is a fine example of such a critic. In book 8 of his *Enquiry concerning Political Justice,* Godwin dismisses marriage as an evil that checks the independent progress of the mind, that is inconsistent with the natural propensities of human beings, and that dooms people to a lifetime of unnecessary misery.[48] We might note the implicit contrast he makes between the conventions of society as currently constituted and the propensities of the natural state: his claim is that humanity's natural instincts militated against monogamy. To set this in the terms of Rousseau, human beings in the hypothetical state of nature would have known nothing of monogamy and marriage; these are alien, and alienating, impositions placed on people by civilization. For Godwin, "the abolition of marriage will be attended with no evils" because the institution represents the unreasonable bondage and oppression of the individuals involved.[49]

Just in case the reader does not grasp the depth of Godwin's abhorrence of the institution of marriage, at the climax of his argument Godwin declares it to be nothing less than "the most odious of all monopolies" because, by making one woman the exclusive property of one man, it creates the context for jealousy, subterfuge, and general social corruption.[50] These are, of course, akin to the vices that Rousseau sees as generated by *amour propre* in the artificial and competitive context of society. In Godwin's proposed utopia, no man would be joined exclusively to one woman, but all would share in each other in one sexual community. Anticipating the obvious objection in terms of family relationships—that this would lead to problems of deciding who was the father of which child—Godwin responds by stating that this would not be an issue because those conditions that make the matter of paternity problematic in the present context (social hierarchy, self-love, family

48. William Godwin, *An Enquiry concerning Political Justice, and Its Influence on General Virtue and Happiness,* 2 vols. (London: G. G. J. and J. Robinson,1793), 2:848–49.

49. Godwin, *Enquiry concerning Political Justice,* 2:850

50. Godwin, *Enquiry concerning Political Justice,* 2:851–52.

pride) are themselves merely social constructs that would vanish. They would simply have no place in the brave new world Godwin envisages.[51]

The parallels with the philosophy of marriage—or perhaps better, the philosophical objections to traditional marriage—of our present day are obvious. Monogamous, chaste marriage is a social construct that runs against the grain of natural human instincts. Therefore, it serves rather to promote problems rather than to solve them. Indeed, it is worse than that: it actually creates the problems that it then purports to solve. Therefore it should be abolished.[52]

Shelley's own work stands as a fine representative of this same tradition of sexual iconoclasm and one that connects aesthetics, freedom, sex, and the artist in a manner that adumbrates so much of our current world. In *Queen Mab* he builds on Godwin's thought to present a view of humanity's coming of age in which all the inequities and injustices created by social conventions will be solved over time as those conventions themselves dissolve. He identifies the underlying cause of inequality and servitude as the commercial marketplace, which, in a manner anticipating Karl Marx, Shelley sees as determining all social relations and as preventing human beings from being truly free. And at the heart of this current commercial oppression that exists in the world is the institution of marriage, undergirded by religious teaching and enforced by religious institutions.[53] Everything now has its value determined by its price, and its price is governed by the forces of the market. Even human relationships, the last vestiges of natural freedom that society allows to its members, have been subjected to this corruption. And at the center of this distortion lies love and that which forces it into the confines of a lifelong, monogamous relationship. Liberty will never be achieved while the market controls everything and while human love is shackled by traditional Christian views of marriage. The destruction of marriage, of the sexual codes that justify it, and of the institutions that enforce

---

51. Godwin here anticipates the kind of dissolution of the family through political liberation that is found in later feminist writings, such as that of Shulamith Firestone. See "The Psychological Transformation of Feminism," p. 254, in chap. 7.

52. Godwin, *Political Justice*, 2:852.

53. Shelley, *Queen Mab*, Canto 5.177–96, in *Shelley's Poetry and Prose*, 46.

and police it is therefore central to the liberation of humanity and to the cause of justice.

Ironically, given his comments on the futility of didactic prose to teach and cultivate a revolutionary consciousness, Shelley attached notes to *Queen Mab*, just in case his readers did not quite understand his message, and his comments on this specific passage of the poem are a concise but pungently phrased summary of his general view of conventional marriage and of the role of religion. "Love withers under constraint," he declares; "its very essence is liberty."[54] Thus, at the very heart of Shelley's political program of liberation lies the matter of sexual love, for it is love that equates to happiness and freedom. Restraints on love may well help the commercial marketplace function better, but they are nonetheless restraints on human flourishing. As happiness is the foundation of morality, so the liberating of love is a moral and political imperative. And as love lies at the core of what it means to be human, unnatural constraints on love effectively prevent human beings from being truly human. They are the primary cause for personal inauthenticity.

Shelley goes further, applying the imperative of happiness to the purpose of marriage as a means of pointing toward how it might be restructured:

> If happiness be the object of morality, of all human unions and disunions; if the worthiness of every action is to be estimated by the quantity of pleasurable sensation it is calculated to produce, then the connection of the sexes is so long sacred as it contributes to the comfort of the parties, and is naturally dissolved when its evils are greater than its benefits. There is nothing immoral in this separation.[55]

The passage has a remarkably contemporary logic to it. Shelley believes that the purpose of life is personal happiness, which he defines as "a pleasurable sensation," or, as we might put it, an inner sense of psychological well-being—the ethic of the therapeutic age. Marriage is therefore not to be understood as a lifelong monogamous relationship for the purposes of

---

54. Shelley, *Poetical Works*, 806.
55. Shelley, *Poetical Works*, 806–7.

procreation, mutual companionship, and exclusive sexual union. Rather, it is for the mutual pleasure and satisfaction of the consenting parties, and that is all. It is, one might say, a sentimental union, and once the pleasurable sentiments that it stimulates have dissipated, it should be dissolved at the will of the contracting parties. This is the essential rationale of our modern thinking on marriage, defined as it is by the logic of no-fault divorce. We should therefore take note: today's understanding of marriage is clearly not a recent innovation; it was explicitly advocated by the likes of Shelley over two centuries ago.

Shelley continues, likening vows taken to lifelong marriage to those taken to religious creeds. To make such vows is to bind oneself in a manner that prevents personal inquiry, precludes improvement, and preempts any possibility of escape if the marriage ceases to be a source of happiness. We might recast his objection and say that the problem with both marriage and creeds is that in each case the individual has to acknowledge the existence of an external authority beyond that of immediate, personal desires. By submitting to such an external authority, individuals plunge themselves into inauthentic existence. To make this point more sharply, Shelley then argues that marriage forces people to be hypocrites and even fosters prostitution. In doing so, he breaks with the dominant view of the time—that prostitutes were in origin the hapless victims of male seduction.[56] Instead, it is the impact of monogamy on the sexual marketplace and the repression of natural sexual instincts that leads women to become prostitutes. That society then chooses to punish women for doing that to which society itself has driven them is for Shelley the height of hypocrisy. Indeed, he cannot think of things more likely to conduce to human misery than the ideals of chastity and lifelong monogamy. Echoing the views of Godwin, he states that the abolition of marriage is the only way sexual relations can be reconstructed in accordance with nature.[57] Finally, in a dramatic rhetorical flourish, Shelley leaves the reader in no doubt about what is to blame for the vile institution of marriage:

---

56. This view was an innovation in the eighteenth century. Prior to that, prostitution was seen as the result of women's predatory sexual appetites. See Dabhoiwala, *Origins of Sex*, 141–42, 160.

57. Shelley, *Poetical Works*, 807–8.

> In fact, religion and morality, as they now stand, compose a practical code of misery and servitude: the genius of human happiness must tear every leaf from the accursed book of God ere man can read the inscription on his heart. How would morality, dressed up in stiff stays and finery, start from her own disgusting image should she look in the mirror of nature![58]

Organized Christianity, with its imposition on humanity of the law code contained in the Bible, is that which has alienated human beings from each other and destroyed true liberty. Christianity must therefore be destroyed and marriage abolished, or at least dramatically redefined, if human beings are to be truly free and truly happy.

We should note the rhetorical strategy Shelley employs here. He presents Christian morality not as wrongheaded or benign but as essentially evil. Christian morality is really immorality dressed up as righteousness. And thus the battle with Christianity is actually a battle with evil. Again, this is a characteristic of our present age, when Christian moral codes are seen as positively immoral. Calls for chastity are an unrealistic response to promiscuity and lead to cruel sexual repression, an irresponsible lack of proper sex education in schools, and the demonizing of unmarried teenage mothers. Opposition to homosexuality stirs up prejudice, forces gay people to live a lie, and can even lead to mental illness and suicide. The list could be extended, but it is not really a new one. The idea that Christian sexual codes prevent people from living free and happy lives—from being true to themselves—is not of recent vintage.

A similar perspective is evident in the work of William Blake. In his *Songs of Innocence and Experience*, Blake plays out the two conditions of human nature against the backdrop of England's Industrial Revolution and its impact on (to borrow a phrase from another of his poems) "England's green and pleasant land."[59] Scenes of rural bliss in the *Songs of Innocence* find their counterparts in the darker scenarios of the *Songs*

---

58. Shelley, *Poetical Works*, 808.
59. The phrase is found in Blake's poem "Jerusalem," Poetry Foundation, accessed March 23, 2020, https://www.poetryfoundation.org/poems/54684/jerusalem-and-did-those-feet-in-ancient-time.

of Experience. While Blake's symbolism often makes interpretation of his poems a tricky enterprise, many of them have strong sexual connotations. There is no debate, however, about the meaning of a poem such as "The Garden of Love," quoted here in full:

> I went to the Garden of Love.
> And saw what I never had seen:
> A Chapel was built in the midst,
> Where I used to play on the green.
>
> And the gates of this Chapel were shut,
> And Thou shalt not writ over the door;
> So I turn'd to the Garden of Love
> That so many sweet flowers bore.
>
> And I saw it was filled with graves,
> And tomb-stones where flowers should be:
> And priests in black gowns, were walking their rounds,
> And binding with briars, my joys and desires.[60]

The simplicity of the meter and the rhyme and the intensification of both in the final extended couplet with its double internal rhyme make this a powerful poetic testimony to Blake's philosophy of life. The chapel is a man-made intrusion into the garden of what was once innocence. Its presence is both alien and oppressive, with Blake picking up on the Decalogue's refrain of "Thou shalt not" as a means of conveying the negative, life-denying nature of Christian morality. Then, in the last couplet, sinister priests impose their external rules on Blake and hinder his realization of his happiness through the actualization of his desires.

The message is clear: external, socially constructed constraints are bad and deny us our real humanity. The garden symbolizes a state of childlike innocence, while the chapel represents the alien intrusion of institutional religion, the essence of which is summarized in the statement "Thou shalt not." Religion is oppressive. Indeed, religion is

---

60. William Blake, *Blake's Poetry and Designs*, ed. Mary Lynn Johnson and John E. Grant (New York: W. W. Norton, 2008), 40.

equated with death—hence the gravestones of the last verse that have taken the place of beautiful, vital, natural flowers. And finally, there are the cadaverous priests, patrolling the area and making sure that Blake's inner desires—the person he really is—are cruelly suppressed. Liberty and personal authenticity are to be found therefore in eschewing such things as institutional Christianity and thereby returning to the child-like and carefree innocence of the natural state where "joys and desires" are unhindered by the cruel "Thou shalt nots" enforced by the officers of the church.

Again, we see the state of nature contrasted with that of civilized society, this time (as with Shelley) epitomized in the church and its en-forcement of a strict and unnatural sexual code. Human desire is thus frustrated at every step, and individuals are not free to be themselves. The result is akin to death. Indeed, in *The Marriage of Heaven and Hell*, Blake offers the maxim "He who desires but acts not, breeds pestilence."[61] For Blake, as for Shelley, the revolution that the world needs is essentially sexual and irreligious at its very core, for it is in the affirmation of free love and the rejection of institutionalized religion that true liberty and personal authenticity are to be found.[62]

From the perspective of today, Shelley and Blake are thus representa-tive of fascinating and significant developments in discussions of sex, freedom, religion, and what it means to be human. In line with think-ers after Rousseau, they see feelings and instinct as lying at the heart of authentic moral action and what it means to be truly free and truly human. External, socially constructed constraints militate against this authenticity of the self in a manner that leads to a curtailment of personal freedom and to various problems in society. And of all socially repressive phenomena, Shelley and Blake consider organized religion, specifically traditional Christianity, to be the worst offender.

---

61. *Blake's Poetry and Designs*, 71.

62. In an even more extreme statement in *The Marriage of Heaven and Hell*, worthy indeed of Fried-rich Nietzsche at his most provocatively rhetorical, Blake declares, "Sooner murder an infant in its cradle than nurse unacted desires." *Blake's Poetry and Designs*, 73. Obviously, from the title alone, the maxims in *The Marriage of Heaven and Hell* are phrased to be both ironic and shocking, but the underlying philosophy is that of Blake himself, as comparison with the poetical works makes clear.

This polemic against Christianity is given a specifically sexual content because the institutional church offends against nature and freedom by unnaturally regulating sexual behavior through its promotion of the ideal of chaste, monogamous marriage and its identification of all other sexual activity as sinful and liable to punishment. For Shelley and Blake, therefore, the attack on religion and the attack on the sexual morality that underpins marriage, if not coterminous, stand in very close relationship to each other. While these two poets do not see sex in itself as a matter of identity in the modern sense (sex for them is still something one does rather than something one is), they do see the question of sexual behavior as one of the central questions of political freedom. It is therefore clear that the historical connection between expressive individualism, sex, and politics, so typical of our own day, was already beginning to be made by Romantic writers such as Shelley and Blake in the early nineteenth century. That particular aspect of our current cultural times is not a recent innovation brought about by the sixties.

Furthermore, as with Wordsworth, both Shelley and Blake see aesthetic productions as key to cultivating the revolutionary imagination that is necessary for what they wish to achieve. The poet, or the artist, thus becomes the central figure in bringing about the transformation of values that is necessary for the liberation of humanity. The poet is, to use Shelley's term once again, the unacknowledged legislator of the world.

Thomas De Quincey: An Aesthetic Postscript

Before moving on from the English literary scene of the early nineteenth century, it is worthwhile to note the contribution of one further figure associated with Romanticism who perhaps inadvertently anticipates some of the significant pathologies of our present age: Thomas De Quincey. While most famous for his memoir, *Confessions of an English Opium-Eater*, De Quincey was also an astute literary critic and something of an aficionado of violent crime. In particular, two of his essays were to prove culturally significant: "On the Knocking at the Gate in *Macbeth*" and "On Murder Considered as One of the Fine Arts." In these he applied with considerable irony and humor the kind of aesthetic arguments that based ethics on empathy that we have noted above. Yet he presses these in the service of a conclusion that is both entertaining and, if taken literally, quite disturbing.[63]

The first, his most famous piece of literary criticism, raises the question of what makes murder interesting, an object of aesthetic contemplation as opposed to a simple object of horror. His starting point is his recollection of his own emotional response to the murder of Duncan in *Macbeth*. These feelings, he comments, gave the murder "a peculiar awfulness and a depth of solemnity," and he wanted to know why.[64] De Quincey's answer is intriguing and significant: the murder must be presented in a manner that creates sympathy for the murderer. Now to create sympathy for a victim is, of course, easy. That is the natural instinct in such situations. But to create sympathy for a murderer, to draw the reader into the narrative in such a way that he has compassion, or at least some degree of fascinated comprehension, for the perpetrator—that is what makes a murder truly great. He must be a seething cauldron of complicated passions and contradictory motives so as to captivate the reader.[65]

It is this idea that De Quincey elaborates in his other famous essay, "On Murder Considered as One of the Fine Arts." Cast as a speech given to the annual meeting of a group that calls itself the Society of Connoisseurs in Murder, it is a Swiftian piece with a serious purpose. Near the start, he makes the following observation:

> Everything in this world has two handles. Murder, for instance, may be laid hold of by its moral handle, (as it generally is in the pulpit, and at the Old Bailey;) and *that*, I confess, is its weak side; or it may also be treated *aesthetically*, as the Germans call it, that is, in relation to good taste.[66]

---

63. Both essays are reprinted in Thomas De Quincey, *On Murder*, ed. Robert Morrison (Oxford: Oxford University Press, 2006).

64. De Quincey, *On Murder*, 3.

65. De Quincey says, "In the murderer, such a murderer as a poet will condescend to, there must be raging some great storm of passion,—jealousy, ambition, vengeance, hatred,—which will create a hell within him; and into this hell we are to look." *On Murder*, 5.

66. De Quincey, *On Murder*, 10–11.

The qualities of the aesthetics of murder in any given age, he then argues, speak to the quality of the age itself. Further, the quality of a philosopher can be gauged by whether he was murdered or at least had an attempt made on his life at some point, an argument that allows him to offer perhaps the most novel, concise, and devastating critique of John Locke[67] and also to express total confusion that Thomas Hobbes was not assassinated, given that he was such a good candidate for such.[68]

De Quincey's essay proved hugely influential. Edgar Allan Poe and G. K. Chesterton both thought highly of it, and it is arguable that its impact on the former led, via his Auguste Dupin tales, to the invention of the modern genre of crime fiction. Indeed, a moment's reflection indicates that this genre is itself morally interesting as it is typically predicated on the idea that murder and murderers are intrinsically fascinating. And this suggests that beneath the humorous hyperboles of De Quincey's sardonic essay lies a serious and perceptive point. Sympathy and empathy are really functions of aesthetics, not moral law. The murderer can be set forth in a sympathetic light by presenting him as sophisticated or at war with himself or as a rebel against society or as a genius engaged in a battle of wits with a detective. In such a context, murder becomes entertaining, intriguing, even attractive in some sense. What De Quincey has done, perhaps inadvertently, is to demonstrate that arguments for sentiments as the foundation for ethics are vulnerable to making aesthetic sense in and of itself the arbiter of what is good and what is bad.

De Quincey is not, of course, advocating murder or really trying to make murder socially acceptable, let alone desirable. But his ironic essays raise an interesting point: once aesthetics is detached from some universal understanding of what it means to be human, from some universally authoritative moral metanarrative, from some solid ground in a larger metaphysical reality, then aesthetics is king. Taste can drive what

---

67. In De Quincey's words, "It is a fact that every philosopher of eminence for the last two centuries has either been murdered, or, at the least, been very near to it; insomuch, that if a man calls himself a philosopher, and never had his life attempted, rest assured there is nothing in him; and against Locke's philosophy in particular, I think it an unanswerable objection, (if we needed any) that, although he carried his throat about with him in this world for seventy-two years, no man ever condescended to cut it." *On Murder*, 16.

68. De Quincey, *On Murder*, 19.

we think to be right and wrong. Ethically speaking, taste becomes truth. This, as we will see, is the argument made by Friedrich Nietzsche, who points out that the death of God demands a transvaluation of all values and that it places taste and desire at the center of this project. It also lies behind Alasdair MacIntyre's claim that modern ethical discourse is really just a way of expressing emotional preferences, with no universal criterion by which competing moral claims can be compared or assessed.

This is the point that Rousseau, Wordsworth, Blake, and Shelley understood. It was why they used poetry as a means of achieving the moral reformation of individuals and of society. It was also the point that De Quincey pressed to its logical conclusion. In a world of empathy-based ethics, the moral sense is ultimately the aesthetic sense. And that means that when the sacred order collapses, morality is simply a matter of taste, not truth. And in a world in which the idea of universal human nature has been abandoned or attenuated to the point of being meaningless, it also means that those who shape popular taste become those who exert the most moral power and set society's moral standards. While he would no doubt have retched at the thought, William Wordsworth stands near the head of a path that leads to Hugh Hefner and Kim Kardashian.

5

The Emergence of Plastic People

Nietzsche, Marx, and Darwin

*The Gods are first, and that advantage use
On our belief, that all from them proceeds;
I question it, for this fair Earth I see,
Warm'd by the Sun, producing every kind,
Them nothing.*

SATAN TO EVE IN JOHN MILTON'S *PARADISE LOST*

Central to the narrative of this book are the gradual emergence and then rise to dominance of the type of person that Philip Rieff calls psychological man and Charles Taylor characterizes as the expressive individual. Without this general concept, it is impossible to understand particular elements of the world as we now know it—the sexual revolution, the current importance of identity politics, or the reasons why once-nonsensical ideas such as transgenderism now have popular currency. As I argue later, the triumph of the therapeutic that psychological man represents depends for much of its success on its cultivation and dissemination through art, whether the elite products of the surrealists or the mass-produced demotic offerings of pop culture. Most people have not read Freud, but many find appealing the message preached in myriad movies and soap operas that life is about finding individual sexual satisfaction and that one's sexual appetites lie at the very center of who one actually is.

Yet while sex provides much of the content of psychological man and the expressive individual of this present age, perhaps the most striking characteristic of today's understanding of what it means to be human is not its sexual content but rather its fundamental plasticity. Psychological man is also plastic person, a figure whose very psychological essence means that he can (or at least thinks he can) make and remake personal identity at will. And for such plastic people to exist and thrive, there must exist both a certain kind of metaphysical framework and a certain kind of society with a particular social imaginary. This brings us to a second narrative strand regarding the emergence of the types of self that now characterize our world, namely, the elimination of the notion that human nature is something that has authority over us as individuals.

The Plausibility of Self-Creation

The idea that we can be who or whatever we want to be is a commonplace today. Consumerism, or late capitalism, fuels this notion with its message of the customer as king and of the goods we consume as being basic to who we are. Commercials communicate this message in the way they present particular products as the key to happiness or life improvement. You have the power to transform yourself by the mere swipe of a credit card. The possession of this thing—that car, that kitchen, that item of clothing—will make you a different, a better, a more fulfilled person. Underwritten by easy credit, consumerist self-creation is the order of the day.

Such self-creation is perhaps more of a myth, or what Freud would have called an illusion, an act of wishful thinking, than a practical reality. Indeed, the underlying dynamic of the consumer marketplace is that desires can never be fully satisfied, at least not in any long-term manner. The consumer may not simply be a hapless dupe of the ruthless capitalist reinventing the market to maintain income streams, as some on the Left would argue, but the negotiation between producer and consumer is ultimately predicated on the fact that the desire for consumption never seems to be met by the act of possession. If the producer creates desires in order to fulfill them, then the consumer seems a willing-enough party in the process. To use Hegelian jargon, the consumer society really does present persons whose being is in their becoming, constantly looking to the next purchase that will bring about that elusive personal wholeness.

This illusion of sovereign self-creation through consumption still has its limitations. All of us are ultimately limited by a variety of factors that are not always susceptible to transubstantiation by credit card. First, there is the range of goods or lifestyles on offer. The marketplace does not have an infinite number of products for sale. The consumer is not an absolute monarch; as noted above, the marketplace involves a negotiation between supplier and consumer. Second, society is constantly changing its mind about what is and is not fashionable, what is and is not cool, and what is and is not acceptable. We might think that we have the power to create ourselves and our own identities, but we are typically subject to the range of options and the value schemes that society itself sets and over which most individuals, considered as individuals, have very limited power. Consumerism makes us believe we can be whoever we want to be, but the market always places limits on that in reality.

Third, there are always specific individual limitations to our ability to invent ourselves. Physiology, intellectual capacity, income, location in time, and geographical location all play their role. I might truly desire to be Marie Antoinette, queen of France—indeed, I might happily decide to self-identify as such—but my body is male, has a genetic code provided by my English parents, is physically located in Pennsylvania, and exists chronologically in the twenty-first century. Being Marie Antoinette is therefore not a viable option for me. My body, not my psychology, has the last word on whether I am the last queen of France in the eighteenth century.

Nevertheless, the idea of self-creation, that we can shape our essences by acts of will, is deeply embedded in the way we now think, to the point that, while I may not be able to overcome the genetic and chronological issues that prevent me from being an eighteenth-century Austrian-born queen of France, I can at least deny the decisive say that my chromosomes might wish to have over my maleness. As Bruce became Caitlyn and was recognized as such by society, so Carl might now become Caroline, if I so wished.

The world in which this way of thinking has become plausible has both intellectual and material roots. Streams of philosophical thought from the nineteenth century have exerted a powerful effect in weakening and even abolishing the idea that human nature is a given, something that has an intrinsic, nonnegotiable authority over who we are. And changes in our material circumstances have enabled the underlying, antiessentialist principles of these philosophies to become plausible and, indeed, perhaps even the default of the way we think about selfhood today; however, I cannot address these material factors but will focus rather on intellectual developments. Thus, here I want to note the thought of three men who, while very different thinkers, helped shape the way we imagine human nature today: Friedrich Nietzsche, Karl Marx, and Charles Darwin. All three in their different ways provided conceptual justification for rejecting the notion of human nature and thus paved the way for the plausibility of the idea that human beings are plastic creatures with no fixed identity founded on an intrinsic and ineradicable essence. While there are others whose thinking also played a role in this shift, these three are arguably the most influential as fountainheads for later developments up to the present day.

Friedrich Nietzsche: Unchaining the Earth from the Sun

Friedrich Nietzsche's thought, given both its frequently aphoristic form of expression and the fact that it underwent some considerable development over his short but remarkably productive professional life, is complicated and subject to a variety of interpretations. As with Freud, some of his terminology—"the will to power," "the Overman," "beyond good and evil," "the genealogy of morality"—has become common currency in the jargon of popular philosophy; yet as with Freud's vocabulary, many of these terms are often used by those who do not know precisely what they mean. Nevertheless, one point on which Nietzsche scholarship is agreed is that he is the man who really calls the bluff of the Enlightenment and challenges those who have sloughed off the shackles of traditional Christianity to have the courage to take the full measure of what they have done.

The most dramatic example of this call is the famous madman passage in book 3 of *The Gay Science* (or, *The Joyful Wisdom*):

The madman.—Have you not heard of that madman who lit a lantern in the bright morning hours, ran to the market place, and cried incessantly: "I seek God! I seek God." As many of those who did not believe in God were standing around just then, he provoked much laughter. Has he got lost? Asked one. Did he lose his way like a child? Asked another. Or is he hiding? Is he afraid of us? Has he gone on a voyage? Emigrated?—Thus they yelled and laughed.

The madman jumped into their midst and pierced them with his eyes. "Whither is God?" he cried: "I will tell you. We have killed him—you and I. All of us are his murderers. But how did we do this? How could we drink up the sea? Who gave us the sponge to wipe away the entire horizon? What were we doing when we unchained this earth from its sun? Whither is it moving now? Whither are we moving? Away from all suns? Are we not plunging continually? Backward, sideward, forward, in all directions? Is there still any up or down? Are we not straying as through an infinite nothing? Do we not feel the breath of empty space? Has it not become colder? Is not night continually closing in on us? Do we not need to light lanterns in the morning? Do we hear nothing as yet of the noise of the gravediggers who are burying God? Do we smell nothing as yet of the divine decomposition? Gods too decompose. God is dead. God remains dead. And we have killed him.

"How shall we comfort ourselves, the murderers of all murderers? What was holiest and mightiest of all that the world has yet owned has bled to death under our knives: who will wipe this blood off us? What water is there for us to clean ourselves? What festivals of atonement, what sacred games shall we have to invent? Is not the greatness of this deed too great for us? Must we ourselves not become gods simply to appear worthy of it? There has never been a greater deed; and whoever is born after us—for the sake of this deed he will belong to a higher history than all history hitherto."

Met with initial mockery and then the astonished silence of his listeners, the madman throws his lantern to the ground, shattering it, and muses that he has come too early, that his audience is not yet ready to understand his message. Later that day, Nietzsche says, the madman enters a number of churches to repeat his message, only to be thrown out. His response is to declare these churches to be nothing other than the tombs of God.[1]

To quote Stephen Williams on this same section of *The Gay Science,* "This is one of those purple passages whose impact is virtually deadened by comment."[2] Yet its compact nature means that its underlying implications are too rich and wide ranging—especially for the arguments of this book—not to be made explicit.

The passage is perhaps most famous for the phrase "God is dead." This is intended as a far more powerful statement than the more matter-of-fact claim that God simply does not exist, because Nietzsche is here imputing a conscious intentionality to the matter of atheism. The underlying idea is that Enlightenment philosophy has quite purposefully rendered God implausible or unnecessary. It has done away with him. But here is the rub: Enlightenment philosophers have failed to draw the necessary, broader metaphysical and moral conclusions from this notion. In fact, we might say that they have had neither the intellectual acumen nor the courage to do so. It is thus polite atheists, not religious believers, whom the madman first engages in the town square, those who wish to have their comfortable, stable, secure lives even as they have removed any foundation on which they might build such. But the nonexistence of God is not like the nonexistence of unicorns or centaurs. Nothing significant has been built on the supposition that those mythological creatures are real. To dispense with God, however, is to destroy the very foundations on which a whole world of metaphysics and morality has been constructed and depends.

---

1. Friedrich Nietzsche, *The Gay Science,* trans. Walter Kaufmann (New York: Vintage, 1974), §125 (181–82). First published in German in 1887.

2. Stephen N. Williams, *The Shadow of the Antichrist: Nietzsche's Critique of Christianity* (Grand Rapids, MI: Baker Academic, 2006), 119.

The madman passage is not the initial place where Nietzsche uses the phrase "God is dead." It occurs for the first time in his writings at the very start of book 3 of *The Gay Science*. There he gives the following story:

> After Buddha was dead, his shadow was still shown for centuries in a cave—a tremendous, gruesome shadow. God is dead; but given the way of men, there may still be caves for thousands of years in which his shadow will be shown. And we—we still have to vanquish his shadow too.[3]

This passage sets the scene for the madman's later intervention. The basic point is that the foundation of religion may have been exposed as false, but the influence of religion, the systems of life and thought built on it, continue to live on, up until the present day. To use Charles Taylor's term, God continues to inform the social imaginary, and Nietzsche wants to put an end to this. Indeed, in the aphorisms between Buddha's shadow and the madman, Nietzsche raises a series of pungent questions about, and challenges to, science, logic, and morality, all of which he clearly regards as being in need of revision in light of the death of God.

For example, he attacks any notion that the universe considered in itself can have any intrinsic meaning. To think of it as a living being is a ridiculous—in fact, nauseating—anthropomorphism, and to regard it as a machine is really no better. In fact, one should not even talk of "laws" in nature, because that would imply a lawgiver and a universe somehow accountable to such.[4] Nietzsche then postulates that "knowledge" is simply a means of giving some kind of specious objective authority to ideas that both have proved useful in preserving humankind and have enjoyed longevity and general acceptance but that are really rooted in instinct and struggles for power.[5] When we claim to explain the universe, we are actually merely describing it and not really penetrating into any essence it may have at any deeper level than our ancestors

---

3. Nietzsche, *Gay Science*, §108 (167).
4. Nietzsche, *Gay Science*, §109 (167–68).
5. Nietzsche, *Gay Science*, §110 (169–71).

did.[6] Nietzsche also applies the same critique to logic[7] and finally to morality. Indeed, he dismisses morality as "herd instinct in the individual," a point that has affinities with Freud's later notion of the relationship between the superego and the ego and also to Rousseau's (and the Romantics') notion of authentic humanity as being that exhibited by the least socialized and civilized.[8]

All this provides the background to the explosive madman passage. To kill God, either by denying his existence or at least the coherence of claims to knowledge of him (as David Hume arguably did) or by making him nothing more than a necessary presupposition for moral discourse, the Enlightenment effectively tore out the foundations from under the polite bourgeois morality that it wished to maintain. You cannot do this, says Nietzsche. You have unchained the earth from the sun, a move of incalculable significance. By doing so, you have taken away any basis for a metaphysics that might ground either knowledge or ethics. In killing God, you take on the responsibility—the terrifying responsibility—of being god yourself, of becoming the author of your own knowledge and your own ethics. You make yourself the creator of your world. Hence Nietzsche peppers the madman's speech with dizzying, vertiginous imagery and the language of blood, murder, and decay. The cheerful and chipper atheism of a Richard Dawkins or a Daniel Dennett is not for Nietzsche because it fails to see the radical consequences of its rejection of God. To hope that, say, evolution will make us moral would be to assume a meaning and order to nature that can only really be justified on a prior metaphysical basis that itself transcends nature, or simply to declare by fiat and with no objective justification that certain things we like or of which we approve are intrinsically good.[9]

---

6. Nietzsche, *Gay Science*, §112 (172–73). It is worth noting that Nietzsche does allow here that the descriptions offered in his day may be better than those offered in earlier times, a point that calls into question interpretations of his thought that see him as a radical epistemological relativist, but the central point—that there is no metaphysics of essence that allows us to get beyond description to ultimate explanation—is nonetheless very significant.

7. Nietzsche, *Gay Science*, §111 (171–72).

8. Nietzsche, *Gay Science*, §§116–17 (174–75). For Rousseau and the Romantics, see chap. 3, and for Freud, see chap. 6.

9. Earlier in *The Gay Science*, Nietzsche notes the connection between opinion and aesthetics: "The change in general taste is more powerful than that of opinions. Opinions, along with all proofs, refuta-

Nietzsche and the Genealogy of Morality

The unavoidable antimetaphysical implications of atheism for morality are what drives Nietzsche to his polemics against both Christianity and Immanuel Kant. In his last work, *The Anti-Christ*, Nietzsche rails against Christianity on two related fronts. First, he attacks what he describes as the "theologian instinct." This is the tendency to give apparent objective and transcendent status to personal tastes and opinions by dressing them up with God language:

> Out of this erroneous perspective on all things one makes a morality, a virtue, a holiness for oneself, one unites the good conscience with seeing *falsely*—one demands that no *other* kind of perspective shall be accorded any value after one has rendered one's own sacrosanct with the names "God," "redemption," "eternity."[10]

This "theologian instinct" is not a monopoly of orthodox Christian theologians but can also be found in philosophers like Kant, whose concept of the "thing in itself"—the metaphysical reality that lies behind and undergirds all perceived reality but whose existence cannot be directly proved—is, for Nietzsche, simply another "God word," a specious transcendent foundation by means of which Kant is able to grant his own epistemological and ethical tastes a universal, objective status.[11] This is consonant with the madman passage: Nietzsche is demanding that both Christianity and Kant realize that their claims to truth are not ultimately claims about objective reality but claims about how they want the world to be in order to suit their own particular ends. For Christians, that is exalting weakness over strength; for Kant, it is to maintain the universal significance of the categorical imperatives that really only constitute his own personal moral preferences.

---

tions, and the whole intellectual masquerade, are merely symptoms of the change in taste and most certainly not what they are still often supposed to be, its causes." Nietzsche, *Gay Science*, §39 (106).

10. Friedrich Nietzsche, *Twilight of the Idols and The Anti-Christ*, trans. R. J. Hollingdale (London: Penguin, 2003), 132.

11. Nietzsche states, "*Decay of God:* God became 'thing in itself.'" *Anti-Christ*, 140. Elsewhere, Nietzsche describes Kant as an "idiot" and a "fateful spider." *Anti-Christ*, 134.

While *The Anti-Christ* is the last book that Nietzsche wrote prior to his complete and permanent mental breakdown, it exemplifies the approach to history that he developed in his earlier *On the Genealogy of Morals*. In this work, Nietzsche traced what he saw as a fundamental shift in ethical thinking, from the basic binary of good and bad to that of good and evil. What made this shift more than a semantic one for Nietzsche was the fact that what was referred to as good in earlier times (spontaneous strength) was that which later came to be denominated as evil, while that which was bad (servile weakness) came to be regarded as good. In short, the move involves a clever linguistic inversion and transformation of tremendous significance.[12]

What this does is transform the discussion of morality from a matter of discovering the nature of objective virtue or of eternal laws into an analysis of psychology. The pressing question is not, Is this right or wrong, good or bad? but rather, Why do people act this way? And that question points toward a host of more critical questions: Who benefits from arguing that action X is considered morally wrong? In fact, does morality actually have any value? As Nietzsche expresses it in the preface to *On the Genealogy of Morals*,

> Let us articulate this *new demand*: we need a *critique* of moral values, *the value of these values themselves must first be called in question*—and for that there is needed a knowledge of the conditions and circumstances in which they grew, under which they evolved and changed (morality as consequence, as symptom, as mask, as tartufferie, as illness, as misunderstanding; but also morality as cause, as remedy, as stimulant, as restraint, as poison), a knowledge of a kind that has never yet existed or even been desired.[13]

This point is far reaching and highly subversive. The game in moral discussion ceases to be that of establishing categorical imperatives and is changed into that of exposing the psychology that underlies any such claims. As Alasdair MacIntyre says in his reflections on Nietzsche's

---

12. Nietzsche develops this argument in various places. See, for example, *On the Genealogy of Morals and Ecce Homo*, trans. Walter Kaufmann and R. J. Hollingdale (New York: Vintage, 1989), 167.

13. Nietzsche, *On the Genealogy of Morals*, 20.

genealogical method, he "did not advance a new theory against older theories; he proposed an abandonment of theory."[14]

Nietzsche's application of this thinking to Christianity is merciless. Christianity represents the instincts of the weakest and most oppressed, and it embodies the very hatred of life and of living;[15] it desires to subjugate the truly noble and strong;[16] it makes men and women sick;[17] and it disvalues everything that is vital and strong and natural.[18] In short, we might say that while for a man like David Hume Christianity is epistemologically indefensible, for Nietzsche it is morally repugnant. Hume dismantles Christianity by analyzing how human beings know things; Nietzsche dismantles it by asking what ulterior motivation lies behind it. Hume might laugh at the claims of the Christian faith; Nietzsche is nauseated by them. With Nietzsche we see clearly two pathologies of our present age receiving philosophical explication: the tendency to be suspicious of any claims to absolute moral truth and a rejection of religion as distasteful.

Nietzsche and the Concept of Human Nature

At root, Nietzsche's attacks on metaphysics, morality, Christianity, and Kant are really attacks on the concept of human nature. Certainly, Nietzsche would have acknowledged human nature as a biological reality, but biology is not metaphysical and does not allow for claims about how all people should live or what purpose and destiny they all share. Again, he expresses this idea powerfully in *The Gay Science*:

> Man has been educated by his errors. First, he always saw himself only incompletely; second, he endowed himself with fictitious attributes; third, he placed himself in a false order of rank in relation to animals and nature; fourth, he invented ever new tables of goods and always accepted them for a time as eternal and unconditional: as a result of this, now one and now another human impulse and state held first place

---

14. Alasdair MacIntyre, *Three Rival Versions of Moral Enquiry: Encyclopaedia, Genealogy, and Tradition* (London, Duckworth, 1990), 49.

15. Nietzsche, *Anti-Christ*, 142.

16. Nietzsche, *Anti-Christ*, 144.

17. Nietzsche, *Anti-Christ*, 147.

18. Nietzsche, *Anti-Christ*, 162.

and was ennobled because it was esteemed so highly. If we removed the effects of these four errors, we should also remove humanity, humaneness, and "human dignity."[19]

In short, the basic error human beings have made is to give themselves a nature, to think in terms of a transcendent category that is prior to and greater than any single individual. In doing so, they have enslaved themselves to moral codes and given themselves a heteronomous teleology that they do not intrinsically possess. Human beings are rather to create themselves, to be free of the demands that the idea of a Creator or a metaphysically grounded morality or an abstract and universal concept of human nature would impose on them. Freedom for Nietzsche is freedom from essentialism and for self-creation.

The importance of self-creation is visible in *The Gay Science*. Two sections in particular are important in this regard. The first is *The Gay Science* §341, where Nietzsche outlines what he himself regarded as one of his most significant breakthroughs. Imagine, he says, that one night you are accosted by a demon who declares that you are going to relive your life—every single moment, the good and the bad, the great and the trivial—for all eternity, again and again and again. How would you react? Would it be a source of immediate horror to you, or would it inspire you?[20]

Nietzsche does not appear to present this notion, that of the *eternal return* or *eternal recurrence*, as an actual physical reality, whereby everything will happen again and again. Rather, it appears to be a rhetorical ploy designed to elicit an existential reaction: If this were true, how would you live? Would it make a difference to you? Nietzsche is challenging individuals to affirm the life they have and to live every moment as if it possessed eternal significance.

This is an important point for this study for two reasons. First, it is a useful reminder that popular characterizations of Nietzsche as a nihilist are typically misplaced. Simply because he rejects the idea that life has

---

19. Nietzsche, *Gay Science*, §115 (174).
20. Nietzsche, *Gay Science*, §341 (273).

any ultimate transcendent meaning does not mean that he believes life is not worth living. The person who thinks every moment is to be treated as if it had eternal significance is no true nihilist.

Second, it focuses on the present, on the here and now. One of the pathologies of our present age is that the pleasure of the instant, the psychological satisfaction of the individual in the here and now, has become primary in how we think about human purpose. It can be seen, for example, in matters as disparate as pornography and the principles underlying legal judgments in the courts. Now the path between Nietzsche and the easy hedonism of our present day is not straightforward: Nietzsche understood that struggling and overcoming obstacles carried with it satisfactions of which the lazy person knows nothing. The woman who climbs the north face of the Eiger feels a pleasure when she reaches the top that is unknown to the man whose sole achievement in life is merely to prop up the bar in the hotel at the foot of the mountain. But personal satisfaction, the basic element of the therapeutic ideal, is there in Nietzsche's conception of what it means to truly live.

That leads to the final point of relevance: the content of self-creation. In *The Gay Science* §290, Nietzsche reflects on the importance of giving style to one's character. Using the metaphor of the self as artist, he plays here with a distinction between original and second natures:

One thing is needful—To "give style" to one's character—a great and rare art! It is practiced by those who survey all the strengths and weaknesses of their nature and then fit them into an artistic plan until every one of them appears as art and reason and even weaknesses delight the eye. Here a large mass of second nature has been added; there a piece of original nature has been removed—both times through long practice and daily work at it. Here the ugly that could not be removed is concealed: there it has been reinterpreted and made sublime. Much that is vague and resisted shaping has been saved and exploited for distant views; it is meant to beckon toward the far and immeasurable. In the end, when the work is finished it becomes evident how the constraint of a single taste governed and formed everything large and small. . . . For one thing is needful: that a human being should attain satisfaction with himself, whether it be by means of this or that poetry and art.[21]

Here Nietzsche acknowledges that no individual is simply a blank slate. Each has natural strengths and weaknesses, but the key is to be intentional in how those are presented and how they are used in relation to the second nature, that nature by which the person invents himself, makes himself into something analogous to a work of art. We are who we choose to be, who we choose to make ourselves. Here the note that will later be struck by Jean-Paul Sartre with such force—that existence precedes essence—finds a voice. And the purpose of this artistic endeavor called life is personal satisfaction. Again, Nietzsche is no nihilist; life is to be lived in a manner that brings about personal satisfaction. But that personal satisfaction is, to risk tautology, deeply personal. It is not a matter of conforming to some heteronomous law or learning to cultivate those virtues to which human nature lends itself as a means to a good life that has an objective, transcendent status beyond the individual. Rather, it is a matter of creating one's own satisfactions and determining one's own form of the good life. Nietzsche, sophisticated thinker that he is, is really giving a critical account of what we might express in the demotic banalities of our time as "Be whoever you want to be, and do whatever works for you."

Karl Marx: Turning Hegel Upside Down

Karl Marx is significant for this part of the narrative because he saw the vital connection between social and economic conditions and the constitution of the world.[22] To understand Marx, however, it is first necessary to connect him to his immediate background in the intellectual ferment precipitated by the thought of G. W. F. Hegel.[23]

---

21. Nietzsche, *Gay Science*, §290 (232–33).

22. In saying this, I am not affirming the detailed content of Marx's philosophy but rather highlighting the fact that he understood that there is a deep and undeniable connection between the material conditions of existence and how human beings think of themselves.

23. A number of good Marx biographies are available in English. Jonathan Sperber, *Karl Marx: A Nineteenth-Century Life* (New York: W. W. Norton, 2013) is excellent at setting him in historical context. Gareth Stedman Jones, *Karl Marx: Greatness and Illusion* (Cambridge, MA: Belknap Press of Harvard University Press, 2016) is perhaps the most thorough historical treatment to date. Sven-Eric Liedman,

I noted in chapter 1 that Hegel's thought is important to Charles Taylor's development of the idea of recognition and its significance in contemporary society. Taylor draws on Hegel's understanding of self-consciousness and as such is indebted to one of the philosopher's most significant contributions: the historical nature of specific manifestations of what it means to be human. Whereas Kant's categories assumed a basic transhistorical and transcultural stability to human nature, Hegel noted that the way people think, their self-consciousness, actually changes over time.[24]

For Hegel, the central dynamic in this historical process is its general character, or "spirit." This spirit has a profound and decisive effect on the material elements of any given culture—its technology, for example.[25] This relationship raises the interesting question whether Hegel believed in human nature as a given. To this inquiry one might respond by saying that human nature for Hegel must be seen as a work in progress, something that is pressing into the future for its full realization. In the language of Christian theology, we might say that for Hegel human nature is something eschatological. Or speaking more philosophically, we might say that human nature here and now finds its being in its becoming. It is dynamic, not static.[26]

Marx was himself closely connected in his early career to the Young Hegelians, disciples of Hegel who were taking the master's thought in directions that were highly critical of the political status quo and of the instruments by which such was maintained, particularly Christianity and the church. Marx, however, was to break with this group, and with idealist trajectories of Hegelianism, in favor of a materialist approach.

A World to Win: The Life and Works of Karl Marx, trans. Jeffrey N. Skinner (London: Verso, 2018) is deeply sympathetic to Marx and also very good on his Hegelian background.

24. This is Hegel's central criticism of Kant: see Joseph McCarney, *Hegel on History* (London: Routledge, 2000), 57–59. Also see G. W. F. Hegel, *Phenomenology of Spirit*, trans. A. V. Miller (Oxford: Oxford University Press, 1977), 64–66.

25. Stephen Houlgate, *An Introduction to Hegel: Freedom, Truth and History*, 2nd ed. (Oxford: Blackwell, 2005), 10.

26. Erich Fromm captures the Hegelian approach to human nature well: "For Spinoza, Goethe, Hegel, as well as for Marx, man is alive only inasmuch as he is productive, inasmuch as he grasps the world outside of himself in the act of expressing his own specific human powers, and of grasping the world with these powers. Inasmuch as man is not productive, inasmuch as he is receptive and passive, he is nothing, he is dead." *Marx's Concept of Man* (London: Continuum, 2004), 26.

He described the relationship between his own materialist thought and the idealism of Hegel in the afterword to the second edition of *Das Kapital* in 1873:

> My dialectic method is not only different from the Hegelian, but is its direct opposite. To Hegel, the life-process of the human brain, i.e., the process of thinking, which, under the name of "the Idea," he even transforms into an independent subject, is the demiurgos of the real world, and the real world is only the external, phenomenal form of "the Idea." With me, on the contrary, the ideal is nothing else than the material world reflected by the human mind, and translated into forms of thought. . . . The mystification which dialectic suffers in Hegel's hands, by no means prevents him from being the first to present its general form of working in a comprehensive and conscious manner. With him it is standing on its head. It must be turned right side up again, if you would discover the rational kernel within the mystical shell.[27]

Put simply (or as simply as possible, given that this is Hegel and Marx), the dynamic dialectical process by which history moves forward is for Hegel an intellectual one, a struggle between ideas in the self-consciousness. For Marx, the basic pattern of Hegelian dialectic is sound, but it is not ideas that drive the historical process; rather, it is material conditions and relations. Hegel must be turned on his head: it is not ideas and the self-consciousness that grasps them that shape the material conditions of the world but the material conditions that shape the ideas and the self-consciousness.

The implications of this move by Marx are far reaching. Writing in the white heat of the nineteenth-century Industrial Revolution, he made the following famous comment in chapter 1 of *The Communist Manifesto* (1848):

> The bourgeoisie, wherever it has got the upper hand, has put an end to all feudal, patriarchal, idyllic relations. It has pitilessly torn asunder the motley feudal ties that bound man to his "natural superiors," and has left remaining no other nexus between man and man than naked self-interest, than callous "cash payment." It has drowned the most heavenly

---

27. Karl Marx, *Das Kapital*, in *The Marx-Engels Reader*, ed. Robert C. Tucker, 2nd ed. (London: W. W. Norton, 1978), 301–2.

ecstasies of religious fervour, of chivalrous enthusiasm, of philistine sentimentalism, in the icy water of egotistical calculation. . . . The bourgeoisie has stripped of its halo every occupation hitherto honoured and looked up to with reverent awe. It has converted the physician, the lawyer, the priest, the poet, the man of science, into its paid wage-labourers. . . . Constant revolutionising of production, uninterrupted disturbance of all social conditions, everlasting uncertainty and agitation distinguish the bourgeois epoch from all earlier ones. All fixed, fast-frozen relations, with their train of ancient and venerable prejudices and opinions, are swept away, all new-formed ones become antiquated before they can ossify. All that is solid melts into air, all that is holy is profaned, and man is at last compelled to face with sober senses, his real conditions of life, and his relations with his kind.[28]

Cry "Havoc!" and let slip the dogs . . . not of war but of capitalism! Perhaps as no other person in the nineteenth century, Marx was aware of how industrial production and the capitalism it represented were overturning traditional social structures and remaking society. More than that, however, he saw that this transformation had profound significance for the way human beings related to each other and understood themselves. What is most remarkable about this passage—which, as with Nietzsche's anecdote of the madman, is almost doomed to be rendered less powerful by any commentary on it—is the way it makes human nature and all that depends on such a notion to be functions of the economic structure of society. That makes human nature a plastic thing, subject to historical change as the economic dynamics of society change. And just as significantly for our overall narrative, everything becomes profoundly political, from the laws of the land to the moral codes by which a society regulates itself to organizations that, on the surface, would not appear to have political significance. As all social phenomena involve social relations, and the nature of social relations rests on economic relations, and as economic relations are dialectical (or perhaps we might say adversarial), so all social phenomena have political

---

28. Karl Marx and Friedrich Engels, *The Communist Manifesto*, in Tucker, *Marx-Engels Reader*, 475–76.

significance. From the Boy Scouts to the Federal Reserve, all human organizations and relationships play their part in the political drama that
is human history.

One obvious example of this dynamic is religion. Marx is well known
for describing religion as "the opium of the people," a statement that is
typically understood as claiming that religion is a means of keeping the
masses in a state analogous to drug-induced passivity and false happiness. Certainly, the idea that religion provides an ideology by which the
ruling classes are able to keep others in their place has a role in Marxist
thinking. Friedrich Engels's *The Peasant War in Germany* (1850) offered
an interpretation of the Peasants' War of 1525 in terms of both religion's disruptive and revolutionary potential and its social conservatism.
Commenting on Martin Luther's abandonment of the peasants and his
use of the Bible to do so, Engels remarks that he "turned it [the Bible]
against them, extracting from [it] a real hymn to the God-ordained authorities such as no bootlicker or absolute monarchy had ever been able
to achieve."[29]

Yet there is more to Marx's view on religion than simply seeing it as a
means of ideological oppression. When set in context, the original quotation regarding the opium of the people reveals a richer and arguably
more sympathetic understanding, if not of religion as a phenomenon,
then at least of the religious themselves. The full statement occurs in
Marx's *Critique of Hegel's Philosophy of Right* (1844):

> The foundation of irreligious criticism is: Man makes religion, religion
> does not make man. Religion is indeed the self-consciousness and self-
> esteem of man who has either not yet won through to himself or has
> already lost himself again. . . . The struggle against religion is there-
> fore indirectly the struggle against that world whose spiritual aroma is
> religion.
>
> Religious suffering is at one and the same time the expression of real
> suffering and a protest against real suffering. Religion is the sigh of the

---

29. Friedrich Engels, *The Peasant War in Germany*, in *Marx on Religion*, ed. John Raines (Philadelphia: Temple University Press, 2002), 210.

oppressed creature, the heart of a heartless world and the soul of soulless conditions. It is the opium of the people.

The abolition of religion as the illusory happiness of the people is the demand for their real happiness.[30]

Marx here is building on the argument of his contemporary Ludwig Feuerbach that the existence of religion points to the fact that human beings are living in an alienated condition. For Feuerbach, talk about God is really talk about human beings. Religion involves the perfection and projection of human attributes onto a fictitious being, God, who is then worshiped. If human beings are ever to reach their full potential, they must therefore realize that they should really ascribe the glory they give to God to themselves. Religion hinders human beings from being fully human.[31]

Feuerbach's critique of religion is not simply a debunking of religious language. It is also a pungent criticism of moral arguments based on religious premises:

> Wherever morality is based on theology, wherever the right is made dependent on divine authority, the most immoral, unjust, infamous things can be justified and established. I can found morality on theology only when I myself have already defined the Divine Being by means of morality. . . . To place anything in God, or to derive anything from God, is nothing more than to withdraw it from the test of reason, to institute it as indubitable, unassailable, sacred, without rendering an account *why*. Hence self-delusion, if not wicked, insidious design, is at the root of all efforts to establish morality, right, on theology.[32]

Like Nietzsche after him, Feuerbach sees God as an illusory foundation for morals, the result of either delusion or malicious intent on the part

---

30. Karl Marx, *Marx on Religion*, 171.
31. See Ludwig Feuerbach, *The Essence of Christianity*, trans. George Eliot (New York: Harper and Row, 1957). Feuerbach summarizes his view of Christianity as follows: "Religion, at least the Christian, is the relation of man to himself, or more correctly to his own nature (i.e., his subjective nature); but a relation of it, viewed as a nature apart from his own. The divine being is nothing else than the human being, or, rather, the human nature purified, freed from the limits of the individual man, made objective—i.e., contemplated and revered as another, a distinct being. All the attributes of the divine nature are, therefore, attributes of the human nature" (14).
32. Feuerbach, *Essence of Christianity*, 274.

of those who make such arguments. To address the matter of religion is, for Feuerbach, to raise questions of human psychology.

Marx takes Feuerbach's basic idea but refracts it through his own radically materialist lens. In other words, for Marx religion is a function of alienation, but it is not so much alienation from human nature as specifically the alienation generated by the material inequities of the economic system. As he comments, it is a cry of pain, but that pain is real. And as he notes in the above quotation, it makes the criticism of, and the struggle against, religion a political struggle because religion is the ideological mask that the specific inequities of the current economic structure of society wear to give themselves a mystical, metaphysical disguise. Religion offers false happiness to an unhappy world; the tearing down of religion is thus the precondition for offering true happiness through the establishment of an economic system that does not alienate the workers from the fruits of their labor. For Marx, as for Nietzsche and Feuerbach, religion is not so much a matter of metaphysical interest, for it is an illusion. Rather, it poses questions regarding human psychology.

Marx and the Concept of Human Nature

Students of Marx debate if and when Marx ever had an essentialist understanding of human nature. Certainly, many of the traditions of later Marxist thought have little patience with the idea, seeing human nature and personhood not as matters of essence but purely as a function of the wider social and economic structures of society.[33] Human nature is for them a purely historical phenomenon. Yet as Erich Fromm argues, it does seem that Marx was not an entirely anti-essentialist thinker.[34] As with Hegel, Marx believes that the idea that human beings have certain physical needs (food, sleep, etc.) is clear; he also believes that they have a nature that is defined in its actual instantiated reality by that which they produce, or their relation to the means of production, and that this is what separates

---

33. For the development of Marx's thought on this point in relation to Feuerbach, see Gregory Claeys, *Marx and Marxism* (New York: Nation Books, 2018), 52–54.

34. See Fromm, "The Nature of Man," in *Marx's Concept of Man*, 23–36; Fromm, "The Concept of Man and His Nature," in *Beyond the Chains of an Illusion: My Encounter with Marx and Freud* (New York: Trident, 1962), 27–32.

human beings from other creatures.[35] For example, we might say that it is of the nature of human beings to desire money; we might even say that that is a human distinctive, something that no lizard or cat ever experiences—but that desire can only exist in a world in which money is already present. Prior to the development of money, such desire was no part of what it meant to be human.

This means that while there is a human nature, it can never be considered in abstraction from the specific historical context in which particular humans occur. It is the concrete conditions in which human beings exist that determine who they are. And thus, in a sense, human nature is always in a state of potential flux. As the economic conditions and relations in society change, so does the instantiation of human nature.[36]

For Marx, observing the Industrial Revolution, it seemed clear that, as industrial capitalism tore apart and remade society in terms of its own revolutionizing of the means of production through technology, so human beings found themselves—and their very identities—caught up in the frenetic changes that industry, particularly its technological innovations relative to production, involved.

It is here that Marx's understanding of the importance of technology proves remarkably prescient. In chapter 1 of *The Communist Manifesto*, he makes this statement:

> The less the skill and exertion of strength implied in manual labour, in other words, the more modern industry becomes developed, the more is the labour of men superseded by that of women. Differences of age and sex have no longer any distinctive social validity for the working class. All are instruments of labour, more or less expensive to use, according to their age and sex.[37]

---

35. See Marx, "Critique of Hegel's Dialectic and General Philosophy," in Fromm, *Marx's Concept of Man*, 140–42.

36. Fromm perhaps best sums up the problem of finding a stable doctrine of human nature in Marx: "Marx was opposed to two positions: the unhistorical one that the nature of man is a substance present from the very beginning of history, and the relativistic position that man's nature has no inherent quality whatsoever and is nothing but the reflex of social conditions. But he never arrived at the full development of his own theory concerning the nature of man, transcending both the unhistorical and relativistic positions; hence he left himself open to various and contradictory interpretations." *Beyond the Chains of Illusion*, 31.

37. Marx and Engels, *Communist Manifesto*, in Tucker, *Marx-Engels Reader*, 479.

Marx's words here have proved more prophetic than he could ever have anticipated. In terms of the basic economic trajectory that he is describing, we see the fruit of the elision of the gender difference in the gains made by first-wave feminism in the wake of World War I, where the fact that women had done vital wartime work in the munitions factories dramatically strengthened the case for granting them the vote, equal rights under law, and so on. But since then, technology has assumed a key role in the more radical context of making plausible the separation of biological sex and the concept of gender. This separation is now basic to much of the modern social imaginary and that clearly rests on the psychologized notion of self that emerged in the seventeenth and eighteenth centuries and now dominates our contemporary world. Marx was thinking only in terms of the relationship of the sexes to the means of production. But thanks to surgery and hormones and modern medical breakthroughs, we can now plausibly separate gender from sex and even revise the relationship of the sexes to the means of reproduction.[38]

It is also important to note one more implication of Marx's materialist criticism of religion, his view of human nature, and his understanding of the importance of technology: ethics and moral codes, like religion, are functions of the material structure of society at any given point in time and serve the interests of maintaining that structure by justifying the form of life that suits the status quo. Thus, as for Nietzsche, morality for Marx has a genealogy—a specifically economic one but a genealogy nonetheless. Therefore, the criticism of morality, like the criticism of religion, is a vital part of the political struggle. The critical spirit, the suspicion that metaphysical claims are not as innocent or as morally neutral as they may appear, thus finds a philosophical foundation in Marx's dialectical materialism, as it does in Nietzsche's psychology.

---

38. I note in chap. 7 that this connection of technology to the question of gender is something picked up by later feminists, most notably Simone de Beauvoir and Shulamith Firestone. See "The Psychological Transformation of Feminism," p. 254.

Darwin and the End of Teleology

The last figure in this chapter, Charles Darwin, was someone with whom both Nietzsche and Marx were familiar. Nietzsche appreciated Darwin's theory of evolution because its antimetaphysical implications were very similar to those of his own later thought.[39] Marx, unlike Darwin, believed that history had a telos, an end.[40] But he still appreciated that Darwin's theories were another blow struck against traditional religion and metaphysics in favor of atheistic materialism.[41] Engels even connected the two men's achievements in his speech at Marx's graveside in 1883.[42] Darwin was, of course, neither a philosopher nor an economist, but his account of the origin of human beings dealt a decisive blow to those systems that granted special essential status and significance to humanity. As Nietzsche rejected human nature as a manipulative metaphysical trick and Marx redefined it relative to an ongoing historical process, so Darwin provided an account of it that allowed no room for inferring that it had a special destiny or significance.[43]

Darwin was far from the first person to advocate evolution as the means by which human beings emerged on the earth. Most famously, Jean-Baptiste Lamarck had argued for evolution of species via the inheritance of adaptations to creatures caused by environmental factors. But prior to Darwin, such theories had all had some form of teleology embedded within them, even if often a rather murky one—the notion that a divine Creator was providentially guiding the process or, as with

---

39. Nietzsche's late work *Twilight of the Idols* contains polemic by "the anti-Darwin," but as Julian Young comments, this opposition is to social, not biological, Darwinism. *Friedrich Nietzsche: A Philosophical Biography* (Cambridge: Cambridge University Press, 2010), 198, 545–46.

40. Stedman Jones, *Karl Marx*, 567.

41. Sperber, *Karl Marx*, 396.

42. Engels stated, "Just as Darwin discovered the law of development of organic nature, so Marx discovered the law of development of human history." In Tucker, *Marx-Engels Reader*, 681.

43. Engels, who mentioned Darwin positively in his 1883 speech at Marx's graveside, made precisely this point about Darwin's metaphysical significance in his 1880 pamphlet *Socialism: Utopian and Scientific*: "Darwin must be named before all others [i.e., natural scientists]. He dealt the metaphysical conception of Nature the heaviest blow by his proof that all organic beings, plants, animals, and man himself, are the products of a process of evolution going on through millions of years." In Tucker, *Marx-Engels Reader*, 697. For the graveside speech, see Tucker, *Marx-Engels Reader*, 681–82.

Lamarck, the idea that adaptations moved toward some kind of vague notion of increasing perfection or progress.[44]

Francis Ayala sums up Darwin's distinctive contribution as follows:

> It was Darwin's greatest accomplishment to show that the complex orga-
> nization and functionality of living beings can be explained as the result
> of a natural process—natural selection—without any need to resort to a
> Creator or other external agent. The origin and adaptations of organisms
> in their profusion and wondrous variations were thus brought into the
> realm of science.[45]

In other words, Darwin's theory of natural selection effectively made any metaphysical or theological claim concerning the origins of life irrelevant. One could, if one wished, believe that a divine hand guided the process, but the process itself could be adequately explained without the need of any such supernatural hypothesis.[46]

Darwin outlines his central concept at the start of *The Origin of Species*, chapter 4:

> How will the struggle for existence . . . act in regard to variation? . . .
> Let it be borne in mind in what an endless number of strange pecu-
> liarities our domestic productions, and, in a lesser degree, those under
> nature, vary; and how strong the hereditary tendency is. . . . Can it,
> then, be thought improbable, seeing that variations useful to man have
> undoubtedly occurred, that other variations useful in some way to each
> being in the great and complex battle of life, should sometimes occur
> in the course of thousands of generations? If such do occur, can we
> doubt (remembering that many more individuals are born than can
> possibly survive) that individuals having any advantage, however slight,
> over others, would have the best chance of surviving and of procreating

---

44. See Michael Ruse, *The Darwinian Revolution: Science Red in Tooth and Claw*, 2nd ed. (Chicago: University of Chicago Press, 1999), 10–11.

45. Francis J. Ayala, "Darwin's Greatest Discovery: Design without Designer," *Proceedings of the National Academy of Sciences of the United States of America* 104 (2007): 8567.

46. Near the end of *The Origin of Species*, Darwin comments, "I see no good reason why the views given in this volume should shock the religious feelings of anyone. . . . A celebrated author and divine has written to me that 'he has gradually learnt to see that it is just as noble a conception of the Deity to believe that He created a few original forms capable of self-development into other and needful forms, as to believe that he required a fresh act of creation to supply the voids caused by the action of His laws.'" *The Origin of Species and The Descent of Man* (New York: Modern Library, n.d.), 367–68.

their kind? On the other hand, we may feel sure that any variation in the least degree injurious would be rigidly destroyed. This preservation of favourable variations and the rejection of injurious variations, I call Natural Selection.[47]

In short, the great variety and beauty of animal species that we see in this world is the result of a natural process of selection, whereby the fittest—or perhaps better, the best adapted—survive and the rest slowly but surely die out. The important factors are biological and environmental. One could argue that the chances of the world developing the way that it is are billions to one, but Darwinians would simply respond that the internal rationality of the process of natural selection dramatically attenuates such odds. The question is not so much about the statistical likelihood of this world being the way it is; it is rather one of how the world as it now is came to be.

And therein lies the genius of Darwin's approach: the world as we have it does not need a designer or divine architect. It can be explained without any reference to the transcendent. It is an immanent process involving variations and adaptations over vast periods of time. More significantly for the concerns of this book, Darwin thus takes his place among others, such as Nietzsche and Marx, as one who dealt a brutal blow to the idea of human nature. By dispatching the idea of teleology from nature, Darwin inevitably dispatched it from human beings too. And to take away teleology from the concept of humanity is to demand a fundamental revision of the understanding of who and what human beings are. Coming from earlier species by way of an immanent process of natural selection, they cease to be the crown of creation and to enjoy some kind of special, God-given status among (and above) other creatures. And having no God-given destiny, they have no transcendent ethical standards, either laws or virtues, to which they need to conform themselves. What Nietzsche did through his iconoclastic approach to the Enlightenment, and Marx did by turning Hegel upside down, Darwin did through observation and scientific theorizing.

---

47. Darwin, *Origin of Species*, 63–64.

This treatment of Darwin is brief, but this is not to imply that he is not as important—if not in some ways more so—than Nietzsche and Marx. In fact, it is the intuitive simplicity of his theory that has made him so influential. The science may have proved far more complicated than Darwin ever imagined, but the basic idea is easy to grasp. And it has come to shape the way many people who are quite incompetent to assess the science have come to imagine the world.

Concluding Reflections

Few people among the general public today have firsthand familiarity with the writings and thought of Nietzsche, Marx, and Darwin, but many of the key ideas of these men profoundly shape the way that that elusive but omnipresent creature, the average man or woman on the street, imagines the world to be. The social imaginary is thoroughly permeated by the ideas and attitudes of these three men, or at least the implications thereof.

Darwin is likely the most influential. Setting aside the question whether evolution—or, to be more precise, one of the numerous forms of evolutionary theory that looks back to Darwin's work as an initial inspiration—is true, there is no doubt that vast numbers of people in the West simply assume that it is so.

There are numerous reasons for this. While the various theories themselves rest on interpretations of the geological record and on complex genetic science, the basic idea—that one species can evolve from another—is easy to grasp. Indeed, the most popular example— that human beings descended from an ape ancestor—seems to make eminent sense. Apes look like humans; why should there not be a connection? As the world seems very old, there would surely be time enough for an incredibly slow process to take place. And this view has been pressed home in the accessible science writings of men like Richard Dawkins and in the play and movie *Inherit the Wind*. The latter especially helped fix in the popular mind the image of the Scopes Monkey Trial and the issue of evolution as a battle between religious obscurantism and scientific freedom.

Whether evolution can be argued from the evidence is actually irrelevant to the reason most people believe it. Few of us are qualified to opine on the science. But evolution draws on the authority that science possesses in modern society. Like priests of old who were trusted by the community at large and therefore had significant social authority, so scientists today often carry similar weight. And when the idea being taught has an intuitive plausibility, it is persuasive.

The obvious implications of this situation are, first, that the sacred account of human origins given in Genesis is undermined and, second, that human beings are therefore relativized in relation to other creatures. Descent from a prior species excludes special creation of man and woman, and natural selection renders teleology unnecessary as a hypothesis. In short, human nature as a significant foundational category for understanding human purpose is annihilated. And in a world in which belief in evolution is the default position, the implications for how people imagine that world, and their place within it, are dramatic.

The influence of Nietzsche is perhaps less obvious in terms of it being a source—I suspect many more have heard of Darwin—but no less pervasive. As we noted, he, too, attacks the idea of human nature, though from the perspective of his assault on metaphysics. Nevertheless, the result is much the same: neither human nature nor human destiny any longer have any transcendent or objective foundation; in fact, they were never anything more than manipulative concepts developed by one group, most notoriously the Christian church, to subjugate another.

This points to two further pathologies of this present age that can be seen as finding some inspiration in the work of Nietzsche. First, his genealogical approach to morals carries with it a basic historicist relativism and a deep suspicion of any claims to traditional authority. Both of these are now basic to our contemporary world. From the casual iconoclasm of pop culture to the dethroning of traditional historical narratives, from the distrust of traditional institutions such as the church to iconoclastic attitudes to sex and gender, we can see the anarchic outworking of the challenge posed by Nietzsche's madman and the ruthless critical spirit of *On the Genealogy of Morals*. The average twelve-year-old girl attending an Ariana Grande concert may never even have heard of Nietzsche, but the amoral sexuality of the lyrics she hears preach a form of (albeit unwitting) Nietzscheanism.

And that leads to the second area where Nietzsche's thinking is reflected in current social attitudes: living for the present. When teleology is dead and self-creation is the name of the game, then the present moment and the pleasure it can contain become the keys to eternal life. While Nietzsche himself may have had a view of hedonism that was different from that which grips the popular imagination today (he understood the pleasure to be gained from struggle and from triumphing over adversity), the idea that personal satisfaction is to be the hallmark of the life—or perhaps better, moment—well lived is basic to our present age. Again, Nietzsche's books may not be widely read, but his central priorities have become common currency.

That brings us to Marx. As with Darwin and Nietzsche, he assaults the metaphysics on which traditional religions and philosophies have built their views of the moral universe. Again, as with Nietzsche, he not only relativizes ethics via a form of historicism, he also presents moral codes as manipulative, as reflecting the economic and political status quo and therefore designed to justify and maintain the same. Modern suspicion of traditional authority owes a debt to Marx, as to Nietzsche, for its theoretical foundations.

This wariness of tradition connects to another legacy of Marx: history is the history of oppression. Whether it is politics, economics, or ideas, history is a matter of dominant, powerful groups marginalizing and silencing others. In a strange way, both Marx and Nietzsche help serve this cause by making power a central category in their analyses of history. Who has power, how they are using it, and how their view of the world can be destabilized as a means of stripping them of it are now standard fare in Western approaches to history and sociology. Again, as noted above, the notion of suspicion—the attitude that no claim to truth or judgment of value is as disinterested as it appears—finds powerful theoretical expression in both Nietzsche and Marx. But it is no monopoly of the intellectual classes: it is now a basic part of the social imaginary, and the deep cynicism about tradition and traditional authorities that pervades our culture in general points to demotic expressions of much the same attitude.

Marx also makes another major contribution that is now basic to how we think about society: he abolishes the prepolitical, that notion that there can be forms of social organization that stand apart from, and prior to, the political nature of society. For Marx—and even more for later Marxists—all forms of social organization are political because all of them connect to the economic structure of society. By Marx's account, the family and the church exist to cultivate, reinforce, and perpetuate bourgeois values. In today's world, this thinking helps explain why everything—from the Boy Scouts to Hollywood movies to cake baking—has become politicized. And one does not need to be an ideological Marxist to be pulled into this tussle, for once one side gives a particular issue or organization political significance, then all sides, left, right, and center, have to do the same.

In closing, it is worth noting that these observations on the connection between Nietzsche, Marx, and Darwin and the pathologies of our present age can be fruitfully assessed through the grids provided by Charles Taylor and Philip Rieff. Certainly, Nietzsche's notion of self-creation represents a philosophical rationale for a form of expressive individualism. In this, he stands in the line of thinkers to which men like Rousseau and the Romantics belong, but what he has done is call the bluff on the metaphysical assumptions that they used to limit the implications of such psychologizing of selfhood. He also points toward the age of the therapeutic, where psychological well-being is deemed to be the purpose of life and where happiness in the present moment is the overwhelming priority.

Further, all three men offer rationales for a world imagined in terms of poiesis rather than mimesis. Darwin strips the world of intrinsic meaning through natural selection; Nietzsche, through his polemic against metaphysics; Marx, through his rejection of Hegel's idealism in favor of a radical and consistent materialism. But the net result is the same: the world in itself has no meaning; meaning and significance can thus be given to it only by the actions of human beings, whether through the Nietzschean notion of self-creation and eternal recurrence or through the Marxist notion of dialectical materialism and class struggle. In both cases, meaning is created, not given.

Finally, the cultural iconoclasm of all three thinkers is notable. Darwin is perhaps the least culpable in this regard: his thought relativizes culture but is not directly iconoclastic. For Nietzsche and for Marx, however, history and culture are tales of oppression that need to be overthrown and overcome. If ever the Rieffian deathworker of today needed a philosophical rationale, then the thought of Marx and Nietzsche and the traditions of cultural and political reflection they helped birth certainly provide it. These men shattered the metaphysics for the sacred order that underlay the Rieffian second world of nineteenth-century Europe and thus challenged the culture to maintain itself purely on the basis of an immanent frame of reference—something that Rieff declares to be impossible. In light of this, the words that Nietzsche applied to himself in his autobiography, *Ecce Homo*, might easily be applied to all three:

> I know my fate. One day my name will be associated with the memory of something tremendous—a crisis without equal on earth, the most profound collision of conscience, a decision that was conjured up *against* everything that had been believed, demanded, hallowed so far. I am no man, I am dynamite.[48]

---

48. Nietzsche, *Ecce Homo*, 326.

Epilogue to Part 2

Reflections on the Foundations
of the Revolution

Is there a thing of which it is said,
"See, this is new"?
It has been already
in the ages before us.

ECCLESIASTES 1:10

Much in the narrative of part 2 adumbrates the world in which we now
live as conceptualized by the thought of Philip Rieff, Charles Taylor, and
Alasdair MacIntyre. The modern self and the culture of the modern self
clearly find their immediate roots in the intellectual developments that
took place in the eighteenth and nineteenth centuries.

The most obvious aspect of this influence is the inward, psychological turn with regard to the nature of the self. Jean-Jacques Rousseau is
central to this development, though it would be easy to set him against
the backdrop of previous thinkers, such as René Descartes and John
Locke, who exemplified the Enlightenment concern with epistemology and thus with the inner mental life of the knowing subject. But
with Rousseau and then the Romantics, this inward turn plays out in a

profoundly ethical manner and is used as the basis for a critique of the way society—and particularly the highly organized society of the urban elites and later the Industrial Revolution—forced individuals to conform to its conventions, to be untrue to their inner impulses, and therefore to be untrue to themselves and inauthentic. This is where expressive individualism (to use the terminology of Taylor and the later MacIntyre) or psychological man (to use that of Rieff) starts to assert itself as a significant type. If individuals today—be they avid sports fans, shopaholics, or transgender people—place an inner sense of psychological well-being at the heart of how they conceptualize happiness, then they stand in a cultural line that includes Rousseau and the Romantics. The therapeutic society did not originate with the 1960s. Its origins go back centuries.

Yet the thinkers addressed in part 2 are not merely significant for adumbrating the expressive individualism and the psychological man of contemporary culture. It is also clear that the whole notion of sacred order, so critical according to Rieff for the preservation and transmission of culture, also begins to collapse. If Jean-Jacques Rousseau, William Wordsworth, Percy Bysshe Shelley, and William Blake had confidence that nature itself possessed an intrinsic, sacred order on which an ethical life could be built if only the hypocritical accretions of civilized society could be stripped away, then Friedrich Nietzsche, Karl Marx, and Charles Darwin proved lethal to such an idea. Nietzsche's madman demanded that polite Enlightenment atheists face up to the consequences of killing God and abandon any attempt to build on the basis of any kind of metaphysics. Marx saw sacred order—the belief in God—both as a means by which the poor and the suffering could be manipulated and as a function of those same groups' alienation. For both Nietzsche and Marx, then, sacred order was a sign of psychological sickness. And Darwin dealt the real death blow: by removing teleology from the story of humankind, he eliminated the notion of human exceptionalism, provided scientific support for Nietzsche's antimetaphysical stand, and, like Marx, demanded that whatever meaning life might have, had to be considered in purely material terms. That his idea could be expressed in a manner that was intuitively easy for even the scientifically uneducated to understand—that human beings descended from the apes whom they physically resembled—made his thought perhaps the most widely influential of all. And as Rieff would argue, the death of sacred order ushers in the unstable cultures, or better, "anticultures," of what he calls third worlds. These worlds, with nothing beyond themselves by which they can justify their beliefs and practices, are doomed to be volatile, entropic, and self-defeating. Again, the seeds of this outlook were present in the nineteenth century, and—at least with Nietzsche, Marx, and Darwin—there are numerous direct connections to the antireligious and antimetaphysical thinking that dominates our contemporary world.

This death of metaphysics also connects to Alasdair MacIntyre's claim that moral discourse today is so fruitless because it lacks any commonly accepted basis on which moral differences can be discussed and assessed. Certainly, Rousseau and the Romantics placed a high premium on emotions for moral education. But their assumption was that there was a common human nature that could lead to agreement on what things should arouse appropriate empathy and sympathy or anger and outrage. Take away the notion of human nature, and all that is left is free-floating, subjective sentiment. The seeds of today's moral anarchy, where personal emotional preferences are constantly confused with moral absolutes, is thus to be found in the nineteenth century. Nietzsche, Marx, and Darwin each, in their different ways, abolished metaphysics, and at least the first two demanded that human beings face that fact and rebuild their meaning and identity in that new light.

All this led to another shift: that from mimesis to poiesis. If society/culture is merely a construct, and if nature possesses no intrinsic meaning or purpose, then what meaning there is must be created by human beings themselves. Now, the subjugation of nature to human beings was not invented in the nineteenth century. Hand tools and ploughs are hardly inventions of Victorian vintage. But the direct challenge to create meaning posed by Nietzsche, along with the explosive technological power of the Industrial Revolution, fueled a view that the world was increasingly the raw material of human creativity, not the act of divine creation. The social imaginary emerging in the nineteenth century was one that intuitively placed human beings as the sovereigns at the center of a universe to which they could give shape and significance.

There are other aspects of our modern Western social imaginary that also find their roots in the thought of the men discussed in part 2. The idea that religion, specifically Christianity, is a corrupt ideology used by hypocritical religious leaders to hinder human beings from being truly happy is a commonplace today. It finds pungent philosophical expression in Nietzsche and Marx. And the idea that moral codes, specifically sexual codes, are oppressive and actually militate against human happiness and create social ills is also an intuitive part of the way many in Western society now think. Again, Shelley, Blake, Nietzsche, and Marx all in their different ways offered rationales for thinking in such ways about morality. And here we see one of the seeds of Rieff's anticulture: if cultures are defined by those sexual behaviors that they forbid, then those who seek to overthrow all sexual taboos or who regard "Thou shalt not" as intrinsically life denying and wicked, are offering not an alternative culture but an anticulture.

Rieff's anticultures exhibit another characteristic that we see emerging in the eighteenth and nineteenth centuries: they are antihistorical. This sentiment manifests itself in two ways. First, there is the psychological emphasis in Rousseau and the Romantics, with its notion that society/culture deforms and corrupts the authentic individual. This means that history—that which is constitutive of society/culture—must be seen as something that needs to be overcome or transcended or erased if the individual is to be truly who he or she is. This is the basic logic of transgenderism, as I will note in chapter 10. But it is of long-standing vintage and has clear affinities with Romanticism.

The second manifestation of this antihistorical tendency occurs in the thought of Nietzsche and Marx. Both men see power as the key to history. For Nietzsche, modern Christian society is the result of the manipulative use of religious ideas by the weak to subjugate the strong. Morality has a historical genealogy and studying that genealogy reveals it to be a scam, a confidence trick, used to make the strong feel guilty about being strong and the weak feel proud about being weak. Good has been turned into evil, and bad has been made into good. For Marx, history is the story of class struggle and of the oppression and marginalization of the working class. Morality is simply the ideology by which the ruling class keeps its subjects in a state of submission.

What Nietzsche and Marx do is offer a view of history in which the traditional heroes of the story are actually the villains and in which even the narrating of history becomes part of a wider discourse of power that keeps the marginalized on the margins. In their different philosophies, then, we see the early emergence of critical philosophies of history that turn things on their head, make the villains and victims into the true heroes, and make the purpose of history that of overcoming and transcending history. In Rieffian terms, they provide the philosophical rationale for an anticulture. And later generations of thinkers would use them for precisely that end.

Finally, there is one further distinctive of our modern age of which Marx's thought is an early and influential harbinger: the abolition of the prepolitical. In seeing the identity of human beings as constituted by economic relations and in regarding history as a political struggle determined by economic relations, Marx makes all intentional human activity political. Everything, from religious organizations to the structure of the family, is politicized. There is no private, prepolitical space in Marx's world. And that is now basic to the world of today, where all things are politicized, from kindergartens and Girl Scout troops to adoption agencies, sports teams, and pop music.

Is our age unique? In some ways, perhaps. But the eighteenth and nineteenth centuries are foundational to the intuitions of the contemporary social imaginary. The past may be "a foreign country," as L. P. Hartley wrote in *The Go-Between*, but it provided fertile soil for the seeds of the present.[1]

---

1. L. P. Hartley, *The Go-Between* (London: Penguin, 1958), 7.

Part 3

SEXUALIZATION OF THE REVOLUTION

6

Sigmund Freud, Civilization, and Sex

These days, sexuality is equated with the truth of the individual, which is arguably our era's most prominent fiction regarding the nature of truth.

RÜDIGER SAFRANSKI, *NIETZSCHE: A PHILOSOPHICAL BIOGRAPHY*

Given the narrative in part 2, it is clear that certain key elements of our modern world were already being put in place in the thought of nineteenth-century writers. The inward turn that places the inner psychological life of the individual at the heart of what it means to be a self is well established by the end of the nineteenth century. In the work of William Wordsworth, Percy Bysshe Shelley, and William Blake, we have a continuation of the connection of aesthetics or sentiments to ethics that we noted in Jean-Jacques Rousseau. And particularly with Shelley and Blake, we find early examples of the modern commonplace identification of sexual freedom with authentic human freedom in general. The latter was also, for obvious reasons, connected to polemics against traditional marriage and traditional, institutionalized Christianity. On these points, the affinities with the dominant intuitions of today's society seem obvious. Then, with Friedrich Nietzsche, Karl Marx, and

Charles Darwin, we see assaults on any static or transcendent notion of human nature. The groundwork for the rejection of morality based on some form of sacred order—whether that of Christianity or that of the view of nature offered by the Romantics—is thus in the ascendant.

Nevertheless, there is a key subsequent development that is necessary for us to understand if we are to appreciate fully the way our contemporary culture thinks, and that is the move from understanding sex as an activity to seeing it as absolutely fundamental to identity. When men such as William Godwin, Percy Bysshe Shelley, and William Blake proposed the dissolution of the traditional idea of marriage as a lifelong, monogamous, chaste bond, they did so because they saw it as restrictive of humanity's natural sexual instincts. They did not think of it primarily as an assault on a personal identity conceived of in sexual terms. Marriage was simply one aspect of the way society unnaturally restricted human desire and forced people to live inauthentic lives. The development of sexuality as identity was not part of their thought world.[1]

To understand how this development occurred, it is important to engage with the thought and influence of the father of psychoanalysis, Sigmund Freud. While his psychological theories are today largely rejected, his thinking is an important influence on the whole notion of sex as identity that now grips the popular social imaginary. This idea has been successfully detached from any specific commitment to his broader thought and his more speculative notions, such as the Oedipus complex. In addition, his work as a philosopher of culture remains a helpful lens with which to assess our current society. The genius of Freud, like that of Darwin, lay in his ability to articulate the kind of notions we noted as foreshadowed in Shelley and Blake but to do so in a scientific idiom that carries rhetorical power in this modern age.[2]

---

1. One might argue that they regarded traditional marriage as an assault on human identity because the curbing of the sexual instincts inevitably made human beings inauthentic or false to their natures. Nevertheless, the foundational nature of such things as sexual orientation to identity—indeed, the idea of sex as intrinsically determinative of personal identity—is at best an inference of their positions, an inference they did not themselves draw out.

2. Philip Rieff comments, "With Montaigne begins the modern distrust of civilization; in Freud that distrust found its theoretician." *Freud: The Mind of the Moralist* (New York: Viking, 1959), 66.

It is arguable that Freud is actually the key figure in the narrative of this book. So much should be obvious, given that his ideas also provide the background to the cultural analysis and critique offered by Philip Rieff that I am using as part of the conceptual framework for my argument.[3] But his importance to the story of the modern self is much broader than his influence on Rieff. He is the person who offered an account of what it means to be human that stands in continuity both with elements of Rousseau and the Romantics in seeing civilized humans as artificial social constructions and with Nietzsche in terms of what we might describe as an emphasis on the darker irrationality that drives much of human behavior. He is also a decisive influence on subsequent generations in terms of political thinking. As I note in chapter 7, the fusion of elements of Marxist and Freudian thought is central to the rise of the so-called New Left in the twentieth century. This in turn provides the basic theoretical foundations for much of the radical identity politics that shapes our current environment. Yet his influence was much wider than the realms of psychoanalysis and political theory. He also exerted a profound impact on art and literature (see the discussion of surrealism in chap. 8) and, through the work of his nephew Edward Bernays, on the rise of the modern advertising and public relations industries as well as—in a much more overtly sinister form—the propaganda of Joseph Goebbels. Freud's fingerprints are all over the Western culture of the last century, from university lecture halls to art galleries to television commercials.

Freud and the Modern Myth

Freud was very much a man of the Enlightenment, from his repudiation of traditional religion to his confidence in analytical reason, even as his work on the subconscious helped lay the groundwork for the later hermeneutics of suspicion that served to undermine Enlightenment notions of rationality in lethal ways. For him, as for Rousseau or David Hume, the goal of human existence was to be happy. But Freud gave this idea of happiness a specifically sexual turn in identifying it with

---

3. For an account of Freud's influence on American sociology in general, including Rieff, see Philip Manning, *Freud and American Sociology* (Cambridge: Polity, 2005).

genital pleasure. This move is obviously of huge consequence for the understanding of key aspects of our present-day culture, where sexual satisfaction is promoted as one of the key components of what it means to be living the good life.

Freud's theories have, of course, been subject to repeated and devastating criticism over many years, from the methodological critique of Karl Popper to the rival theories of psychoanalysis proposed by contemporaries such as Carl Jung.[4] Yet there is a very real sense in which the question of the truth (or not) of his approach is irrelevant. Freud provided a compelling rationale for putting sex and sexual expression at the center of human existence and all its related cultural and political components in a way that now grips the social imaginary of the Western world. Even if his theories are myths in the sense of not being factually correct, that does not prevent them from possessing powerful and continuing cultural influence.

Freud has, in fact, provided the West with a compelling myth—not in the sense of a narrative that everybody knows is false but in the sense of a basic idea by which we can understand the world around us, regardless of whether it is "true" in the commonsense way of understanding the word. That myth is the idea that sex, in terms of sexual desire and sexual fulfillment, is the real key to human existence, to what it means to be human. Nobody looking at Western society today could fail to see how sex dominates the culture in a way unknown to our ancestors in the Middle Ages or the early modern age. From art to politics, sex is omnipresent. And thinking of human beings as fundamentally defined by their sexual desire is now virtually intuitive for us all. We are categorized as straight, gay, bi, queer, and so on; and sexual preferences, once considered private and personal, are now matters of public interest, means by which we are recognized, in Taylor's sense, by the world around us. And this makes the task of tracing the origins and nature of the sex myth an important part of understanding the modern self and the modern world.

---

4. See Karl Popper, *Conjectures and Refutations: The Growth of Scientific Knowledge* (London: Routledge and Kegan Paul, 1963); Carl G. Jung, *Symbols of Transformation*, vol. 5 of *The Collected Works of C. G. Jung*, trans. Gerhard Adler and R. F. C. Hull (Princeton, NJ: Princeton University Press, 1977).

In part 2, I have already traced a foundational part of this myth: the idea that selfhood is to be understood in inner, psychological terms. This understanding leads to a focus on aesthetics, on feelings, as central to human life. Happiness is a psychological state. It is this state that provides the background to Freud, who takes the important next step of identifying happiness with sexual pleasure. In his important essay *Civilization and Its Discontents*, Freud makes the following comment:

> Man's discovery that sexual (genital) love afforded him the strongest experiences of satisfaction and in fact provided him with the prototype of all happiness, must have suggested to him that he should continue to seek the satisfaction of happiness in his life along the path of sexual relations and that he should make genital erotism the central point of his life.[5]

If happiness is the desired goal of all human beings, then for Freud the pleasure principle—the quest for pleasure focused on sexual gratification—is central to what it means to be a self. The purpose of life, and the content of the good life, is personal sexual fulfillment. This principle also reorients thinking on the purpose of sex: the purpose of procreation is subordinated to the purpose of personal pleasure.

Such a position is in itself radical. In making this claim, Freud is asserting that true happiness *is* sexual satisfaction, and therefore the way to be happy is to engage in behavior that leads one to be sexually—that is, genitally—satisfied. Rousseau saw unhappiness as the result of the corrupting power of civilized society in fueling *amour propre*, which prevented people from being true to themselves by forcing them to engage in the artificial conventions and hypocrisies that such demanded. Freud stands in basic continuity with this idea, but he radically sexualizes and darkens it. He focuses this contrast between the natural authentic self and the civilized inauthentic self specifically on the conflict between natural sexual desires and the sexual restrictions demanded by life in civilized society. And if for Rousseau the natural

---

5. Sigmund Freud, *Civilization and Its Discontents*, trans. James Strachey (New York: W. W. Norton, 1989), 56.

man was fundamentally good, empathetic, and rational, Freud sees him as dark, violent, and irrational.[6]

We will return to this point later when discussing Freud's essay *Civilization and Its Discontents*, but there is a second related aspect of his thinking on sex that is also important to grasp: Freud not only places sex and sexual gratification at the center of adult human identity, he also extends sexuality back to infancy.

The Sexualization of Children

If sexuality, sexual desire, and the quest for sexual gratification begin at some point during life—say, at puberty during the teenage years—then to be human is not, in and of itself, to be sexual any more than to be human is to have hair under one's arms. But if children and infants are sexual from birth, then to be human is always to be sexual, even prior to the onset of puberty. One might say that it is part of the very essence of humanity to be a sexual being. And as Freud makes sexual desire fundamental to human happiness, one might go as far as to say that sexuality is the primary and most important part of being human.

This sexualization of children is, of course, something with which we today are very familiar as it lies behind debates about, for example, the nature and timing of sex education, the treatment of children with gender dysphoria, and the respective rights of children and parents when it comes to doctors prescribing birth control. It also informs tastes in fashion: the sight of even prepubescent girls dressed in a manner that is apparently designed to indicate their sexuality is an unexceptional commonplace today, albeit a somewhat vexing one in a world in which pedophilia is one of the few remaining sexual taboos and something that generates considerable

---

6. In this view, Freud can be seen as an heir to the Marquis de Sade as much as to Rousseau. For Rousseau and his followers, human beings in the state of nature are essentially benign and benevolent. But as Camille Paglia perceptively comments, "Every road from Rousseau leads to Sade." There is a darkness to human nature for which Rousseau simply cannot account, and the amorality of nature and its instinctual violence make Sade and Nietzsche more compelling as analysts of the human condition— a tradition of thought that finds its expression in a scientific idiom in Freud. An Augustinian Christian can find clear affinity with such approaches but sees this condition as the result not of nature but rather of fallen nature. For the connection between Rousseau, Sade, Nietzsche, and Freud, see Camille Paglia, *Sexual Personae: Art and Decadence from Nefertiti to Emily Dickinson* (New York: Vintage, 1990), 14.

public outrage. But as routine and as common an assumption as child-hood sexuality now is, this sexualization of childhood and even infancy is a relatively recent—and profoundly revolutionary—phenomenon and owes more to Freud than to any other individual thinker.

In this normalizing of infant sexuality, Freud was not so much a trailblazing innovator as he was the most sophisticated and influential representative of a late nineteenth-century tendency. The latter decades of the eighteenth century had witnessed a general decline in belief in the Christian notion of original sin and thus of belief in the innate depravity of children. As a result, educational regimes based on the need to crush the enemy within the child slowly gave way to those that emphasized protecting the child from the enemy without. This was a classic Rousseauesque paradigm, where the purpose of education is less to enforce social conformity and more to encourage the development of natural talents.

Such approaches, predicated on the innate innocence of the child, saw children as asexual and regarded childhood sexual activity as there-fore an alien, corrupting force, something that was not part of the child's natural condition. This in turn led to a significant emphasis on treating the archetypal and rather common sexual practice of children and ado-lescents: masturbation. With the shift away from notions of original sin, however, masturbation came to be seen not so much as a moral problem arising from within the child, which was therefore to be handled by traditional moral authorities such as the church, but rather as a medi-cal issue, to be policed and treated using medical methods. It was also thought to be the precursor to unhealthy adult sexual deviancy, a physi-cal act that could lead to later behavioral problems.[7]

The language of "self-abuse" is emblematic of how the activity was regarded in the nineteenth century: masturbation was something that involved self-inflicted damage on the individual's psyche and, quite pos-sibly, the body—hence the popular myth that it caused its practitioners

---

7. On the sexualization of childhood prior to Freud, see Lutz D. H. Sauerteig, "Loss of Innocence: Albert Moll, Sigmund Freud and the Invention of Childhood Sexuality around 1900," *Medical History* 56, no. 2 (2012): 156–83.

to go blind. It was also one reason why parents started to defer to the experts of the medical profession rather than the churches in matters of child-rearing, something of great social significance down to the present day. The movement of sexual problems from the sphere of morality to the sphere of medicine is one that continues today, as society's strong preference for technical, rather than moral, approaches to everything from AIDS to teenage pregnancies indicates. But stripping sex of its moral fabric did not begin with the pill or HIV treatments; it began in earnest in the nineteenth century with attitudes to childhood masturbation.

The late nineteenth century witnessed a further significant change to this medicalized approach to masturbation. Research by the German psychiatrist Albert Moll among Berlin youth found that there was no discernible causal relationship between childhood masturbation and later homosexual tendencies, as had previously been assumed to be the case.[8] And Moll's findings played an important role in Freud's thought, as Freud himself acknowledged in a letter to his friend Wilhelm Fliess in 1897.[9] Indeed, the result of work such as Moll's was that by 1900 masturbation was no longer considered by the medical profession to be either a moral or even a medical problem. It had come to be seen simply as a harmless childhood activity, a perfectly natural, if infantile, form of sexual behavior. And it was in this context that Freud articulated his theory of childhood sexuality.

On the basis of Moll's work, Freud was now able to provide a scientific rationale that made masturbation an explicable and normal part of a child's behavior, a routine element in growing up. Freud's recent biographer Élisabeth Roudinesco describes his approach: "A masturbating child was envisaged, from this new perspective, not as a savage creature whose evil instincts had to be tamed, but as a prototypical human being in progress."[10] Again, it is helpful to connect Freud's thinking here with the kind of view of the self proposed by Rousseau and the Romantics.

---

8. Sauerteig, "Loss of Innocence," 164.

9. Sauerteig, "Loss of Innocence," 168.

10. Élisabeth Roudinesco, *Freud in His Time and Ours*, trans. Catherine Porter (Cambridge, MA: Harvard University Press, 2016), 109.

If the authentic self is the one whose outward actions are the expression of inward, uncoerced instincts, thoughts, and desires, then Freud's view of children is a sexualized version of the idea of humanity in Rousseau's hypothetical state of nature. The authentic human—the authentic child—is the one whose inner sexual desires are naturally expressed and satisfied by outward behavior consistent with them.[11]

In fact, we can actually draw an even more radical conclusion from Freud's sexualization of children. In normalizing masturbation and childhood sexuality, what Freud was in effect doing was precisely what I noted earlier: making sex the central element in what it means to be human. The quotation above from his later work *Civilization and Its Discontents* makes genital pleasure the archetype of human happiness, and as Freud extended sexuality back into childhood and even into infancy, so the purpose of human life at every stage becomes that of finding happiness via sexual satisfaction. And that means that sex is basically that which constitutes what it means to be human and that which defines the purpose of life. For Freud, the taxonomy of all life's stages is sexual. The nature of human relationships is always determined at some profound level by sexuality. The growth of a person from infancy to childhood to adolescence to adulthood is marked by shifts in the nature and range of sexual expression, but the goal—sexual gratification—always remains the same. And Freud's classic statement of this idea occurs in his *Three Essays on the Theory of Sexuality* (1905).

Three Essays on the Theory of Sexuality

In the words of one commentator, Freud's *Three Essays on the Theory of Sexuality* helped bring to an end "that epoch of cultural innocence in which infancy and childhood were regarded as themselves innocent."[12] In

---

11. It should be noted that Freud did not regard sexuality as in itself possessing fully formed and unified content from birth. The sex drive is a complicated and composite force. Hence his development of a taxonomy for describing the sexual development of children. See Peter Gay, *Freud: A Life for Our Time* (New York: W. W. Norton, 1988), 146–48.

12. Steven Marcus, introduction to *Three Essays on the Theory of Sexuality*, by Sigmund Freud, trans. and ed. James Strachey (New York: Basic Books, 2000), xxxii. Anthony Giddens also credits this work with playing an important role in demolishing the notion of *perversion*, a clearly pejorative term when applied to nonmonogamous, nonheterosexual sexual activity, and therefore with providing a scientific foundation

this work Freud categorized sexual development as taking place through a series of stages, each of which was marked by fixation on a particular part of the anatomy. First comes the oral stage, in which the mouth is the primary erogenous zone. Breast feeding is thus an activity with sexual significance, as is the act of thumb sucking.[13] Next there is the anal stage, when the control of defecation becomes something of a focus and also the child, now beginning to interpret the world around in more reflective ways, becomes enamored of ideas such as a baby's emerging from a mother's anus.[14] After this, there is the phallic phase, marked by masturbation. Then there is a period of latency, when there is little or no motivation for sexual activity.[15] And finally, there is the genital phase, marked by a turning away from the primarily autoerotic impulse exemplified in masturbation and toward finding a sexual partner, with engagement in full sexual intercourse as its consummation.[16]

Two things are important here. First, as noted above, the concept of what it means to be human is being recast in thoroughly sexual terms. "Growing up" is consequently characterized by phases in the transformation of sexual expression. There is no stage in life in which sexual desire and its satisfaction are not foundational to human behavior. All that changes is the means by which individuals find this satisfaction. Second, behind the narrative of individual sexual development is also a narrative of social development, to which the individual connects. It is society that exerts a decisive impact on the later phases of sexual development. What occurs in the period of latency and then the genital phase is the rise and influence of what Freud later dubs the superego.

In Freud's psychoanalytic taxonomy as he articulated it from the 1920s, there are three elements of human psychology that interact with each other. There is the id, present from birth, which one might characterize as

---

for the social acceptance of sexual diversity in Western society. Giddens, *The Transformation of Intimacy: Sexuality, Love, and Eroticism in Modern Societies* (Stanford, CA: Stanford University Press, 1992), 32–34.

13. Freud, *Three Essays*, 45–47.
14. Freud, *Three Essays*, 51–53.
15. Freud, *Three Essays*, 42–45.
16. Freud, *Three Essays*, 73–74.

the basic instinctual drives of the individual. The id is in itself unregulated and disorganized, a dark, unknowable sea of chaotic, irrational desires.

Then there is the individual's ego, which develops over time and operates as a mediator between the drives of the id and the reality of the world around it. The ego has the task of satisfying the desires of the id in a manner that brings happiness and not grief to the individual. Its task is therefore to negotiate a balance between the impulses of the id and the consequences of personal behavior. It also offers rationalizations for behavior when the real motivation may just be an irrational impulse. Thus, for example, the man who cheats on his wife and ruins his life thereby might well have been driven by immediate and uncontrolled lust for another woman, but he may offer as a rationale (and may even come to believe) that it was because his wife did not understand him (or other such sentiments) that he sought sexual consolation with another.

Finally, there is the superego. The superego is that which over time internalizes the customs, conventions, expectations, and general rules of society such that they become an integral part of the individual. So, for example, the idea that monogamy is the only legitimate context for sexual expressions is an external cultural construct that the individual nonetheless comes to believe is natural and normative via the influence of the superego.

Freud's theory of the id, ego, and superego may be nonsense, but it is nonetheless a most helpful tool in understanding how his own thinking came to shape contemporary cultural and political discourse. Take, for example, the following passage from *Three Essays* that adumbrates what he later sees as the role of the superego. Here he articulates an important argument concerning the role of taste or aesthetics in the construction of morality:

> Those who condemn the other [sexual] practices (which have no doubt been common among mankind from primeval times) as being perversions, are giving way to an unmistakable feeling of *disgust*, which protects them from accepting sexual aims of the kind. The limits of such disgust are, however, often purely conventional: a man who will kiss a

pretty girl's lips passionately, may perhaps be disgusted at the idea of
using her tooth-brush, though there are no grounds for supposing that
his own oral cavity, for which he feels no disgust, is any cleaner than the
girl's. Here, then, our attention is drawn to the factor of disgust, which
interferes with the libidinal over-valuation of the sexual object but can
in turn be overridden by libido. Disgust seems to be one of the forces
which have led to a restriction of the sexual aim.[17]

Here Freud's thinking stands in line with the kind of aesthetic morality
that we noted earlier in Rousseau and then in Wordsworth, Shelley, and
Blake. The role of taste in ethics is therefore hardly innovative at this point.
Yet it is worth noting that Freud sees morality as fundamentally irrational
and ultimately subjective. It is not, as with Rousseau and company, that
sentiments and aesthetics prepare the heart to think in ways that are truly
correct and that enable the right ordering of reason. That view assumes a
basically positive, moral view of human nature, one that Freud rejects. Yes,
he sees ethics as rooted in taste, but he regards such as irrational and even
inconsistent with other human behaviors, a point that he thinks would
be obvious if anyone ever cared, or had the courage, to reflect on them.
Why would a man enjoy kissing a girl and yet gag at the thought of using
her toothbrush? The difference is not rooted in any medical consideration
regarding hygiene. It is purely a matter of social convention that has been
internalized via the superego that a kiss is considered a good and desirable
thing, while a communal toothbrush is a disgusting abomination. Morality is from this perspective simply a matter of socially conditioned taste,
which has no transcendent, objective foundation.

Again, the connection to the world of today is obvious. We will see in
chapter 9 that the Supreme Court of the United States has in one of its
judgments codified the notion that objection to homosexuality and gay
marriage is ultimately rooted in animus—or basic, irrational prejudice—
against homosexuals. That idea stands within the tradition of critiquing
moral convictions that we see influentially espoused by Freud. To this can
be added the modern penchant for words ending in *phobia* as a means of

---

17. Freud, *Three Essays*, 17–18.

exposing the alleged irrational bigotry of positions of which society does not approve: homophobia, transphobia, Islamophobia, and so on.

Freud's claim, then, is that morality draws its strength from the fact that these irrational tastes and preferences are internalized and thereby made to seem natural and thus rational. In this, he is making a point very similar to that of Nietzsche, whose concept of "herd morality" bears comparison to Freud's notion of the superego: the individual comes to believe that certain arbitrary social conventions are transcendent moral imperatives merely because everyone believes and practices them.[18] What Freud does, however, is express this idea in a scientific idiom and, most importantly, in terms of human sexual development: the specific formation of this internalized sense, the individual cultivation of this "herd instinct," to use Nietzschean terminology, takes place during the phase of childhood sexual development, when feelings of shame and distaste for sexual activity emerge as a potent means of curbing the child's basic sexual instincts.[19]

Yet moral codes, while ultimately irrational, are not for Freud purely arbitrary or random. In this context it is interesting to compare him to Godwin and Shelley. These two both regarded monogamy, for example, as immoral because of the bad social consequences that they considered it to bring in its wake—the personal frustration, the prostitution, the adultery, the subjugation and commodification of women, and so on. Freud, however, sees codes of sexual behavior as problematic not so much because of their bad social consequences—to the contrary, as we will see below, he actually thinks the social consequences of traditional sexual codes are better than the alternatives. Rather, he sees them as problematic because of their individual consequences—they inhibit the basic drive for personal sexual satisfaction and therefore preclude the possibility of society allowing individuals to achieve true happiness.

The question of morality and its connection to taste thus finds a more elaborate foundation in Freud than in previous writers and also one that is more comprehensively sexual than even that offered by Godwin,

18. See, for example, Friedrich Nietzsche, *The Gay Science*, trans. Walter Kaufmann (New York: Vintage, 1974), §116 (174–75). First published in German in 1887.

19. Freud, *Three Essays*, 42–44.

Shelley, and Blake. Yet at the same time, it points toward a conflict that Freud sees as lying at the very heart of the human condition: the conflict between the needs of society for order and the needs of the individual for sexual satisfaction as the goal of the pleasure principle and the essence of happiness. And that brings us to the next important move made by Freud for our narrative: his connection between the psychology of infants and the phenomenon of religion.

Religion as Infantile

Freud himself was an avowed atheist with a deep disdain for organized religion as any kind of ultimate and true explanation of the world, an attitude he exhibited with some militancy even in his youth.[20] And yet he realized that religion played a significant role in maintaining civilization as he understood it. Like Nietzsche and Marx, Freud regarded religion as a psychological issue, and he set forth the matter in his major work on the subject, *The Future of an Illusion*, within the context of his broader theory of sexuality and civilization.[21]

If, according to Freud, the function of civilization is to protect human beings from nature, then religion finds its purpose in precisely that task. As the infant or child fears her parents but also has to trust them for protection, so she comes to project onto the forces of nature both the fear that such can destroy her and also the hope that, if approached and appeased in the proper way, such can also protect her and cause her to prosper. Religion thus becomes the answer to a psychological need and a kind of wish fulfillment expressed through more or less elaborate idioms and practices.

---

20. Gay, *Freud*, 525. Rieff comments, "Against no other strongpoint of repressive culture are the reductive weapons of psychoanalysis deployed in such open hostility. Freud's customary detachment fails him here. Confronting religion, psychoanalysis shows itself for what it is: the last great formulation of nineteenth-century secularism. . . . What first impresses the student of Freud's psychology of religion is its polemical edge. Here, and here alone, the grand Freudian animus, otherwise concealed behind the immediacies of case histories and the emergencies of practical therapeutics, breaks out." *Mind of the Moralist*, 257. It is worth remembering in this context that Freud's early and primary exposure to religion would have been that of the Viennese Catholic Church with its overt anti-Semitism. Rieff, *Mind of the Moralist*, 257.

21. Sigmund Freud, *The Future of an Illusion*, trans. and ed. James Strachey (New York: W. W. Norton, 1961).

Commenting on the origin of religion, Freud declares,

> A store of ideas is created, born from man's need to make his helplessness tolerable and built up from the material memories of the helplessness of his own childhood and the childhood of the human race. It can clearly be seen that the possession of these ideas protects him in two directions—against the dangers of nature and Fate, and against the injuries that threaten him from human society.[22]

A number of comments are in order. First, Freud regards religion as literally infantile: it is the result of the carrying over of childish hopes and fears into adulthood. It is therefore, strictly speaking, a sign of immaturity and a failure to develop into an adult. We might therefore add a noun to the adjective: it is for Freud an infantile *neurosis*. In this, his attitude stands within a well-established tradition of thought that identifies traditional religion both with childishness and with psychological problems, from the French philosophes to Feuerbach, Marx, and Nietzsche.[23] What Freud does that marks an important contribution is, once again, to express this attitude toward religion using a scientific idiom. In doing so, he gives scientific respectability to the idea that religious belief represents some form of mental deficiency or emotional immaturity. What Marx and Nietzsche expressed with memorable philosophical rhetoric, Freud expressed with the cool, dispassionate prose of the scientist. And this has certainly informed the basic intuitions of the modern social imaginary. Such attitudes to religion and its implications now pervade contemporary culture, from legal judgments that see a desire to maintain Christian marriage as the result of irrational animus to comments by politicians about those who cling to guns and religion as a means of justifying and fueling their resentment and bitterness toward society in general. The idea that religious belief represents either personal immaturity or some form of psychological defect is now such a deeply embedded cultural commonplace that it is rarely considered

---

22. Freud, *Future of an Illusion*, 22.
23. Gay, *Freud*, 532–33.

necessary to offer any justification for what is deemed a self-evident, objective, undeniable truth.[24]

Second, in the quotation above, Freud points toward his underlying idea that religion is an illusion. It is an illusion not in the sense that it is necessarily untrue (though Freud has no doubts on that score) but in the sense that it represents a form of wish fulfillment. This means that religious belief is motivated not by rational proof but by irrational human desire; as a result, its adherents are not vulnerable to rational refutation.[25]

Third, Freud does grudgingly acknowledge that religion has historically fulfilled a useful purpose: "Religion has clearly performed great services for human civilization. It has contributed much towards the taming of the asocial instincts."[26] Freud may well have disdain for religion as an infantile neurosis, but he concedes that it has played an important role in maintaining civilization by providing a rationale for morality. It has held men and women back from indulging in very dark and destructive desires they may have. He also sees, however, that it has not done this perfectly. He continues his argument by declaring that religion has failed to provide happiness for people, that strongly religious eras exhibited no more, and often less, general satisfaction with life than his own increasingly irreligious age.[27]   •

What is his alternative? Freud has tremendous confidence that science, including (of course) psychoanalysis, will help fill the void left by the death of religion. He is well aware that if belief in God is the only reason for maintaining moral codes, then when God dies (to use Nietzschean terminology), the morality that depends on him dies too.[28] Therefore, Freud sees scientific reason as the means by which human beings can be reconciled to civilization in a way that avoids the burdens of guilt and anxiety that religion brought in its wake. The id can

---

24. On the judicial use of the idea of irrational animus as a basis on which to dismiss opposition to gay marriage, see "The Supreme Court and Gay Marriage," p. 302, in chap. 9.

25. Freud, *Future of an Illusion*, 39–40.

26. Freud, *Future of an Illusion*, 47.

27. Freud, *Future of an Illusion*, 48.

28. Freud, *Future of an Illusion*, 50.

be controlled in a postreligious world by scientific knowledge. Yet this optimistic view of science is uncharacteristic for Freud and, indeed, in his later work gives way to a pessimism that is arguably more consistent with his thought as a whole. *The Future of an Illusion* provides a scientific rationale for modern disdain for religion as childish and irrational, but even Freud had to move beyond it in his thinking about sex, morality, and civilization. It is not the optimism of *The Future of an Illusion* but Freud's later pessimism that is his greatest contribution to social theory and something that has had ramifications far beyond the medical world. This impulse finds its most important expression in his classic essay *Civilization and Its Discontents*.[29]

Civilization and Its Discontents

Given that, for Freud, human beings are at base sexual and that the libido, or sex drive, is the most powerful force in motivating their behavior, it is nonetheless clearly true that the world does not consist of human beings outwardly indulging every sexual whim or desire they might have in order to make themselves happy and properly satisfied. Were they to do so, the possibility for personal happiness would be in theory great but also in practice short lived and restricted to those aggressive enough and sufficiently strong to be the dominant figures in any given social arrangement. As Freud describes it,

> Primitive man was better off in knowing no restrictions of instinct. To counterbalance this, his prospects of enjoying this happiness for any length of time were very slender. Civilized man has exchanged a portion of his possibilities of happiness for a portion of security.[30]

Here Freud gives the ideal man of nature that underpins Rousseau's theory of society a distinctly Freudian sexual identity. As with Rousseau, Freud imagines a world in which primitive man knew no restrictions, in this case sexual, and was therefore very happy. But then

---

29. Gay describes *The Future of an Illusion* as reading "like a rehearsal for *Civilization and Its Discontents.*" *Freud*, 527.

30. Freud, *Civilization and Its Discontents*, 73.

Freud's pessimism comes to the fore: such happiness would be short lived and risky precisely because it played into the hands of only the most immediately powerful individuals and left the rest vulnerable and hopelessly unsatisfied.

One might think here of the animal kingdom, where the dominant male in, say, a band of gorillas is the one with exclusive sexual access to the females. Other males are driven away and thus doomed to be (in anthropomorphic terms) sexually frustrated. Thus, happiness for the Freudian primitive man would in practice have been a virtual monopoly of whoever happened to be the dominant male. Other men would live lives of total frustration, and women would clearly function as nothing more than instruments for the sexual gratification of the strongest male. And even the dominant male would have a relatively short reign: another stronger, younger one would inevitably arise to overthrow him. And yet society—civilized society—is not like that at all. It involves far more activities than simply the spontaneous satisfaction of sexual desire and is far more complicated and structurally diverse than a community ruled by one dominant male.

This dynamic points to the great trade-off that Freud sees at the heart of civilization: the curbing of the sex drive in order to make society possible; for if this drive is not curbed, a situation of chaos or of domination by one strong individual must inevitably ensue, both of which cases are worse scenarios for the majority of people than sacrificing sexual satisfaction for a degree of security. The social contract of Rousseau is, in the hands of Freud, turned into a sexual contract, exchanging uninhibited sexual license for sexual restraint. And the result is civilization.[31]

---

31. In this context it is important to note that the popular misunderstanding of Freud as considering sexual repression to be a bad or negative thing is entirely misplaced. It is true that Freud sees society's traditional sexual codes as too restrictive—such codes, in banning homosexuality, incest, premarital sex, etc., repress far more than is necessary for civilization to exist, and thus he does anticipate Herbert Marcuse's later concept of surplus repression. See the comments of Scott Yenor, *Family Politics: The Idea of Marriage in Modern Political Thought* (Waco, TX: Baylor University Press, 2011), 166–68; see also chap. 7 of this volume. Yet for Freud repression as a general principle is actually a necessary thing in order for civilization to exist and to do many of the great things for which it is known. The sublimation of sexual desire leads not only to the ability of human beings to live together but also to phenomena such as art and music, as sexual energy is redirected to other activities. Sarah Coakley makes this point with

Society develops various means of enforcing this contract—external moral codes designed to cultivate social shame among its members for their transgressions of it and an internalized conscience whereby behavior is regulated by the individuals themselves.[32] It is the natural instinct of human beings to seek to live in social formations, and thus guilt is increasingly important as the means of reinforcing the codes necessary to make such formations possible.[33] Furthermore, if sexual codes are vital for social cohesion, then the need to police sexuality from infancy onward is of critical importance. It is this idea that lays the foundation for adult codes of sexual behavior: unless children are schooled in the sexual mores of society from an early age, they will not conform to such as adults.[34] And again, central to each of these is the notion of guilt: by cultivating a feeling of guilt for transgression of sexual codes among members of society from chilhood, society is able to maintain broad control of the way people behave. Guilt is the internal regulator of the individual's sexual conduct.[35]

What is important to understand here, however, is that this curbing of the sexual instinct comes at significant cost, for it means that it is impossible for the civilized ever to be truly happy. If happiness depends on the fulfillment of personal sexual desires, then to the extent that such desires are curbed and thereby frustrated, to that extent the individual will be unfulfilled and unhappy. Civilization thus has at its very core the impossibility of human beings ever being truly happy and content. Hence the title of Freud's essay: *Civilization and Its Discontents*. To be civilized is inevitably to be discontented at some deep level because that sexual satisfaction that constitutes human happiness is impossible to achieve in any absolute or lasting sense. Civilization is the answer

---

great clarity in her recent discussion of Freud in *The New Asceticism: Sexuality, Gender and the Quest for God* (London: Bloomsbury, 2015), 39–45.

32. Freud, *Civilization and Its Discontents*, 94–96.

33. Freud states, "Since civilization obeys an internal erotic impulse which causes human beings to unite in a closely-knit group, it can only achieve this aim through an ever-increasing reinforcement of the sense of guilt." *Civilization and Its Discontents*, 96.

34. Freud explains, "A cultural community is perfectly justified, psychologically, in starting by proscribing manifestations of the sexual life of children, for there would be no prospect of curbing the sexual lusts of adults if the ground had not been prepared for it in childhood." *Civilization and Its Discontents*, 60.

35. Freud, *Civilization and Its Discontents*, 99.

to the unhappiness that sexual chaos would involve, but it itself creates another kind of unhappiness, that of sexual repression and frustration.[36]

This unhappiness, this discontent, is itself the foundation of culture. Freud's biographer Élisabeth Roudinesco expresses it well:

> Freud emphasized that those human beings who had given up the religious illusion could expect nothing from any return to "nature." As he saw it, the only way to achieve wisdom, that is, the most exalted of freedoms, consisted in an investment of the libido in the highest forms of creativity: love (Eros), art, science, knowledge, and the ability to live in society and to commit oneself, in the name of a common ideal, to the well-being of all.[37]

Thus the pleasure principle, the desire for sexual fulfillment, has to find within society different outlets either for its release or its sublimation. These outlets can never fully satisfy—and therefore the experience of discontent is pervasive—but they do serve to lessen that feeling somewhat by temporarily distracting from it.

Freud sees a number of such substitutive distractions in civilized society that ameliorate the unhappiness caused by the frustration of sexual desire. Science and art both offer avenues that allow individuals to take pleasure in life. In addition, for the ordinary person, there is religion—for Freud, as noted above, surely a fiction in terms of its referential truth claims but one that purports to be useful in offering wish fulfillment and supplying the illusion of a transcendent meaning to the experience of this immanent world.[38] It also—most importantly—not only cultivates that internalized sense of guilt that is necessary for the maintenance of civilization in terms of the trade-off involved in sexual taboos, but it also claims to offer a solution to it, albeit a specious and inadequate one—in the case of Christianity, its notion of a substitutionary

---

36. As Freud states, "It is impossible to overlook the extent to which civilization is built upon a renunciation of instinct, how much it presupposes precisely the non-satisfaction (by suppression, repression or some other means?) of powerful instincts. This 'cultural frustration' dominates the large field of social relationships between human beings." *Civilization and Its Discontents*, 51–52.

37. Roudinesco, *Freud*, 347.

38. Freud, *Civilization and Its Discontents*, 22–25.

atonement for sin in the person and work of Jesus Christ.[39] Then there are also intoxicants—alcohol and drugs—both of which numb the body to the painful realities of civilized life and, indeed, to the body's own weakness and inevitable mortality.[40] All these things are useful in ameliorating the pain that the trade-off between happiness and civilization requires.

Concluding Thoughts on Freud

In terms of the overall argument of this book, Freud occupies a pivotal position. In the introduction, I stated that the rise of the sexual revolution was predicated on fundamental changes in how the self is understood. The self must first be psychologized; psychology must then be sexualized; and sex must be politicized. The first move is exemplified by Rousseau and his Romantic heirs. The second is the signal achievement of Sigmund Freud. Of critical importance to the modern age is his development of both a theory of sexuality that places the sex drive at the very core of who and what human beings are from infancy and the theories of religion and of civilization that he connects to that theory—and that he does so through the scientific idiom of psychoanalysis, an idiom that makes his theories, like those of Darwin, inherently plausible in a modern social imaginary in which science has intuitive authority. And the result is that, before Freud, sex was an activity, for procreation or for recreation; after Freud, sex is definitive of who we are, as individuals, as societies, and as a species.

It does not matter that the strictly scientific status of Freud's theories is now methodologically and materially discredited. The central notion—that human beings are at core sexual and that that shapes our thinking and our behavior in profound, often unconscious, ways—is now a basic part of the modern social imaginary. From the sexualized tools of the advertising industry to the increasingly explicit products of Hollywood, we all know that sex sells. And it sells because sexual desire is something that human beings experience as among the most powerful

---

39. Freud, *Civilization and Its Discontents*, 99–100.
40. Freud, *Civilization and Its Discontents*, 26–27.

and irrational forces in life. Cultural artifacts, whether works of great literature such as the *Iliad* or the raunchy lyrics of some throwaway pop song by the latest girl or boy band, reflect the human preoccupation with all things erotic. And Freud stands as the grand theorist of this fixation and, most important, as the man who offered an analysis of civilization and culture that takes this obsession into account.

It is also important to note that Freud's emphasis on sexual fulfillment as the essence of human happiness also leads to a reconfiguration of human destiny. The end of human life is no longer something set in the future; rather, it is enclosed within the present. To be satisfied is to be sexually fulfilled here and now. The happiest person is the sempiternal orgiast, the one who is constantly indulging his or her sexual desires. That such a figure is now a normative type in our society is a claim that scarcely needs justifying, given the omnipresence of pornography and the general assumption that sexual activity is that which makes us authentic human beings.

There are other commonplaces of our contemporary culture that Freud did not invent but to which he gave powerful expression and specious scientific plausibility. The idea of religion as childish and of sexual morality as driven by taste, not transcendent divine or natural law, are perhaps the two most obvious. Regarding the latter, he also reinforces the shift that is evident in the work of Nietzsche, Marx, and Darwin: human beings are not naturally "moral," as Rousseau, Wordsworth, and company believed. They lack a "moral" nature; "morality" is always a social construct and cannot be read back into the state of nature in any pure, primeval form. Again, Freud (as Darwin) expresses ideas with explosive metaphysical significance in the apparently objective, cool, dispassionate language of science.

There is one final point worth noting in Freud's *Future of an Illusion*. It is where his convictions on infant sexuality and on the infantile nature of religion come together in one rhetorical question that, in retrospect, has a particularly portentous ring to it:

Is it not true that the two main points in the programme for the education of children today are retardation of sexual development and premature religious influence?[41]

In pinpointing these two aspects of education in his day, Freud anticipates the emphases that emerge in the late twentieth century by way of reaction and reversal, and that are now at the heart of today's educational philosophies. Contemporary education has become in some quarters preoccupied with the liberation of children's sexual instincts and the elimination of any religious influence whatsoever. Today's education as therapy exhibits these two pathologies: a liberation from traditional sexual codes and (given its role in maintaining traditional sexual codes) liberation from religion.

Freud's brief comment here points forward to the next phase in the transformation of the self: now that the self has been sexualized, all that is necessary is that sex be politicized. And that is the topic of the next chapter.

---

41. Freud, *Future of an Illusion*, 60.

7

The New Left and the
Politicization of Sex

*The mind is its own place, and in itself
Can make a heav'n of hell, a hell of heav'n.*

JOHN MILTON, *PARADISE LOST*

The contemporary political scene is dominated by issues of identity—racial, sexual, ethnic, and otherwise. Underlying much of the discussion, and driving much of the stridency, is the cluster of philosophical approaches to such matters known by the umbrella term *critical theory*.

Critical theory is today a diverse phenomenon that draws deeply and variously on strands of Marxist thought, psychoanalysis, feminist theory, postcolonialism, poststructuralism, queer theory, and deconstruction. It embraces a variety of such approaches and continues to develop its conceptual vocabulary and its range of political concerns.[1] Yet at the core

---

1. For example, out of critical theory has arisen the concept of "intersectionality" as a means of articulating the complexity of social and political categories, which are marked by overlapping identities among particular groups or individuals of varying status within the hierarchy of society. The term was coined by Kimberlé Crenshaw in her important essay "Demarginalizing the Intersection of Race and Sex: A Black Feminist Critique of Antidiscrimination Doctrine, Feminist Theory and Antiracist

of the various approaches of critical theorists lies a relatively simple set of convictions: the world is to be divided up between those who have power and those who do not; the dominant Western narrative of truth is really an ideological construct designed to preserve the power structure of the status quo; and the goal of critical theory is therefore to destabilize this power structure by destabilizing the dominant narratives that are used to justify—to "naturalize"—it.[2]

While critical theory is a vital tool in the modern LGBTQ+ movement in terms of its political engagement, my focus in this chapter is not on its contemporary manifestations. Such a task is well beyond the necessary scope of my argument. Rather, I want to look at its origins and some of its earliest iterations as a means of pinpointing key developments in the overall narrative of the self with which this book is preoccupied. And that means that the discussion is focused on the way Freud's thinking came to be modified and appropriated by the Marxist Left in the mid-twentieth century. Critical theory may have moved well beyond the writings of those I discuss in this chapter—Herbert Marcuse, Wilhelm Reich, Simone de Beauvoir, and Shulamith Firestone—but the work these earlier thinkers did both established and exemplified the trajectories along which later critical theory has moved.

An Odd Couple: Marx and Freud

Freud's theories are intriguing but in themselves insufficient for understanding why sexual identity has played such a significant role in the politics of the West for more than fifty years. How did the psychoanalytic speculations of a Viennese physician come to shape the logic of the contemporary political landscape to the point that matters of sexuality now look set to overwhelm traditional concerns of liberal societies, such as freedom of speech and religious liberty? To explain that, it is first necessary to grasp the manner in which Freudian ideas came to occupy

---

Politics," *University of Chicago Legal Forum* 1, no. 8 (1989), accessed July 2, 2019, https://chicago unbound.uchicago.edu/uclf/vol1989/iss1/8.

2. For a very accessible introduction to critical theory, see Stephen Eric Bronner, *Critical Theory: A Very Short Introduction* (Oxford: Oxford University Press, 2017); see also Fred Rush, ed., *The Cambridge Companion to Critical Theory* (Cambridge: Cambridge University Press, 2004).

a prominent place in the development of Marxist philosophy in the twentieth century.

As noted in chapter 5, Karl Marx's philosophy of history is at its core a materialist revision of the idealism of G. W. F. Hegel. Like Hegel, Marx envisaged history as a forward-moving dialectical process, but for him this would culminate in the triumph of the working class (the proletariat) over the middle class (the bourgeoisie). This shift involved the replacement of the capitalist system with a communist one, in which the means of production would be held in common ownership by the workers in the form of the state.

Marx's theory of the triumph of the proletariat depended on two other historical developments as preconditions. First, the capitalist system would have to collapse under the weight of its own economic contradictions. Essentially, the increasing concentration of wealth in the hands of fewer and fewer people would create a situation in which the system simply broke down. And second, the proletariat would need to develop a political self-consciousness that would allow it to understand that its best interests were not served by it supporting the capitalist system and the bourgeoisie but rather that these had to be overthrown and replaced with common ownership of the means of production. In other words, the workers would need to realize that their interests and those of their bosses were antithetical to each other and that overthrowing their bosses would therefore be to their distinct advantage.

This latter point is where a crucial lacuna in Marx's thought exists. What Marx never explained was how this second development, this rise of proletarian self-consciousness, was to take place. This gap in Marx's thought was made only more problematic by the events of history itself. As Europe moved through the early part of the twentieth century, it became apparent that crises in world capitalism (e.g., the stock market crash of 1929 and the subsequent Great Depression) were not proving sufficient in themselves to create the necessary class consciousness required. Material conditions clearly did not determine class consciousness in a direct, simple fashion. This issue—of how proletarian class consciousness was to be developed in order to facilitate the advent of a communist society—was in many ways the key theoretical question that drove the development of Marxism in the twentieth century.

The problem was faced in one form by Vladimir Ilyich Lenin, leader of the Russian Revolution. Russia, as a predominantly peasant society, had not undergone the necessary capitalist development that was supposed to be the precondition for the advent of communism; Lenin was also convinced that economic conditions in themselves would not produce revolutionary consciousness among the working class. At best, it would lead the workers to form trade unions, not to overthrow the bourgeoisie and seize the means of production.

Not to be deterred by a mere detail, Lenin revised Marxism somewhat to allow for revolutionary leadership to be assumed by the Communist Party, led by bourgeois intellectuals who understood the dialectics of history and were able therefore to teach and thereby stir up the proletariat for revolution.[3]

But if this had worked in Russia, it did not do so elsewhere. The Spartacist uprising of 1919 in Germany was a dismal failure, despite the fact that Germany had a developed industrial working class and, defeated in the war, was subject to considerable internal conflict and potential instability—both of which made it ripe (according to Marxist theory) for communist revolution. Then, as European and American capitalism continued to survive even in the wake of the Wall Street Crash of 1929, and as the New Deal in the United States and the welfare state in Britain seemed to defuse the class conflict, the possibilities of a naturally developed political consciousness among the proletariat looked more and more remote. And this was rendered only more complicated by the rise of Stalinism. The routing of Leon Trotsky, the purging of the Old Bolsheviks, and the establishment of brutal totalitarianism of a kind never seen before indicated that the path to a socialist utopia might not be straightforward, even within the poster-boy

3. On Lenin, see Leszek Kołakowski, *Main Currents of Marxism*, trans. P. S. Falla (Oxford: Oxford University Press, 1978), 2:381–412.

Marxist state of the Soviet Union.[4] Further, the rise of Fascist and Nazi parties in Italy, Germany, and central and eastern Europe and the clear appeal of these movements to the working classes indicated that the dialectics of history were not operating quite as smoothly as Marx and his followers had once hoped.

One response to this problem that was to have a significant impact on later generations of leftist thinking came from a prison cell in Benito Mussolini's Italy. There the Italian Marxist Antonio Gramsci attempted a response to this theoretical lacuna by focusing on the role of intellectuals in society. Rejecting the idea that intellectuals were a class apart, he developed the notion of "organic intellectuals," whose task was to articulate and shape the political consciousness of a class through the development of a specific class culture that stood in opposition to that of whatever the dominant or (in his term) hegemonic class happened to be. In Gramsci, therefore, we see the roots of the modern approach to political revolution via the transformation of cultural institutions such as schools and the media. Once the levers of cultural power were in the right hands, the path to forming appropriate political self-consciousness was fairly straightforward. But one needed a vanguard of intellectuals to accomplish this aim.[5]

Another approach, however, was that developed by members of the so-called Frankfurt School, the name given to those associated with the Frankfurt Institute for Social Research. This institution, founded in 1923, was to be the focus of a major reworking of Marxist theory, fueled variously by the turmoil of Germany's interwar years, by the rise of Nazism, and intellectually by the publication in the 1930s of early works of Karl Marx, most notably his *Economic-Philosophical Manuscripts* and *The German Ideology*. These texts presented a view of Marx's thinking that stood more clearly in continuity with the idealist thought of Hegel

---

4. A further problematic aspect of Stalinism from a Marxist perspective was its nationalist focus, which stood in conflict with the class-based, transnational categories and ambitions of traditional Marxism. I am grateful to my Grove City College colleague Professor Andrew Mitchell for bringing this aspect of the Left's disillusionment with Stalinism to my attention.

5. Gramsci's major statement on the role of intellectuals is found in his essay "The Intellectuals," in *Selections from the Prison Notebooks*, ed. and trans. Quintin Hoare and Geoffrey Nowell Smith (New York: International Publishers, 1971), 5–23.

and also offered the possibility of using Marx for developing forms of social and cultural criticism that might address the apparent resilience of capitalism in the face of its various shortcomings.[6]

The influence of the Frankfurt School has been far reaching, from contributing to discussions of aesthetics to possibly inspiring the central character in Thomas Mann's *Doctor Faustus*.[7] The schools of critical theory that it has spawned have offered the world both some of the most opaque and bombastic prose ever written and also some of the most intriguing criticisms of the role of popular culture in forming society's dominant beliefs. Its significance for our narrative, however, lies in the way it brought together the political concerns of Marxism with the psychoanalytical claims of Freud.[8]

The Shotgun Wedding of Marx and Freud

The story of the fusion of Marxist and Freudian thought, which historian of the Frankfurt School Stuart Jeffries has described as a "shotgun wedding," begins with two of the early members of the school, Max Horkheimer and, more importantly, Erich Fromm.[9]

For Fromm, the point of useful contact between Marx and Freud lay in the fact that both saw human character (selfhood) in dynamic terms, Marx in the material social conditions in relation to which human self-consciousness developed, Freud in terms of the psychological development of the sex drive as individuals matured and took their place in

---

6. An excellent history of the Frankfurt School is Stuart Jeffries, *Grand Hotel Abyss: The Lives of the Frankfurt School* (London: Verso, 2016).

7. Jeffries suggests that it is the Frankfurt School philosopher Theodor Adorno and not the composer Arnold Schoenberg (the more usual identification) who stands at least in part behind the character of the composer Adrian Leverkühn in Mann's *Doctor Faustus*. *Grand Hotel Abyss*, 242.

8. For an extremely negative assessment of the role of critical theory, see Michael Walsh, *The Devil's Pleasure Palace: The Cult of Critical Theory and the Subversion of the West* (New York: Encounter Books, 2015). For a critical assessment that highlights the inability of many of the Frankfurt School acolytes to write a pellucid sentence, see Roger Scruton, *Fools, Frauds, and Firebrands: Thinkers of the New Left* (London: Bloomsbury, 2015). For a more appreciative and avowedly Marxist, though still critical, perspective, see Terry Eagleton, *After Theory* (New York: Basic Books, 2004).

9. For Horkheimer, Freud's notion of the Oedipus complex and the domineering function of the father was helpful in explaining the irrational appeal of Nazism and Fascism in otherwise outwardly sophisticated Western European societies, particularly Germany. See his *Eclipse of Reason* (1947; repr., London: Continuum, 2004), esp. 74–79. For Fromm's fusion of Marx and Freud, see his autobiographical account, *Beyond the Chains of an Illusion: My Encounter with Marx and Freud* (New York: Trident, 1962).

society. For both, the process was evolutionary, and this allowed Fromm to draw fruitfully on the work of both men. Freud was particularly useful to him because of his taxonomy of character types.

While Horkheimer and Fromm attempted to bring together Marxist and Freudian insights in order to address the rise of Fascism and Nazism, this union, like most shotgun marriages, was not an entirely comfortable one. There were, after all, some very basic problems of compatibility between the two approaches. First, there was the complexity of welding together an approach to human life that prioritized the material and economic in the context of society at large with one that focused on the psychological and the individual. Then there was also the deeper disparity, even contradiction, between what we might call the teleological expectation of the two. Marxism offered a fundamentally optimistic view of the world because, whatever the suffering and traumas that might characterize the road to the worker's paradise, that paradise was surely coming at some point in the future. For Freud, however, civilization was impossible except for a society that was prepared to repress the most fundamental of human instincts, the desire for sexual satisfaction via unhindered sexual activity. Marx and his progeny were optimists; Freud—certainly the later Freud of *Civilization and Its Discontents*—was a pessimist. Finally, there was the prominent place of libido, the sex drive, in Freud's thought that Fromm, for example, rejected as a key category for understanding human beings, regarding it as taking insufficient account of the historical and social origins of character types.[10]

The transformation of the marriage of Freud and Marx, however, from shotgun status to one of genuine love was to take place at the hands of two men, one informally associated with the Frankfurt School, the other perhaps its most significant and influential activist intellectual: Wilhelm Reich and Herbert Marcuse, respectively. These two figures are central to any understanding of modern political discourse and also to many cultural attitudes even beyond the bounds of left-wing ideology.[11]

---

10. Don Hausdorff, *Erich Fromm* (New York: Twayne, 1972), 54–59.

11. It is interesting to note that Reich regarded America, with its deep tradition of individualism, as the place where the sexual revolution was most likely to take root; see the discussion of Reich in

Wilhelm Reich and Revolutionary Sex

Wilhelm Reich's combining of Freud and Marx was initiated through his desire to understand the rise of Fascist ideology. In his book *The Mass Psychology of Fascism* (1933), Reich developed the concept of what he called sex economy, in which he used Marx's notion of class conflict to deepen Freud's notion of sexual repression and develop it for a specifically political end.[12]

In this work, Reich is particularly interested in a standard Marxist problem: Why do members of a certain class act against their own class interests? He draws a specific example from Lenin, who had noted how soldiers in the 1905 rebellion in Russia had gained power but had then used it in effect to reinstate those they had overthrown. Reich comments that a religious mystic would interpret this as a sign of humanity's innate morality, which ultimately prevents full rebellion against the divinely established order. The vulgar Marxist would reject this interpretation but would not be able to offer any adequate alternative based on strictly economic premises.[13] Reich regards Freud as helpful here: he offers a fruitful line of reflection through seeing such behavior as the effect of guilty ambivalence toward a father figure, a kind of sociological Oedipus complex. The soldiers supported the tsar, against their real political interests, because they instinctively both feared and desired to please him as a kind of father figure. And yet Reich does not think that Freud went far enough because he did not ask the deeper question of the sociological origin or political function of such behavior.[14]

Reich then highlights four elements of Freud's work that he thinks are particularly pertinent to answering these latter questions: (1) Freud

Charles J. Chaput, *Strangers in a Strange Land: Living the Catholic Faith in a Post-Christian World* (New York: Henry Holt, 2017), 87.

12. Wilhelm Reich, *The Mass Psychology of Fascism*, ed. and trans. Mary Higgins and Chester M. Raphael (New York: Farrar, Straus, and Giroux, 1970).

13. "Vulgar Marxism" is typically a pejorative term used to refer to those Marxists who attempt to reduce human action to a very simple cause-and-effect structure based on purely economic foundations. As noted above, this was found by many, most notably Lenin, to be wholly inadequate as a means of creating and cultivating revolutionary self-consciousness among the working class.

14. Reich, *Mass Psychology*, 24–25.

pointed to the subconscious as that which provides the context, and thus the real meaning, of all thought and actions; (2) he sexualized infancy and childhood; (3) he discovered that sexual repression was central to the authority relationship that existed between parent and child; and (4) he realized that adult morality was not some absolute, transcendent reality but was itself derived from the educational measures taken by parents and those acting in the place of parents (e.g., nannies, teachers) in the education of children.[15]

What Reich then does with these insights is a critical move in the synthesizing of Marxist and Freudian ideas: he applies the Marxist notion that ideas are themselves the ideological expression of specific historical circumstances to Freud's thought in a way that connects Freud's insights to the political structure of the society in which the psychological phenomena they describe occur:

> It becomes apparent that it is not cultural activity itself which demands suppression and repression of sexuality, but only the present *forms* of this activity, and so one is willing to sacrifice these forms if by so doing the terrible wretchedness of children could be eliminated.[16]

What Reich does here is adopt Freud's basic point about civilization/culture—that it is the product of sexual repression—while refusing to make this a transcendent truth, preferring to relativize it. Sexual codes are part of the ideology of the governing class, designed to maintain the status quo so as to benefit those in power. To be specific: the present shape of this civilization-happiness trade-off involves preventing children from engaging in sexual self-expression, but this particular historical form of moral prescription is not in itself a necessary absolute and could well be configured differently. The question therefore emerges as to how and why the current sexual codes, specifically here relating to children, have come to be the way they are. More generally, why is a culture or civilization built on such specific forms of repression considered necessary, and by whom?

---

15. Reich, *Mass Psychology*, 26–27.
16. Reich, *Mass Psychology*, 29.

Reich answers the question first by asking when this form of sexual repression began to take shape as a historical reality. His answer, stated rather than supported with any evidence, is that it began with the rise of authoritarian patriarchy and was subsequently reinforced by the rise of a sex-negating church. This is not a new notion: I noted it in chapter 4 in the thought of both Percy Bysshe Shelley and William Blake. Now, however, the idea is expressed using the scientific language of Freudian and Marxist philosophy.

Reich then goes further: current repressive sexual codes are intimately connected to the exploitation of labor, and to understand this point, he argues, one must understand the basic institution that is used to inculcate this repression:

> *The interlacing of the socio-economic structure with the sexual structure of society and the structural reproduction of society take place in the first four or five years and in the authoritarian family.* The church only continues this function later. Thus, the authoritarian state gains an enormous interest in the authoritarian family. *It becomes the factory in which the state's structure and ideology are moulded.*[17]

Here Reich strikes a note that will be of great significance in Marxist thinking (and, one might argue, eventually across the political spectrum in general): the traditional patriarchal family is a unit of oppression. This is a function of both Freud's belief in childhood sexuality and his understanding of how sexual repression connects to the culture of civilization. In the hands of Reich it becomes a potent starting point for reflecting on what political revolution and liberation might look like and how these might be accomplished. By implication, those who argue for the traditional family as a societal good are really lackeys, witting or unwitting, of the current oppressive status quo.

Reich is not unique or original in identifying the traditional family unit as oppressive. I noted in chapter 4 that William Godwin and Percy Bysshe Shelley regarded monogamy and its subsequent emphasis on the family as a fundamentally oppressive construction. This was also

---

17. Reich, *Mass Psychology*, 30; emphasis original.

the view of Friedrich Engels, Marx's financier and colaborer in the communist cause. Engels's *The Origin of the Family, Private Property, and the State* (1884), connected the rise of the monogamous patriarchal family to changing economic conditions. The emergence of the family, he argued, created "the cellular form of civilized society," which anticipated in microcosm the larger conflicts that would develop in society at large.[18] His focus, however, was on not the status of children so much as that of women: the family turned women into chattels, virtual pieces of property, and their emancipation would come about only when they were allowed to take their place as workers in the public means of production.[19]

Reich therefore stands in a line of Marxist thinking that sees the family as a problematic bourgeois institution. What Reich does, however, is radicalize and psychologize this notion by appropriating Freud's insights and then presenting this sexualized understanding of the family's social significance as a means of helping explain the psychology of Fascism and Nazism: the traditional family with its bourgeois sexual morality and repression of children's instincts helps produce the kind of pliant, submissive individual who offers no resistance but rather supine obedience to authority figures:

> Morality's aim is to produce acquiescent subjects who, despite distress and humiliation, are adjusted to the authoritarian order. Thus, the family is the authoritarian state in miniature, to which the child must learn to adapt himself as a preparation for the general social adjustment required of him later.[20]

This connection between the family and political oppression is of lasting significance for left-wing politics: the dismantling and abolition of the nuclear family are essential if political liberation is to be achieved. It also offers an answer to that lacuna in Marx's thought as to how the proletariat can develop a proper political self-consciousness:

---

18. Friedrich Engels, *The Origin of the Family, Private Property, and the State*, in *The Marx-Engels Reader*, ed. Robert C. Tucker, 2nd ed. (London: W. W. Norton, 1978), 739.

19. Engels, *Origin*, in Tucker, *Marx-Engels Reader*, 744.

20. Reich, *Mass Psychology*, 30.

working-class people must be disabused of their commitment to the bourgeois sexual codes that make the traditional family an unquestioned and necessary good.

Reich's *Sexual Revolution*

This latter point, that sexual morality and political consciousness are intimately connected, is one that Reich makes in greater detail in the work that is in many ways the manifesto of his thinking, *The Sexual Revolution*.[21] First published in 1936, the book articulates the importance of childhood sexuality and sexual identity for the political struggle, prophetically anticipating many of the elements of the radicalism of the 1960s and beyond.[22]

In this work, Reich is explicitly critical of aspects of Freud's thought. Again, he makes the point that Freud was correct in seeing the role of sexual repression as the basis for civilization but that he was incorrect in generalizing this to all cultures and not simply to societies built around the patriarchal family. From Reich's perspective, Freud failed to be sufficiently historicist in his approach.[23]

In *The Sexual Revolution*, Reich argues that attitudes to the family among youth are a gauge of the level of political radicalism that exists: conservative political conformists regard the family as an unquestionably good thing; radicals see it as something that needs to be overcome or destroyed.[24] And so at the heart of Reich's revolutionary program is sex education and the need for children and adolescents to be allowed sexual freedom. This is simply because these are the bases for political freedom, as their absence is the basis for political oppression. In a key passage Reich states the matter as follows:

---

21. Wilhelm Reich, *The Sexual Revolution: Toward a Self-Regulating Character Structure*, trans. Therese Pol (New York: Farrar, Straus, and Giroux, 1974).

22. Gabriele Kuby notes that Reich's extraordinary influence was essentially postmortem, in the 1960s. *The Global Sexual Revolution: Destruction of Freedom in the Name of Freedom*, trans. John Patrick Kirchner (Kettering, OH: Angelico, 2015), 25–26. See also E. Michael Jones, *Libido Dominandi: Sexual Liberation and Political Control* (South Bend, IN: St. Augustine's Press, 2000), 262, 277, 508.

23. Reich, *Sexual Revolution*, 10.

24. Reich, *Sexual Revolution*, 75.

The free society will provide ample room and security for the gratification of natural needs. Thus, it will not only not prohibit a love relationship between two adolescents of the opposite sex but will give it all
manner of social support. Such a society will not only not prohibit the
child's masturbation but, on the contrary, will probably conclude that
any adult who hinders the development of the child's sexuality should
be severely dealt with.[25]

The closing phrase of the above quotation is interesting because it makes
clear what Reich is really doing here. While asserting that the patriarchal
family is the single most important unit of ideological control for an oppressive and totalitarian regime, Reich also believes that the state must be
used to coerce families and, where necessary, actively punish those who
dissent from the sexual liberation being proposed. In short, the state has
the right to intervene in family matters because the family is potentially
the primary opponent of political liberation through its cultivation and
policing of traditional sexual codes.

Of course, it is generally accepted that when a child or an adolescent
is being seriously maltreated or abused by a parent, then the state has an
obligation to intervene. What is significant in Reich's comment is not so
much the principle of state intervention to stop abuse but the underlying
definition of abuse with which he is operating. It is a psychological one,
specifically one rooted in a highly sexualized psychology. Freud has here
been used to transform the classic understanding of oppression, one understood in material terms regarding the well-being of the body, to one
that really focuses on the well-being of the mind. And once oppression
becomes primarily psychological, it also becomes somewhat arbitrary
and subjective.

The importance of Reich's point here can scarcely be overestimated.
It has had a decisive influence on Western political thought, most obviously for the Left but, as it connects to the rise of a psychological conception of victimhood, for Western society in general. When oppression
comes to be thought of as primarily psychological, then victimhood

---

25. Reich, *Sexual Revolution*, 23.

becomes a potentially much broader—and much more subjective—category. This affects everything, from reasoning in Supreme Court cases to ethics to campus politics and beyond.[26]

Italian philosopher Augusto Del Noce noted this psychologizing of victimhood in his important essay "The Ascendance of Eroticism."[27] There he underscores the key connection between the understanding of the significance of sex and the radical transformation of left-wing politics. Del Noce quotes as part of his argument a passage from the preface to the 1945 edition of Reich's *Sexual Revolution*, which culminates in the following important statement:

> Social concepts of the nineteenth century which were defined purely in economic terms no longer fit the ideological stratifications in the cultural struggles of the twentieth century. In its simplest formulation: today's social struggles are being waged between those forces interested in the safeguarding and affirming of life and those whose interests lie in its destruction and negation.[28]

The affirmation of life is, of course, for Reich the same as the lifting of the sexual taboos that maintain the authoritarian culture of the patriarchal family and bourgeois society. Del Noce draws the obvious, though nonetheless significant, conclusion:

> It is clear that what today is called the left fights less and less in terms of class warfare, and more and more in terms of "warfare against repression," claiming that the struggle for the economic progress of the disadvantaged is included in this more general struggle, as if the two were inseparable.[29]

Del Noce wrote that sentence in 1970, but we can now see how prescient his observation was. Today, political discussion is dominated by talk of hate speech, microaggressions, and so on, all of which arise out of

---

26. See chap. 9 of this volume.

27. The essay, originally published in Italian in 1970, is included in the collection of Del Noce's writings in *The Crisis of Modernity*, ed. and trans. Carlo Lancelotti (Montreal: McGill-Queen's University Press, 2014), 157–86.

28. Reich, *Sexual Revolution*, xvi.

29. Del Noce, *Crisis of Modernity*, 166.

a culture in which psychological categories give the fundamental shape to what is understood to be oppressive. My grandfather might have felt oppressed in the 1930s by his inability at points to find a job or by the fact that he did not receive what he considered an honest day's pay for an honest day's work. Today, those basic economic categories of oppression still exist, but they are generally eclipsed in the media by discussions of psychologically oppressive actions: the refusal to bake a cake for a gay wedding, for example, does not push the gay couple into starvation or any other form of economic hardship; rather, it offends against their dignity and inflicts psychological harm by refusing to recognize them on their own terms. And that is regarded as very serious because it is politically oppressive in a world in which psychological categories have come to dominate discussion. Reich's Freudian focus on sex opens the way for precisely the kind of discourse of oppression that now touches so many other areas of life and forms an important part of the modern social imaginary.

This is why arguments about sex that default to statements such as "It is nobody's business what consenting adults do in the privacy of their own home" miss the point. Sex is no longer a private activity because sexuality is a constitutive element of public, social identity. Patterns of private sexual behavior are not simply private; they are public and political because they constitute a significant part of how our culture thinks of identity. And it is only through public acknowledgment of their legitimacy that those identities are recognized and legitimated. To outlaw, for example, gay sex or merely to tolerate it, is to outlaw or merely tolerate a certain identity. Both are ultimately forms of oppression, albeit the one more overtly so than the other.

Reich anticipates this thinking. To return to his statement about the need for society to support the sexual relationships of teenagers, it is clear that this also legitimates increasing government encroachment on the private sphere, both of the family and of the mind. The sexual education of the child is simply of too much social and political consequence to be left to the parents. After all, it is the parents as those in authority who actually constitute the problem. The family as traditionally understood needs to be dismantled.[30] It is stating the obvious to note that what Reich was arguing on this score in the 1930s is now the increasingly dominant view of our own contemporary society, where questions of childhood and adolescent sexuality and gender identity raise immediate and significant questions about the respective rights and responsibilities of parents and of the state.

Further, the logic of Reich's argument means that the holding of views on sexual matters that deviate from Reichian orthodoxy is not simply a matter of legitimate difference of opinion. Rather, it is profoundly political because it is both a sign of repression and a tool of the repressive state. For example, to deny one's teenage son the right to have sex with his girlfriend is to perpetuate the iniquitous and oppressive political structure that is built on the patriarchal family and its associated sexual regulations. Even to think that one has the right to corral the sexual behavior of one's teenage child represents an oppressive bourgeois mentality that must be opposed and rooted out. In Reich's world, it is a thought crime, to be uttered aloud at one's peril.

Anthony Giddens summarizes the connection between politics and sex in Reich as follows: "Reich believed that sociopolitical reform without sexual liberation is impossible: freedom and sexual health are the same thing."[31] If Freud identified happiness with sexual gratification, then the way to create a happy society, one untainted by selfishness and craven pursuit of power, was to allow for a maximum amount of sexual gratification. That was Reich's basic idea. The political question of freedom could therefore only be answered through sexual liberation.

Again, this is of great importance for understanding why sex is now so political and why even holding personally to traditional sexual codes

---

30. Del Noce's comment on Reich and the family is apposite: "But, what is the repressive social institution *par excellence*? To Reich it is the traditional monogamous family; and, from his standpoint, certainly he cannot be said to be wrong. Indeed, the idea of family is inseparable from the idea of tradition, from a heritage of truth that we must *tradere, hand on. Thus, the abolition of every meta-empirical order of truth requires that the family be dissolved.* No *merely sociological* consideration can justify keeping it." *Crisis of Modernity*, 161; emphasis original.

31. Anthony Giddens, *The Transformation of Intimacy: Sexuality, Love, and Eroticism in Modern Societies* (Stanford, CA: Stanford University Press, 1992), 163.

is regarded as dangerous. It might seem odd to a religious conservative that a call for chastity is seen as positively harmful to society, but that is because the religious conservative does not look at society through the type of lens that is provided by Reich and that is now an intuitive part of much political discourse. Yes, the sexual act may be the most private and intimate encounter two people ever have, but within the kind of framework offered by Reich, how that act is understood, policed, legislated, and recognized (or not) is the most pressing and public of political issues. Reich politicized sex and is thus an important harbinger of the world in which we now all have to live.

Reich and the Limits of Sexual Freedom

For all his calls for the demolition of traditional sexual codes designed to support the traditional family, it is noteworthy that Reich is not a complete sexual anarchist. He does have some kind of moral sexual code, albeit arguably a somewhat incoherent one. As an example of an inappropriate sexual relationship, he takes the case of a fifteen-year-old boy who wants to have sex with girls. If the object of this boy's desire is a thirteen-year-old girl, Reich would see such a relationship not only as permissible but as one that should be encouraged and actively supported. Not all sexual relationships for this boy, however, would be legitimate, and Reich offers this example to demonstrate his point:

> If the same boy of fifteen were to induce three-year-old girls into sexual games or if he tried to seduce a girl of his own age against her will, such conduct would be antisocial. It would indicate that he is neurotically inhibited in his capacity to choose a partner his own age.[32]

This is, of course, assertion and not argument. Why pedophilia would be outlawed as neurotic and antisocial is not at all evident from Reich's thinking. Perhaps the issue of consent is important from a social perspective, as the second example implies, but then that raises the question of the nature of consent—a philosophically, politically, culturally, and

---

32. Reich, *Sexual Revolution*, 24.

legally complicated matter, particularly, one would have thought, for a psychoanalytic Marxist. If the issue is consent, then the first obvious objection is that children are often made to do things to which they do not consent, from receiving immunizations and eating their vegetables to attending kindergarten and having to go to bed at a certain time. Why should sex be privileged as requiring consent? Further, how does Reich know that his own objection to pedophilia is not simply a holdover from the sexual mores of the capitalist society he so despises, with its need to keep children carefully corralled within the oppressive structure of the traditional family? Could Reich's own objection here not be based simply on his own false sexual consciousness, a vestige of bourgeois morality determined by the times in which he lives? Conveniently, Reich does not care to parse the issue at all but simply roots his objection in the age difference of the participants and their status relative to the process of puberty.

Just a few lines later he makes this dramatic statement:

> The existence of strict moral principles has invariably signified that the biological, and specifically the sexual, needs of man were not being satisfied. Every moral regulation is in itself sex-negating, and all compulsory morality is life-negating. The social revolution has no more important task than finally to enable human beings to realize their full potentialities and find gratification in life.[33]

This statement is quite unequivocal: strict moral principles negate sex and negate life, and the demolition of such repressive sexual codes is the primary task of revolutionary politics. It is therefore hard to understand how this is at all consistent with Reich's apparent moral distaste for pedophilia. But then surely that is the key: Reich's objections to it are ultimately ones of taste. The Rousseau-Hume-Shelley pattern of aesthetic taste as moral truth is alive and well in Freudian Marxism, granted a veneer of apparent objectivity by being couched in the language of psychoanalysis and "scientific" socialism.

---

33. Reich, *Sexual Revolution*, 25.

The question of taste touches on another interesting implication of Reich's thinking that helps explain some of what we now witness in contemporary society: the matter of modesty. It might be tempting to relativize the sexual revolution by interpreting it as essentially redefining the boundaries of traditional concepts such as modesty. For example, where once it was regarded immodest for a woman to wear a skirt that revealed her knees, now this is generally acceptable. What constitutes modesty has simply been broadened, but the concept itself remains. Yet to see the sexual revolution that Reich proposes as merely calling for a revision of the concept of modesty would be to underestimate his proposal in a startling way. Reich's revolution does not want to redefine modesty; rather, it wants to outlaw the concept altogether, for the very idea depends on a framework of sexual taboos that are in themselves oppressive and to be demolished. Del Noce points this out in "The Ascendance of Eroticism," and it is perhaps one of the most socially significant elements of the sexual revolution. To be truly human requires that one is immodest, for to be otherwise—to be modest—is to be abnormal. I will return to this point in the discussion of pornography in chapter 8.[34]

Reich ultimately marginalized himself as he indulged in stranger and stranger obsessions. Even Freud, for whom Reich worked for a while, regarded him as odd and something of an obsessive sexual maverick.[35] In later years he became interested in UFOs, developed a machine for concentrating sexual energy, and was eventually imprisoned in Pennsylvania for fraud. He died there, still in prison, in 1957, paranoid and widely dismissed as crazy. Yet the insanity of his disastrous end should not detract from the huge impact that his thinking has had on the relationship between Freud, Marx, and revolutionary politics. It should also not distract from how his thinking in many ways adumbrated the popular connection between sexual liberation and political freedom that is now

---

34. Del Noce, *Crisis of Modernity*, 158.

35. Writing to Lou Andreas-Salomé in 1928, Freud declared, "We have here a Dr. Reich, a worthy but impetuous young man, passionately devoted to his hobby-horse who now salutes in the genital orgasm the antidote to every neurosis." Quoted in Élisabeth Roudinesco, *Freud in His Time and Ours*, trans. Catherine Porter (Cambridge, MA: Harvard University Press, 2016), 340.

the presupposition of many of the debates of our own age. A number of the basic assumptions of post-1968 modern Western society find their initial articulation in his works of the 1930s.

Herbert Marcuse and Surplus Repression

While Reich was only loosely associated with the Frankfurt School, Herbert Marcuse, along with Theodor Adorno, was one of the school's two leading lights in its efforts to reconstruct Marxism against the background of the twin disasters of Soviet Stalinism and of the proletariat's failure to respond appropriately to the various crises in capitalism that marked the twentieth century. Indeed, Marcuse became a key figure in the student unrest that characterized 1968, and he exerted a deep influence on many younger radicals and thinkers, including Angela Davis and Fredric Jameson.[36]

Marcuse's two most influential books are his critique of consumer society, *One-Dimensional Man* (1964), and his appropriation of Freud for Marxist social analysis and politics, *Eros and Civilization* (1955).[37] Both became standard fare for the '68ers. The former addressed the question as to why the cheap satisfactions of consumerism seemed to have defused any grand political aspirations toward great political freedom in the West. But it is the latter, embodying Marcuse's appropriation of Freud for revolutionary politics, that is of particular interest here.

Marcuse is critical of Reich's work because of what he perceives to be a failure to make a necessary distinction. Both men fundamentally agree with the general principle of Freud's understanding of the relationship between civilization as now constituted and sexual repression. But against this shared background, there is an important difference between the approaches of the two men. Reich tends to see untrammeled sexual liberation in itself as the necessary constituent element of political freedom,

---

36. See the essays in Andrew T. Lamas, Todd Wolfson, and Peter N. Funke, eds., *The Great Refusal: Herbert Marcuse and Contemporary Social Movements* (Philadelphia: Temple University Press, 2017). Angela Davis contributed the foreword to this volume.

37. Herbert Marcuse, *One-Dimensional Man: Studies in the Ideology of Advanced Industrial Society* (London: Routledge, 2002); Marcuse, *Eros and Civilization: A Philosophical Inquiry into Freud* (Boston: Beacon, 1966).

even though (as noted above) he is somewhat arbitrary in how he identifies the limits of legitimate sexual expression. Marcuse, however, considers this notion of sexual liberation to lack necessary nuance.[38]

To understand Marcuse on this matter, it is important to grasp two basic concepts of his thinking: that of the performance principle and that of surplus repression.

As with Reich, Marcuse views Freud as failing to see the historically conditioned nature of forms of repression because he lacked the Marxist insight into the impact of socioeconomic relations on how people think and act. Freud's thought was insufficiently historicist in method, abstracting human nature and desire from its historical conditions. Thus, while the concept of repression is a universal constituent of civilization, the specific forms of repression at any given moment in time are connected to the specific forms of civilization that exist at that particular point in history. Here, however, Marcuse makes a further distinction, that between domination and the rational exercise of authority. The latter is necessary in any form of social organization, if there is not to be anarchy. It is based on knowledge and confined to the organization of those matters necessary for the well-being of the whole of society. Domination, by contrast, is the power exerted over others by a particular group within society in order to maintain its own privileged social position. In short, the rational exercise of authority has the goal of the common good. It is exemplified, for instance, in the bureaucratic administration of resources to achieve the best results for society as a whole. Domination, by contrast, refers to the exercise of power for the good of a specific group. And it is domination with which Marcuse, as a Marxist, is most interested, because domination constitutes what he calls the specific historical form of Freud's *reality principle*.[39]

In his argument about civilization, Freud argued that the pleasure principle needed to be tamed by what he dubbed the reality principle.

---

38. Marcuse dismisses Reich in a single paragraph, expressing appreciation for his insights into repression but then dismissing him for his rejection of Freud's notion of the death instinct and for the "wild and fantastic hobbies" (UFOs, sex-energy machine) of his later years. *Eros and Civilization*, 239.

39. Marcuse, *Eros and Civilization*, 36.

This was the form of the trade-off between sexual satisfaction and civilized life, rooted in such basic matters as scarcity, the need for survival, bearable common life, and so on. What Marcuse does is historicize this concept, pointing to the fact that the reality principle might itself look different at different stages of society's economic development. Marcuse was, after all, a Marxist who was particularly sensitive to the Hegelian roots of Marx's thought and therefore to historicist thinking.[40]

For Marcuse, economies motivated by private profit will have a different reality principle from those that are centrally planned. Each will cultivate particular forms of behavior in order to ensure the outcome desired by the dominant class. And these historical instantiations of the reality principle Marcuse refers to as the "performance principle," a term that brings out nicely the constructed nature of what it involves.[41] There is no transcendent form of the performance principle, only specific local manifestations of behavior shaped by the economic context.[42]

And this performance principle has a significant impact on sexual relations in that these are part of the behavior that is designed to serve the economic status quo. In fact, Marcuse argues that "the organization of sexuality reflects the basic features of the performance principle and its organization of society."[43] One does not need to be a Marcusan Marxist to acknowledge this point in its most generic sense, that sexual codes connect to the economic structure of society in general. We noted earlier that Engels was aware of how the notion of the family had developed in relation to social and economic relations. And we might look at our own society and compare it to that of one hundred years ago: the fact that many women now go out to work and enjoy financial independence means that our understanding of the relationship between men and

---

40. The reconnection of Marxism with its Hegelian roots was a significant part of the early Frankfurt School's work, as exemplified in, for example, Erich Fromm, *Marx's Concept of Man* (London: Continuum, 2004). Marcuse himself sees precedent for his understanding of the historical development of domination in relation to self-consciousness in Hegel's *Phenomenology of Spirit*. See Marcuse, *Eros and Civilization*, 113–18.

41. Giddens explains, "[Marcuse's] performance principle is the principle implied in facing, not 'reality' as such, but the (impermanent) historical reality of a particular social order." *Transformation of Intimacy*, 165.

42. Marcuse, *Eros and Civilization*, 34–35.

43. Marcuse, *Eros and Civilization*, 48.

women and the roles that each plays in the family—indeed, our whole understanding of what constitutes normal family life—has changed dramatically over the last century in concert with changing economic expectations. The type of family that a society considers normative stands in positive relation to the economic possibilities that that society represents. And of course, a normative understanding of what constitutes a family is inextricably connected to normative codes of sexual conduct.

But Marcuse does not stop there. He then draws Freud into the specifically political question by claiming that, in addition to the repression needed for the rational exercise of power, there is what he dubs "surplus repression," which is the result of domination. In short, the ruling, dominant class imposes repression well beyond that which is strictly necessary for the rational management of resources for all. This is because the dominant class has a vested interest in maintaining its own special status and control over others. And true to his positive appreciation of Freud, Marcuse sees as central to domination sexual desire and the need for any given culture to curb this desire in such a way as to preserve itself.[44]

Thus, as with Reich, the demolition of bourgeois society is predicated on the demolition of the sexual regulations that maintain it. Marcuse describes the situation this way:

> Within the total structure of repressed personality, surplus-repression is that portion which is the result of specific societal conditions sustained in the interest of domination. The extent of the surplus-repression provides the standard of measurement: the smaller it is, the less repressive is the stage of civilization.[45]

In theory, therefore, Marcuse offers a more nuanced view of the sexual liberation of humanity than that of Reich. Some level of sexual repression is necessary for the maintenance of society. The problem is that the sexual mores of late capitalism, focused as they are on the maintenance of monogamy and the patriarchal family, are actually no longer as necessary as they once were. Thus, their continuation has more to

---

44. Marcuse, *Eros and Civilization*, 38–44.
45. Marcuse, *Eros and Civilization*, 87–88; cf. 36.

do with the bourgeoisie controlling the proletariat than with the ratio-nal organization of society. Taboos and the concept of perversions are means by which the bourgeoisie demonizes any type of sexual behavior that threatens this control.[46] And behavior deemed by bourgeois society to be perverted or deviant is therefore by inference actually part of the subversive protest against the status quo. Sex focused on procreation and family is the repressive weapon of bourgeois capitalist society. And free love and untrammeled sexual experimentation are a central part of the revolutionary liberation of society.[47]

The problem is, as Alasdair MacIntyre points out in a pungent critique of Marcuse's thought, that Marcuse does not actually provide any vision of what this sexual liberation might look like.[48] At least Reich offered some specific examples—for example, that of teenagers being helped to have sexual relationships through the positive support of wider society and therefore not being subject to the authoritarian control that comes with the monogamous, patriarchal family unit. Marcuse, by contrast, never rises above the level of arcane references to various sexual perversions and taboos.[49] Nor will it suffice to excuse him by playing the eschatological escapologists' favorite card—"We will not know what the end of history looks like until the end of his-tory arrives"—because we cannot really know that the current regime of sexual practices and taboos is in fact repressive unless we have access to a vision of what liberated, unrepressed sexual freedom might actu-ally look like.

Nevertheless, even with this gaping lacuna in Marcuse's manifesto, we can say with confidence that, as with Freud, he sees sex at the center of what it means to be human. With Marx's historicism as foundation, Marcuse then (like Reich) makes sexual codes and practices fundamental to understanding the political nature of culture and of humanity at any given point in time. That he cannot describe what the end of history will

---

46. Marcuse, *Eros and Civilization*, 48–51, 202–3.
47. Marcuse, *Eros and Civilization*, 49–50.
48. Alasdair MacIntyre, *Herbert Marcuse: An Exposition and a Polemic* (New York: Viking, 1970), 50–51.
49. Marcuse, *Eros and Civilization*, 202–3.

specifically involve in terms of socially sanctioned sexual behavior may be a lethal flaw in his argument but does not seem to have unnerved him for a second.[50]

Yet if the sexual details of the political eschaton are somewhat murky in Marcuse's thought, the overall purpose of his argument is clear. Reich's immediate background was the rise of Nazism and therefore the need to explain the way one of the most technically and culturally advanced nations on the planet submitted so easily to barbaric totalitarianism. Marcuse, however, having left Germany in the early 1930s to escape Nazism, spent much of his career teaching in the United States. His real concern, then, was somewhat different from that of Reich. Like his colleague Adorno, he wanted to provide the tools for a critique of America and American capitalism that debunked the Cold War notion that the United States represented the triumph of individual freedom as opposed to the oppressive statism of the Soviet Union. Drawing on a well-worn literary analogy, we might say that the two men were aiming at the two alternative models of political oppression: Reich was targeting the kind of world envisaged in George Orwell's *1984*, where the jackboot crushed opposition, and Marcuse that of Aldous Huxley's *Brave New World*, where pleasure lulled the population into political inertia. Both were addressing the psychological lacuna in Marx's own thinking, but Marcuse did so in the context of postwar consumerism and material prosperity: Where was the political self-consciousness of the proletariat to come from in a world in which the class struggle seemed to have been defused by a surfeit of consumer goods?

This is where the issue of sexuality and the issue of politics fused in Marcuse's thought to form a potent revolutionary mix that has come to exert significant influence over today's political discourse and behavior. The notions that political freedom is sexual freedom and that shattering

---

50. See Leszek Kołakowski's comment on Marcuse: "He seeks to provide a philosophical basis for a tendency already present in our civilization, which aims at destroying that civilization from within for the sake of an apocalypse of the New World of Happiness of which, in the nature of things, no description can be given." Needless to say, Kołakowski is not commending this as a point of strength. *Main Currents*, 3:415.

heterosexual norms is a vital part of transforming society for the better are now intuitive cultural orthodoxies.

Marcuse and the Wider Implications of the Sexual Revolution

To follow Rousseau is to make identity psychological. To follow Freud is to make psychology, and thus identity, sexual. To mesh this combination with Marx is to make identity—and therefore sex—political. And, at the risk of offering a truism, the politics that is produced thereby has a distinctive character precisely because the reality that it thinks it is addressing is at base a psychological one. To transform society politically, then, one must transform society sexually and psychologically, a point that places psychological categories at the heart of revolutionary political discourse. Where once oppression was seen in terms of economic realities (e.g., poverty, lack of property) or legal categories (e.g., slavery, lack of freedom), now the matter is more subtle because it relates to issues of psychology and self-consciousness. The political sphere is internalized and subjectivized. And Marcuse was not slow to see this or draw the necessary conclusions for revolutionary action.

Marcuse's approach to politics is summarized neatly in his essay "Repressive Tolerance" (1965).[51] The oxymoron of the title reflects the provocative thesis of the work as a whole: the notion of tolerance and its concomitant elements, such as freedom of speech, is really a sham that serves the interests of the status quo and thus of those who hold power in the present and wish to defuse any significant challenges to their position.[52] Indeed, the traditional liberal concept of tolerance is part of the false consciousness that the ruling bourgeois class has cultivated in order to maintain its power. Through the propagandizing of the rulers, the oppressed essentially internalize this and other values, assuming them to be natural truths and not realizing that they are ideological constructs

---

51. "Repressive Tolerance" was reprinted, with an afterword reflecting on the student unrest of 1968, in Robert Paul Wolff, Barrington Moore Jr., and Herbert Marcuse, *A Critique of Pure Tolerance* (Boston: Beacon, 1970), 81–123.

52. E.g., Marcuse states, "I call this non-partisan tolerance 'abstract' or 'pure' inasmuch as it refrains from taking sides—but in doing so it actually protects the established machinery of discrimination." "Repressive Tolerance," 85.

designed to make them politically impotent and in so doing render themselves nothing more than passive dupes within the system.[53]

One of the obvious implications of this perspective is that educational institutions become key places for dismantling this false consciousness and encouraging a true understanding of reality. In a remarkable passage, Marcuse expresses his view on education as follows:

> Surely, no government can be expected to foster its own subversion, but in a democracy such a right is vested in the people (i.e. in the majority of the people). This means that the ways should not be blocked on which a subversive majority could develop, and if they are blocked by organized repression and indoctrination, their reopening may require apparently undemocratic means. They would include the withdrawal of toleration of speech and assembly from groups and movements which promote aggressive policies, armament, chauvinism, discrimination on the grounds of race and religion, or which oppose the extension of public services, social security, medical care, etc. Moreover, the restoration of freedom of thought may necessitate new and rigid restrictions on teaching and practices in the educational institutions which, by their very methods and concepts, serve to enclose the mind within the established universe of discourse and behavior—thereby precluding a prior rational evaluation of the alternatives.[54]

For anyone brought up to consider freedom of speech a virtue, this statement is shocking and profoundly counterintuitive: How can the restoration of freedom of thought be advanced by "new and rigid restrictions" on what can and cannot be said and done in educational institutions? And yet it makes perfect sense if one accepts Marcuse's underlying premises. The struggle to cultivate the right form of political consciousness or psychology means that things such as education and speech need to be carefully regulated in order to ensure the correct outcome. In a world in which psychology perverted by false

---

53. In Marcuse's words, "Universal toleration becomes questionable when its rationale no longer prevails, when tolerance is administered to manipulated and indoctrinated individuals who parrot, as their own, the opinion of their masters, for whom heteronomy has become autonomy." "Repressive Tolerance," 90.

54. Marcuse, "Repressive Tolerance," 100–101.

consciousness is the key problem, oppression becomes a psychological category. This means that words and ideas then come to be the most powerful weapons available—for good and for ill. Thus, it becomes necessary to make sure that good words and ideas are not simply promoted but are, if possible, enforced and given a monopoly in public discourse. Why, after all, would bad words and ideas be allowed when their only purpose is to inflict psychological damage on and cause oppression of the marginalized, the dispossessed, and other victims of the ruling class's practices of domination?

Unless we understand this point, we will not understand the increasing popularity of the view that free speech is itself not simply *not* a political virtue but is in fact positively harmful. Few of the campus protesters of recent years may have read Marcuse, but the basic ideas that he promulgated have penetrated the popular consciousness in such a way that challenges to classical liberal thinking are commonplace and often well received.[55]

Of course, there is an obvious elitism to Marcuse's proposals and indeed to the politics of the New Left that takes its cue from him. The Left, and it alone, is competent to see through the false consciousness of Western consumerist culture and to perceive what the political realities truly are. And only the Left has a monopoly of knowledge as to what political strategies must be adopted to advance the cultural revolution necessary for freedom. It is therefore no surprise that Marcuse's work is full of disdain for American popular culture, which he sees as promoting the false consciousness required to preserve bourgeois society. It tricks the populace into thinking that the status quo is in their best interest. Buying consumer products from a market that continually reinvents itself through built-in obsolescence, through creating needs that it then satisfies only temporarily as it generates new ones, distracts the individual from the harsher realities of life and the oppressive nature of the regime. It gives cheap and ultimately transient pleasure to people to keep

---

55. For further discussion of free speech on college campuses, see "Campus Anticulture," p. 325, in chap. 9.

them in a state of political passivity and acquiescence to the established authorities.[56]

In his sneering at this culture, his claims to be the one who truly understands it, and his view of its impact, Marcuse also thereby ironically shows his disdain for ordinary people. It is clear that he does not think they have the critical faculties necessary to resist the ideological propaganda that television and the media use to shape their minds. Within a Marcusan framework, the election victory of a populist such as Donald Trump would be a perfect example of how this confidence trick plays out among ordinary people who happily vote against their own class interests. So who, one might ask, knows the truth and would thus be able to decide what should be taught in schools and universities? The answer, of course, is Herbert Marcuse and those who agree with him. Marxism's notion of false consciousness is in essence a sophisticated rationale for justifying not simply a type of intellectual snobbery but also a form of gnostic knowledge, such that all and any criticism of Marcuse and company is merely sure evidence of the false consciousness of the critic. And how is this gnostic knowledge to be imposed? In the short term, by destabilizing the status quo through the constant critiquing of dominant narratives that support the established order and through transgressive actions, such as the practical shattering of bourgeois sexual codes. Ultimately, one assumes, this will all require coercion by government force. Marcuse may have started out in part motivated by a desire to present an alternative to Stalinism, but he really ends up practically in much the same totalitarian place. The only real difference is that Marcuse is certain that he has the truth and just as certain that Stalin does not.[57]

---

56. Marcuse states, "The growing productivity of labor creates an increasing surplus-product which, whether privately or centrally appropriated and distributed, allows an increased consumption—notwithstanding the increased diversion of productivity. As long as this constellation prevails, it reduces the use-value of freedom; there is no reason to insist on self-determination if the administered life is the comfortable and even the 'good' life. This is the rational and material ground for the unification of opposites, for one-dimensional political behavior. On this ground, the transcending political forces within society are arrested, and qualitative change appears possible only as a change from without." *One-Dimensional Man*, 53. To translate this statement into English, as long as people are allowed to buy the things they want and live a comfortable life, they will not be politically self-conscious and will passively accept the status quo.

57. Again, a comment by Kołakowski is apposite here: "The only feature of the millennium that we can deduce from Marcuse's work is that society is to be ruled despotically by an enlightened group

Totalitarian elitism aside, the main significance of Marcusan politics for us lies in the way it makes sex politically important, as did Reich before him. Even though Marcuse does not mention sexual minorities in his list of the oppressed in the above quotation, he understands that sexual codes are foundational to the structure of society, which means that sexual identity is clearly going to be part of precisely the same program of educational reform that he proposes. In fact, it *should* form a major part because the dominant group maintains its power in the status quo primarily by repressing certain expressions of sexual identity.

The Psychological Transformation of Feminism

If appropriating elements of Freud's thought by Marxists such as Reich and Marcuse is an important development in the politicization of the psychological self, then other thinkers and philosophical traditions also played important roles in this move as well, as the development of feminist thinking in the second half of the twentieth century indicates. Indeed, it is in feminist theory that the radical implications of the anti-essentialism and critical approaches of thinkers such as Nietzsche and Marx come to fruition. It is in feminism that a fundamental challenge is issued regarding what might have seemed to be intuitively the most obvious fact about human beings—that they exist as two sexes, male and female, with differences and distinctions clearly rooted in biology.

Nietzsche's antimetaphysical philosophy demanded that human beings become self-creators and thereby transcend themselves. This theme was picked up and developed by one of the influential philosophical streams of the mid-twentieth century, that of existentialism, most famously associated with the work of Martin Heidegger and Jean-Paul Sartre. Sartre's famous saying "Existence precedes essence" captures the heart of this philosophy beautifully: to be a "human" in the sense of

---

whose chief title to do so is that its members will have realized in themselves the unity of Logos and Eros, and thrown off the vexatious authority of logic, mathematics, and the empirical sciences. . . . Marcuse's thought is a curious mixture of feudal contempt for technology, the exact sciences, and democratic values, plus a nebulous revolutionism devoid of positive content." *Main Currents*, 3:415–16.

merely existing as a particular genetic phenomenon is really nothing; rather, men and women are condemned to be free, to move themselves by their decisions and their intentional actions into the future. While a dog is a consciousness, it is a creature of instinct; men and women, however, are able to constitute themselves by their self-conscious, intentional actions.

Yet for all of its popularity at the time, Sartre's existentialism now looks more like a museum piece or a staging post to later schools of French theory than a living philosophy in its own right. As for contemporary relevance, it is the thought of his longtime companion and lover, Simone de Beauvoir, that is of far more significance, especially as expressed in her major text of feminist theory, *The Second Sex* (1949).[58]

Feminism in the early twentieth century operated along lines of what we might characterize as the concerns of economic man, to use Rieff's terminology, with labor law, pay, and voting rights being the central points of concern. With de Beauvoir, a new, more philosophical and psychological form of feminist thinking emerges.

The Second Sex is a text of massive historical and philosophical learning. The first volume, *Facts and Myths*, deals with the notion of woman in terms of what we might call the great metanarratives—biological, psychological, and economic/material; then the history of the status of women; and finally, mythology, that is, the cultural representation of women via literature. The burden of this first volume is to show that the standard metanarratives of what it means to be a woman cannot explain the diversity of what it actually is to be a woman in various cultures, that the notion of womanhood has changed over time, and that the various literary representations of women reveal themselves to be ideological constructs, not reflections of essential reality.

This discussion sets the stage for de Beauvoir's dramatic opening sentence in the second volume, *Lived Experience*:

---

58. Simone de Beauvoir, *The Second Sex*, trans. Constance Borde and Sheila Malovany-Chevallier, with an introduction by Judith Thurman (New York: Vintage, 2011).

One is not born, but rather becomes, woman. No biological, psychic, or economic destiny defines the figure that the human female takes on in society; it is civilization as a whole that elaborates this intermediary product between the male and the eunuch that is called feminine.[59]

This statement is consonant with much of the thinking I have outlined in previous chapters, which assumes the fundamental artificiality of human identity as formed by social relations. One might describe it perhaps as an extreme application of Rousseau's notion that it is society that civilizes us, that makes us into who we are. Marx, too, regarded our identity as the result of our social relations, specifically as determined by our place in the economic structure of society. Above all, de Beauvoir's statement connects to Freud and to the advent of psychoanalysis. Indeed, de Beauvoir opens her chapter on psychoanalysis in *The Second Sex* with the following paragraph:

> The enormous advance psychoanalysis made over psychophysiology is in its consideration that no factor intervenes in psychic life without having taken on human meaning; it is not the body-object described by scientists that exists concretely but the body lived by the subject. The female is a woman, insofar as she feels herself as such. Some essential biological givens are not part of her lived situation: for example, the structure of the ovum is not reflected in it; by contrast, an organ of slight biological importance like the clitoris plays a primary role in it. Nature does not define woman: it is she who defines herself by reclaiming nature for herself in her affectivity.[60]

While de Beauvoir is no uncritical supporter of psychoanalysis, she here acknowledges the importance of Freud for the study of women. By shifting attention away from empirical biological facts to the inner psychological life, he opened up entire new vistas for reflection—something that de Beauvoir and subsequent feminists were to develop in radical directions.[61]

---

59. De Beauvoir, *The Second Sex*, 283.
60. De Beauvoir, *The Second Sex*, 49.
61. De Beauvoir was, of course, aware that Freud himself was not a particularly profound thinker when it came to the matter of women, regarding them as rather inferior versions of men. See *The Second Sex*, 50.

What is of significance for this study is the way that de Beauvoir makes a clear separation between gender and sex. The latter is biological, while the former is psychological. Consonant with her basic commitment to the anti-essentialist assumptions of existentialism, she here brings the implications of these assumptions to bear not simply on the notion of human nature but also on the basic biological division between the sexes. Being a woman is something that is learned through assimilating society's expectations of what a woman should be.

This separation of sex and gender is entirely consistent with patterns of thought I have noted previously, particularly the anti-essentialist thinking of Nietzsche and the implications of Hegel's historicizing of human nature, which in turn underlies the thought of Marx and Marcuse. But it is also perhaps the most radical move in the narrative so far. If human nature is not something we are given but something we do or something we determine for ourselves via our free decisions and actions, why should we tie gender identity to an objective physiological basis? Such would seem to be a move motivated more by the demands of society than by any mysterious essence in which the individual must inevitably participate. Indeed, in the passage above, it is noteworthy that to be a woman is to feel that one is a woman, a notion that has obvious roots in the psychologized self and continuities with today's issue of transgenderism.

Again, as with Reich and Marcuse, we see here the way that politics and a psychologized understanding of the self come together. De Beauvoir is clearly operating within the same post-Freudian framework, seeing oppression as a basically psychological category and the result of the structures of society. Central to this point is the role of women in childbearing: it is, says de Beauvoir with heavy sarcasm, reproduction that allows women to fulfill their natural destiny.[62] And this points to another significant element in her argument: the role of technology.

---

62. De Beauvoir states, "It is through motherhood that woman fully achieves her physiological destiny; that is her 'natural' vocation, since her whole organism is directed toward the perpetuation of the species." *The Second Sex*, 524.

In chapter 5, I noted Marx's remark in *The Communist Manifesto* that technology, in the form of the automation of labor, would inevitably relativize and then eliminate the differences between the sexes.[63] In context, it is clearly little more than the relativizing of the physical strength of men and women that he had in mind; his was not a world that even dreamed of the possibilities offered by hormone treatment and gender reassignment surgery. But as twentieth-century Marxist thought shifted into the psychological realm, the scope for technological possibilities to elide and then eliminate gender differences beyond the area of the workplace emerges. And de Beauvoir stands as a signal and early example of one providing a theoretical framework for such.

For her, the main issue is birth control. This is hardly surprising: reproduction is the most obvious evidence that there is a clear distinction in function between men and women that is rooted in biology. It also has obvious implications for personal behavior. To put it crudely, men have always been more sexually free than women because they are able to have sex with whomever they please and never run the risk of conception. Promiscuity without penalty has long been a male possibility, which has become available to women only with easy access to the pill and abortion. And given the way that sex, from Shelley and Blake to Reich and Marcuse, became increasingly associated with notions of freedom, it seems in retrospect to have been inevitable that a woman's control of her own reproductive function would eventually become a matter of pressing political concern. De Beauvoir summarizes her position on the importance of reproductive technology as follows:

> With artificial insemination, the evolution that will permit humanity to master the reproductive function comes to completion. These changes have tremendous importance for woman in particular; she can reduce the number of pregnancies and rationally integrate them into her life, instead of being their slave. During the nineteenth century, woman in

---

63. Cf. the comment by de Beauvoir in a 1976 interview in the journal *Society*: "As technology expands—technology being the power of the brain and not of the brawn—the male rationale that women are the weaker sex and hence must play a secondary role can no longer be logically maintained." Simone de Beauvoir, interview by John Gerassi, "The Second Sex 25 Years Later," *Society* (January–February 1976), https://www.marxists.org/reference/subject/ethics/de-beauvoir/1976/interview.htm.

her turn is freed from nature; she wins control of her body. Relieved of a great number of reproductive servitudes, she can take on the economic roles open to her, roles that would ensure her control over her own person.[64]

Both the content and the tone of this statement are significant. As to the content, it is clear that freedom for economic activity is understood by de Beauvoir as freedom from the (natural) consequences of sexual activity. We see here that which is now a basic given of the politics of our own day: reproductive rights are rights precisely because of the nature of the freedom that is presupposed.[65]

As to the tone, de Beauvoir's rhetoric reinforces the idea that biology is ultimately regarded as a form of tyranny, a potentially alienating form of external authority. Rather than seeing reproduction as the fulfillment—or at least a fulfillment—of what it means to be a woman, de Beauvoir sees it instead as a potential obstacle to the identity of any individual woman. The body is something to be overcome; its authority is to be rejected; biology is to be transcended by the use of technology; who or what woman really *is* is not her chromosomes or her physiology; rather, it is something that she becomes, either as an act of free choice or because society coerces her into conformity with its expectations. Reich and Marcuse's assault on sexual codes as constitutive of bourgeois tyranny find their counterpart in de Beauvoir's assault on the idea that biological differences between men and women should exert decisive influence on their respective roles. Everything, even the male-female binary, must be revised in the world of the psychologized self.

This distinction between gender and sex is now a basic element of contemporary notions of identity. The whole transgender question depends

---

64. De Beauvoir, *The Second Sex*, 139.

65. See de Beauvoir's comment on childbearing: "There is no way to directly oblige a woman to give birth: all that can be done is to enclose her in situations where motherhood is her only option: laws or customs impose marriage on her, anticonception measures and abortion are banned, divorce is forbidden." *The Second Sex*, 67. Though de Beauvoir would presumably allow that a woman may *choose* to conceive even in a feminist utopia, the language she uses about childbearing is typically so negative that it is hard not to regard her as resenting the fact that women can produce children and men cannot.

on it, for if sex and gender are inextricably connected, then a mismatch between what one is biologically and who one is psychologically must inevitably be regarded as a dysfunction of the mind. Once the two are detached from each other—something that can only really be plausible in a world in which psychology rather than biology is seen as fundamentally determinative of identity—then the problem becomes one of the body, to be treated with medication and surgery. Technology therefore makes the whole claim plausible. Technology, one might even say, defines ontology.

Catholic thinker Michael Hanby makes precisely this point when summarizing the connection between technology and the philosophical attitude to biology that feminism (and, he argues, homosexuality) involves:

> Underlying the technological conquest of human biology, whether in its gay or feminist form, is a dualism which bi-furcates the person into a meaningless mechanical body made of malleable "stuff" and the affective or technological will that presides over it. The person as an integrated whole falls through the chasm. This is the foundation of the now orthodox distinction between "sex" which is "merely biological" and "gender" which is socially constructed, as well as the increasingly pervasive (and relentlessly promoted) idea that freedom means our self-creation of both.[66]

At the heart of de Beauvoir's feminism—indeed, at the heart of any system that makes a hard distinction between biology and gender—is a metaphysical (or, perhaps better, antimetaphysical) commitment to denying the authority of the physical body and its significance for personal identity. That is a dramatic move, and as de Beauvoir well knew (and Hanby points out), it can be sustained only on the basis of technological power.[67]

We can see the logical extension of de Beauvoir's thought in the writing of another second-wave feminist, Shulamith Firestone. Her book *The*

---

66. Michael Hanby, "The Brave New World of Same-Sex Marriage: A Decisive Moment in the Triumph of Technology over Humanity," *The Federalist*, February 19, 2014, https://thefederalist.com /2014/02/19/the-brave-new-world-of-same-sex-marriage/.

67. Earlier in the same *Federalist* article, Hanby makes the striking claim that "the sexual revolution is, at bottom, the technological revolution and its perpetual war against natural limits applied externally to the body and internally to our self-understanding."

Dialectic of Sex: The Case for Feminist Revolution (1970) draws on both Marx and Reich, among others, to make what might arguably be called the most consistent application of Reichian ideas to a political cause such that even the most basic elements of traditional social organization will be abolished. The following passage is worth quoting in full:

> And just as the end goal of socialist revolution was not only the elimination of the economic class privilege but of the economic class distinction itself, so the end goal of feminist revolution must be, unlike that of the first feminist movement, not just the elimination of male privilege but of the sex distinction itself: genital differences between human beings would no longer matter culturally. (A reversion to an unobstructed pansexuality—Freud's "polymorphous perversity"—would probably supersede hetero/homo/bi-sexuality.) The reproduction of the species by one sex for the benefit of both would be replaced by (at least the option of) artificial reproduction: children would be born to both sexes equally or independently of either, however one chooses to look at it; the dependence of the child on the mother (and vice versa) would give way to a greatly shortened dependence on a small group of others in general, and any remaining inferiority to adults in physical strength would be compensated for culturally. The division of labour would be ended by the elimination of labour altogether (through cybernetics). The tyranny of the biological family would be broken.[68]

Firestone published this passage in 1970, at a point in time when the predictions it contains should have looked like sheer lunacy to anyone reading it, given that the technological developments required for its vision to be conceivable were then unavailable. Notice the various elements that she says will be swept away—that *must* be swept away—in the revolution. First, the distinction between genders based on the physical difference of genitalia will be eliminated. That was implicit in de Beauvoir but is now made explicit as something necessary for true liberation. Second, the norm of heterosexual sex will be replaced by polymorphous pansexuality—essentially a free-for-all in which sex acts

---

68. Shulamith Firestone, *The Dialectic of Sex: The Case for Feminist Revolution* (1970; repr., New York: Farrar, Straus and Giroux, 2003), 11.

are no longer constrained by heteronomous moral codes built around traditional heterosexual norms. Again, de Beauvoir was herself bisexual, and *The Second Sex* contains appreciative discussion of lesbianism and criticism of Freud on that very point.[69] Third, reproduction will, via the application of technology, be available to both men and women. Again, de Beauvoir hints at this notion with her reference to artificial insemination, but Firestone makes this an explicit goal of feminist liberation. Fourth, the role of the mother will thereby be abolished, replaced with a more communal form of education. The attack on traditional notions of family and of motherhood is basic to de Beauvoir's case, but as noted earlier, it is present in the works of earlier radicals such as Godwin and Shelley. From that perspective, de Beauvoir and Firestone stand as the latest exemplars of iconoclastic thought on marriage. Fifth, differences in physical strength between children and adults will be eliminated by cultural means, though in the tradition of Marxist utopian thinking, Firestone does not care to elaborate on exactly what form this will take. Sixth, and finally, technology will remove the need for human beings to work.

These predictions range from the hopelessly naive to the remarkably prophetic. Of the first kind, technology may have replaced human workers in a variety of industries, but there is no sign that this is leading to a Shangri-La of leisure time. Of the second, the notion that the gender distinction will be abolished and that reproduction will be available to both biological sexes—that must have appeared to be completely delusional at the time, but it is now coming to pass. Even the claim on transgender reproduction no longer looks particularly far fetched.

The most interesting aspect of the statement, however, comes at the very end: the purpose of this revolution is to abolish the "tyranny" of the biological family. Firestone targets the same enemy as Godwin, Shelley, Reich, Marcuse, and de Beauvoir: the sexual revolution

---

69. Freud regards lesbians as women who have failed to mature correctly in terms of their sexuality, a view that de Beauvoir excoriates as rooted in "moralizing conformity" that leads him to regard lesbianism as never "anything but an inauthentic attitude." *The Second Sex*, 418–19. For a good discussion of Freud's views of lesbianism, set in the context of personal relationships with, and his professional attitudes to, women, see Lisa Appignanesi and John Forrester, *Freud's Women* (London: Penguin, 2000), 182–89.

ultimately has one great goal, the destruction of the family. It makes sense, of course, for the family is the primary means by which values are transmitted from generation to generation. From a Marxist perspective, that makes the family the means by which false consciousness is passed on and replicated over time. Its demolition is thus essential. And the means to this demolition are, for Firestone, to be found in the tools provided by technology.

Conclusion

The marriage of Freud and Marx at the hands of the New Left may well have started out as a shotgun wedding, but it is very clear that it has proved a long, happy, and fruitful relationship. The fact that sex is now politics is in large measure the result of this unusual marriage, and the latest iteration of that—the transgender movement—also takes its cue from the psychologizing and historicizing of human nature, combined with the now-standard leitmotif of oppression as society's imposition of its own values and norms on the individual. For any who wonder why private sexual behavior has great public and political significance today, the story of the New Left makes it all clear.

What is perhaps most striking, however, is that the politicized sexuality of our day is detached from its sophisticated roots in the anti-essentialist thought of the likes of Nietzsche, the psychoanalytic cultural criticism of Freud, and the Hegelian-Marxist thinking of Marcuse. Society now intuitively associates sexual freedom with political freedom because the notion that, in a very deep sense, we are defined by our sexual desires is something that has penetrated all levels of our culture. Even the typical songs of teenage pop stars now proclaim that idea as truth, as do the commercials that use sex appeal to sell us consumer goods. Modesty and sexual codes do not need to be merely expanded or redefined; for humans to be truly liberated and truly human, they need to be abolished altogether. That was the gospel of the sexual revolution of the sixties, and this has become the gospel of the consumerist world of today. Sex as revolution or sex as commodity: both are predicated on the idea of sex as the answer to human ills, and both assume the kind of psychologized, sexualized self that has emerged over the last three hundred years.

And that raises a matter of great significance: when we start to think about sexual morality today, we need to understand that we are actually thinking about what it means to be human. Discussions of what does and does not constitute legitimate sexual behavior cannot be abstracted from that deeper question. On that point, the thinkers of the New Left are correct. One may disagree with their conclusions—and I do so vehemently—but one must give them credit for understanding that when we address matters of sexual morality, we are actually addressing questions about the nature and purpose of human beings, the definition of happiness, and the relationship between the individual and wider society and between men and women. As Archbishop Charles Chaput summarizes the matter:

> Once the genie is out of the bottle, sexual freedom goes in directions and takes on shapes that nobody imagined. And ultimately it leads to questions about who a person is and what it means to be human.[70]

The acceptance of Freud's basic insight, that sexual desire is constitutive of identity, and this from infancy onward, is therefore an anthropological, philosophical, and political watershed. To concede this point means that debates about the limits of acceptable sexual expression become almost pointless because any attempt to corral sexual behavior is then rendered an oppressive move designed to make the individual inauthentic. And as is (ironically) clear from Reich's own uncharacteristic squeamishness on the matter of pedophilia, any attempts to set such limits based on the intrinsic nature of certain sexual acts are ultimately arbitrary and politically motivated.

---

70. Chaput, *Strangers in a Strange Land*, 88.

Epilogue to Part 3

Reflections on the Sexualization
of the Revolution

Many waters cannot quench love,
neither can floods drown it.

SONG OF SOLOMON 8:7

In the introduction, I pointed out that recourse to the concept of expressive individualism is not in itself sufficient to explain why the expressivist revolution in the understanding of the self has taken the specific form that it has, that is, one that is highly sexualized. The same applies to other attempts to identify the villains of Western culture. The breach between faith and reason, for example, to which Pope Benedict XVI famously pointed in his Regensburg Address in 2006, is no doubt important for understanding the fact that Western culture has unraveled, but it does not in itself explain the precise forms of that unraveling.[1]

This is why the figure of Sigmund Freud is so important. His theories may have been contested in their own day and largely repudiated in the years since then, but his identification of human beings as essentially

---

1. Pope Benedict XVI, "Regensburg Address: Faith, Reason and the University—Memories and Reflections," *Catholic Culture*, September 12, 2006, https://www.catholicculture.org/culture/library/view.cfm?id=7155.

sexual has proved to be revolutionary as few other ideas in history. In his hands, Jean-Jacques Rousseau's natural man becomes something more akin to the characters of the Marquis de Sade's darkly perverse and sexually anarchic novels. Unlike Rousseau and Sade, however, Freud expressed his theories in the objective language of the scientific idiom, something that has proved very compelling to the intellectual elites of the modern age.

Freud's ideas were not to remain confined to the elites, however, or to the lecture theaters and clinics of Vienna. Rather, they have come to shape the social imaginary of Western culture at large in profound ways. One might ask why this is so, given that his psychoanalytic theories are now largely discredited, but the answer is surely that in giving such a key place to human sexual instincts, he did identify something that is incontestable: sex is a powerful motivating factor in human action and always has been, as is witnessed by its constant presence in the great art and literature of the world.[2] If sex sells, one might add that it is also easily sold—sold to the public imagination as a primary factor in that which shapes much of human behavior. After Freud, the idea that sex is not simply an activity but is foundationally constitutive of our very identity becomes extremely plausible.

Once identity was understood to be sexual, then it was only a matter of time before sex became political. And in the hands of Wilhelm Reich and Herbert Marcuse, that is exactly what happened. Their genius lay in the way they took the Marxist category of oppression and refracted it through the Freudian notion of repression. In so doing, they psychologized the notion of oppression, turned sexual repression into something negative (therefore turning Freud on his head, as Karl Marx had done with G. W. F. Hegel), made political liberation essentially dependent on sexual liberation, and thereby established the framework for today's psychosexual politics.

---

2. See, for example, Camille Paglia, *Sexual Personae: Art and Decadence from Nefertiti to Emily Dickinson* (New York: Vintage, 1990); Norman O. Brown, *Life against Death: The Psychoanalytical Meaning of History*, 2nd ed. (Hanover, NH: Wesleyan University Press, 1985); Leslie A. Fiedler, *Love and Death in the American Novel* (Normal, IL: Dalkey Archive, 1997). One does not need to accept the specifically Freudian premises of these scholars to agree with their general point, that sex is central to human culture as evidenced in its art and literature.

In the context of the overall argument of this book, then, the Marx-Freud connection is of singular importance in understanding why expressive individualism has come to have a central sexual component. It set the stage for the politics of sex, of which the LGBTQ+ movement is the latest and most influential example.

It is also important to note that a number of the other concepts outlined in part 1 are embodied in the Marx-Freud revolution. With the ruthless assault by Nietzsche and Freud on the inconsistencies of moral codes and their psychologizing of these as being a matter of culturally conditioned aesthetics, they opened the way for what are in essence claims of emotivism to be a way of subverting traditional moral stands: "Your objection to homosexual behavior is simply an irrational, emotional stand based on social conditioning." In the hands of the New Left, this takes on a moral stridency: "And your irrational, emotional stand based on social conditioning reflects the politically repressive interests of bourgeois society." The concept now dubbed emotivism allows one to explain and dismiss the moral claims of anyone with whom one happens to disagree. Emotivism for thee, but not for me.

The psychologizing of oppression and the placing of it at the center of the history of human society plays directly to the idea that history is something to be overcome. After all, the history of humanity is the history of oppression and victimhood. In Marx this was understood in economic terms, but from the mid-twentieth century onward it became psychological, as in the various manifestations of critical theory that grew from the seeds planted by the Frankfurt School—poststructuralism, postcolonialism, critical race theory, and so on. As these gained hold in academia and in political discourse, so the standard historical narratives of Western culture and the traditional social mores and communal attitudes and practices that such narratives have been designed to justify came to be treated simply as instruments of oppression, to be deconstructed, destabilized, and thereby demolished. The marriage of Marx and Freud provided an intellectual basis for the broader anticulture.

It is also important to note that the sexualizing of children and the politicizing of sex sets the stage for a struggle between parental rights and those of the state, and for the dismantling of traditional sexual codes. This is yet another aspect of the Rieffian third-world anticulture. As Marx's thought abolished the prepolitical by making human beings the product of economic forces, so the New Left furthered this abolition by making them the product of sexual codes that are first inculcated when they are infants and children. The expressive individual is now the sexually expressive individual. And education and socialization are to be marked not by the cultivation of traditional sexual interdicts and taboos but rather by the abolition of such and the enabling of pansexual expression even among children. One might regard this change as obnoxious, but it reflects the logic of expressive individualism in the sexualized world that is the progeny of the consummation of the Marx-Freud nuptials.

Finally, one point of great importance is that in the post-Auschwitz, postcolonial world of the latter half of the twentieth century, victimhood came to possess huge cachet in the *Sittlichkeit* of the West. At the same time, the psychologizing of oppression by the New Left massively expanded the potential number of victims. One did not need to be in a concentration camp or a gulag or to be subject to segregation or even to have experience of serious poverty to claim such status. Now one could point to other forms of nonrecognition as constituting victimization— not having one's sexual preferences positively affirmed by wider society, for example, or not being allowed to marry a same-sex partner. And merely tolerating certain sexual proclivities and activities would not be enough, for tolerance is not the same as recognition. Indeed, it actually implies a degree of disapproval, of nonrecognition by society. Only full equality before the law and in the culture at large can provide that. When the political struggle became a psychological struggle, it also became a therapeutic struggle.

In sum, in the work of the New Left one finds philosophical justification for what are now intuitive commonplaces of our culture: to be free is to be sexually liberated; to be happy is to be affirmed in that liberation. Our narrative has therefore reached the point at which the basic philosophical elements behind the modern social imaginary are in place.

Part 4

TRIUMPHS OF
THE REVOLUTION

8

The Triumph of the Erotic

Pornography is the attempt to
insult sex, to do dirt on it.

D. H. LAWRENCE, *PHOENIX*

With the advent of the New Left, the revolutionary politics of Karl Marx took on a decidedly sexual form. As I note in chapter 10, the most obvious manifestation of this impulse has been the LGBTQ+ movement, which has moved well beyond Herbert Marcuse in its political philosophy and indeed entered the mainstream life of middle America. It has even accommodated itself to the consumer society in a manner that would no doubt have elicited an ambivalent response from the true revolutionaries had they lived to see it.[1]

Sex now pervades every aspect of life, from elementary education to commercials to Congress and the Supreme Court. Everywhere one looks,

---

1. It is, of course, arguable that it is consumer society that has accommodated itself to the sexual revolution, finding there simply one more set of commodities and one more marketplace. See, for example, the rise of so-called "woke capitalism," connected to various social causes, including that of LGBTQ+, and the massive economic significance of internet pornography, with even the lowest estimates of how much money it makes for the US economy being around $6 billion. Ross Benes, "Porn Could Have a Bigger Economic Influence on the US Than Netflix," *Quartz*, June 20, 2018, https://finance.yahoo.com /news/porn-could-bigger-economic-influence-121524565.html.

the erotic—sexual desire—has triumphed. And yet very few people, outside of sectarian groups on the Left or the occasional postgraduate seminar in the history of politics or psychology, have read Wilhelm Reich and Herbert Marcuse. Sexual mores have been transformed in the last sixty years, from a time when the Rolling Stones had to change the lyrics of "Let's Spend the Night Together" to "Let's Spend Some Time Together" in order to perform on *The Ed Sullivan Show* to Miley Cyrus simulating a sex act with a microphone on stage at the Glastonbury Festival, to the approval of audience and media alike. The erotic has triumphed as sex has come to grip the popular imagination, but this has not been through scientific argument. It has been through other cultural media.

This part of the story is as complicated as any. A full account of the triumph of the erotic would need to take into account the wider breakdown of social hierarchies in the twentieth century under the impact of economic and social changes, not least those generated by two world wars. Technology—from easy access to the pill and the legalization of abortion to the internet and the consequent ability to access pornography with little risk of social stigma—is also critical. To these should also be added the impact of documents such as *The Kinsey Reports* and the later *Hite Report* on sexuality.[2]

Given the vast nature of the topic, I want to focus on two specific aspects of the sexual revolution that serve as a bridge between its various theoretical foundations that I have traced thus far and the way its basic tenets have become an intuitive part of how people imagine the world is: the artistic movement of surrealism and the popularization and increasing social acceptance of pornography.

Art, Politics, and the Cultural Ascendance of the Erotic: Surrealism

The choice of surrealism as an example of the cultural ascendance of the erotic demands justification. Art has, of course, been a signal in-

---

2. For an account of the sexual revolution that addresses the significance of a number of these matters, see Alan Petigny, *The Permissive Society: America, 1941–1965* (Cambridge: Cambridge University Press, 2009). Also useful are the articles and documents in Mary E. Williams, ed., *The Sexual Revolution* (San Diego: Greenhaven, 2002).

fluence in challenging sexual norms and in bringing explicit sexual content into the realm of public discourse and common social consciousness.[3] I noted in chapter 4 that poets such as Percy Bysshe Shelley were very self-conscious and intentional about the politically transformative ambitions of their work. Then, in the late nineteenth century, Oscar Wilde's flamboyant aestheticism laid the groundwork for the later rise of camp and then gay culture.[4] Other authors—James Joyce, Henry Miller, and D. H. Lawrence, for example—placed sex and the psychology of sex at the heart of their literary projects and were consequently subject to censorship. Any comprehensive history of the modern sexual revolution would need to address both the content of their literary works and the legal actions that surrounded them.[5]

Nevertheless, the Italian philosopher Augusto Del Noce has pinpointed surrealism as being of particular importance to what he characterizes as "the ascendance of eroticism" for reasons that will become clear below.[6] Certainly, the works of surrealists such as Salvador Dalí hang in many houses of people who know little of the philosophy that drove the movement. So surrealism has clearly crossed from the realm of elite culture to that of commonplace kitsch, quietly extending its influence and its basic ideas far beyond art galleries and the private collections of the wealthy.

---

3. See Eve Kosofsky Sedgwick, *Epistemology of the Closet*, rev. ed. (Berkeley: University of California Press, 2008), which is a fascinating study of how late nineteenth- and early twentieth-century literature influenced the formation of concepts of gender and sexuality.

4. See Camille Paglia, *Sexual Personae: Art and Decadence from Nefertiti to Emily Dickinson* (New York: Vintage, 1990), 512–71.

5. Joyce's *Ulysses* was subject to various legal actions in the United States in the 1920s and 1930s. Miller's *Tropic of Cancer*, published in Paris in 1934, was not published in the United States until 1961, triggering a legal case that culminated in a Supreme Court ruling in 1964 that the book was not obscene. Lawrence's *Lady Chatterley's Lover* was not published in the United Kingdom until 1960 and was then the subject of a famous trial, Regina v. Penguin Books Ltd, at which the work was found to be not obscene. The result of the latter case was the advent of an era of much more liberal policies regarding published materials in Britain, at the very point when other social and cultural forces were also pushing toward an overturning of traditional sexual mores. See, for example, Philip Larkin's poem "Annus Mirabilis," *Michigan Quarterly Review* 9, no. 3, accessed February 24, 2020, http://hdl.handle.net/2027/spo.act2080.0009.003:02.

6. This quotation is the title of the important essay on the sexual revolution that Del Noce published in 1970. It is reprinted in Augusto Del Noce, *The Crisis of Modernity*, ed. and trans. Carlo Lancelotti (Montreal: McGill-Queen's University Press, 2014), 157–86.

DEFINING SURREALISM

Surrealism is the name given to a school of artistic expression that emerged in the first half of the twentieth century and whose leading figures included the poet André Breton, the film director Luis Buñuel, and, perhaps most famously, the painter Salvador Dalí. There were many aspects to the surrealist project, but the nature of the self and of identity was central.[7] And given that surrealists promoted their understanding of the self through their artwork, the nature and purpose of the selfhood they proclaimed is of great interest both in terms of its ambition and its methods.

At the foundation of the surrealist movement was the thought of Sigmund Freud. The artistic philosophy that it espoused sought to give concrete, artistic expression to the unconscious, following Freud's idea that everything there—everything—is significant.[8] In the first *Manifesto of Surrealism* (1924), André Breton declares that at the start of the surrealist movement, he was "completely occupied with Freud" and was particularly impressed that the psychoanalyst had drawn attention to the importance of dreams for understanding human existence.[9] Indeed, Breton comments that he has always "been amazed" at the fact that people attach more importance to things that happen when they are awake than to what they dream about when they are asleep.[10] One of the reasons for this is significant:

> The mind of the man who dreams is fully satisfied by what happens to him. The agonizing question of possibility is no longer pertinent. Kill, fly faster, love to your heart's content. And if you should die, are you not certain of reawaking among the dead? Let yourself be carried along,

---

7. Dawn Ades and Michael Richardson observe, "Issues of identity and the constitution of the self run through surrealism. Long before Foucault announced 'the death of the subject' or Barthes proclaimed that the author was dead, the surrealists had implicitly taken both notions for granted. Indeed, an essential element of surrealism's coming into being was precisely the recognition that Enlightenment individualism had ceased to be a tool of human emancipation and was displaying increasingly oppressive aspects." Dawn Ades and Michael Richardson, eds., *The Surrealism Reader: An Anthology of Ideas*, with Krzysztof Fijałkowski (Chicago: University of Chicago Press, 2015), 24.

8. Herbert S. Gershman, *The Surrealist Revolution in France* (Ann Arbor: University of Michigan Press, 1969), 19.

9. André Breton, *Manifestoes of Surrealism*, trans. Richard Seaver and Helen R. Lane (Ann Arbor: University of Michigan Press, 1969), 12, 22.

10. Breton, *Manifestoes of Surrealism*, 11.

events will not tolerate your interference. You are nameless. The ease of everything is priceless.[11]

We might summarize this sentiment by saying that the great attraction of dreams is that the dreamer is able to be whoever or whatever she wants to be in whatever kind of world she chooses to envisage. Of course, the identity of the dreamer is somewhat complicated, given that dreams are not the actions of a conscious individual but rather the manifestations of the unconscious. And that points to the basic contention that it is the unconscious that is the real bedrock of individual identity, the thing about the person that is most real. There is therefore an inversion of normal assumptions here, perhaps something we might describe as the logic of Jean-Jacques Rousseau's self pressed to its ultimate end: the most authentic self is the self that is totally detached from, and uninhibited by, any of the conditions of material life. Thus, one of Breton's earliest ambitions was to produce a monologue that was essentially a stream of consciousness, unfiltered by any critical faculties.[12]

The interest in dreams permeates surrealist art. There is the dream-like, and sometimes nightmarish, quality of the paintings of Dalí, and his dramatic, often confusing, use of symbols. Perhaps the most famous example of this fixation on dreams in popular culture is the sequence in Alfred Hitchcock's movie *Spellbound*, in which Gregory Peck's character recalls a dream and thereby becomes the key to solving a murder. The sequence was designed by Dalí and consists of a series of bizarre, portentous, and, yes, surreal scenes. The message is clear: the unconscious is the guide to truth. For the surrealists, it was key to individual authenticity. One might also add this: the truth is therefore arcane and hidden; opaque depth is to be understood as truth; that which has always been assumed to be obvious is to be regarded as inauthentic or problematic. The antihistorical aspect of an anticulture is evident. And that is even clearer from the movement's revolutionary social and political aspirations.

---

11. Breton, *Manifestoes of Surrealism*, 13.
12. Breton describes the experiment in the first *Manifesto*, in *Manifestoes of Surrealism*, 22–24.

SURREALISM AND REVOLUTION

There was far more to surrealism than a desire to give aesthetic expression to Freudian notions of the unconscious. In fact, even the philosophy underlying the usefulness of dreams had implications well beyond the mere aesthetic. Preoccupation with dreams was not, for the surrealist, a case of art for art's sake. Again, Breton in the first *Manifesto*:

> Why should I not grant to dreams what I occasionally refuse reality, that is, this value of certainty in itself which, in its own time, is not open to my repudiation? Why should I not expect from the sign of the dream more than I expect from a degree of consciousness which is daily more acute? Can't the dream also be used in solving the fundamental questions of life? Are these questions the same in one case as in the other and, in the dream, do these questions already exist?[13]

Dreams are therefore to be regarded as a potential source for thought and for solving the most basic problems of life. And as the movement developed, these "problems" came to be seen in a distinctly political light and positively framed in relation to revolutionary Marxist concerns. Before we address this thinking, however, it is worth noting that, like Freud, the surrealists regarded sex as providing the basic dynamic for the unconscious.

Perhaps nothing points to the moral and sexual iconoclasm that the surrealists desired to unleash on society through their art than their rehabilitation of the most notorious theorist and practitioner of perverse sexual chaos, the Marquis de Sade. Indeed, in the first surrealist *Manifesto* (1924), Breton lauded Sade as the great sexual surrealist because his behavior in the sexual realm was free from any control by reason, aesthetics, or morals.[14] Eroticism—the glorification of sexual desire and the establishment of it as the subversive norm and impulse for reconstructing human personhood

---

13. Breton, *Manifestoes of Surrealism*, 12.

14. Breton, *Manifestoes of Surrealism*, 26. Cf. the comment by Maurice Nadeau: "Twenty centuries of Christian oppression have not been able to keep man from having desires, and from longing to satisfy them. Surrealism proclaims the omnipotence of desire, and the legitimacy of its realization. The Marquis de Sade is the central figure of its pantheon. To the objection that man lives in society, surrealism replies by the total destruction of the bonds imposed by family, morality, religion." *The History of Surrealism*, trans. Richard Howard (New York: Macmillan, 1965), 50.

and society—was at the very center of the surrealist political project, and this focus made the rehabilitation of Sade an obvious move.[15]

Sade himself had emerged as a popular author in the heady days of the early French Revolution, when pornography and a taste for the sexually explicit and perverse were part and parcel of the revolutionary ethos.[16] The political power of sex is not a new thing, nor is the role of popular literature in promoting revolutionary social change. Sade's novel *Justine* was a best seller in the later eighteenth century and was owned and read by Lord Byron and by Algernon Swinburne in the nineteenth. That Sade became the "Divine Marquis" to the surrealists in the twentieth was, in retrospect, predictable. Political freedom has often been equated with sexual freedom, as we noted with William Godwin, Percy Bysshe Shelley, and William Blake, and Sade is still this idea's most infamous advocate.[17]

Sade therefore provides an explicit link between the sexual and political ambitions of the surrealists. In his *Speech to the Congress of Writers* (1935), Breton lists Sade, along with Arthur Rimbaud and Freud, as a writer whose works need to be defended and expounded in the public square. Nothing, he says, should make the surrealists deny their importance—and significantly, he adds that nothing can make them deny the importance of Marx and Lenin either. Having cited these names, he then starts his concluding paragraph:

> From where we stand, we maintain that the activity of interpreting the world must continue to be linked with the activity of changing the world. We maintain that it is the poet's, the artist's role to study the human problem in depth. . . . It is not by stereotyped declarations against fascism and war that we will manage to liberate either the mind or man from the ancient chains that bind him and the new chains that threaten him. It is by the affirmation of our unshakeable fidelity to the powers of emancipation

---

15. J. H. Matthews, *An Introduction to Surrealism* (University Park: Pennsylvania State University Press, 1965), 156.

16. See Faramerz Dabhoiwala, *The Origins of Sex: A History of the First Sexual Revolution* (Oxford: Oxford University Press, 2012), 339.

17. E. Michael Jones, *Libido Dominandi: Sexual Liberation and Political Control* (South Bend, IN: St. Augustine's Press, 2000), 30.

of the mind and of man that we have recognized one by one and that we will fight to cause to be recognized as such.

"Transform the world," Marx said; "change life." Rimbaud said. These two watchwords are one for us.[18]

The unacknowledged legislator mentioned by Shelley here combines with the political revolutionary of Marx to offer works of art that do not simply describe the world, reflect the world, or entertain the world. The purpose is to change the world and that, in the surrealist mind, by a sexual revolution. The purpose of surrealism was profoundly and aggressively political: to overthrow Christianity (and its corollaries—families and moral codes governing sexual behavior). And it was to do this via an emphasis in its various works of art on human desires and their attainment through the self-actualization of the individual.

The role of Freud in this movement was not so much inspiration as providing insightful tools into how the political transformation could be achieved. Describing the surrealists' ambitions, Herbert Gershman writes,

> Years before existentialism was known in France the surrealists had evolved an existential line of criticism: not only society but the author (or artist) too must be transformed by his work. To illustrate or illuminate was no longer sufficient. An active engagement leading toward a radical transformation of society and its individual parts must be the goal of all who worked in ink, paint, or clay. To this end the lamp of reason, reflecting traditional techniques and serving as society's searchlight, would have to be modernized so as to accept the real insights, the pure revelations of the Id. What to Freud had been a therapeutically useful hypothesis derived from experience became for the surrealists a portrait of Man suggesting a philosophy of life.[19]

---

18. Breton, *Manifestoes of Surrealism*, 240–41.

19. Gershman, *Surrealist Revolution*, 18. Cf. the comment of Augusto Del Noce: "Surrealism should not be regarded as an artistic phenomenon, in the sense in which art is distinct from other forms of spiritual life, but above all as a revolutionary phenomenon, characterized as such by totalizing categories; in fact, it intends to carry out not just a revolution *in* art, but a revolution *through* art." *Crisis of Modernity*, 211.

In other words, surrealism attempted to achieve through art what Reich attempted to do in his writings: promote social revolution through the application of aspects of Freudian theory to life. The difference, of course, is that copies of paintings by Dalí and company found their way into far more living rooms of far more ordinary people than did volumes by Reich and Marcuse. Surrealism, with its blurring of boundaries, its accent on the subconscious, and its obvious sexual connotations, easily penetrated the territory of popular culture, as the dream sequence in Hitchcock's *Spellbound* indicates.

Philosopher Augusto Del Noce is therefore surely correct to identify surrealism as a key element in the rise of eroticism and also in the fight against orthodox Christianity. That it has not featured more significantly in narratives of the sexual revolution is, for Del Noce, a significant oversight. Like Marxism in general, he argues, surrealism sought to overturn Christianity. Christianity represented precisely the oppressive bourgeois ideology par excellence and therefore needed to be overthrown. And at the heart of Christianity lay its sexual codes, the means by which it regulated individual lives. Then, as with the Reichian turn in Marxism, surrealism wanted to do this via a redefinition of human beings as fundamentally sexual beings, a redefinition that required a corresponding rejection of the strictures of Christian morality. As Del Noce summarizes his position:

> Surrealists were almost the only ones to *realize a fundamental truth: the decisive battle against Christianity could be fought only at the level of the sexual revolution.* And therefore the problem of sexuality and eroticism is today the fundamental problem from the moral point of view.[20]

And this takes us to the heart of another significant issue: surrealism, like other forms of sexualized art, did not simply trade in sexual images in a manner that made what had always existed more available. Pornography is a perennial of human society, and so one might be tempted to see the surrealist movement as just a clever spin on an already existent

---

20. Del Noce, *Crisis of Modernity*, 177–78; emphasis original.

phenomenon. But that is not the case. What surrealism did was play a part in the general and radical eroticization of modernity. It did not simply make sexual images more widely available under cover of intellectual respectability; it actually served to help the process by which society's judgment of the cultural value of pornography changed from something bad and detrimental to something good and healthy. This is the process Del Noce categorizes as "the ascendance of eroticism," something predicated on the idea that sexual taboos and restraint were fundamentally negative in their effects. The sexual revolution is just that—a revolution—and its artistic vanguard represents a qualitative, not merely quantitative, change.[21] And in surrealism this change is rooted in the marriage of the Freudian notion that the unconscious is the true determinant of who we are and the Marxist idea that human liberation can be achieved only through the revolutionizing of social relations. And this requires art to transform attitudes toward sexuality and toward identity. With surrealism, the struggle against Christianity in which Western culture had been engaged since the Enlightenment found a specific artistic form—one that now adorns the walls of respectable middle-class houses.

Yet if surrealism turned the sexually radical politics of the twentieth century into a popular art form, the real success story of the sexual revolution is far less philosophically articulate and far more extensive: the triumph of pornography, the consumption of which is no longer restricted to the shadows of society or to seedy nightclubs and cinemas but something that now forms a basic part of recreational activity for many—children as well as adults.

The Pornification of Mainstream Culture
By the time of his death, aged ninety-one, in 2017, Hugh Hefner was a classic example of a hero of the anticulture so ably described by Philip

---

21. In reflecting on criticism of antipornography demonstrations in Paris, Del Noce comments, "The claim here is that the erotic wave is just a quantitatively larger diffusion of pornography. There is greater consumption of all types of products, and therefore . . . Not true: what has changed is the judgment of value. With eroticism, what until yesterday was regarded as a dis-value is now affirmed as a value." *Crisis of Modernity*, 178. In Rieffian terms, this philosophy is an anticulture.

Rieff. His life had been dedicated to overthrowing the sexual codes of earlier generations, and his career proved the truth of the old adage "Sex sells." Though his central contribution to American publishing, the magazine *Playboy*, now looks remarkably tame in comparison to the pornography routinely available on the internet and even, one might add, to the kind of sexually explicit antics featured in many mainstream television shows such as *Game of Thrones*, there is little doubt that Hefner played a key part in making pornography part of the cultural mainstream and thus in dismantling traditional public attitudes to sex.[22] Indeed, historian Alan Petigny points to the success of the Playboy Clubs that Hefner founded as probably the single most important sign of "the emergence of a bolder, less reticent culture during the early sixties."[23]

Hefner's genius lay in the way he was able to remove the social stigma typically attached to pornography and the selling of sex as a commercial interest. This was exemplified in the way *Playboy* was constructed, with its combination of titillating photographs and serious interviews with individuals of cultural significance, the latter of which Hefner added to the magazine in 1962. Thus, between 1962 and 1969 interviewees included figures of popular culture (Bob Dylan, Bill Cosby, Frank Sinatra); politicians of various stripes, nationality, and degrees of respectability (Eldridge Cleaver, Fidel Castro, George Lincoln Rockwell, George Wallace, Jawaharlal Nehru); famous art house directors (Federico Fellini, Ingmar Bergman); movie stars (Marcello Mastroianni, Jack Lemmon, Michael Caine); philosophers (Bertrand Russell, Jean-Paul Sartre); men of letters (Jean Genet, Henry Miller, Norman Mailer, Truman Capote); and so on.[24]

---

22. Gail Dines, professor emerita of sociology and women's studies at Wheelock College, comments, "Today there is almost no soft-core porn on the internet, because most of it has migrated into pop culture." Quoted in the Boston Women's Health Book Collective, *Our Bodies, Ourselves* (New York: Touchstone, 2011), 59.

23. Petigny, *Permissive Society*, 118.

24. For a complete list, see Playmate Hound, "A List of Playboy Interviews of the '60s," Ranker, updated June 8, 2017, https://www.ranker.com/list/a-list-of-playboy-interviews-of-the-_60s/playmate-hound. Anthony Giddens notes that the insertion of orthodox advertising along with nonsexual stories and news items in soft-core magazines played a significant role in normalizing the erotic objectification of women. *The Transformation of Intimacy: Sexuality, Love, and Eroticism in Modern Societies* (Stanford, CA: Stanford University Press, 1992), 119.

Combining interviews of figures such as Orson Welles, Salvador Dalí, and the Beatles with nude pictures of beautiful women was a brilliant marketing ploy. The old joke—that people bought *Playboy* for the interviews—was funny precisely because it had a ring of plausibility to it. And the presence of women on the interview roster (Grace Kelly, Ayn Rand) also helped undermine claims that it represented the unacceptable objectification of women. *Playboy* did not appear sleazy; nor did it appear to be exploiting women; rather, it presented itself as epitomizing a certain kind of lifestyle—an image of discerning, thoughtful, engaged artistic hedonism. And the fact that the interviews often contained surprising and salacious personal admissions did not damage sales at all.

When then presidential candidate Jimmy Carter confessed in his *Playboy* interview to having committed adultery in his heart, it caused a minor sensation. But the admission was not the most important thing, given that it was scarcely a spectacular or exceptional sin to which he was confessing. What was significant was that he did so publicly and in a magazine committed to mainstreaming erotic pictures. Carter was a function of the age of expressive individualism, in which authenticity demands that private thoughts become part of public performance; he was also emblematic of an age when pornography was beginning to seep into the mainstream of public life.

Even the type of nudity in *Playboy* fulfilled the function of blending the culturally mainstream with sexual titillation of a kind that had previously been the preserve of the seedier corners of society. The list of popular and well-known women who have posed for the magazine over the years is a long one, and it includes figures such as singer Nancy Sinatra, Bond girls Ursula Andress and Barbara Bach, movie actress Natassja Kinski, game-show hostess Vanna White, and prime-time TV stars Joan Collins, Donna Mills, and Linda Evans. The very first edition carried a famous nude picture of Marilyn Monroe. These women all qualify as household names, not because they removed their clothes for *Playboy* but because they are part of the mainstream, respectable entertainment industry of the latter half of the twentieth century. The crossover into teen culture was also represented by a figure such as Geri Horner (formerly

Halliwell), better known as Ginger Spice from the girl band the Spice Girls. And by posing for *Playboy*, these figures of mainstream pop culture helped bring the kind of sexualized entertainment that *Playboy* represents into the zone of respectability.

By the time of his death in 2017, Hugh Hefner was himself a figure of mainstream popular American culture, a staple of talk shows and television. In 2003, he had become a spokesman for the Carl's Jr. fast-food chain and appeared in commercials along with a selection of Playboy Bunnies. This move provoked some reaction among the religious sectors of society but appears to have fortified the company's sale of its Six Dollar Burger. As a company spokesperson commented in a press release, "As a pop icon, Hefner appeals to our target audience and credibly communicates our message of variety." Sex sells. It even sells something as prosaic as a burger. Especially when the face selling it is that of Hugh Hefner, pop icon.[25]

The sexualization of pop culture, of which *Playboy* was an important part, is now all-pervasive but is something of a comparatively recent development. Commenting on American women's magazines in 1946, George Orwell made the following observation:

> Someone has just sent me a copy of an American fashion magazine which shall be nameless. It consists of 325 large quarto pages, of which no fewer than 15 are given up to articles on world politics, literature, etc. The rest consists entirely of pictures with a little letterpress creeping round their edges: pictures of ball dresses, mink coats, step-ins, panties, brassieres, silk stockings, slippers, perfumes, lipsticks, nail varnish— and, of course, of the women, unrelievedly beautiful, who wear them or make use of them. . . .
>
> One striking thing when one looks at these pictures is the overbred, exhausted, even decadent style of beauty that now seems to be striven after. Nearly all of these women are immensely elongated. . . .
>
> A fairly diligent search through the magazine reveals two discreet allusions to grey hair, but if there is anywhere a direct mention of

---

25. See the article "Carl's Jr.," Encyclopedia.com, updated March 12, 2020, https://www.encyclopedia.com/marketing/encyclopedias-almanacs-transcripts-and-maps/carls-jr.

fatness or middle-age I have not found it. Birth and death are not mentioned either: nor is work, except that a few recipes for breakfast dishes are given.[26]

The description speaks eloquently of the American preoccupation with physical beauty, but what is really interesting about Orwell's commentary is how unsexy it is. There is a matter-of-fact, nonerotic aspect to the manner in which he describes the few articles the magazine contains and even the representation of the female form. Were he writing about magazines today, it is hard to imagine he could do so in such terms. *Cosmopolitan* is typically full of advice on sexual matters, and its covers usually involve a highly sexualized image of a beautiful woman. The cult of beauty has become the cult of sexuality.

Of course, the sexualization of pop culture that Hefner played such a signal role in starting has gone well beyond any vision for the main-streaming of sex offered by *Playboy*. The culture in which we now live has absorbed into the mainstream much more extreme sexual content than that which his magazine, videos, and clubs offered. Our world has developed technological means of accessibility to pornography whereby even previous social controls on access to such material no longer apply. In the past, the adolescent terror of being spotted in the shop buying a copy of *Playboy* or the fear of being seen by a neighbor entering an adult bookstore or cinema exerted significant restraint on behavior. Now the internet has made pornography more easily available and has made it a matter involving much less personal risk to the consumer. As a result, more extreme pornography is more readily accessible by more people than at any previous point in history. The overall social effects are numerous and dramatic.

The slow arrival of hard-core pornography as a consumer item that carries little or no social stigma began in the early 1970s.[27] Now the process seems near to completion. Perhaps the most obvious evidence

---

26. George Orwell, "As I Please 60," in *Essays*, Everyman's Library (New York: Alfred A. Knopf, 2002), 1118–19.

27. See Jones's comments on the audience for *Deep Throat*, a famous pornographic movie. *Libido Dominandi*, 525.

for pornography now being part of mainstream popular culture is the manner in which key players in the pornographic industry are today considered well-known celebrities. In the introduction to her book *Pornified* (2005), Pamela Paul notes how adult movie stars have become household names: for example, Jenna Jameson's autobiography was a best seller, and Ron Jeremy has been the subject of a reality show and a documentary and is a regular on the university lecture circuit.[28] And that was in 2005, before such names as Stormy Daniels became part of prime-time news reporting. Today, the "porn chic" that Hefner helped birth grips much of the cultural imagination. In 2014, an exclusively online show, *The Sex Factor*, allowed contestants to compete for the chance to become a porn star.[29] Even Hugh Hefner, the doyen of the mainstream sexual revolution, today looks conservative in the context of the world that he, perhaps more than anyone, helped create. Porn is now the norm.[30]

PORNOGRAPHY AND FEMINISM

The instinctive Christian response to pornography is fundamentally correct: pornography involves the promotion of lust and the objectification of women. Increasingly, porn also promotes a view of sexual activity that sets violence against women at its core.[31] Further, there is strong evidence

28. Pamela Paul, *Pornified: How Pornography Is Damaging Our Lives, Our Relationships, and Our Families* (New York: Holt, 2005), 7–8.

29. See "The Sex Factor: Mainstreaming and Normalizing the Abuse and Exploitation of Women," Collective Shout, July 24, 2014, https://www.collectiveshout.org/the_sex_factor_mainstreaming_and _normalising_the_abuse_and_exploitation_of_women.

30. See Pamela Paul, "From Pornography to Porno to Porn: How Porn Became the Norm," in *The Social Costs of Pornography: A Collection of Papers*, ed. James R. Stoner and Donna M. Hughes (Princeton, NJ: Witherspoon Institute, 2010), 3–20.

31. The National Center on Sexual Exploitation released a report in February 2018, *The Public Health Harms of Pornography*, which is an extremely useful summary of the research findings of key peer reviewed studies and other papers presented at the US Capitol. The subtitle provides a helpful précis of the whole: *How Pornography Fuels Child Sexual Abuse, Compulsive Sexual Behavior, Violence against Women, Commercial Sexual Exploitation, and More*. One of the (many) chilling comments in the report is the observation on page 7 that what is described as "mainstream pornography" has come to "coalesce around a homogenous script involving violence and female degradation." The whole report is available for download at https://endsexualexploitation.org/wp-content/uploads/NCOSE_SymposiumBriefing Booklet_1-28-2.pdf, accessed April 8, 2019. The connection between pornography and the objectification of and violence against women has been a staple of much feminist literature for many years; see the classic statement of the case by Andrea Dworkin, *Pornography: Men Possessing Women* (New York: Plume, 1989).

emerging that pornography shapes the sexual expectations, behavior, and relationships of those who consume it.[32]

To this we can add that it is often closely connected to sex trafficking.[33] The advent of the term "ethically sourced pornography"—even among some professing Christians like the Lutheran pastor Nadia Bolz-Weber—is something of an oxymoron.[34] The sheer stupidity of this idea ignores the fact that there is no way to tell the difference between pornography involving willing participants and that which is essentially a recording of rape. Just as significant, it also ignores the fact that however (to use their term) "ethical" the source, there is an established connection between the use of pornography by men and their likelihood to use prostitutes.[35]

Comments like those of Bolz-Weber no doubt serve to keep her name in the headlines as an irritant of socially conservative Christians, but she is thereby building her public reputation on a mortgage whose interest is being paid by the suffering of the victims of sex trafficking. Perhaps one might say that such celebrity is hardly itself "ethically sourced."

32. See Norman Doidge, "Acquiring Tastes and Loves: What Neuroplasticity Teaches Us about Sexual Attraction and Love," in Stoner and Hughes, *Social Costs of Pornography*, 21–56, esp. 30–31. Mark Regnerus has offered one of the most powerful and depressing analyses of the impact of pornography on human relationships: see his *Cheap Sex: The Transformation of Men, Marriage, and Monogamy* (Oxford: Oxford University Press, 2017).

33. The connection of pornography to prostitution is an area of philosophical debate: see the essays in Jessica Spector, ed., *Prostitution and Pornography: Philosophical Debate about the Sex Industry* (Stanford, CA: Stanford University Press, 2006).

34. See Bolz-Weber's comment in an interview with the LGBTQ+ magazine *Out in New Jersey*: "Now, there are issues of justice and exploitation within the porn industry, no question, but it doesn't mean consumption of pornography should be shamed. There is ethically sourced porn. There are people who say it's sexual immorality, but if you take Liberals and Conservatives who show outrage and made a Venn diagram of those who consume pornography, you'd see a huge overlap." Johnny Walsh, "Nadia Bolz-Weber Does Ministry Differently," *Out in New Jersey*, October 21, 2018, https://outinjersey.net /nadia-bolz-weber-does-ministry-differently/. Bolz-Weber is no doubt correct when she sees a level of hypocrisy in much of the outrage about pornography. But the hypocrisy of the consumer does not negate the validity of arguments against pornography as immoral, nor relativize the exploitative relationships on which the pornographic industry depends.

35. See "How Porn Fuels Sex Trafficking," Fight the New Drug, August 23, 2017, https://fight thenewdrug.org/how-porn-fuels-sex-trafficking/. Also see "The Porn Industry's Dark Secrets," Fight the New Drug, August 23, 2017, https://fightthenewdrug.org/the-porn-industrys-dark-secrets/. In a 2015 article, John-Henry Westen quotes feminist sociologist Dr. Gail Dines as saying, "The biggest sex educator of young men today is pornography, which is increasingly violent and dehumanizing, and it changes the way men view women." Westen, "Want to Stop Sex Trafficking? Look to America's Porn Addiction," *Huffington Post*, updated March 30, 2015, https://www.huffpost.com/entry/want -to-stop-sex-traffick_b_6563338?ncid=engmodushpmg00000006.

Nevertheless, Bolz-Weber's simplistic headline grabbing notwithstanding, shifting feminist attitudes to pornography do point to changes in the overall attitude of society to its social acceptability. An earlier generation of feminists such as Andrea Dworkin and Catherine MacKinnon regarded pornography as part of the male domination of women within a patriarchal society:

> Women are in pornography to be violated and taken, men to violate and take them, either on screen or by camera or pen, on behalf of the viewer. . . .
>
> If pornography has not become sex to and from the male point of view, it is hard to explain why the pornography industry makes a known ten billion dollars a year selling it as sex mostly to men.[36]

Recent decades, however, have seen the emergence of pro-pornography feminists, perhaps most famously Camille Paglia, who declares herself to be "radically pro-pornography and pro-prostitution."[37]

Less emphatically, but perhaps more significantly, the Boston Women's Health Book Collective declares the following concerning pornography in what is arguably the sacred text of modern American feminism:

> What it comes down to at a personal level is that what some women consider arousing, others may consider unappealing or demeaning. As with fantasies, what you see in erotica/porn may help you explore and enjoy an aspect of your sexual desire without having to act on it.[38]

This speaks eloquently of the impact of the therapeutic and of expressive individualism on feminism: the moral status of pornography is irrelevant; the big question is whether it works for the individual, whether it enhances the individual's understanding or experience of her own

---

36. Catherine A. MacKinnon, *Toward a Feminist Theory of the State* (Cambridge, MA: Harvard University Press, 1989), 139. Cf. Dworkin, *Pornography*, 200–201: "The word whore is incomprehensible unless one is immersed in the lexicon of male domination. Men have created the group, the type, the concept, the epithet, the insult, the industry, the trade, the commodity, the reality of woman as whore. Woman as whore exists within the objective and real system of male sexual domination. The pornography itself is objective and real and central to the male sexual system. The valuation of women's sexuality in pornography is objective and real because women are so regarded and so valued."

37. Camille Paglia, *Sex, Art, and American Culture: Essays* (New York: Vintage, 1992), 11.

38. Health Book Collective, *Our Bodies, Ourselves*, 80.

sexuality, whether it gives pleasure. This feminism is a long way from the world of Dworkin and MacKinnon and yet reflective both of the therapeutic dynamic of modern culture and the extent to which pornography has become part of the mainstream. In fact, the major criticism of pornography that the Boston Women's Health Book Collective makes is in chapter 3 of *Our Bodies, Ourselves*, which discusses body image. Pornography's major crime is that it creates unrealistic expectations regarding the perfection of the female form. In other words, it is not bad because it contravenes traditional codes of sexual morality. It is bad because it may have a detrimental effect on some women's inner sense of well-being with their physical appearance. It is bad as and when it fails the therapeutic test.[39]

THE SOCIAL SIGNIFICANCE OF PORNOGRAPHY

Setting aside the question of its origins and "sourcing," we should also note that pornography has deeper social significance. From this perspective, the question whether the people engaged in the sexual acts depicted in pornographic pictures and films have consented to such things is irrelevant to the message that is being communicated. Fantasy worlds left unchecked have a habit of impinging on reality and remaking it in their own image. And that applies as much, if not more, in the realm of sexuality as it does in any other area.

As Roger Scruton has pointed out, real sexual encounters are interpersonal:

> The "reality" principle by which the normal sexual act is regulated is a principle of personal encounter, which enjoins us to respect the other person, and to respect, also, the sanctity of his body, as the expression of another self.[40]

Scruton—no Marxist!—proceeds to apply the Marxian term "fetishized" to that which sexual fantasy (and therefore, *a fortiori*, pornography) does to sexual acts: the other person becomes not an end but rather a means

---

39. Health Book Collective, *Our Bodies, Ourselves*, 58–60.
40. Roger Scruton, *Sexual Desire: A Moral Philosophy of the Erotic* (New York: Free Press, 1986), 346.

to an end, that of the personal pleasure and sexual satisfaction of the individual consumer.[41] In short, the sexual fantasies displayed in pornography have potent metaphysical and ethical implications: they project a very specific vision of the world and of other selves. In Taylor's terms, they profoundly shape the social imaginary.

Perhaps the most obvious point in this context is that pornography detaches sex from real bodily encounter. Traditional sexual morality, which saw sexual activity as being restricted to that between a man and a woman in a lifelong relationship, assumed that legitimate sexual activity had to involve actual interpersonal bodily encounter within the context of a larger, ongoing social relationship. That meant that some kind of respect for the needs and wishes of the other person was necessary in any sexual act. This continues even in our own day of chaotic sexual ethics in the form of consent as providing the one necessary precondition for rendering a sexual encounter morally acceptable. Where this respect is lacking, the act is regarded as rape, as an assault on the other person. And we might note that sexual assault always has been—and is still—typically regarded as more serious than other forms of unwanted physical attention. A slap in the face might be most unpleasant, but it does not carry the social stigma and legal consequences of a rape, and that for good reason: sexual assault strikes deeply at who we are at the very core of our being. It denies our full selfhood and our identity. Yet pornography, too, strikes against all this. It detaches the observer's sexual pleasure from bodily encounter and thus renders it a private, personal matter, and it trivializes the sexual act portrayed by making it significant only as a matter of third-party entertainment.

This message—that sex is all about the individual and what personal satisfaction and pleasure he or she can derive from it without reference to the other—is consonant with what we have noted concerning the rise of psychological man and the therapeutic society, in which happiness is an inwardly directed sense of personal psychological

---

41. Scruton states, "In his [the sexual fantasist's] world, the sexual encounter has been 'fetishised,' to use the apt Marxian term, and every other human reality has been poisoned by the expendability of the other." *Sexual Desire*, 346.

well-being. One does not have to read Freud and Reich to be persuaded of that view of life. One can simply watch porn—or, indeed, the myriad sexual plotlines of countless movies, sitcoms, soap operas, and even commercials. If freedom and happiness are epitomized in sexual satisfaction, then pornography becomes a medium, perhaps the obvious and certainly the easiest and least personally costly medium, of liberation and fulfillment.

Closely connected to this detachment of sex from bodily encounter is the detachment of sex from interpersonal narrative. Again, one of the characteristics of traditional moral codes that restricted legitimate sexual activity within the bounds of marriage was that it also meant that sexual acts received their significance in large part because of the wider narrative context in which they occurred. Within such a framework, the relationship between a husband and wife is unique precisely because it is the only relationship they each have that is marked, or sealed, by sexual intimacy. And that sexual intimacy therefore possesses significance because of its ongoing context. It is the one thing that makes the friendship of a husband and wife unique compared to any of the other relationships and any of the other interpersonal narratives that shape their identities. The traditional Anglican wedding vows—for richer, for poorer, in sickness and in health, till death us do part—bear witness to this distinguishing quality. The sexual encounters between a husband and wife find their deeper meaning not in the personal pleasure of the moment but in the way those encounters are intended to strengthen and reinforce the unique relationship that exists between the two partners, one shaped by a shared past and present and open to a shared future.

Again, pornography, with its message that sex is about personal satisfaction, focuses on the pleasure of the present moment, without reference to past or future. It promotes a view of sex as being the activity of the sempiternal orgiast, the one who lives for sexual pleasure in the here and now with no thought about the future. It presents a view of sex whereby the participants move effortlessly from one encounter in the present to the next without any significant consequences. In this sense, it is continuous with the countless movie, soap opera, and sitcom plots in which sexual relationships are made and broken with minimal emotional cost to those involved. The pornification of culture inevitably involves the trivialization of sex.

Much evidence also suggests that pornography has exerted a dramatic effect on sexual expectations, especially those of men, and has served women particularly badly in this regard. This observation has been a staple of traditional feminist criticism. Commenting on the role of pornography in promoting sexual violence, feminist theorist Adrienne Rich notes,

> Pornography does not simply create a climate in which sex and violence are interchangeable; *it widens the range of behavior considered acceptable from men in heterosexual intercourse*—behavior which reiteratively strips women of their autonomy, dignity, and sexual potential, including the potential of loving and being loved by women in mutuality and integrity.[42]

One might build on what Rich says here to posit a connection with lesbianism: As pornography encourages men to treat women like objects and to abuse them, is it not likely that women will seek from other women the kind of emotional companionship on which properly ordered sexual activity is meant to be the seal?

Yet even among the sempiternal orgiasts of the pornography culture, it is interesting to note in passing that there is evidence to suggest that the need for narrative—the need to know something about the person with whom one engages in sexual activity, the need for history, for a past—is something of which the commercial sex industry is aware. Evidence for this sentiment comes from an unlikely source. In 2017 the Foundation for Responsible Robotics issued a report titled *Our Sexual Future with Robots*, in which it addressed the issue of what would make

---

42. Adrienne Rich, "Compulsory Heterosexuality and Lesbian Existence," *Signs* 5 (1980): 641; emphasis original. There is mounting empirical evidence that Rich's philosophical claim is correct: see Mary Anne Layden, "Pornography and Violence: A New Look at the Research," in Stoner and Hughes, *Social Costs of Pornography*, 57–68; A. J. Bridges, R. Wosnitzer, E. Scharrer, C. Sun, and R. Liberman, "Aggression and Sexual Behavior in Best-Selling Pornography Videos: A Content Analysis Update," *Violence against Women* 16, no. 10 (2010): 1065–85.

a sexual encounter with a machine truly satisfying. The following comment is interesting:

> It is an empirical question whether or not a robot can generate the same experience that a human being can. This is doubtful when we listen to the narratives of some sex workers suggesting that the pleasure of another human can often be tied to getting inside the life and emotional links of another human and to feel their enjoyment. As one sex worker puts it,
>
>> My clients always used to like to push boundaries. They like the fact that they are getting under your skin. . . . They also like to know the real you. . . .
>
>> Other sex workers tell us that clients like to party with them by joining them in drug taking and getting their back story just like a real girlfriend.[43]

For robotics experts, this relational element poses the specific challenge of making robots with a fake life story, but it surely points to the general fact that sex might not be reducible to a merely physical release after all. As the attempt to make sex simply a matter of instantaneous, punctiliar personal bodily pleasure stands at odds with our intuitive understanding that sex is more significant than that, and as we all know that sexual assault is intrinsically more heinous than a simple slap, so at least anecdotal evidence suggests that the detachment of sexual encounters from a deeper interpersonal narrative removes something that human beings want. Sex is not reducible to a moment of personal physical pleasure; there is a psychological dimension to it that has reference to the other person involved in the encounter. Sex is relational, for good or for ill, as the robotics report and such modern phenomena as the #MeToo movement indicate.

But if pornography detaches sex from past narrative context, it also detaches it from future consequences. It could be argued that this is

---

43. Noel Sharkey, Aimee Van Wynsberghe, Scott Robbins, and Eleanor Hancock, *Our Sexual Future with Robots: A Foundation for Responsible Robotics Consultation Report* (The Hague, Netherlands), 13, accessed April 6, 2019, https://responsible-robotics-myxf6pn3xr.netdna-ssl.com/wp-content/uploads/2017/11/FRR-Consultation-Report-Our-Sexual-Future-with-robots-.pdf.

true of abortion and contraception as well and that pornography is thus part of a larger culture of the detachment of sex from any broader context. There is some plausibility to this charge since both abortion and contraception allow for the detaching of sex from the production of children, the most obvious consequences of sex. But pornography involves a much more radical detachment of sex from the future even than that provided by abortion. The consumer of pornography is completely removed from any necessary consequences on the grounds that he is not personally participating in any sexual act with another person at all. This allows him to feel that he is not vulnerable to consequences. The man who has a one-night stand or uses the services of a prostitute still exposes himself at some level to interpersonal risk and concomitant consequences. He has to hand over money; he knows there is the danger of the woman telling his wife; he may be caught by the police; and so on. The solitary man sitting in front of a computer screen in the privacy of his own home is easily able to persuade himself that he risks virtually nothing.[44] Nothing is demanded of him, and he gives nothing in return. It is, to use Mark Regnerus's term, very cheap sex.

Finally, pornography detaches sex from any ethical context. Ethics are a function of narrative, a function of relationships, a function of context and consequences, and because all these are absent in the consumption of pornography, the constant message being projected is that sex itself has no ethical context or intrinsic moral content.[45] Again, for Bolz-Weber to refer to "ethically sourced porn" and thus to raise the issue of its origin as the only criterion by which to judge the morality of pornography is to betray the fact that she regards pornography in itself, as a concept, as having no

---

44. Of course, such a man may actually be taking significant risks, given the reality of web tracking and even of inadvertently viewing illegal content. But it is much easier for him to convince himself that such contemporary risks are remote than for a member of an earlier generation to do so relative to the more obviously immediate risks that he faced. And the actors on the screen pose no danger to him at all.

45. The words of Catholic philosopher Dietrich von Hildebrand regarding sex outside the context of the marriage relationship have clear implications for the underlying metaphysical significance of pornography: "The moment I treat physical sex as something complete in itself and take no account of its profoundest function, namely, in wedded love, I falsify its ultimate significance and become blind to the mystery it contains. Physical sex is certainly something distinct from love, but, nevertheless, between it and wedded love there subsists a preestablished harmony. Its true significance as an experience is inseparable from its character as the expression and flower of a specific kind of love." *In Defense of Purity: An Analysis of the Catholic Ideals of Purity and Virginity* (Steubenville, OH: Hildebrand, 2017), 7.

moral value one way or the other beyond that relating to whether the acts depicted are consensual. This belief misses the point made by Mona Charen, that pornography is degrading, and not simply to the women involved—a point she sees as missed even by feminist critiques:

> Feminists saw porn—accurately, in my judgment—as a degradation of women. Yet they always interpret life through the narrow lens of women's oppression by men, which prevents them from seeing that its harm is to human dignity and not just to women as a class. Porn encourages immorality because it treats people as means, not ends— which is exactly what casual sex does. Porn is, in a sense, the logical end point of the sexual revolution because it completes the separation of sex from love and relationships. Sexual release is commodified, packaged, and sold. The right to pleasure may be assured, 24/7, but it carries with it the debasement of human beings.[46]

Charen's final point is most perceptive: pornography epitomizes the sexual revolution because it presents sex as merely a physical, pleasurable act that is divorced from any greater relational significance.

And that, in turn, means that pornography is simply one manifestation of our contemporary world of therapy and expressive individualism, where sex itself has no intrinsic moral content and sexual ethics hangs on the spider-web-thin thread of consent. We might therefore conclude that the likes of Bolz-Weber, while obviously not to be listed among the profoundest thinkers on the issue of sexual ethics, are nonetheless great examples of the therapeutic, expressivist spirit of the age: if porn works for you, if it promotes that sense of inner well-being that is the basic moral imperative of the therapeutic age, then as long as nobody was harmed in its production, as long as everybody on the film set consented (and let us not worry overmuch about the problematic nature of defining

---

46. Mona Charen, *Sex Matters: How Modern Feminism Lost Touch with Science, Love, and Common Sense* (New York: Crown Forum, 2018), 53. Roger Scruton makes a similar observation in terms of the aesthetic difference between erotic art and pornography: "In distinguishing the erotic and the pornographic, we are really distinguishing two kinds of interest: interest in the embodied person and interest in the body. . . . Pornography, like slavery, is a denial of the human subject, a way of negating the moral demand that free beings must treat each other as ends in themselves." Roger Scruton, *Beauty: A Very Short Introduction* (Oxford: Oxford University Press, 2009), 159.

and discerning consent), then all is good. This thinking is a basic element of how sex is envisaged in our modern social imaginary.

PORNIFIED POP CULTURE

If the burden of this chapter has been to show that the marketing of sex has a foundational role in modern society, whether through the pretentious ambitions of the surrealists or the pure hedonism of Hefner and his spiritual children, then it is worth reflecting for a moment on how total the triumph of the erotic has been.

I noted in chapter 6 that one of Freud's major contributions was his claim that children are sexual beings, that sexuality cannot be something that is sequestered in the period of life after puberty. That idea grips the popular educational imagination, where every sexual issue, from teen pregnancy to sexually transmitted diseases, has to be addressed from the perspective of more sex education—and that of a merely technical kind, divorced from any traditional moral framework. The advent of gay rights, and now transgender rights, has served only to intensify the pressure for such sex education earlier and earlier in a child's life.[47]

Yet it is not only in the field of education that we see the triumph of the erotic, or perhaps better the pornographic. The realm of pop culture also provides plenty of evidence for this. Reality TV, the apotheosis of expressive individualism as entertainment, is full of sexual themes, as are soap operas, sitcoms, and movies. The old joke about actresses only appearing nude "when the plot demands it" now seems somewhat pointless; in a world in which the erotic has triumphed, the plot is likely always to demand it because that is what the audience has come to expect as a sign of authenticity. #MeToo has raised obvious questions about how to film such scenes in the modern age, but one might respond that such questions occur only in a world in which nude sexual encounters on screen have become apparently indispensable—a world in which the erotic has already triumphed.

---

47. See, for example, Colleen Shalby, "Controversial Sex Education Framework for California Approved despite Protest," *Los Angeles Times*, May 10, 2019, https://www.latimes.com/local/lanow/la-me-sex-education-california-20190510-story.html.

Pop music is particularly interesting in this regard. It is perhaps one of the quintessential products of the sexualization of our expressive individualist culture that is focused on public performance of any and all inner feelings. It is also a great example of the way youth has become a priority of our culture, both because of the philosophical underpinnings of expressive individualism—in which society is that which corrupts, which thus bestows on childhood a certain authenticity that adulthood lacks—and because of the importance of youth marketing to the consumer economy. And the lyrics, aesthetics, and preoccupations of many of its leading examples are profoundly sexual.

When a terrorist bomb exploded at Ariana Grande's concert in Manchester, United Kingdom, in 2017, *The New York Times* reported on the tragedy and made the passing observation that the audience was made up of "adoring adolescent fans."[48] That statement is hardly surprising since Grande is marketed to teenage girls. What is interesting, however, is that her lyrics are very sexually explicit, with frequent references to sexual intercourse, insatiable sexual desire, and casual sexual encounters. In her song "Right There," featuring a gentleman known as "Big Sean," she even offers a pithy and pellucid summary of how expressive individualism and the therapeutic find expression in a highly sexualized culture. Grande's concise clarity in this regard should surely make the more prolix Charles Taylor and opaque Philip Rieff green with envy, as she celebrates individual desires and asks how something that "feels so right" can be wrong.[49] Of course, it might be objected that people buy pop music for how it makes them feel, not for the lyrics. But there is surely something significant in the fact that pop artists now market sexually explicit songs, often accompanied with erotic videos, to teenagers. If the lyrics do not matter, why are so many of these songs preoccupied with sex? This reality surely indicates something of the way sex has come to be the dominant idiom for expressive individualism in our contemporary

---

48. Rory Smith and Sewell Chan, "Ariana Grande Manchester Concert Ends in Explosion, Panic and Death," *New York Times*, May 22, 2017, https://www.nytimes.com/2017/05/22/world/europe/ariana-grande-manchester-police.html.

49. For the song lyrics, see Ariana Grande, "Right There," AZLyrics, accessed July 23, 2019, https://www.azlyrics.com/lyrics/arianagrande/rightthere.html.

culture. These singers would be mocked if they produced songs with lyrics advocating celibacy or criticizing premarital sexual activity. The erotic/pornographic has triumphed in our culture to the point that it is precisely the advocacy of traditional sexual mores that has come to be regarded at best as ridiculous, at worst as downright immoral and oppressive. When Nadia Bolz-Weber issued her call for people to send her purity rings so that she could melt them down and have them remade into a giant model vagina, she was not simply engaging in one of her typically desperate attempts to grab a shocking headline, she was also playing to the priorities of our contemporary *Sittlichkeit*, which rewards and lionizes those who set their faces against anything resembling traditional modesty or sexual codes. The social imaginary has made Reichian thinking intuitive.

The philosophical claim I am making here is that the normalization of pornography in mainstream culture is deeply connected to the mainstream culture's rejection of any kind of sacred order. Pornography carries with it a philosophy of sex and of what it means to be human that is inimical to traditional religious perspectives, in the West's case primarily Christianity. It is therefore both symptomatic and constitutive of the decreated, desacralized world that emerges in modern times, with roots in Rousseau and Romanticism, and given sharp expression in philosophical and scientific idioms by Marx, Nietzsche, Darwin, Freud, and the New Left. The triumph of pornography is both evidence of the death of God and one means by which he is killed.[50]

The Triumph of the Erotic and the Anticulture

Rieff, following Freud, sees cultures as defined by that which they forbid, specifically those sexual activities and relationships that they prohibit.

---

50. Empirical evidence is emerging that supports my philosophical point concerning the metaphysical implications of pornography. In an important 2017 article, sociologists Samuel L. Perry and George M. Hayward argue that there is a clear link between pornography use and the rejection of traditional religious belief, particularly among teenagers. See Perry and Hayward, "Seeing Is (Not) Believing: How Viewing Pornography Shapes the Religious Lives of Young Americans," *Social Forces* 95, no. 4 (2017): 1757–88, https://www.ncbi.nlm.nih.gov/pmc/articles/PMC5439973/.

From this perspective, then, the triumph of the erotic, with its comprehensive rejection of traditional sexual codes, marks the death of traditional culture and the advent of the anticulture. Expressed in other Rieffian terminology, it embodies the death of first and second worlds, built on sacred order, and the rise of a third world, built on the rejection of any sacred order whatsoever. It is not that third worlds build on second worlds; they repudiate them and demolish them.

Surrealism and the mainstreaming of pornography are both central to this development. For the surrealists, the project was intimately connected to the idea of socialist revolution, and Breton and his colleagues correctly identified the overturning of sexual morality as the means of overturning a Western culture that was built on a Christian sexual ethic. Hugh Hefner and those who followed him may not have had the same self-conscious political aims as the surrealists, but their impact has been no less revolutionary. Pornography and the pornification of pop culture has been critical to the destruction of sexual norms, to the reinforcement of an expressive individualist view of selfhood, and to the transformation of the West. At its heart, it makes individual sexual gratification the gold standard of personal human happiness and thereby makes sex a matter of the therapeutic ideal, not of any kind of objective morality; it prioritizes the present instant over either the past or the future; and it promotes a view of history that plays precisely to the kind of narrative that grips the popular imagination—the past is a land of sexual repression and therefore oppression. The present and the future offer the chance of freedom precisely through the rejection of that past's sexual mores and related social practices. And the root-and-branch nature of this revolution should not be underestimated: it seeks not simply to expand traditional moral categories but to demonize and destroy them. Hugh Hefner was not seeking to broaden the definition of modesty any more than Miley Cyrus or Ariana Grande are seeking to broaden the concept of chastity through their raunchy stage performances and explicit lyrics. Debating skirt lengths or the acceptability of bikinis assumes a concept of modesty and then seeks to find where its limits might lie at any given point in time. Pornography seeks to make the very concept of modesty a laughable, unrealistic notion in its entirety. Whether the attack comes from the New Left, with its view of modesty as an ideological instrument of oppression, or from hedonists, for whom the idea is simply a tool used by killjoys to stop others having fun and being who they want to be, the result is the same: modesty is immoral, and modest people are repressed, incomplete, and less fulfilled than they could or should be.

One might respond by saying that other cultures—first and second worlds—had a place for sex that we might characterize today as pornographic. The Sanskrit text *Kama Sutra* might be one such example, to which we might add the sexual escapades of the Greek gods. The difference between these ancient examples and sex in the modern world, however, is that pornography detaches sex from any kind of transcendent meaning. *Kama Sutra* sought to set sexual pleasure in the broader context of a happy life well lived, and the sexual escapades of the Greek gods were not intended as normative patterns of behavior by which society might be organized. No one can deny that sex has been a powerful cultural force. But the detachment of sex from any larger metaphysical narrative and its placement at the center of how we think of ourselves is new—and, one might add, lethal to cultures of the first and second worlds.

This brings me to the question of how this shift shapes the social imaginary. This transformation of sexual mores has profoundly affected the *Sittlichkeit* of society, that framework of values that provides the grammar and syntax of recognition, that by which the individual expresses his or her personal identity in a way that is acknowledged by others. As noted in part 3, the idea that sexuality is identity is now basic and intuitive in the West, and this means that all matters pertaining to sex are therefore matters that concern who we are at the deepest level. Sex is identity, sex is politics, sex is culture. And central to this thinking is the notion that traditional sexual codes that value celibacy and chastity actually militate against authenticity, something that is now intuitive. I noted in the introduction that nobody has to have seen the film *The 40-Year-Old Virgin* to know that it is a comedy, for the idea of a middle-aged virgin is today self-evidently comical. In our world, it speaks of someone who is somehow inadequate or who has failed to be a fully rounded and fulfilled human being. To reach forty without being sexually active is indicative of a failed life. That is the result of a culture, of a social imaginary, in which personal sexual satisfaction in the context of sexual freedom corralled only by the notion of consent is presented as the aspirational norm for proper human selfhood.

Yet this triumph of the erotic through the crudity of pornography and the vulgarity of the society in which pornography can plausibly enter the mainstream of culture is also, to use a phrase from Mario Vargas Llosa, the disappearance of eroticism. The disappearance of taboos and the public display of that which should be most private and intimate destroys any mystery—and transcendent significance—that might be applied to sex and sexuality. Where sex is reduced to nothing more than a pleasant biological function, a recreational activity with no intrinsic significance beyond the immediate pleasure it involves, and is restricted by nothing more than the often-nebulous and complicated concept of mutual consent, then human beings are themselves reduced. To quote Llosa,

> The inanity and vulgarity that has been undermining culture has also damaged in some way one of democratic society's most important achievements in our day and age: sexual liberation, the disappearance of many taboos and prejudices surrounding erotic life. Because, as in art and literature, the disappearance of the idea of form in matters of sex is not progress but rather a backward movement that denatures freedom and impoverishes sex, reducing it to something purely instinctive and animalistic.[51]

That crude, vulgar society is the world in which we now live and, if we are honest, of which we are a complicit part. The modern social imaginary on which the sexual revolution is profoundly influential is the social imaginary of us all.

---

51. Mario Vargas Llosa, *Notes on the Death of Culture: Essays on Spectacle and Society*, trans. John King (New York: Picador, 2012), 99.

The Triumph of the Therapeutic

Glory to man in the highest! For Man is the master of things.
ALGERNON SWINBURNE, "HYMN OF MAN"

If the triumph of the erotic is evident through the prevalence and influence of pornography in today's society, it must also be understood as part of the much wider change in the dominant notions of selfhood and human fulfillment. This was famously characterized by Philip Rieff as "the triumph of the therapeutic," the phrase he used for the title of his important 1966 book; in retrospect, however, the triumph had only just begun by the mid-1960s. The more than fifty years since that date have witnessed the slow and steady transformation of all areas of public life by the therapeutic. And nowhere is this more evident than in matters of public ethics, whether defined by the law, by the most influential thinkers in the field, or in the behavior that has come to be almost routine on college campuses. Indeed, if one wishes to see just how deep the pathologies identified in the narrative in parts 2 and 3 run in modern Western culture, then one need look no further than the Supreme Court of the United States, the classrooms of the Ivy League, and the student behavior and campus protests that have seized so many headlines in the last few years. The logic of all three is essentially the same: it is that of expressive individualism working out in the public sphere and often driven by therapeutic concerns.

The Supreme Court and Gay Marriage

In theory, it is the role of law courts to interpret the law and apply it to contemporary questions and problems as they present themselves. Yet it is precisely that matter of interpretation that makes legal judgments such an interesting historical phenomenon. Judges, too, are human beings; they have a historical context and a historically shaped consciousness; and they are therefore subject to having their opinions and their approach to the meaning of legal texts shaped by the culture around them and by the way they understand society to have developed. When it comes to the American Constitution, originalism—the conviction that law must be read according to the understanding of those who originally drafted it—may have been given new life through the work of Antonin Scalia, but it has scarcely carried the day on a number of key decisions. In fact, numerous Supreme Court decisions provide first-class evidence of the pervasive nature of a variety of the themes we have explored in earlier chapters, from the rise of expressive individualism and the psychologizing of the self to the antihistorical tendency that ironically has often clothed itself under the guise of being on "the right side of history."

Perhaps the most obvious example of this shift is the 2015 majority ruling in *Obergefell v. Hodges*, which found a right to gay marriage in the Constitution. This decision captures the spirit of our age in numerous ways, given that it reflects changing attitudes to sex and marriage. Yet the ruling did not arise in a vacuum but represented the culmination of a trajectory of legal decisions that began some decades earlier, most obviously in the Supreme Court decision in the case of *Planned Parenthood of Southeastern Pennsylvania v. Casey*, 505 U.S. 833, 851 (1992). When the *Obergefell v. Hodges* decision is set against the background of this longer narrative, it becomes clear just how deep seated are the changes in our culture that *Obergefell v. Hodges* reflects and on which it depends. Gay marriage did not make gay marriage plausible; the Supreme Court did not make gay marriage plausible. Gay marriage is plausible because of the wider transformation of the social imaginary that we have noted in earlier chapters, and the background to and justification offered by the majority for the *Obergefell* decision demonstrate this fact.

PLANNED PARENTHOOD OF SOUTHEASTERN PENNSYLVANIA V. CASEY (1992)

The Supreme Court case of *Planned Parenthood of Southeastern Pennsylvania v. Casey* was brought by a number of Planned Parenthood abortion clinics against a Pennsylvania bill passed into law that sought to impose restrictions on abortion, such as the need for preabortion counseling and spousal consent. It was historically significant as an opportunity, after several appointees by pro-life Republican presidents, for *Roe v. Wade*, 410 U.S. 113 (1973), to be overturned as a precedent by the Supreme Court. In fact, it proved something of a disappointment from that perspective because it did nothing to overturn the central holdings of *Roe*. But that is not the concern here. The decision's real interest for my argument in this book lies not so much in the details of its findings regarding abortion as in the definition of personal freedom it expressed and also in the way in which it applied the principle of legal precedent.

The statement about personal freedom and self-definition that it contained has since become infamous for the way it effectively gives legal status to a subjective and plastic notion of what it means to be a human. Poiesis here triumphs decisively over mimesis. The key passage reads as follows:

> At the heart of liberty is the right to define one's own concept of existence, of meaning, of the universe, and of the mystery of human life. Beliefs about these matters could not define the attributes of personhood were they formed under compulsion of the State.[1]

---

1. Planned Parenthood of Southeastern Pennsylvania v. Casey, 505 U.S. 833, 851 (1992), https://www.law.cornell.edu/supremecourt/text/505/833.

This is a concise articulation of the expressive individualism and psychological subjectivity regarding the self that we have traced in its development from Jean-Jacques Rousseau to the present day. Such a statement should really be deemed incoherent when it comes from a legal body because it is arguably mystical in its approach to personhood. And what does law exist for if it is not to establish or maintain under some kind of compulsion or restraint a broader notion of human personhood that transcends the personal convictions of any given individual? Serial killers and child molesters still (thankfully) do not have the right to "define their own concept of existence" in twenty-first-century America. Their right to define their own concept of existence is restricted by the fact that their chosen callings are illegal and subject to severe legal penalty. Yet this statement sounds so plausible and features as part of what is supposed to be a serious legal argument because it so accurately captures the way most people—including, it would seem, a number of Supreme Court justices—imagine themselves to be. It is consistent, we might say, with the *Sittlichkeit*, the ethical framework, of wider society and is thus immune to significant challenge. It resonates with the intuitions of the modern social imaginary. And its significance for the subsequent rulings on homosexuality and gay marriage lies in the fact that it cements into law the notion of individual freedom that underlies the modern concept of selfhood we find expressed in the sexual revolution.

The second significant aspect of the court's opinion is the weight placed on the precedential nature of *Roe v. Wade* in shaping the decision. The *Casey* opinion begins with the statement that "liberty finds no refuge in a jurisprudence of doubt" and then proceeds to comment that the fact that *Roe v. Wade* established a clear legal precedent on the matter of abortion rights had formed a major part of the court's reasoning. Of course, legal precedents are not absolute and can be overturned, but specific criteria need to be used in order to make sure that these are not common occurrences. Casual overturning of precedent would indeed undermine the authority and stability of the court. The standard used in this case to decide whether precedent should be overturned was whether the central holding in *Roe* had proved unworkable or had been undermined by developments in constitutional law in the years since the ruling. The opinion stated that this was not the case, and therefore the precedent held.

The intricacies of the application of precedent in this specific case are not what is of most interest in the development of constitutional law in the years leading up to *Obergefell v. Hodges*. Rather, it is the arbitrary application of this principle, as revealed by a later case, that is so revealing about the way legal decisions reflect the dynamics of the culture—or, to use Rieff's term, the anticulture—of our day. The flip-flop on precedent that the later case of *Lawrence v. Texas*, 539 U.S. 558 (2003), involved speaks eloquently of what really drives some of these key decisions.

LAWRENCE V. TEXAS (2003)

The second important Supreme Court decision, one that provides more direct legal background for *Obergefell v. Hodges*, is the 2003 case of *Lawrence v. Texas*. Texas law at the time prohibited certain intimate sexual contact between people of the same sex, and this was being challenged by two men who had been apprehended while engaged in such conduct in their own home and were subsequently convicted of sodomy. The Supreme Court ruled in favor of the two men and thus overthrew a previous judgment in the 1986 case of *Bowers v. Hardwick*, 478 U.S. 186 (1986), in which the court had upheld a Georgia law forbidding oral and anal sex between consenting adults.[2]

What makes the ruling in *Lawrence v. Texas* interesting is both its clear move to legitimate homosexual activity and also the willingness of certain of the justices to overthrow legal precedent in a manner that would seem antithetical to the logic that provided the justification for the ruling in *Planned Parenthood v. Casey*. This concern formed a central part of the dissenting opinion of Justice Antonin Scalia.

In his dissent, Scalia points out that three members of the majority in *Planned Parenthood v. Casey* had argued in that decision that the

---

2. Bowers v. Hardwick, 478 U.S. 186 (1986), https://www.law.cornell.edu/supremecourt/text/478/186; Lawrence v. Texas, 539 U.S. 558 (2003), https://www.law.cornell.edu/supremecourt/text/02-102%26amp.

precedent of *Roe v. Wade* should be upheld because if the Supreme Court allowed its decision to be affected by widespread popular opposition to its decisions, then it would lose its legitimacy.[3] By way of contrast, the ruling in *Lawrence v. Texas* made such popular criticism a basis for overturning the precedent of *Bowers v. Hardwick*. Scalia quotes from the decision as follows: "Bowers, the Court says, has been subject to substantial and continuing [criticism], disapproving of its reasoning in all respects, not just as to its historical assumptions."[4] Scalia first points out that this criticism is not specified by the majority and that such also applies to the ruling in *Roe v. Wade*. Then he proceeds to point out that another reason cited for overturning the *Bowers v. Hardwick* decision is that there is no significant individual or social reliance on it that would prevent it from being overturned. In this context, Scalia notes that the principle it reflects—the belief that certain sexual behavior is immoral and unacceptable—has been basic to the legal regulation of sexual morality since ancient times. Furthermore, this principle, specifically as represented in the decision in *Bowers v. Hardwick*, was an important source for the ruling in the case *Barnes v. Glen Theatre, Inc.*, 501 U.S. 560 (1991).[5] In short, overturning *Bowers v. Hardwick* is an extremely significant move on the part of the court.[6] Later in his opinion, Scalia even goes so far as to be specific (and, in hindsight, prophetic) about what social and legal institutions might be affected by the logic of the decision: "This reasoning leaves on pretty shaky grounds state laws limiting marriage to opposite sex couples."[7]

---

3. Scalia quotes the following from the controlling opinion in *Planned Parenthood v. Casey*: "Where, in the performance of its judicial duties, the Court decides a case in such a way as to resolve the sort of intensely divisive controversy reflected in *Roe*[,] . . . its decision has a dimension that the resolution of the normal case does not carry. . . . [T]o overrule under fire in the absence of the most compelling reason . . . would subvert the Court's legitimacy beyond any serious question." *Scalia's Court: A Legacy of Landmark Opinions and Dissents*, with edits and commentary by Kevin A. Ring (Washington, DC: Regnery, 2016), 359.

4. *Scalia's Court*, 360.

5. This case involved the constitutionality of an Indiana law that banned full nudity in public places and that had been applied to clubs that hosted nude dancers for the entertainment of customers. The Supreme Court ruled that a state has the constitutional authority to ban public nudity, even when it was part of an artistic activity, such as dancing, because the law in question "furthers a substantial governmental interest in protecting societal order and morality." See Barnes v. Glen Theatre, Inc., 501 U.S. 560 (1991), https://www.law.cornell.edu/supremecourt/text/501/560.

6. *Scalia's Court*, 361.

7. *Scalia's Court*, 371.

Scalia's closing comment on the section of the ruling that dealt with the status of legal precedent goes to the very heart of the matter. The inconsistent approach to precedent has, he declares, "exposed *Casey's* extraordinary deference to precedent for the result-oriented expedient that it is."[8]

While the details of the role of precedent in legal interpretation are well beyond the scope of this book, this last comment clearly resonates with another aspect of our earlier argument. As Anthony Kennedy's mystical definition of personhood in *Planned Parenthood v. Casey* represents the assumptions of the wider culture of expressive individualism in a judicial context, so the philosophical flip-flop that Scalia notes between that earlier ruling and the approach in *Lawrence v. Texas* would seem to indicate the kind of pragmatic approach to legal decisions that a culture of psychologized selfhood and an ethics based on personal happiness would engender. The key issue is not philosophical consistency in the interpretation and application of the law but the therapeutic result that needs to be achieved by any plausible means necessary. If society needs abortion rights to keep women happy, then the law must be made to yield such results. If society requires the affirmation of certain sexual activities and identities to affirm certain classes of individuals, then the law must be made to yield those results—even if the methods used to achieve these two results are inconsistent with each other and perhaps even antithetical. Scalia does not use the language of therapy, but his verdict on the reasoning of his colleagues indicates that what he is describing is the culture of therapy manifesting itself in the judgments of the Supreme Court. The stage is clearly being set in such a way that legal resistance to gay marriage will prove futile: personhood has been redefined, and the therapeutic goal of legal decisions has been established.

Before turning to the *Obergefell v. Hodges* case, however, there is one more significant Supreme Court case that is relevant.

---

8. *Scalia's Court*, 362.

UNITED STATES V. WINDSOR (2013)

The background to *United States v. Windsor* was provided by the 1996 Defense of Marriage Act (DOMA), signed into law by President Bill Clinton, which excluded same-sex partnerships from the federal definition of marriage. In 2007, Edith Windsor married her same-sex partner, Thea Spyer, in Ontario, Canada. The couple lived in the United States, in New York State, and when Spyer died in 2009, Windsor tried to claim the federal estate tax exemption to which legally recognized spouses are entitled. This claim was denied under the terms of section 3 of DOMA, which excluded same-sex partnerships, and Windsor sued. Her claim was upheld by both a district court and the Court of Appeals for the Second Circuit in 2012. Then, with the case pending for the Supreme Court, the Justice Department announced that it would not seek to defend DOMA. At this point, a bipartisan legal advisory group of the House of Representatives voted to take up the suit with a view to determining the constitutionality of section 3.

The Supreme Court ruled, by a five-four majority, that section 3 was unconstitutional and thereby effectively overturned the central principle of DOMA, that marriage was to be exclusively defined as being between one man and one woman. Given the way that cultural attitudes to gay marriage had changed since the passage of DOMA, the decision was perhaps not a surprise. What was surprising, however, was the characterization by the court's majority of the motive of the opponents of gay marriage that underlay DOMA. The relevant passage reads as follows:

> DOMA's unusual deviation from the usual tradition of recognizing and accepting state definitions of marriage here operates to deprive same-sex couples of the benefits and responsibilities that come with the federal recognition of their marriages. This is strong evidence of a law having the purpose and effect of disapproval of that class. The avowed purpose and practical effect of the law here in question are to impose a disadvantage, a separate status, and so a stigma upon all who enter into same-sex marriages made lawful by the unquestioned authority of the States.[9]

---

9. For the full text of the decision, see United States v. Windsor, 699 F. 3d 169 (2013), https://www.law.cornell.edu/supremecourt/text/12-307.

In technical legal terms, the court is here claiming that the motivation behind DOMA was unconstitutional animus. That means that the sole reason that in DOMA the federal government took it on itself to regulate marriage—a matter traditionally left to individual states—was to marginalize a particular group otherwise protected by the law, that is, homosexuals.

What is striking about this claim is that it effectively denies that there is any rational basis for defining marriage as between one man and one woman. This is interesting from the perspective of the emotivism that Alasdair MacIntyre has identified as the way ethical discussion typically operates today. What we have here is an example of such emotivism being used polemically to dismiss arguments for DOMA, a claim that sees emotivism as the preserve of one side (DOMA supporters) as opposed to the rational arguments of the other (those who seek to strike down DOMA). Yet supporters of traditional marriage have numerous arguments that they would consider rational—for example, the overwhelming consensus of tradition regarding marriage as between one man and one woman and the role of procreation and family life. That such matters can be dismissed so easily as irrational and (presumably) as nothing more than a specious cover for marginalizing gay couples, points toward the triumph of the kind of cultural pathologies delineated in earlier chapters. The standard of rationality with which the majority of the justices is operating is not the standard of rationality in, say, the Book of Common Prayer, which argues that marriage is ordained to fulfill three basic functions: the procreation and nurture of children, mutual comfort and support, and a context for legitimate sexual relations. One might disagree with the Book of Common Prayer's definition, but to dismiss it as irrational and as a cloak for bigotry involves both a particular understanding of what constitutes a rational argument and a remarkable act of telepathy by which the hidden motivations of certain groups can be discerned by members of the Supreme Court. The latter is highly unlikely; the former requires an act of cultural hubris whereby the elites of contemporary culture have an apparent monopoly on what can be declared rational.

A further noteworthy aspect of the *United States v. Windsor* judgment is the majority's concern that DOMA enshrines inequality. This in itself is an argument that rests on interesting shifts in the notion of what human beings and marriage are for. Under DOMA, every individual enjoyed the same rights and labored under the same restrictions as everyone else. Men, heterosexual and gay, could marry women and could not marry men. Women, heterosexual and lesbian, could marry men and could not marry women. So how is it that this can be interpreted as enshrining inequality? It would seem that such a judgment can be understood only in a situation in which equality is defined as the ability of every individual to redefine marriage in the manner in which he or she chooses. This notion is presumably not what the Supreme Court was consciously trying to achieve, but there are some obvious questions to ask about the ruling in this regard. Why can marriage not be between one man and two or more women? Why should marriage be restricted to a relationship that is exclusively human? Could the case not be made that to refuse to recognize polygamy or a marriage between a man and a dog would marginalize in turn the polygamous and zoophilic communities?

Such questions might seem distasteful, but that takes us to the heart of what is happening here. The rejection of traditional arguments for marriage and the assertion that DOMA enshrines inequality are really a function of the wider tastes of the culture in which the judgment takes place. Polygamy and (even more so) bestiality still stand outside the current framework of what is socially acceptable. And it is that framework that ultimately determines what is rational judgment and what is irrational animus.

In sum, the three Supreme Court rulings above set the scene and established the logic for the gay marriage decision in *Obergefell v. Hodges*. The court essentially affirmed expressive individualism in *Planned Parenthood v. Casey*, revealed through its flip-flop in the use of legal precedent in *Lawrence v. Texas* that the principles guiding its rulings were profoundly shaped by the therapeutic outcomes desired by the wider culture, and demonstrated by an act of willful cultural amnesia in *United States v. Windsor* that traditional marriage advocates could plausibly be dismissed as motivated by irrational prejudice. Indeed, in the wake of these three rulings, it is hard to believe that there was ever any doubt about how the court would rule in *Obergefell v. Hodges*.

OBERGEFELL V. HODGES (2015)

After the judgment in *United States v. Windsor*, numerous cases involving gay marriages made their way up through the court system until, in 2015, the Supreme Court ruled on the matter in the case of *Obergefell v. Hodges*. It found, again by a five-four majority, that gay marriage was protected by the Constitution.

The ruling that gay marriage is constitutional and therefore to be recognized by the states rests on four particular principles as stated in the majority opinion:

> A first premise of the Court's relevant precedents is that the right to personal choice regarding marriage is inherent in the concept of individual autonomy. . . . A second principle in this Court's jurisprudence is that the right to marry is fundamental because it supports a two-person union unlike any other in its importance to the committed individuals. . . . A third basis for protecting the right to marry is that it safeguards children and families and thus draws meaning from related rights of childrearing, procreation, and education. . . . Fourth and finally, this Court's cases and the Nation's traditions make clear that marriage is a keystone of our social order.[10]

These four points—autonomy, the fundamental nature of a two-person union, the safeguarding of children and families, and the importance of the nation's tradition—offer an eloquent though rather odd combination of reasons for legitimating gay marriage.

The first point, that the right to personal choice in marriage is inherent in the concept of individual autonomy, represents the triumph of expressive individualism in society, as reflected in the court's reasoning, which we saw in Kennedy's infamous passage on self-definition in

---

10. Obergefell v. Hodges, 576 U.S. ___ (2015), https://www.law.cornell.edu/supremecourt/text/14
-556#writing-14-556_OPINION_3.

Planned Parenthood v. Casey. This is not unique to the LGBTQ+ community but is rather something that pertains to us all and points to one of the underlying arguments of this book—that the sexual revolution is a manifestation of a much deeper revolution in what it means to be a self. This helps explain in part why gay marriage is so plausible: it connects with the prevalent understanding of what it means to be a free individual that pervades modern culture.

The second point, that the right to marry is fundamental because it supports a two-person union like no other, is vulnerable to the criticism we noted in the section on *United States v. Windsor*. Yes, it is true that marriage has traditionally been a two-person union. Yet historically its uniqueness has typically been connected both to procreation and to its being a lifelong bond, both of which no longer apply in modern society, given the existence of no-fault divorce laws.

It has also traditionally been a two-person union between people of the opposite sex. The matter of number has actually been less important than the matter of sex. Polygamy, for example, is historically attested as a practice. But the concept of marriage that polygamy assumes is one of the relationship between different sexes, typically a man and two or more women. So why does the traditional view of the number of parties involved enjoy the status of a normative, rational position while the traditional notion of the sex of the persons involved does not? The answer is surely that the canons of reason that are operative here are determined not by the definition of marriage but rather by the contemporary tastes of the wider culture. And these tastes are themselves a function of the sexual mores and expressive individualism of the time. They are intuitions of the modern social imaginary. While it is still distasteful to argue for polygamy (and hence the normative two-person marriage is an easy position to assume, given that it is less likely to be challenged), it is also distasteful to argue against gay marriage, given that this would involve depriving gay people of the chance of happiness that marriage involves and that they are being denied.

To put the argument in a slightly different way: by 2015 society had already accepted the legitimacy of homosexual sexual activity, which in turn assumes the divorce of sexual activity from its traditional context within marriage for the purpose of procreation. Gay marriage is therefore an easy matter to sell to the wider culture on the grounds that the bases for objecting to it have already been conceded. Polygamous marriage, however, is still outside the bounds of the acceptable because society simply has not had enough time to accustom itself to the idea of polygamy as a legitimate lifestyle choice. This is no doubt reinforced in the popular imagination by, among other things, its connotations of Mormon fundamentalism and also the exploitation of women, neither of which will help it gain in popularity, given the general tendency in today's society to regard religious conservatism in general as something sinister and its abhorrence of anything that might appear to involve male exploitation of women.[11]

The third point, that marriage protects families and children, is no doubt reassuring rhetoric—who wants to support what might be seen to undermine families or jeopardize children? But the fact is that American law does not prioritize the protection of children in its marriage laws. The existence of no-fault divorce, by which marriages can be dissolved at will without any grounds beyond the desire of the contracting parties (or, in some jurisdictions, effectively just one of them), meant that by 2015 marriage was already an extremely weak institution as far as its role in protecting children was concerned, laws regarding obligations for post-divorce child support notwithstanding. Therefore, when the court points to the meaning that the institution draws from its various related rights, this argument seems to have more to do with the feelings of personal value that the spouses might derive from marriage and its concomitant elements than anything to do with really supporting the institution of the family as in itself a social good. In short, this reason uses attractive and traditional-sounding language that, when set in the wider cultural and legal context, is really a mask for an underlying therapeutic concern. And it should go without saying that a gay marriage cannot produce children. It can be gerrymandered to do so via adjusting adoption and surrogacy

---

11. See, for example, Libby Copeland, "Is Polygamy Really So Awful?," *Slate*, January 30, 2012, https://slate.com/human-interest/2012/01/the-problem-with-polygamy.html.

laws, but it is itself inherently sterile. So granting a gay couple the right to marry does not, in itself, bring in its wake the existence of a family; that depends on other laws and social practices—again, pointing to the fact that this ruling cannot be isolated from a host of other social practices and beliefs that already enjoy status within the social imaginary. It is as much a symptom of the changing definition of marriage within society as it is a contributing cause.

The fourth and final point, that the nation's tradition points to the role of marriage as a keystone of society, is yet another example of the selective use of tradition and the plastic definition of marriage with which the majority operates. When tradition can be edited in such a way as to confirm modern taste, then tradition apparently has authority. When tradition runs counter to the exigencies of contemporary taste—for example, when it defines marriage as between a man and a woman—it is to be dismissed as having no rational basis, as motivated by animus, as perpetuating inequality, as an affront to the dignity of the gay and lesbian community, and as denying fundamental freedoms essential to what it means to be a human.

To the extent that marriage has been a keystone of the social order, it has been marriage defined in a particular way, as a lifelong bond between a man and woman until death parts them or some extreme cause—adultery or abuse—provides grounds for dissolution. It is therefore illegitimate to change the meaning of marriage into something unprecedented and then claim that tradition indicates that this has proved so vital to society over time. One could do the same with any historic institution or idea. For example, representative democracy has proved a keystone of society; therefore, we are going to grant the vote to dogs and cats. This kind of argument, cloaking itself in the language of history in order to overthrow precisely the history on which it purportedly rests its case, represents a form of nominalism that is as breathtaking in its audacity as it is incoherent in its logic. It uses an appeal to tradition to overthrow key elements of the tradition by fundamentally changing, without sufficient acknowledgment, the very meaning of a key term.

But what is really interesting is not that the reasoning is problematic; we noted before the flexible, even contradictory, use of precedent in the rulings that provide the background to *Obergefell v. Hodges*. Rather, it is the fact that such reasoning is not considered problematic at all. That it proved plausible—more than that, that the court majority believed it to be a sound argument and actually quite compelling—speaks eloquently of the ethical logic of the society within which it was formulated. It is emotivism. Those parts of tradition that support contemporary tastes are proof positive of the correctness of the opinion; those that are not useful to supporting the desired conclusion or that stand in opposition to contemporary tastes can be dismissed as outmoded or motivated by bigotry or simply ignored. And the court can safely do this because it is speaking to a society at large that thinks in precisely the same way. The ruling and its supporting arguments are absolutely connected to, and indeed dependent on, the changes in thinking about selfhood, human nature, sexuality, and the nature of oppression and liberty that we have traced in earlier chapters. The sexual revolution is, as we have noted before, simply one manifestation of the wider revolution in selfhood that has taken place over the last four hundred years.

Ivy League Ethics

If the rulings of the Supreme Court on the matter of gay marriage reflect many of the cultural pathologies that we have noted in previous chapters, it is arguable that these receive some of their most consistent and sophisticated expression in the ethical thought of Peter Singer, the Ira W. DeCamp Professor of Bioethics at Princeton University. As the Supreme Court can be fairly understood to represent the general tendencies of the legal establishment, so an Ivy League ethicist can surely be accorded the same status in the world of academia. Some of Singer's views, such as those in favor of infanticide, are ahead of the tastes of contemporary society, but as he argues, they are consistent with arguments he offers for matters with which much of society has little or no problem, such as abortion.

Singer is famous for holding a number of positions that mark him out as controversial, such as his early work on animal rights, which is now regarded as having been fundamental in the rise of the modern animal liberation and vegan movements.[12] While Singer's thinking has undergone development in recent years—with his acceptance of the idea that there are such things as objective moral standards, something he earlier rejected—this is not of concern to my argument. Rather, it is his views on abortion, infanticide, and euthanasia that are of interest here. In these areas, Singer has the distinction of writing with great clarity and of not hesitating to draw the obvious logical conclusions of his basic premises. And these issues also press toward the heart of both what it means to be a person and what it means to be living a fulfilled life. As dramatic as his views in these areas might appear, he is at least someone surprisingly unencumbered with sentiment when pressing his arguments, something that makes his position—and thus the implications of the culture of which he is a part—remarkably clear. Singer also adamantly refuses to rest his arguments on standard liberal premises, in part because he understands that such premises are often parasitic on, or at least allow the terms of debate to be set by, attitudes rooted in a Christian metaphysic.[13] Singer is a modern version of Friedrich Nietzsche's madman, demanding that the polite liberals of his day face up to the dramatic implications of the death of the Christian way of imagining the world.

Yet what makes Singer particularly interesting for this book is not the arguments he proposes for justifying abortion, infanticide, and euthanasia but rather the grounds on which he believes such things might be allowed to be wrong. To understand this, we first need to see why he finds standard liberal arguments in favor of such things as abortion ultimately unpersuasive.

---

12. See Peter Singer, *Animal Liberation* (1975; repr., New York: Ecco, 2002).

13. See Singer's perceptive comment: "During the centuries of Christian domination of European thought, the ethical attitudes [toward killing] based on these doctrines [i.e., human exceptionalism and immortality] became part of the unquestioned moral orthodoxy of European civilization. Today the doctrines are no longer generally accepted, but the ethical attitudes to which they gave rise fit in with the deep-seated Western belief in the uniqueness and special privileges of our species, and have survived." *Writings on an Ethical Life* (New York: Ecco, 2000), 129–30.

PROBLEMS WITH PRO-CHOICE ARGUMENTS

In addressing the matter of abortion, Singer lists a number of standard liberal arguments for abortion. First, he points to the moment of birth as the most obvious way of setting a point at which killing the fetus becomes unacceptable. This is the one, in his words, that "would suit liberals best" because it is instinctively harder to agree to the killing of a being that "we can all see, hear, and cuddle" than one to which these do not apply.[14] In short, Singer points to the fact that this dividing line really reflects what we might call an aesthetic issue, and given the arguments from earlier chapters in this book, it should not be a surprise that aesthetics offers a plausible foundation for ethical thinking.

Yet, as he proceeds to comment, birth is still somewhat arbitrary. The fact that children can be born prematurely and survive birth indicates that at some point in the womb they have the same features and the same capacity for awareness and for experiencing pain.[15] We might recast this as saying that the aesthetic arguments on which the "birth as dividing line" view rests are based simply on our inability to see the child in the womb, and thus, they are demonstrably arbitrary. This is one of the reasons why sonograms have significantly changed attitudes to abortion: they have not changed the nature of the child in the woman, but they have changed the aesthetic experience of such children by adults. Passing through the birth canal really does not change anything except the immediacy of others' experience of the child.[16]

A second liberal argument for abortion that Singer examines is that of viability, the point at which the Supreme Court ruling in *Roe v. Wade* drew the dividing line. Singer finds this position lacking on two counts. First, there is a need to provide a justification for why viability should hold such a key place in the pro-choice argument. Second, viability is itself an elastic category, subject to the level of available medical science

---

14. Singer, *Writings on an Ethical Life*, 147.
15. Singer, *Writings on an Ethical Life*, 147.
16. Pro-life advocate and philosopher Francis J. Beckwith cites Singer in support of his own argument that location (in the womb / out of the womb) makes no difference to the moral status of the child. *Defending Life: A Moral and Legal Case against Abortion Choice* (Cambridge: Cambridge University Press, 2007), 154.

and care and thus subject to the vicissitudes of both time and space. A viable fetus in the twenty-first century may not have been viable in the sixteenth, and a viable fetus in modern Manhattan may well not be viable in today's Mogadishu. Are the metaphysics of personhood and concomitant questions of the sanctity of life to be simply the functions of happenstance regarding where and when the woman conceives? Nor is total dependence on the mother for existence an argument that gives the mother sovereign rights of life and death over the child. There are numerous contexts in which one person is totally dependent for survival on another in which we do not regard the latter as having the right to kill the former.[17]

Singer also addresses other ways in which liberals have attempted to establish a decisive boundary beyond which abortion is unacceptable. He dismisses the idea of "quickening," or the moment when the soul enters the body of the child, signaled by the baby's first movement, as a piece of theological mystification. He also rejects the moment at which the child feels pain as arbitrary—though here he points to the fact that the pain argument achieves neither what pro-lifers desire (protection of the child from harm from the very moment of conception) nor what pro-choicers desire (because it pushes the boundary for abortion back to the very early stages of pregnancy when the woman might not actually know that she has conceived).[18]

Singer also rejects the argument that abortion laws simply drive abortions underground, making them illegal but not stopping them. That, he notes, is an argument against abortion laws, not an argument in favor of the moral legitimacy of abortion considered in itself.[19] He also rejects the idea that, as a "victimless crime" analogous to homosexual acts between consenting adult males, it should be outside the scope of legislation. This notion falls because the very debate about abortion is really a debate about the status of the baby in the womb

---

17. Singer, *Writings on an Ethical Life*, 148.
18. Singer, *Writings on an Ethical Life*, 149–50.
19. Singer, *Writings on an Ethical Life*, 150–51.

and thus about whether abortion can therefore be categorized as not involving a victim.[20]

Finally, he addresses the standard feminist argument that the fetus is part of the woman's body, for her to deal with as she chooses. In the cases of rape and incest, this reasoning is particularly powerful: the woman can then argue that she has an alien being in her body, parasitically dependent on her for its existence. Singer rejects this argument on utilitarian grounds: if the overall effect of aborting the child was worse than keeping the child (viewed in terms of the overall happiness that would accrue to the world through the birth of another human being), then the woman has no absolute right to dispose of the child as she chooses, however difficult the situation might be in which she has found herself through no fault of her own.[21]

Given that Singer's debunking of the classic liberal arguments for abortion is one with which pro-life advocates can find much common ground, why is it that he is probably the most notorious intellectual advocate of abortion and infanticide? If the standard rationales for abortion are so lacking, what arguments does he consider to be compelling?

THE REJECTION OF HUMAN EXCEPTIONALISM

At the heart of Singer's ethical view of abortion is a fundamental distinction that he makes between being human and being a person. He does not deny that the fetus is a human being; rather, he rejects the idea that merely belonging to the species *Homo sapiens* is sufficient to make one a person and therefore subject to the rights that attach to personhood.

There are two basic strands to this argument. First, there is Singer's rejection of what he calls "speciesism." For him, the idea of human exceptionalism—that which places humanity in a different category from that of, say, iguanas or chimpanzees—is highly problematic and confusing, built as it is on illegitimate metaphysical or religious grounds:

---

20. Singer, *Writings on an Ethical Life*, 151–52.
21. Singer, *Writings on an Ethical Life*, 152–55.

The belief that mere membership in our species, irrespective of other characteristics, makes a great difference to the wrongness of killing a being is a legacy of religious doctrine that even those opposed to abortion hesitate to bring into the debate.[22]

In short, sanctity-of-life arguments as they operate in the abortion debate are in practice sanctity-of-*human*-life arguments, constructed on a false premise, that of the unique status of humanity. This conviction—that the difference between human beings and other animals needs to be relativized—underlies Singer's earlier work on animal rights and has come to characterize the radical wing of the contemporary movement for animal liberation.[23] Human beings are, according to Singer, generally in thrall to speciesism, which, like racism, posits an innate superiority of one group over others on an ultimately unjustifiable foundation. Thus, neither consciousness nor the ability to feel pain allows us to separate our species definitively from others. This is clear in our practices relative to ending life. We kill healthy cows for food, we kill dogs and cats and other animals when they are old and infirm, but we preserve the life of people who are suffering greater pain through cancer or who have less self-awareness thanks to the ravages of Alzheimer's disease than a healthy sheep. Yet we are happy to send the latter to slaughter simply in order to provide food for our tables. In light of this, what Singer wishes to do is to make animals, too, part of the discussion of the ethics of life and to avoid any argument based on human exceptionalism.[24]

Second, having rejected human exceptionalism as a basis for discussion about life issues, Singer proposes instead the matter of consciousness as the foundation for understanding a creature as a person. This Singer parses

---

22. Singer, *Writings on an Ethical Life*, 156.

23. See, for example, the provocative title of a 2012 article by Ingrid Newkirk on the website of the People for the Ethical Treatment of Animals (PETA), "A Rat Is a Pig Is a Dog Is a Boy," PETA, August 28, 2012, updated March 6, 2015, https://www.peta.org/blog/rat-pig-dog-boy/. Newkirk had first used this phrase in an interview with the *Washingtonian* magazine in 1986. See also Wesley J. Smith, *A Rat Is a Pig Is a Dog Is a Boy: The Human Cost of the Animal Rights Movement* (New York: Encounter Books, 2010), 3.

24. Singer, *Writings on an Ethical Life*, 44–46. Wesley Smith comments that although Singer is not technically an animal-rights advocate (e.g., he allows for medical experimentation on animals for human benefit in circumstances where there is no alternative approach), it is his rejection of human exceptionalism that is the precondition of the philosophy and strategy of the modern animal-rights movement. *A Rat Is a Pig*, 33.

under several headings. First, following John Locke, he argues that a person has a sense of its own existence over time. It is aware that it has a past, a present, and a future. As a consequence, such a creature will also have the capacity for desires, for moving itself intentionally into the future.[25] Second, to be a person, a creature has to be autonomous; that is, it has to be capable of making decisions. The most critical decision in this matter is that of continuing to live rather than to die, which itself assumes that the creature is consciously aware of the difference between life and death. We might therefore say that autonomy also assumes a level of rationality in that the decisions that the autonomous creature can make are done so on the basis of a process of reasoning rather than by instinct.[26] For example, the mouse who flees the cat is doing so on the basis of an instinctive reaction, not via discursive reasoning based on the conscious desire to stay alive. The woman who does not jump into the cage to pet the hungry lion is acting on the basis of reason: she knows hungry lions eat people, that being eaten will kill her, and that she desires to avoid death and stay alive.

Given these criteria, it is clear that for Singer a child in the womb is not a person. The child has no consciousness of a past, present, or future; is not autonomous; and has no capacity for rational reflection. In short, for Singer it is not a person and therefore does not possess the rights that personhood entails. This is where Singer's rejection of human exceptionalism, of speciesism, becomes singularly important: the child in the womb should be given no more special status than that which is given to other creatures at a similar stage of development:

> My suggestion, then, is that we accord the life of a fetus no greater value than the life of a nonhuman animal at a similar level of rationality, self-consciousness, awareness, capacity to feel, etc.[27]

Given that we routinely kill animals for no more reason than that we want to put meat on our plates, Singer's point is that we have no basis for protecting children in the womb. Do they feel pain? Well, so does

---

25. Singer, *Writings on an Ethical Life*, 130.
26. Singer, *Writings on an Ethical Life*, 137–38.
27. Singer, *Writings on an Ethical Life*, 156.

the deer shot by the hunter, and the deer is arguably as self-conscious as the child in the womb. So why discriminate between the two? Once the exceptional status of the human species has been rejected, there seem to be no grounds on which to do so.

Of course, the implication of Singer's views of personhood goes beyond the matter of abortion. The same problem of personhood applies to newborn children too. We noted earlier that he (like pro-life advocates) regards the mere act of having passed through the birth canal as irrelevant to the question whether the child should be protected from killing. Singer does not hesitate to draw the obvious implications for infanticide:

> I do not regard the conflict between the position I have taken and widely accepted views about the sanctity of infant life as a ground for abandoning my position. These widely accepted views need to be challenged.[28]

To this we can add the issue of the killing of those who never gain personhood (as Singer defines it) such as the severely mentally impaired or those who have lost it through the ravages of dementia.[29]

WHEN ARE ABORTION AND INFANTICIDE WRONG?

Singer's arguments that abortion and infanticide are not necessarily wrong do not, of course, logically require that such things be regarded as always legitimate. Singer himself is very clear on this point. But on what basis, then, would Singer argue that specific cases of infanticide would be deemed legitimate? The answer is straightforward: where the effect on the parents would be a profoundly negative one. In a passage worth quoting in full, Singer makes this point very clear:

> The difference between killing disabled and normal infants lies not in any supposed right to life that the latter has and the former lacks, but in other

---

28. Singer, *Writings on an Ethical Life*, 161.

29. In an interview on his website, Singer makes the following comment in answer to a question about those with dementia: "When a human being once had a sense of the future, but has now lost it, we should be guided by what he or she would have wanted to happen in these circumstances. So if someone would not have wanted to be kept alive after losing their awareness of their future, we may be justified in ending their life; but if they would not have wanted to be killed under these circumstances, that is an important reason why we should not do so." "Frequently Asked Questions," Peter Singer, accessed June 25, 2019, https://petersinger.info/faq/.

considerations about killing. Most obviously there is the difference that often exists in the attitudes of the parents. The birth of a child is usually a happy event for the parents. They have, nowadays, often planned for the child. The mother has carried it for nine months. From birth, a natural affection begins to bind the parents to it. So one important reason why it is normally a terrible thing to kill an infant is the effect the killing will have on its parents.

It is different when the infant is born with a serious disability. Birth abnormalities vary, of course. Some are trivial and have little effect on the child or its parents, but others turn the normally joyful event of birth into a threat to the happiness of the parents and any other children they may have.[30]

Singer's philosophical tradition is that of utilitarianism, with its belief that the rightness or wrongness of a particular course of action is intimately connected to whether it promotes happiness. But in the context of the argument of this book, we can see that such a philosophical approach is also closely connected to the psychologizing of selfhood that we have noted as a distinct part of the modern therapeutic age. Happiness as an inner sense of psychological well-being is the hallmark of the therapeutic age, and here we see it being deployed as the primary criterion for deciding whether an infant should live or die.

Singer is not prepared to make the immediate psychological well-being of the birth parents the only criterion as to whether an infant should live or die, though he refuses to make the killing of an infant to be morally equivalent to that of a person even when that killing is illegitimate by his criteria. The practical reality of the existence of parents who are willing to adopt unwanted infants, and the happiness that this would bring to such, makes the willy-nilly killing of newborns something that is wrong. To do so deprives others of happiness. Again, to quote Singer himself, in answer to the question whether it would be right to kill a perfectly healthy baby,

> Most parents, fortunately, love their children and would be horrified by the idea of killing it. And that's a good thing, of course. We want to encourage parents to care for their children, and help them to do so.

---

30. Singer, *Writings on an Ethical Life*, 187.

Moreover, although a normal newborn baby has no sense of the future, and therefore is not a person, that does not mean that it is all right to kill such a baby. It only means that the wrong done to the infant is not as great as the wrong that would be done to a person who was killed. But in our society there are many couples who would be very happy to love and care for that child. Hence even if the parents do not want their own child, it would be wrong to kill it.[31]

What is noteworthy here is that Singer is consistent with his basic premise, that infants are not persons and therefore are not entitled to the rights that real persons have. The issue of the legitimacy of infanticide has nothing to do with the intrinsic quality of infant life and everything to do with the psychological impact this may or may not have on those who already exist as real persons: birth parents, siblings, potential adoptive parents. This is the ethics of the therapeutic.

Of course, Singer's position raises immediate problems for the question of abortion: if the fetus is perfectly healthy, then the argument that it should be brought to term so that it could be adopted at birth by infertile parents who want a child and would thus be made happy would seem to apply. As Singer himself has stated numerous times, the mere act of passing through the birth canal does not alter the status of the child considered in itself in any significant manner. Yet Singer, while acknowledging complications in the matter of infanticide, does not press the logic here back into the womb itself. Presumably, the therapeutic triumphs unconditionally in utero: the mental health and the desires of the woman carrying the child are the only decisive factors in whether the child in the womb is allowed to live.

As with the Supreme Court's progress toward gay marriage, the ethics of Peter Singer is driven by the imperative of the personal happiness of those with sufficient self-consciousness to qualify as persons. The only authority that really counts is the feeling of psychological well-being of the parties involved. Perhaps more significantly, the positive reception

---

31. "Frequently Asked Questions," Peter Singer, accessed June 25, 2019, https://petersinger.info/faq/. Cf. Singer, *Writings on an Ethical Life*, 193: "Killing a disabled infant is not morally equivalent to killing a person. Very often it is not wrong at all."

of his ethics, like that of Supreme Court rulings on gay marriage, indicates just how deeply the basic pathologies of expressive individualism and psychological man have come to permeate the social imaginary.

Campus Anticulture

If the expressive individualism of psychological man is evident both in key judicial decisions of the Supreme Court and in the ethics of an influential thinker such as Peter Singer, it is also a powerful force in shaping university and college campuses. In chapter 3, we noted that Rousseau's reconstruction of the relationship between nature and culture was such as to demand a new understanding of the purpose of education. If society was the problem, not the solution, then education needed to focus on allowing individuals to express themselves naturally rather than forcing them to learn the beliefs, values, and customs that would actually lead them to be false to themselves and thus inauthentic. To this we might add the later sharpening of this basic idea—that society corrupts and does so by naturalizing certain culturally generated ways of thinking—refracted through the thought of Nietzsche and Marx, whereby the history of culture becomes a narrative of power and exploitation, a tale in which the apparent heroes are really the villains and the true heroes are those who have been exploited, marginalized, and even erased from the dominant narratives. Bring these two strands together and you have another important sign of the widespread and deep transformation in society that has been taking place: a transformed culture of higher education. This is particularly evident in recent high-profile debates about freedom of speech that have taken place on certain college campuses. Yet in context, these debates are entirely explicable, given the way we have argued in this book that Western society has changed.

FREEDOM OF SPEECH

Something odd but entirely explicable happens when the self is psychologized: things that were previously regarded as unquestioned goods come to be seen as bad and detrimental to society. This is because the changing understanding of selfhood brings with it a changed understanding of what does and does not constitute an assault on the self. For example, in a world in which the dominant understanding of the self is one formed by the polis, as for Rieff's political man, then assaults on the polis or civic institutions will be regarded as serious crimes. Thus, in times of national war, when people come to think of themselves very self-consciously in terms of patriotism, being a traitor to the national cause is the supreme evil. We might also think of the fate of Socrates in ancient Athens, sentenced to death for denying the traditional gods on which Athenian identity in part rested. In a world in which religious affiliation is foundational to selfhood, blasphemy becomes a very serious social crime, as, for example, the controversies surrounding Salman Rushdie's *The Satanic Verses* and the *Charlie Hebdo* affair demonstrate. And where economic categories prevail, crimes against property will have particular cachet.

In a world in which the self is constructed psychologically and in which the therapeutic is the ethical ideal, we should therefore expect the notion of good and bad, of what is appropriate and inappropriate behavior, to change accordingly. The notion of assault on the person becomes not simply—or even perhaps primarily—a matter that involves damage to the body or to property; it becomes psychological, something that damages the inner self or hinders that sense of psychological well-being that lies at the heart of the therapeutic. In such a context, freedom of speech becomes not so much part of the solution as part of the problem. Liberal democracies have long assumed that the free exchange of ideas in society is a means of preventing totalitarianism and promoting the common good. In the world of psychological man, however, it serves rather to give legal protection to (verbal) assaults on the person.

We noted in chapter 7 that Herbert Marcuse regards tolerance and freedom of speech as part of the repressive ideology of modern capitalist society and that this thinking has implications for how the New Left views education. Here he is again, making essentially the same point with unambiguous clarity:

> When tolerance mainly serves the protection and preservation of a repressive society, when it serves to neutralize opposition and to render

men immune against other and better forms of life, then tolerance has been perverted. And when this perversion starts in the mind of the individual, in his consciousness, his needs, when heteronomous interests occupy him before he can experience his servitude, then the efforts to counteract his dehumanization must begin at the place of entrance, there where the false consciousness takes form (or rather: is systematically formed)—it must begin with stopping the words and images which feed this consciousness. To be sure, this is censorship, even precensorship, but openly directed against the more or less hidden censorship that permeates the free media.[32]

What is of note is that one does not have to hold to the psychologized Marxism that Marcuse espouses to concur with what he is saying here. One need only hold to the idea that the self is to be regarded as a primarily psychological phenomenon to agree that words and images that promote or reinforce psychologically unhealthy views should be censored or silenced.

There are other cultural phenomena that point to this basic psychologizing tendency relative to behavior that society at large considers acceptable. The advent of the concepts of hate crimes and hate speech grants significant status to the psychological dimensions of a criminal action. If David murders Michael because he is gay or black, then Michael is no more dead than if David murdered him because he wanted to steal his wallet or his wife, because he had ginger hair, or simply because he wanted to take some random person's life. But the law now regards hate as compounding a crime, and so David will be charged with such and face potentially escalated penalties. It is the same with the category of hate speech. Certain forms of speech have been criminalized in some democracies precisely because of their connection to violence. And once violence comes to be seen to include the psychological, these laws become somewhat elastic in scope.[33] And it is the latter, hate speech,

---

32. Herbert Marcuse, "Repressive Tolerance," in Robert Paul Wolff, Barrington Moore Jr., and Herbert Marcuse, *A Critique of Pure Tolerance* (Boston: Beacon, 1970), 111.

33. In the United Kingdom (which has no written constitution enshrining the right to freedom of speech), the Public Order Act 1986 has been revised over the years and now includes provisions against certain forms of speech likely to stir up hatred and violence against individuals on the grounds

that is proving so problematic a concept on campuses precisely because it cuts across standard notions of free speech as a social good in the service of protecting the various identities that have come to enjoy privileged status in the world of psychological man.[34]

THE CASE OF MIDDLEBURY COLLEGE
AND CHARLES MURRAY

Perhaps the most dramatic example of campus conflict over free speech in recent years involved the invitation of the political scientist Charles Murray to speak to the American Enterprise Club at Middlebury College in March 2017. The lecture sparked passionate student protests that ultimately led to the evening being abandoned and the protesters actually injuring Allison Stanger, the left-leaning Middlebury faculty member who had agreed to be Murray's interlocutor.[35] Murray's crime was that he had argued earlier in his career that intelligence played a role in America's economic divisions, a point seen by his opponents to justify both racial and class prejudice.[36]

It is easy to dismiss the Middlebury incident as an example of what has come to be called "the snowflake generation," a pejorative term used to describe the alleged inability of the rising generation of college students to engage with any viewpoint with which they happen to disagree. This simplistic approach fails to take into account two important factors. First, such sensitivity must have a prior cause

---

of race, religion, or sexual orientation. Given the flexible way hatred and violence can be construed, the law has a potentially very wide range.

34. There are other aspects of the law that indicate the rising importance of psychological categories in our therapeutic age, such as the awarding of damages for "emotional distress," where such used to be a function of loss to body or to property. One might also add the use of victim-impact statements in the penalty phase of criminal cases, whereby the "value" of someone's death is essentially assessed by its impact on family and close friends. To be clear, I am not here arguing about the validity or merits of the phenomena described; I am merely highlighting the fact that such things arise within a society that thinks of itself in certain ways.

35. Peter Beinart, a liberal journalist, provides a useful account of the event, along with reflections on its cultural and political significance: "A Violent Attack on Free Speech at Middlebury," *The Atlantic*, March 6, 2017, https://www.theatlantic.com/politics/archive/2017/03/middlebury-free-speech-violence /518667/.

36. See Richard J. Herrnstein and Charles Murray, *The Bell Curve: Intelligence and Class Structure in American Life* (New York: Free Press, 1996); Charles Murray, *Coming Apart: The State of White America, 1960–2010* (New York: Crown Forum, 2012).

or causes within the broader culture in which it occurs. Second, this explanation ignores the self-conscious ideological underpinnings of such protests by reducing them to the equivalent of infantile temper tantrums.

As to the first, the burden of this book has been to explain the pathologies of our culture and the reasons why speech itself has come to be considered violence. That is a function of the psychologized society in which we live and which has been in the making now for many centuries. Criticism of "snowflakes" by those who themselves live and breathe the atmosphere of expressive individualism is therefore a cause for all of us to engage in self-examination.

As to the second, these ideological underpinnings are made explicit on one of the prominent web pages hosted by Middlebury students opposed to events such as the Murray lecture. The mission statement of the online publication *Beyond the Green: Collective of Middlebury Voices* contains the following passage:

> We feel as though individually, our voices are often ignored in the face of the hegemonic Middlebury discourse, but collectively we will be able to engage with the Middlebury community more effectively. We are a radical, anti-racist, anti-sexist, anti-classist, anti-ableist, and anti-homophobic (as well as strongly opposed to all forms of oppression) group that rejects the structurally conservative "liberal" paradigm that exists at Middlebury. The reasons behind our formation are many, but the predominate [*sic*] one is a feeling of alienation within the campus dialogue—the so-called "free market of ideas" on campus is an illusion, one which exists only to support one strong ideology. We may not always agree, and we want to allow space to challenge each other. However, ultimately we share the same principles and intentions, and are committed to moving forward with solidarity and purpose. Moreover, we acknowledge the potential and probability that the articles we publish may be messy and emotional because the things we write about will be so close to our lived experiences. Rather than espousing the idea that all written work in the public eye must be dispassionate, we welcome the fact that our articles will be written with passion, with love, with anger, and overall, with purpose. We are tired of having to

engage with those who repeatedly devalue our experiences and values—by creating our own platform, we are unifying in the face of this intentional disregard, and rejecting the idea that we must conform to the dominant Middlebury narrative.[37]

The passage is a quite superb example of the radicalized politics of the therapeutic society. First, it is worth noting the language of feeling that permeates the statement and that is assumed to carry tremendous argumentative force: articles will likely be "messy and emotional" because they are connected to "lived experiences" and written with "passion, with love, with anger," and the enemies are those who "devalue our experiences." This is the language of subjective emotions, expressive individualism, and the therapeutic ideal that society has been cultivating. It also renders reason irrelevant—or irrelevant until people are attuned to the proper emotions. These Middlebury students might be described as channeling the spirits of Rousseau and Shelley but without their underlying belief in a normative human nature as the universal horizon of engagement. There is no metanarrative of human nature as a whole or a unity here, only that provided by the oppression of certain marginalized groups.

Second, the statement also assumes that the basic categories of modern identity politics are indisputable. Clearly, anyone who disagrees with the students' stand on LGBTQ+ rights is going to be dismissed not simply as wrong but as bigoted. The standard language of *phobia* is here, ruling out from the very start any notion that objecting to the fluidity that marks current notions of sex and identity could be based on any kind of rational reflection. Akin to the Supreme Court opinion in *United States v. Windsor*, it is irrational animus that these students regard as motivating advocates of traditional sexual mores.

Third, the reference to Middlebury's "structurally conservative 'liberal' paradigm" and to the illusory nature of the "so-called 'free market of ideas'" indicates that this is clearly Marcusan territory. Free speech, that which most of us would intuitively regard as a basic social good, is part

---

37. "Mission," *Beyond the Green: Collective of Middlebury Voices*, accessed June 27, 2019, https://beyondthegreenmidd.wordpress.com/mission/.

of the problem, not the solution. And only by restricting speech will the marginalized voices of the oppressed be heard.

The *Beyond the Green* website also hosts a letter challenging the college over allowing Murray to visit campus. Again, the language is precisely what one would expect from the kind of culture that has emerged over the last couple of centuries. Here is one particularly interesting passage:

> I understand that as an institution of learning, you have a responsibility to challenge your students and provide an atmosphere open to intellectual debate. In general, I believe it is important to include some viewpoints that differ from the general political atmosphere of the campus. However, you also have a responsibility to uphold the humanity and dignity of your students of color, which is not possible if that dignity and humanity are considered an appropriate topic of debate on campus.[38]

The specific concerns of the letter are comments made by Murray regarding students of color on a previous visit. What is noticeable is the language of dignity that the writer uses. I noted in chapter 2 that Charles Taylor sees the rise of dignity as an ethically normative concept to be directly connected to the rise of expressive individualism stemming from Rousseau. I would add that dignity is itself an inference from the Christian teaching that all human beings are made in the image of God. But in our current climate, this universal dignity has been psychologized, and the granting of dignity has come to be equated with the affirmation of those psychologized identities that enjoy special status in our culture. Here we see such a psychologized notion of dignity applied to the matter of Murray's lecture (even his mere presence) at Middlebury, both of which are seen as inherently oppressive. Again, to declare this to be the reaction of a snowflake is to trivialize the deep cultural and philosophical roots that underlie this language and this attitude. The fruit of the psychologizing of selfhood and the politicization of certain identities

---

38. Erica Robinson, "Open Letter to Middlebury Leadership regarding the Recent Protest," *Beyond the Green: Collective of Middlebury Voices*, accessed June 27, 2019, https://beyondthegreenmidd.word press.com/2017/03/15/open-letter-to-middlebury-leadership-regarding-the-recent-protest/.

within this psychologized culture lead to precisely this kind of concern regarding freedom of speech. Those of us who believe freedom of speech is a necessary social good may dislike what we read here, but we cannot claim that it does not make sense, given the wider culture within which we all now live. Indeed, it reflects in a radical political form the intuitions of the social imaginary.

It is also important to note that the increasing intolerance on campuses that the Middlebury protests represent cannot be isolated from the broader issue of educational philosophy. The teaching of history, for example, is now dominated in many places by advocates of critical theory and thus preoccupied with categories of power and marginalization. The current state of the discipline of history provides a good example of this thinking.

THE STATE OF THE HISTORICAL DISCIPLINE

A visit to Harvard University's Department of History website reveals that there is no basic course focused exclusively on the Reformation or the Renaissance anywhere but that there are courses titled Asian American History, Native American History, and British Colonial Violence. While the entire history of early modern Europe is dealt with in a single course, covering the years 1450 to 1789, another offering, Feminisms and Pornography, devotes an entire semester to a mere two decades, 1975 to 1995.[39] In short, it would appear that one can today pay vast sums of money in order to emerge from one of America's preeminent educational institutions with a deeper knowledge of the cultural significance of Gloria Steinem and skin flicks from the end of the twentieth century than of Martin Luther and the seismic intellectual, cultural, economic, and political changes of the sixteenth and seventeenth centuries.

Let me be clear: I am not here saying that topics such as British colonial violence and even pornography are illegitimate objects of historical inquiry. But I am intrigued as to the priorities that such curricula

---

39. Harvard University Department of History, accessed March 5, 2020, https://history.fas.harvard .edu.

represent. It is not that the various theoretical approaches that underlie the priorities they indicate—whether postcolonial, queer, or feminist—are supplementing previous lacunae within the historical discipline. It seems to me that they are rather destabilizing it as a whole. If it is the case that a course on porn and feminism is simply expanding the canon of topics to be studied or the boundaries that constitute the discipline of history, then a solid grasp of the central core subjects and methods of the discipline would surely be the necessary prerequisite for addressing these topics. Instead, the lack of such suggests that the game is to abolish boundaries and canons entirely—presumably as constructs of various previous imperialisms, cultural, sexual, and otherwise. The purpose is the destabilization of the discipline, and this all serves to institutionalize the cultural amnesia that is part of our third-world anticulture.

I argue below that this is a political matter. But it is also important to note that it is a therapeutic matter too. Disciplinary traditions and canons come with a given, external authority, and the purpose of education and study involves submitting oneself to these as a discipline in order (to put it somewhat paradoxically) to be able to develop a level of mastery over them. The purpose of such study is not ultimately the affirmation of the self of the student; rather, it is the transformation of the self of the student through engagement with something external to her that makes demands on her. And so this transformation of the historical curriculum is of a piece with wider debates on campuses about freedom of speech and safe spaces. These, too, are really functions of a wider cultural commitment to the therapeutic and to the idea that human beings are most authentic when their inner life is lived outwardly, without oppressive interference from society at large.

This connects to the second area in which the therapeutic ideals and expressive individualism of this present age are significant in education: the transformation of the authority of educational institutions. Again, this is an area in which much could be said if we had unlimited time, but as that is not the case, I want to focus on just one aspect of the changing nature of traditional institutions in our time. Once they were authoritative contexts for personal formation through curricula that served to help individuals better understand and operate within their societies. To an extent, that still applies in the STEM disciplines because they train students for specific vocations, unlike the humanities and social sciences—yet even there, the divorce of STEM from the humanities in many institutions points to an unfortunate instrumentalization, and therefore reduction, of human reason.

Numerous factors have subverted institutional authority, and higher education is in many ways simply one aspect of a much wider cultural phenomenon. For example, the fact that students pay for their education is generally seen as a good thing. It makes professors and institutions accountable. But it is arguable that it also plays into the idea that education is a commodity and the student is a consumer. That is a very different model from, say, that which gave birth to the university in the Middle Ages and even to that which I myself experienced at Cambridge in the 1980s—I was never left in any doubt by the university authorities that the institution did not need me, that I was privileged to be there, and that I therefore had to follow the rules. In a world in which students take out vast loans for education, there are advantages: as I mentioned, professors, for example, can theoretically be held much more to account. And if the student doesn't pay, there is the big question of who does. But there are also disadvantages of which we need to be aware—most obviously, in a world in which the therapeutic ideal and expressive individualism mark the ethical structure of society, students as customers may well feel entitled to have educational norms conform not to traditional educational goals but rather to those that play directly to that inner sense of psychological well-being that is central to the idea of the therapeutic.

It is also important to note that the matter of college curricula connects to the abolition of the prepolitical; in other words, as noted in part 3, in our era all areas of life are of political significance. Now, many conservatives would wish to dissent from this view. They would argue that the "little platoons" of Edmund Burke's world—those mediating institutions for social organization, such as the church, the sports club, even the gatherings in the local pub—provide a prepolitical context for interaction outside the political field. But unfortunately, once one side in the political debate chooses to politicize an issue, then all sides have to play that game. And the radical individualism of the libertarian Right, as much as the Marxist communitarianism of the Left, tends in this direction, because any corralling of individual behavior can be seen as a political assault on personal sovereignty. The truth is, we now live in a world in which everything is politicized, and we have no choice in the public square but to accept this and engage accordingly.

Again, this politicization connects both to the purpose of education and to the curriculum. To pick on Harvard history again, it is clear that the curriculum reflects the political concerns of the present day. Porn, feminism, colonial violence, racism, and minority histories are all prominent, even as the Reformation and the Renaissance are not. Of course, the response will be that traditional curricular priorities also reflected the political interests of the dominant class of the period in which they were developed. They were the curricula of dead, white, Western, heterosexual males. And therein lies the problem: for the one for whom everything is political, there is no context for discussing such things as the content of a curriculum in a pre- or nonpolitical manner. The content is simply part of the political struggle. This is why such debates are so fruitless—they typically involve the clash of two or more utterly incommensurable ways of looking at the world. As Alasdair MacIntyre would say, they represent the assertion and counterassertion of emotional preferences dressed up in the flimsy clothing of academic objectivity.

This also helps explain the reason why the current disciplinary diversity in the humanities is not simply an expansion or broadening of that which has gone before. It is not that queer history is merely supplementing the lacunae in previous historical narratives; its intention is rather to destabilize the received narratives of the past and the alleged power structures in the present that depend on them, and that is a political purpose predicated on the abolition of the prepolitical as a workable category. It is part of the same educational culture that rioted to silence Charles Murray at Middlebury.

Conclusion

If there is any doubt about the pervasive way expressive individualism and the therapeutic concerns of psychological man have come to shape the *Sittlichkeit* of modern society, then this should be dispelled by a moment's reflection on the Supreme Court's path to finding gay marriage in the Constitution, by the Ivy League ethics of Peter Singer, and by the current pressure on freedom of speech on college campuses. All three are functions of a notion of selfhood that places self-expression and individual psychological well-being at the heart of what it means to be human.

All three also reflect particular aspects of both the emotivism noted by MacIntyre and the anticulture described by Rieff. Underlying the road to *Obergefell* is a fundamentally different understanding of what a person is, as exemplified by the contrast between the arguments of Kennedy and Scalia in *Casey*. For Singer, there is no human essence that makes talk about personhood for a fetus, or even a newborn baby, meaningful, unlike the pro-life advocates whose position he rejects. And for the campus protesters, free speech is simply a license to oppress others with hateful language and arguments—not, as their opponents would claim, the only means by which bad ideas can be scrutinized and rejected. In each case, there is no common ground on which to build a consensus. Particularly in the case of the Supreme Court's claim that religious objections to homosexuality are really driven by animus, it is clear that the idea of emotivism can now function in a polemical setting as something used to discredit the opposition: "*Your* views are irrational and rooted in emotion; *mine* are rooted in reason." The same logic seems to be used by Singer in seeing pro-life arguments as ultimately grounded in sentiment ("Newborn babies are cute . . .") and by campus protesters against free speech ("Why give a platform to irrational bigots . . . ?"). Emotivism explains why the other side is wrong.

As to the anticulture, what is most striking about all three case studies in this chapter is the rejection of history. In each one it takes a different form, but the antihistorical trajectory is there. In the case of the Supreme Court and *Obergefell*, precedent functions in the arguments only when it is useful for it to do so. When it is problematic, it can be ignored.

With Singer, the matter is more complicated. First, any proabortion position is inevitably to some degree antihistorical because it demands the elimination of the consequences of history, namely, conception. That is Rieff's basic point about abortion in *My Life among the Deathworks*. But Singer goes further with his advocacy of infanticide, justified on the basis of the happiness of the parents, and of euthanasia. These are deliberately iconoclastic rejections of past practice and belief. Neither abortion nor infanticide are unprecedented in history, but they have not been widely sanctioned in the West since ancient times, and Singer's argument is predicated on two very modern notions: the rejection of human exceptionalism and the imperative of personal happiness. As to campuses, the protests against free speech are part of a much wider educational pathology. The transformation of the humanities into disciplines by which the past is not so much examined as a source of wisdom but rejected as a tale of oppression is key to this anticultural impulse. Denying free speech on campus is simply an extension of seeing all history as a hegemonic discourse designed to keep the powerful in power and to marginalize and silence the weak. It is the combined result of the abolition of the prepolitical and the advent of a culture in which oppression is conceptualized as psychological. Both of these are pathologies of Rieff's anticulture because both militate against any notion of traditional external authority. And as Rieff comments, "Forgetfulness is now the curricular form of our higher education."[40] That, he says, guarantees that this generation will be the first of the new barbarism, committed to the denigration, destruction, and erasure of the past—not only its artifacts but also its values and social practices.[41]

In recent decisions of the Supreme Court, in the writings of Peter Singer, and in the antics of the denizens of the modern college campus, it would seem clear that Rieff is correct. Cultural amnesia is the order of the day, a political imperative, a fundamental aspect of the social imaginary.

---

40. Philip Rieff, *My Life among the Deathworks: Illustrations of the Aesthetics of Authority*, ed. Kenneth S. Piver, vol. 1 of *Sacred Order / Social Order* (Charlottesville: University of Virginia Press, 2006), 106.

41. See "Forgetfulness," p. 100, in chap. 2.

The Triumph of the T

Girls will be boys and boys will be girls.
It's a mixed up, muddled up, shook up world.

RAY DAVIES, "LOLA"

As I stated in the introduction, this book is not so much a study of the LGBTQ+ movement as it is a prolegomenon to such discussion. My purpose throughout has been to show how ideas that today permeate both the conscious philosophies and the intuitions that dominate the social imaginary have deep historical roots. That a claim so counterintuitive as "I am a woman trapped in a man's body" now makes sense to people who are not schooled in critical theory or poststructuralism reveals the depth of the penetration of many of those schools' sophisticated ideas into the basic fabric of society.

It is appropriate, however, to offer some reflections on how the various analytical concepts and ideas I have described in previous chapters can be applied to the LGBTQ+ movement in a way that helps make sense of it. Therefore, in this chapter I want to look at a number of specific matters: the odd nature of the LGBTQ+ coalition and how the history of its formation reflects a number of the cultural pathologies I have noted; the challenge that the addition of transgenderism to the alliance has brought in its wake, especially to more traditional forms of feminism; and the so-called *Yogyakarta Principles* and how they embody a sexual manifestation of expressive individualism. In doing so, it should become clear that the LGBTQ+ alliance represents the latest and most powerful example of an anticulture, a deathwork, and a rejection of nature, underpinned by the aesthetic and emotive ethics that are so typical of a therapeutic age.

The Enemy of My Enemy Is My Friend

The familiar acronym LGBTQ+ has expanded over the years to keep pace with the range of sexual minorities that it represents, such that it often now ends with a "+" sign to indicate its somewhat open-ended nature. Yet as much as the initials are presented in our culture as indicating a natural alliance, and as much as the groups they represent typically present themselves to the wider world as such, it is in fact the case that the acronym has emerged from historical circumstance rather than from characteristics intrinsic to each category.

All the groups represented in the LGBTQ+ do share a number of things in common. From the perspective of my earlier narrative, they are clearly psychological and sexual in terms of their understanding of selfhood. To identify oneself by one's sexual orientation or to identify one's gender by inner psychological conviction locates the LGBTQ+ within the world of expressive individualism and psychological man. Reality is inward and psychological, not outward and natural. But to say that is not really to say very much at all. As I argue in the final chapter, all twenty-first-century Westerners are expressive individuals and psychological selves. That general fact does not gain anyone membership in any particular Western community, and the LGBTQ+ is a very specific community.

The first and perhaps the most obvious matter to discuss is the odd nature of the LGBTQ+ alliance. So familiar has this acronym become that it is possible to miss completely the fact that it is far from an obvious or natural confederation of sexual minorities. This is perhaps most evident in the matter of the T and Q, as both transgenderism and queer theory are predicated on a basic denial of the fixed nature of gender, something that the L and the G by contrast assume. Thus, unlike the L and the G, the T and the Q are transgressive ideologies in the sense that they aim at the demolition of any construction of reality that takes the idea of male and female as representing something that is at root essential.

In fact, however, even the connection between the L and the G is far from a natural or obvious one, despite the tendency to think of both under the general category of homosexuality or same-sex attraction. This point is clear from an influential 1980 essay by the feminist author Adrienne Rich on the topic of what she calls "compulsory heterosexuality."[1] This is her term for what she perceives as the establishment of heterosexuality as culturally normative, particularly heterosexuality as defined by men's erotic desires and sexual practices, which has created a situation in which all sexual activity is understood in relation to that standard.[2] Central to her argument is the notion that male homosexuality and female lesbianism are radically different phenomena, both in terms of the physical expressions of sexual desire that they involve and in terms of the social behavior of the two groups. Each group experiences, and responds to, the dominant heterosexual culture in different ways.

One example that Rich offers to clarify this point is the different ways in which gay men and lesbian women experience the workplace. The lesbian is required to *act* like a heterosexual, to make herself attractive to men, in order to survive in the workplace, while the homosexual is not required to make himself attractive to women. The lesbian therefore has to deny her identity, indeed contradict her identity, in her social interactions. The male homosexual does not have to do so; there is no analogous requirement placed on him to be attractive to a female colleague; he is therefore free in the workplace to be who he really is. In short, the

---

1. Adrienne Rich, "Compulsory Heterosexuality and Lesbian Existence," *Signs* 5 (1980): 631–60.

2. Rich describes her overall approach and argument as follows: "My organizing impulse is the belief that it is not enough for feminist thought that specifically lesbian texts exist. Any theory or cultural/political creation that treats lesbian existence as a marginal or less 'natural' phenomenon, as mere 'sexual preference,' or as the mirror image of either heterosexual or male homosexual relations is profoundly weakened thereby, whatever its other contributions." "Compulsory Heterosexuality," 632.

dominant heterosexual and patriarchal structure of society means that there is no equivalence between gays and lesbians; their experience of the world is profoundly different.[3]

One can disagree with Rich's basic argument—that heterosexuality and patriarchy define everything in our world—but that is not relevant to my point here. What is important is the fact that we have in Rich a representative thinker arguing that homosexuality and lesbianism are not simply the male and female versions of a single broader phenomenon (erotic attraction to the same sex). She is saying that they are actually two different phenomena because of how they stand in relation to the broader power structures of society that lead inevitably to entirely different experiences of that society. And that indicates that there is nothing intrinsic to the L and the G in LGBTQ+ to suggest that they are automatically going to be partners in a common cause.

Rich presses this point further, going as far as to suggest that to bracket lesbians and gays together is nothing less than an act of oppression against the former:

> Lesbians have historically been deprived of a political existence through "inclusion" as female versions of male homosexuality. To equate lesbian existence with male homosexuality because each is stigmatized is to deny and erase female reality once again.[4]

What Rich claims here is that lumping together lesbians and male homosexuals in a common category is, ironically, an act of male domination that denies female identity. Again, the truthfulness of the claim is not what is important; rather, what is significant is the fact that this claim is made at all. We should not allow our familiarity with the reality of the LGBTQ+ alliance to blind us to the fact that none of the elements out

---

3. Rich states, "[There is] a specific difference between the experiences of lesbians and homosexual men. A lesbian, closeted on her job because of heterosexist prejudice, is not simply forced into denying the truth of her outside relationships or private life; her job depends upon her pretending to be not merely heterosexual but a heterosexual *woman*, in terms of dressing and playing the feminine, deferential role required of 'real' women." "Compulsory Heterosexuality," 642.

4. Rich, "Compulsory Heterosexuality," 649.

of which it is constituted was automatically destined to be the natural partner of any of the others.

Yet the reasons for keeping homosexuality and lesbianism separate go beyond matters of social and economic status. They connect to the erotic as well. Rich again:

> I perceive the lesbian experience as being, like motherhood, a pro-foundly *female* experience, with particular oppressions, meanings, and potentialities we cannot comprehend as long as we simply bracket it with other sexually stigmatized existences. . . . But as we deepen and broaden the range of what we define as lesbian existence, as we delineate a lesbian continuum, we begin to discover the erotic in female terms: as that which is unconfined to any single part of the body or solely to the body itself, as an energy not only diffuse but, as Audre Lorde has described it, omnipresent in the "sharing of joy, whether physical, emotional, psychic," and in the sharing of work; as the empowering joy which "makes us less willing to accept powerlessness, or those other supplied states of being which are not native to me, such as resignation, despair, self-effacement, depression, self-denial."[5]

Two things are important here. First, there is an assumed link in Rich's mind between the physical experience of being a woman and the distinction between male homosexuality and lesbianism. That means that the L and the G cannot be intrinsically united because bodies, and bodily differences, are important. Put simply, women experience the world differently because they are physically different from men. The link here between lesbianism and feminism is significant—a feminism, that is, that assumes bodily distinctions between men and women are important and that experiences unique to the female body, such as menstruation, pregnancy, and so on, are vital to the feminist cause. By implication, then, this link indicates that when the L and the G do come together, as they have done in the LGBTQ+ movement, bodily differences must be sidelined or attenuated in some way. In 1980 Rich could not have known that she was

---

5. Rich, "Compulsory Heterosexuality," 650.

here identifying a matter that would have great significance for feminism as a whole once lesbianism attached itself to the broader LGBTQ+ cause.

Second, Rich points to an erotic difference between male homosexuals and lesbians. For her, the two groups are also distinguished by the form of sexual satisfaction that they favor. Though she is not explicit here, the underlying issue is that male homosexuality is focused on penetrative sex and genital orgasm. For the lesbian, sexual satisfaction is something different. It is a much broader category that is not focused exclusively on genital contact. In Rich's terms, lesbianism is characterized less by genital activity and more by a deep and erotic emotional relationship.

The same kind of concern is found in the Boston Women's Health Book Collective volume *Women and Their Bodies: A Course* (1970), a book that, through its numerous revisions, expansions, and reprintings, has become a standard feminist text.[6] The section on sexuality was in part a vigorous critique of allowing male interests and categories to dominate discussion of female sexuality, particularly as this related to the perceived violence of penetration. From doctors to pornographers, the authors found that the dominant view of sex was that promoted and policed by patriarchal society, with the focus on virginity as effectively reducing women to objects to be conquered and colonized by men. This was something that even the sexual revolution had simply exacerbated through its promotion of the promiscuous woman as an ideal—a male ideal.[7] The whole text, even in its discussion of female homosexuality, is designed to separate the discussion of female experience of the world from any male influence, and the idea that lesbians and gays might have some common cause is never countenanced. And this separation is connected to biological realities. The emphasis in the book on women's felt experience of the world and on personal narratives clearly points to the importance of psychology for the argument. But this psychological

---

6. The original work was a samizdat typescript. The title was later changed to *Our Bodies, Ourselves*, and the work was officially published in 1973 by Simon and Schuster.

7. Boston Women's Health Book Collective, *Women and Their Bodies* (Boston: New England Free Press, 1970), 16–17, 23–24. The first edition is self-consciously rooted in New Left thinking, as the first sentence of the main text indicates: "Marcuse says that 'health is a state defined by an elite.'" The title of the section is indicative of the ideological framework of the whole: "Women, Medicine and Capitalism." *Women and Their Bodies*, 6.

element is never detached from the physiological constitution of what it means to be a woman. Indeed, the authors criticize Sigmund Freud for laying the groundwork of denigrating the female body through his theory that women, because of their lack of male genitalia, constructed the female identity as being that of an incomplete man.[8] They further argue that it is precisely women's ignorance of the biology of their reproductive organs that makes them vulnerable to, and victims of, men's control. A feminism that gives such a place to biology provides a context for a lesbianism that cannot see itself as analogous to male homosexuality precisely because it is *male* homosexuality.[9]

So if there is a strong case for lesbians and gays not being commensurable, how is it that they have become allies in the political and cultural struggles of our time? In the 1970s, lesbians and gays had a very fraught relationship that created serious questions as to whether they could ever work together as two parts of a unified movement for sexual liberation. And it was not simply the philosophical incommensurability of lesbianism and male homosexuality that was the problem. Sexism, too, was rampant in the gay community in a way that kept women out of significant positions of power within the movement.[10] Nevertheless, in the 1980s, a united movement for gay liberation, comprising both lesbians and gays, emerged. And the reason for this is quite simple: their shared victimhood as marginalized sexual minorities ultimately proved stronger than the social, economic, biological, and philosophical differences that theorists such as Adrienne Rich noted.

I observed in part 3 that victimhood emerged as a key virtue, perhaps *the* key virtue, out of the Marxist tradition of New Left thinking. Fused to the sexualized notion of selfhood pioneered by Freud and reinforced by the collapse of European colonialism in the decades after the Second World War, a shared sense of victimhood provided an obvious

---

8. Health Book Collective, *Women and Their Bodies*, 8.

9. Health Book Collective, *Women and Their Bodies*, 9–10. By 2011, the book contained sections on transgender women, indicating a seismic shift in the importance of female biology for feminism, a shift brought about by the common cause that lesbians and gays formed in the 1980s.

10. Eric Marcus, *Making Gay History: The Half Century Fight for Lesbian and Gay Equal Rights* (New York: HarperCollins, 2002), 154.

foundation for building a political movement among gay and lesbian people and also one that would resonate with the *Sittlichkeit* of a Western society that felt guilt about its past history of slavery, exploitation, and marginalization of minorities. All that was needed for an LG alliance was a catalyst.

Two key catalytic moments stand out in the narrative: the Stonewall riots of 1969 and the AIDS crisis of the 1980s. As to the former, the police raid on the Stonewall Inn, a gay bar in Greenwich Village, and the subsequent riots and protests are the stuff of LGBTQ+ legend and are generally regarded as the moment when gay militancy emerged as a self-conscious political force. Of course, the story is not that simple: gay rights activism was not invented in June 1969, but the moment has come to function as something of a historical watershed.

Prior to Stonewall, the 1950s and 1960s had witnessed a growing political self-consciousness and activism among gays and lesbians. For example, in 1956, a group in Washington, DC, known as the Council for the Repeal of Unjust Laws had complained that the civil rights legislation that Congress was then considering took no account of homosexuals nor of the fact that many leading advocates of black civil rights were antihomosexual.[11] In the 1960s, such protests continued but remained relatively small, even as they were noted by the FBI. Thus, in October 1965, there was a protest outside the White House staged by the East Coast Homophile Associations against federal policies of discrimination with regard to gays and lesbians. The FBI noted that the picket consisted of "thirty-five individuals"—not exactly a mass movement but indicative of a movement beginning to gain some notoriety.[12]

Stonewall, however, was a signal moment in male gay activism. For a start, it marked a new set of ambitions. The so-called homophile organizations of previous years had argued for gay rights on the basis that homosexuals were as committed to American ideals as anyone, that, for

---

11. Linda Hirshman, *Victory: The Triumphant Gay Revolution* (New York: HarperCollins, 2012), 52.

12. Marcus, *Making Gay History*, 71. Part 3 of Marcus's book (an oral history composed of firsthand testimony from numerous gay activists) covers the years 1961 to 1968 and is an excellent source for tracing the rising self-confidence of the movement for gay rights in the years immediately prior to Stonewall.

example, being gay was quite compatible with being patriotic and with clean living; it did not therefore mean that one should be considered a greater security risk when it came to government employment. This homophile movement could therefore fairly be described as conservative and as desiring assimilation to the cultural status quo. It was not revolutionary in any deep political sense. After Stonewall, however, gay activism became analogous to (and was deeply influenced by) the New Left thinking that shaped the general political protests of the late 1960s. It was self-consciously radical and revolutionary. It sought not accommodation with the culture but a fundamental transformation of the culture. Neil Miller expresses the matter as follows:

> More than anything, the gay revolution [of the late 1960s] represented a change in consciousness. It advocated nothing less than the complete transformation of society. What distinguished the new generation of gay liberationists from the homophiles was more than just an increased degree of militancy. As Dennis Altman, the Australian writer who was the most perceptive chronicler of the ideas behind the early gay liberation movement, observed, "No longer is the claim made that gay people can fit into American society, that they are as decent, as patriotic, as clean-living as anyone. Rather, it is argued, it is American society itself that needs to change." To the young radicals there was no need to create a "favorable" public image. . . . Now Blatant was Beautiful.[13]

It is arguable—in fact, incontestable—that the eventual triumph of gay rights, in the form of gay marriage, was predicated not so much on "Blatant is Beautiful" as on reassuring images of gay domesticity such as those presented in sitcoms like *Will and Grace*. Those images are more akin to the homophile strategies of the pre-Stonewall era. But it is also surely the case that the political self-consciousness and subsequent powerful political organization that prepared the ground for gay marriage only really emerged in the post-Stonewall era as a result of the aggressive self-confidence of a movement determined to occupy a large place in the cultural imagination. Furthermore, the Stonewall riots provided

---

13. Neil Miller, *Out of the Past: Gay and Lesbian History from 1869 to the Present* (New York: Alyson Books, 2006), 339–40.

one more key element to the gay narrative that resonated deeply within Western culture: victimhood. The image of the police gratuitously raiding a bar where gay men were simply gathering together and doing no violence or harm to others made it clear who were the bullies and who were the victims. And it is this shared status that was to prove critical to the L and the G finding common cause.

The most important moment in the victimhood narrative, however, was not Stonewall. The key event, that which both brought the L and the G together and which presented powerful images of gay men as victims, occurred over a decade later, with the advent of AIDS in the 1980s.[14]

The AIDS crisis is fascinating for a number of reasons. For example, the gay community was itself deeply split over how to respond to it in the early years as the full enormity of the situation began to dawn and as serious questions over lifestyle and behavior came to the fore. Bill Kraus, a San Francisco politician who was himself to die of AIDS, tried unsuccessfully to promote safe-sex practices by recommending the closure of the city's bathhouses, focal points for uninhibited gay sexual activity. This idea was compared by one gay opponent of the plan as giving "the Moral Majority and the right wing the gasoline they have been waiting for to fuel the flames that will annihilate us!"[15] The rhetoric is interesting: any inhibiting of sexual freedom—even that designed to prevent the transmission of a deadly disease—is considered unacceptable because of its perceived obnoxious moralizing or potential for promoting such. That sentiment is entirely consonant with a therapeutic culture of expressive individualism, in which it is the present moment and individuals' ability to perform their own selves in whatever way they should choose in that moment that are the only significant ethical concerns.

The subsequent history of the AIDS crisis is the history of the battle for access to drugs that again reflects a number of the cultural pathologies I have noted in this book. Sexual activity post-Freud is not, in and of

---

14. An excellent account of the AIDS crisis is that by David France, *How to Survive a Plague: The Story of How Activists and Scientists Tamed AIDS* (New York: Vintage, 2017).

15. Miller, *Out of the Past*, 415–16.

itself, moral or immoral. It is just an activity. To the modern post-Freud, post-Nietzsche mind, those who argue that sex acts have intrinsic moral content are merely expressing irrational aesthetic preferences rooted in cultural conditioning of simple prejudice. Sex becomes morally significant only as it is an expression of the self or of personal identity, and so any moral discussion of sexual acts or their consequences must be set against that background.[16] If gay is an identity, then the narrative becomes one in which AIDS is presented as killing people because of who they are, not because of what they do. They are not responsible for their own illness and death any more than the color of their skin; they are victims.

Against such a background, AIDS is not a moral crisis to be solved by a moral reformation but a technical one to be addressed with technical solutions: instruction on "safe sex," distribution of condoms, and the ready availability of drugs such as AZT.[17] And the battle over funding for AIDS research and for cheap access to drugs such as AZT, which went right to the heart of the Reagan administration, made gay men victims.[18] Television images of emaciated individuals dying painful deaths are always powerful, and when the background narrative is that this is being caused by government obstruction and irrational prejudice against gay men, then that power is greatly enhanced.

It was in this context of shared victimhood and oppression at the hands of a heterosexual establishment that lesbians and gays found common cause: the story was now one in which both groups were being prevented from being who they really were; both were victims of a common conservative enemy. In this milieu, the Lesbian and Gay Community Center in New York was founded in 1983. This in turn led to the founding of the AIDS Coalition to Unleash Power (ACT UP) in 1987,

---

16. For example, in this framework rape is wrong because it does not include the mutual consent of the parties involved and therefore represents the denial of the identity of the victim. The physical act itself, considered from a purely physiological perspective, has no moral content, good or bad.

17. AZT (azidothymidine, or zidovudine), was the first drug licensed for the treatment of AIDS.

18. C. Everett Koop, an evangelical Christian and Reagan's surgeon general, broke with the administration by sending an educational leaflet on AIDS to every household in the United States, calling for compassion for victims. France, *How to Survive a Plague*, 317.

after a speech at the center by AIDS activist Larry Kramer.[19] The rest, as they say, is history.

In sum, therefore, the initial forging of the lesbian-gay alliance is not something that arises out of intrinsic affinities between the two. It is the result of sharing the same enemy and suffering similar marginalization. And virtuous victimhood is a powerful catalyst for political coalitions in the modern world. The whole tenor of the therapeutic society, from its psychologizing of oppression to its historical narratives that make history's victims into the real heroes, serves to cultivate the emotional (and therefore moral) power that claims to victimhood now command. And this is perhaps nowhere more dramatically and significantly evident than in the forging of the LG alliance in the early 1980s around the matter of AIDS. AIDS made middle-class gay men into sympathetic victims, and the debates surrounding the government response to the crisis gave lesbians and male homosexuals a common cause and a common enemy: a conservative culture, epitomized by the Reagan administration, that was effectively subverting their identity and, in many cases, literally condemning them to death. It also set the stage for the later alliance with transgender people and therefore laid the groundwork for the current civil war among feminists.

The T Joins the Party

The rise of transgenderism and its grafting onto the LGB alliance is the second matter that I said needed to be addressed in this chapter. While it had always been a presence in the world of transgressive sexuality, the moment when most people probably became aware that transgenderism was about to become a major public issue occurred in April 2015, when the then Bruce Jenner came out as a trans woman in an interview with Diane Sawyer on the current affairs program *20/20*.[20] By 2017, Jenner had completed gender reassignment surgery, and Bruce was now Caitlyn. Since then, debates about transgender bathroom policy in schools,

---

19. France, *How to Survive a Plague*, 247–53.

20. "Bruce Jenner: The Interview," interview by Diane Sawyer, *20/20*, April 24, 2015, https://abc news.go.com/2020/fullpage/bruce-jenner-the-interview-30471558.

about the appropriate use of pronouns, and about the implications for women's sports have dominated much of the sexual political discussion of the public square.[21]

While Jenner may have been the public face of the transgender movement, it should be obvious from the earlier narrative of this book that his declaration is consistent with cultural tendencies that run fast and deep within Western society. For transgenderism to be coherent, the society in which it occurs needs to place a decisive priority on the psychological over the physical in determining identity. For it to be coherent also involves a correlative downplaying of external authority, whether that of the person's biology or of traditional social expectations. Biological and cultural amnesia must be the order of the day. In addition, its credibility is fueled by a powerful individualism and facilitated by the technological ability to manipulate biological realities. All these factors are present in contemporary Western society. To these we might also add the notion that gender is separable from sex, something that we noted in the work of Simone de Beauvoir and later feminism and that gains plausibility again from the technological attenuation of the difference between men and women in the workplace, as predicted by Karl Marx. In other words, Jenner did not appear out of nowhere, nor is he the result of a single cause. Indeed, the acronym LGBT had established itself as common currency among gay activists by the mid-1990s, many years before Jenner came out.[22]

The connection between transgenderism and the deeper social currents noted in earlier chapters is evident from Jenner's 2015 interview with Diane Sawyer. Here Jenner makes a revealing statement—revealing, that is, about where to locate the transgender issue within the greater narrative of Western thinking on selfhood:

> I look at it this way. Bruce [was] always telling a lie. He's lived a lie his whole life about who he is. And I can't do that any longer. Should I take my ponytail out? Yeah, why not? We're talking about all this stuff. Yeah, let's take the . . . ponytail out. [*Sawyer: Are you a woman?*]

---

21. The standard guide to gender and its various social and political ramifications in contemporary society is Michael Kimmel, *The Gendered Society*, 6th ed. (Oxford: Oxford University Press, 2017).

22. Lisa M. Stulberg, *LGBTQ Social Movements* (Cambridge: Polity, 2018), 68.

Um, yes. For all intents and purposes, I am a woman. People look at me differently. They see you as this macho male, but my heart and my soul and everything I do in life, it is part of me. That female side is part of me. It's who I am. I was not genetically born that way. And as of now, [I] have all the male parts, and all that kind of stuff, so in a lot of ways we're different. But we still identify as female. And that's very hard for Bruce Jenner to say. Cuz why? I don't want to disappoint people.[23]

The language is most significant. It is not so much that of psychological confusion as that of the contrast between inner authenticity and outward hypocrisy. Bruce Jenner was "always telling a lie." In fact, his whole life has been a lie. The outward image projected by Bruce was just a performance required by public expectations of him as a macho male, a performance maintained because Jenner did not "want to disappoint people." This is an expression of that which is evident in Rousseau and the Romantics: society, or culture, forced a role on him that has made him inauthentic, untrue to himself. The real Jenner—Caitlyn, not Bruce—is akin to the noble savage, a being whose inward identity matches their outward appearance, but the demands of polite society forced him to play the hypocrite, to be Bruce.

Another testimony from a transgender person, Joanne Herman, exhibits the same basic characteristics:

I felt like a car running on the wrong kind of gas. I did not fully understand how wrong it was until I replaced testosterone with estrogen when I transitioned genders in 2002. I now have an amazing sense of well-being and harmony that I never knew before. Now my body just hums.[24]

---

23. For a partial transcript of the interview, from which this quotation is taken, see Kate Ward, "Transcript of Bruce Jenner Coming Out as Transgender Will Only Make You Respect Jenner More," *Bustle*, April 24, 2015, https://www.bustle.com/articles/78832-transcript-of-bruce-jenner-coming-out-as-transgender-will-only-make-you-respect-jenner-more.

24. Joanne Herman, *Transgender Explained for Those Who Are Not* (Bloomington, IN: AuthorHouse, 2009), 51; quoted in *Our Bodies, Ourselves*, 79. One obvious question at this point concerns why the body is so important to gender identity (in terms of the administering of hormones and surgery), when the whole point of transgenderism is that the body is not important to gender identity. That is, I am not what my body says I am; I am what I think I am. To put the question more concisely, if gender is merely a social construct, then why the need for physical treatment?

In the case of both Jenner and Herman, this is the language of expressive individualism, connected to the central concern of the therapeutic society, that is, an inner sense of psychological well-being.[25] Bruce was a construct, an inauthentic construct, imposed on Caitlyn, on the inner female self, by society. Herman always felt "the wrong primary sex hormone" was "coursing through my body."[26] The result was a lifetime of pretending to be someone else, someone demanded by wider society and by chromosomes and physiology in contradiction to psychological feelings, and therefore their lives were lived as lies. Now, following her inner psychological convictions and breaking free from culturally imposed norms, Caitlyn is free to be herself, to be authentic, to be outwardly who she has always been inwardly, and Joanne has a wonderful sense of inner happiness and peace. This is the language and framework of the expressive individualism traced in this book from Rousseau onward. That which I first noted in the Genevan philosopher's notion of man in the hypothetical state of nature as opposed to the artificial, inauthentic self cultivated by the demands of society finds its most consistent modern-day exemplar in a figure such as Caitlyn Jenner, transgender woman.

Yet there is an interesting question here: How does the T stand in positive relation to the L, the G, and the B in LGBT? Lesbians and male homosexuals traditionally operated with a gender binary—that there are biologically such things as men and women and that their sexual identity must be understood within that framework. The T (and the Q, for queer) denies such a biologically shaped approach in favor of a much more psychological and free-floating notion of gender.

The short answer is that, as with the alliance between the L and the G, it is a political coalition forged on the basis of a common enemy—a socially and politically enforced heterosexual normativity. Drag queens and transgender people played a role in the earlier movement for gay liberation. They were part of the regular clientele at the Stonewall Inn and were

---

25. *Pace* this anecdote, there is much evidence to indicate that surgery does not alleviate the discomfort associated with gender dysphoria and can even lead to further mental issues; see Ryan T. Anderson, *When Harry Became Sally: Responding to the Transgender Movement* (New York: Encounter Books, 2018), 102.

26. Herman, *Transgender Explained*, quoted in *Our Bodies, Ourselves*, 79.

present on June 28, 1969, when the police raid that triggered the Stonewall riots took place.[27] Yet resentment of transgender people, particularly men claiming to be women, was rife within the lesbian community.[28]

All this, however, was to change in the early years of the twenty-first century. In the first decade, transgenderism was to make dramatic strides toward being normalized, even if it had yet to find a high-profile figure such as Jenner to function as its poster child. In 2008, both the American Psychological Association and the National Association of Social Workers called for the full normalization of transgenderism by society, with the American Psychiatric Association following in 2012.[29] And this normalization is reflected in the acceptance of transgender women by influential sections of the feminist movement.

Take, for example, the 2011 edition of *Our Bodies, Ourselves*, the Boston Women's Health Book Collective's handbook for feminists that had started so many years earlier as the samizdat typescript *Women and Their Bodies* in 1970.[30] The earlier work, as I noted above, was steeped in Marcusan New Left concepts and also placed significant emphasis on the physicality of being a woman as being decisive for the female experience of selfhood and the world around it. Second-wave feminism, as in the thought of Simone de Beauvoir and Shulamith Firestone, separated sex from gender but seems to have envisaged a world in which physical differences came to make no real difference between men and women, not where men could become women and vice versa. The goal for them was more eschatological—a transcendence of gender differences through technology and enhanced political consciousness.

In the 2011 edition of *Our Bodies, Ourselves*, there is an entire section devoted to sex, gender, and transgender issues. The separation of sex from gender is accepted as basic, and transgenderism is now clearly part of mainstream feminism in the present—or, perhaps better, part of a *part* of mainstream feminism. Not all feminists are so enamored of

27. Hirshman, *Victory*, 96–97.

28. Marcus, *Making Gay History*, 152.

29. Darel E. Paul, *From Tolerance to Equality: How Elites Brought America to Same-Sex Marriage* (Waco, TX: Baylor University Press, 2018) 152.

30. Boston Women's Health Book Collective, *Our Bodies, Ourselves* (New York: Touchstone, 2011).

trans women (men who identify as women) becoming part of the feminist cause, as I discuss further below. But for the authors of *Our Bodies, Ourselves*, there is no problem with including transgender women:

> An increasing number of feminists and other activists are advocating for the expansion or elimination of either-or gender norms, in order to allow for a full range of human behavior and expression. Knowing that gender is separate from sexual anatomy enables us to express ourselves in ways that may conflict with how society dictates we should look and act.[31]

This is a quite superb example of the central contention of this book: that the issues we face today in terms of sexual politics are a symptom or manifestation of the deeper revolution in selfhood that the rise and triumph of expressive individualism represents. The language of self-expression and the negative attitude to the norms of society at large are entirely consistent with Rousseau and the Romantics. Now refracted through the lens of the post-Freud preoccupation with sexuality and the post-Marx, post-Nietzsche framework of power and oppression, the spirit of the Romantics finds its home in the radicalism of the transgender lobby, and the transgender lobby finds its home with the L and the G and with feminism.[32]

All this serves to highlight the politically constructed nature of the LGBTQ+ alliance. It is one that emerged over time, not as a result of intrinsic affinities between the various groups involved but rather because of a shared sense of victimhood, a common interest in destabilizing society's heterosexual norms (or, to use Adrienne Rich's term, "compulsory heterosexuality"), and therefore a convenient coalition for political and legal lobbying.

---

31. Health Book Collective, *Our Bodies, Ourselves*, 73.

32. While Herbert Marcuse is not explicitly mentioned in the 2011 edition of *Our Bodies, Ourselves*, the work still stands within the tradition of critical theory that flows from the New Left. Intersectionality is central to many of its arguments: queer fat women and black lesbians receive separate treatment, and an upper-middle-class white "dyke" (her chosen term for self-reference) explains that her white privilege cuts her off from experiencing the queer community as people of color do. This is symptomatic of the fissiparous and deeply destabilizing nature of political categories in a world in which any notion of transcendent human nature rooted in some form of metaphysical reality is rejected, presumably as a hegemonic construct of the dominant elites. See Health Book Collective, *Our Bodies, Ourselves*, 93–94.

These unifying elements are corroborated by firsthand testimony from an LGBTQ+ insider. In private correspondence with Rosaria Butterfield, a former lesbian activist and professor of queer theory, I suggested that these three elements were foundational to the LGBTQ+ coalition. Her response confirmed my analysis but added an interesting insider's perspective:

> Your take on the "T" issue is right, and your latter point [i.e., that its inclusion was driven by the pragmatics of forming a convenient coalition for lobbying against heteronormativity] is crucial to discuss. Really, transgenderism was the bane of queer existence until it was politically expedient to add this to the movement. The Stonewall Riot included drag queens, of course, but the moment of clear inclusion was the fall of DOMA [the Defense of Marriage Act] in 2013. Part of the reason behind this is the warring class and culture differences within the movement. The AIDS crisis (late 1980s until the widespread use of AZT) brought together the L and the G—not because AIDS ever really hit the lesbian community, but because white, middle class, educated men who identified as gay suddenly appeared as victims to us, and that changed everything. While there were a few examples of friendships that crossed lines, most of the distinctive sexual perversions that define the differences within this movement are incommensurable: lesbians eschew penetration, gay men engage in reckless and dangerous penetration, women who want to become transgender men usurp male privilege and turn their backs on women's empowerment, men who want to become transgender women deny the male privilege that has been their invisible birth right and steal false identifications with victimhood. These were some of the things we said about and to each other before the cameras were rolling. But for the sake of creating a political groundswell, one based on the autonomous, freely choosing individual who finds meaning in no one but himself, all distinctions were put aside. SOGI [Sexual Orientation and Gender Identity] laws also point to the clear lines that divide, combined with political coalitioning.[33]

In short, as natural as the LGBTQ+ alliance has come to seem, given its constant presence in the media, its dramatic displays of unity in Pride parades, and its common cause in pressing for the rights of sexual

---

33. Rosaria Butterfield, email message to the author, February 23, 2018. Reproduced with permission.

minorities, it is nonetheless a convenient construct that has emerged because of historical circumstances and a shared sense of victimhood and marginalization. And the confected nature of this alliance is in practice proving insufficient to defuse significant tensions and conflicts that exist within the movement itself.

Conflict within the Camp

In retrospect, the key moment both for making possible the uniting of the various minorities of the LGBTQ+ movement and for guaranteeing that it would not be a stable and coherent alliance was the coming together of the L and the G. The instant that lesbians decided to make common public cause with gay men, they had in effect decided to prioritize opposition to heterosexual normativity over biological sex. The addition of the trans community to the cause is simply an extension of the principle then established, that marginalization by the heterosexual hegemony was the only thing that really mattered when it came to public campaigning. The price paid by orthodox feminism, however, has been costly, and the status of transgender people is today a matter of acrimonious dispute among those who have campaigned for women's rights. The coining of the pejorative acronym TERF, standing for trans-exclusionary radical feminist, in 2008 witnesses to the fact that some feminists refuse to accept that men can be surgically transformed into women. Of particular note in this context are Janice G. Raymond and Germaine Greer.[34]

Raymond's book *Transsexual Empire: The Making of the She-Male* (1979) is, as one writer (hostile to Raymond) has described it, "the exemplary and foundational TERF text."[35] Raymond has no desire to assert a

---

34. On the problems that the separation of gender from biological sex has created for feminism as a movement, see Mona Charen, *Sex Matters: How Modern Feminism Lost Touch with Science, Love, and Common Sense* (New York: Crown Forum, 2018).

35. Stulberg, *LGBTQ Social Movements*, 150. Raymond reissued the work in 1994 with a preface responding to many of her critics: *Transsexual Empire: The Making of the She-Male*, reissued with a new introduction on transgender (New York: Teachers College Press, 1994). The term *transsexual* and its cognates are equivalent to the modern term *transgender*. The book is available for download as a pdf at "The Transsexual Empire," Janice Raymond, accessed July 18, 2019, https://janiceraymond.com/the -transsexual-empire/.

kind of essentialism, where there is some necessary connection between an ideal femininity and female biology. She is well aware that women's roles have been historically constructed: the ideal woman in ancient Athens is not the same as the ideal woman in medieval Paris or Reformation Wittenberg or a middle-class Victorian household or present-day Manhattan. But she is unwilling therefore to reduce being a woman to some kind of gnostic psychological experience that has no connection whatsoever to female biology. In the 1994 preface, she expresses the matter this way:

> Affirming that transsexual surgery cannot change the basic biology of chromosomal sex is not to say that chromosomal sex defines gender. But in some very real senses, female biology shapes female history—a history that men don't have because of their sex—including the history of menstruation, the history of pregnancy or the capacity to become pregnant, the history of childbirth and abortion, the history of certain bodily cycles and life changes, and the history of female subordination in a male-dominant society. Note that I keep saying history. To deny that female history is, in part, based on female biology is like denying that important aspects of Black history are based on skin color. As with biological skin color, female biology doesn't confer an essential femininity; rather it confers a historical reality about what it means to be born with XX chromosomes.[36]

Raymond therefore allows for a separation between sex and gender, where gender refers to the specific roles that women are expected to play in historically particular circumstances, but she will not allow that there is therefore no significance to the bodily constitution of women for their experience of what it means to be female.[37] Menstruation and pregnancy are experiences unique to women and are part of their history. Biology

---

36. Raymond, *Transsexual Empire*, xx.

37. The analogy with race has since become quite important. In 2015, a chapter president of the National Association for the Advancement of Colored People, Rachel Dolezal, was exposed as not actually being black. She claimed, however, that although she was white, she identified as black. At least some of her supporters found that to be a satisfactory claim, and (in light of the prevailing logic of transgenderism) it is hard to see how one could object to her claim, given that race has far less basis in biology than does sex. See Gisele Lamarre and Elisha Fieldstadt, "NAACP Chapter President Rachel Dolezal Plans to Address Race Controversy Monday," NBC News, June 13, 2015, https://www.nbcnews.com/news/us-news/embattled-naacp-president-rachel-dolezal-will-address-race-controversy-monday-n374986.

may not demand a hard essentialism when it comes to social gender norms, but it does provide a distinctly female experience of life that is forever denied to Caitlyn Jenner.[38]

This point is analogous to what I noted in chapter 7 with regard to Erich Fromm's interpretation of Karl Marx. Fromm's point was that Marx's notion (developed from Hegel) that human identity is a function of economic forces means that human nature cannot be abstracted from its historical context—there is for Hegel, Marx, and Fromm no platonic ideal of human nature separable from history. But this does not mean that the Roman slave, the medieval lord, and the modern industrial worker have nothing in common. They have a shared biological constitution that is the foundation for their experience of their (albeit very different) worlds. Raymond is making a similar argument with regard to women: though what constitutes female identity (gender) in different times and different cultures may vary greatly, these various identities are connected to common forms of bodily experience. To reject that, as transgenderism does, is to move gender entirely into the realm of the psychological and to deny, in a quasi-gnostic fashion, any significance to the body.[39]

It is not surprising, then, that Raymond locates the rise of transgenderism as part of the rise of the therapeutic society. Chapter 5 of

---

38. It is possible to imagine a future world in which womb transplants will make it possible for men to give birth, but Raymond would no doubt (correctly) argue that such men are still not experiencing childbirth as women but simply as men who have undergone a surgical procedure.

39. Judith Butler, probably the most influential philosopher of gender behind the transgender movement, argues that the split between gender and sex (such as that made by de Beauvoir and also later second-wave feminists) immediately jeopardizes any notion that one could posit a unity of subject ("woman") for articulating a common experience of what one could designate womanhood or being a woman. Further, building on the work of Michel Foucault, she asserts that gender is not to be understood as "merely the cultural inscription of meaning on sex" but that the very act of making such a connection stands within a broader discourse of power relations and is designed therefore to serve the interests of the powerful. Given Butler's influence, the spirit of Nietzsche's genealogical approach, via the work of Foucault, clearly underlies the demolition of the gender binary in modern thought. See Judith Butler, *Gender Trouble: Feminism and the Subversion of Identity* (London: Routledge, 1990), 6–7. It is not surprising that Butler stands at the head of a tradition of thought that dismisses the claims of Raymond and those like her as essentialism and as built on an untenable commitment to metaphysics. Given the argument that Fromm makes about Marx, it would seem that Raymond can be considered an essentialist only in a very weak sense of the term, in light of the strongly historicist bent of her thought, and that blanket dismissal of antitransgender feminists as "essentialists" is more of a rhetorical cheap shot than a serious philosophical challenge. See Butler, *Gender Trouble*, 16–25, esp. 20–21.

Raymond's *Transsexual Empire* is particularly relevant in this regard. Drawing explicitly on the work of Philip Rieff, Raymond sees the medicalized response to transgenderism as a function of the therapeutic nature of modern society:

> If one's basic approach to the problem of transsexualism is from a psychological and medical basis, then many moral issues, as well as sociopolitical, economic, and environmental problems, are transformed into technical problems.[40]

I have noted this point numerous times in this book. Where a sense of psychological well-being is the purpose of life, therapy supplants morality—or, perhaps better, therapy is morality—and anything that achieves that sense of well-being is good, as long as it meets the rather weak condition that it does not inhibit the happiness of others, or that of a greater number of others.

Raymond's feminist concern here is that transgenderism essentially depoliticizes the matter of being a woman.[41] Being a woman is now something that can be produced by a technique—literally prescribed by a doctor. The pain, the struggle, and the history of oppression that shape what it means to be a woman in society are thus trivialized and rendered irrelevant. More to the point, this depoliticization is clear from the fact that transgenderism still operates within the gender stereotypes generated by patriarchal society.[42] In this context, it is interesting to note that Jenner's 2015 cover for *Vanity Fair* and the accompanying photo shoot all operated within the aesthetic norms of standard American cover girls. Jenner was presented as the kind of woman who might feature in a male fantasy. Such a display both perpetuates stereotypes and would seem to support Raymond's basic thesis that the man who thinks he is a woman

---

40. Raymond, *Transsexual Empire*, 120.

41. Raymond states, "One of the major effects of the medical model has been the de-ethicizing of problems and behavior. De-ethicization occurs when problems that have moral implications are defined as if they had none, or are redefined or reclassified, for example, as 'therapeutic considerations,' or 'health issues,' or 'psychiatric management' problems. The 'triumph of the therapeutic' has made transsexualism the 'territorial imperative' of the psychologist, psychiatrist, and/or mental-health worker." *Transsexual Empire*, 125.

42. Raymond, *Transsexual Empire*, 126–27.

trapped in a man's body really wants to be a woman in accordance with male expectations of what a woman should be.[43]

As with Raymond, Germaine Greer is no essentialist in the simplistic sense of the word. In her first major work, *The Female Eunuch*, she devotes the first chapter to asserting that the role of chromosomes in traditional understandings of the gender difference between men and women has been greatly exaggerated.[44] But in an infamous and oft-quoted paragraph in a later work, she famously declares,

> Governments that consist of very few women have hurried to recognize as women men who believe that they are women and have had themselves castrated to prove it, because they see women not as another sex but as a non-sex. No so-called sex-change has ever begged for a uterus-and-ovaries transplant; if uterus-and-ovaries transplants were made mandatory for wannabe women they would disappear overnight.[45]

Greer's point is that sex-change surgery simply removes the most distinctive elements of the male sexual anatomy; it does not add the critical components of womb and ovaries that provide the experiences that constitute womanhood: menstruation and pregnancy.[46] To claim to transition from male to female, or vice versa, is for Greer to engage in a self-deception, an act. In the closing paragraph of her chapter "Pantomime Dames," she pointedly declares,

> The transsexual is identified as such solely on his/her own script, which can be as learned as any sex-typed behavior and as editorialized as autobiographies usually are.[47]

---

43. Raymond, *Transsexual Empire*, 20.

44. Germaine Greer, *The Female Eunuch* (New York: McGraw-Hill, 1971), 15–19.

45. Germaine Greer, *The Whole Woman* (New York: Random House, 1999), 70. The passage occurs in the chapter "Pantomime Dames"—itself a part of Greer's polemic as it refers to the traditional British pantomime in which the lead comic female character, the Dame, is always played by a man in drag.

46. Since Greer wrote this, the desirability of womb and ovary transplants has actually become part of transgender thinking; see Leah Samuel, "With Womb Transplants a Reality, Transgender Women Dare to Dream of Pregnancies," *Stat*, March 7, 2016, https://www.statnews.com/2016/03/07/uterine-transplant-transgender/.

47. Greer, *Whole Woman*, 80.

In fact, Greer believes, men who transition to become women are simply trying to conform themselves to what they as males think women should be. Ironically, therefore, she sees transgenderism as in some sense profoundly conservative.[48] What is clear is that radical feminism is now divided on this issue, and that division is closely connected to the philosophical sacrifice of the importance of biological sex that occurred in the coming together of the L and the G.[49]

The End of All Stable Categories

The problem that Raymond and Greer identify in the LGBTQ+ movement is far reaching in its implications: as soon as biology is discounted as being one decisive factor of significance for identity, the L, the G, and the B are also destabilized as meaningful categories. One might see this implication from various perspectives. It is, for example, of the nature of intersectionality to make such categories highly volatile and unstable, given its basic assertion that power relations are complex relative to simple taxonomies. The debt such theory owes to Michel Foucault (and therefore to his own inspiration, Friedrich Nietzsche), with his radical questioning of all stable forms of discourse as manipulative bids for power, is evident in the work of influential gender theorists such as Judith Butler.[50] For Butler, gender is a performance and possesses no prior ontological status. To be a woman is not to have a certain biological substance but to repeatedly act like a woman, and the philosophical origins of Butler's idea is clear:

> The challenge for rethinking gender categories outside of the metaphysics of substance will have to consider the relevance of Nietzsche's claim

---

48. Greer, *Whole Woman*, 71.

49. Greer has been consistently and aggressively outspoken on this issue. Her basic position is summarized in comments she made in an interview with transgender actor Rebecca Root: "Just because you lop off your penis and then wear a dress doesn't make you a ******* woman," Greer said in a statement given to the Victoria Derbyshire show. "I've asked my doctor to give me long ears and liver spots and I'm going to wear a brown coat but that won't turn me into a ******* cocker spaniel." Lucy Clarke-Billings, "Germaine Greer in Transgender Rant: 'Just Because You Lop Off Your Penis . . . It Doesn't Make You a Woman,'" *Telegraph*, October 26, 2015, https://www.telegraph.co.uk/news/health/news/11955891/Germaine-Greer-in-transgender-rant-Just-because-you-lop-off-your-penis...it-doesnt-make-you-a-woman.html.

50. See Butler, *Gender Trouble*.

in *On the Genealogy of Morals* that "there is no 'being' behind doing, effecting, becoming; 'the doer' is merely a fiction added to the deed— the deed is everything." In an application that Nietzsche himself would not have anticipated or condoned, we might state as a corollary: There is no gender identity behind the expressions of gender; that identity is performatively constituted by the very "expressions" that are said to be its results.[51]

An obvious riposte might be that menstruation, conception, pregnancy, and childbirth are all gender performances that yet depend on some kind of prior biological essence, and that hormone treatment and gender reassignment surgery also seem to assume the importance of biology for gender identity. But Butler's argument—that gender is doing, not being—stands in line with the antimetaphysical philosophy that now dominates intellectual life in the humanities.

Yet one does not need critical theory to throw traditional categories into confusion. From the perspective of the narrative of the rise of psychological man, I would argue that the subjectivity inherent in the psychological construction of the self serves to render any biologically grounded categories—indeed, any fixed categories, whether economic, racial, or whatever—to be highly unstable. If I am whoever I think I am and if my inward sense of psychological well-being is my only moral imperative, then the imposition of external, prior, or static categories is nothing other than an act of imperialism, an attempt to restrict my freedom or to make me inauthentic. Nietzsche saw this in the nineteenth century. At the same time, Karl Marx and Charles Darwin were also stripping nature of its given metaphysical authority. In this context, transgenderism is merely the latest iteration of self-creation that becomes necessary in the wake of decreation.

It is therefore not surprising that a movement is emerging that is pressing for the abandonment of terms such as *lesbian*, *gay*, and *bisexual* as too rigid to account for the pansexuality and the fluidity of gender that is supposed to characterize the modern world. More than that, it is

---

51. Butler, *Gender Trouble*, 25; cf. 136–41.

argued that the very concept of binary gender is profoundly manipulative. In the words of Judith Butler,

> Gender can denote a *unity* of experience, of sex, gender, and desire, only when sex can be understood in some sense to necessitate gender—where gender is a psychic and/or cultural designation of the self—and desire—where desire is heterosexual and therefore differentiates itself through an oppositional relation to that other gender it desires. The internal coherence or unity of either gender, man or woman, thereby requires both a stable and oppositional heterosexuality. That institutional heterosexuality both requires and produces the univocity of each of the gendered terms that constitute the limit of gendered possibilities within an oppositional, binary gender system.[52]

In plain English, minus the pretentious and arcane syntax, Butler is claiming that the idea of male and female as a natural binary is itself merely a means of maintaining heterosexuality as the norm. On this basis, we could conclude that those alternative sexualities—lesbianism, homosexuality, and bisexuality—are all ultimately defined by, and therefore dependent on, heterosexuality. True sexual revolution thus requires the abolition of all such categories, based as they are on the gender binary.

If the poststructuralist theory expressed in such rebarbative prose is perhaps hard to grasp on a first, second, or even fifteenth reading, there are still clear practical instances of real human experience that demonstrate the problem of traditional categories of sexuality in a gender-fluid world with much greater clarity and emotional force. Take, for example, the following personal testimony of a lesbian living with a partner who transitioned from female to male:

> When my partner began his gender transition my lesbian identity had been central to my life and my sense of self for well over a decade, and I didn't know what his transition made me. Some people told me I was "obviously" still a lesbian, but it was just as obvious to others that I was now straight, or bisexual. It wasn't obvious to me at all, and I struggled with it for a long time. Now I've been the partner of a trans man for

---

52. Butler, *Gender Trouble*, 22.

as long as I was a lesbian, and I've gotten comfortable just not having a name for what I think I am. I think of myself as part of the family of queers and trans people.[53]

This is an extraordinarily instructive testimony to the kind of problem faced within the LGBTQ+ community in the wider context of the expressive individualism and the need for recognition noted in chapter 1. For this individual to continue to affirm her own identity as a lesbian after her partner's transition requires her to deny the identity of her partner. For her to affirm the identity of her partner after the transition means that she must deny her own—the catch-22 of modern sexual politics. Her resolution—to embrace a "queer" identity—essentially involves the repudiation not only of the connection between sex and gender but even of gender itself as a binary construct.[54]

This anecdotal testimony is also a tragic example of what happens when the individual self-consciousness has nothing solid or firm with which to engage dialogically in the construction of the self. There is no clearly defined "other" in relation to which she can define herself. If gender is completely psychologized and severed from biological sex, then categories built on the old male-female binary cease to be relevant, and attempts to maintain them only create problems of the kind described in this testimony.[55] If gender is a construct, then so are all those categories based on it—heterosexuality, homosexuality, and bisexuality. The world of psychological man is a world in which, to borrow Marx's phrase, all that is solid is constantly in danger of melting into air—incuding our selves.

---

53. Health Book Collective, *Our Bodies, Ourselves*, 85.

54. Andrew Sullivan, who is himself gay, notes the importance of biology and biological difference for the gay community while reflecting on the question of transgender rights: "It is not transphobic for a gay man not to be attracted to a trans man. It is close to definitional. The core of the traditional gay claim is that there is indeed a very big difference between male and female, that the difference matters, and without it, homosexuality would make no sense at all. If it's all a free and fluid nonbinary choice of gender and sexual partners, a choice to have sex exclusively with the same sex would not be an expression of our identity, but a form of sexist bigotry, would it not?" "The Nature of Sex," *New York Magazine*, February 1, 2019, http://nymag.com/intelligencer/2019/02/andrew-sullivan-the-nature-of-sex.html.

55. In the words of veteran gay rights advocate and commentator Dennis Altman, "If we accept that gender is fluid, it makes nonsense of a binary division between hetero- and homosexual. This may be why social conservatives feel so threatened by 'gender ideology.'" "The Term 'LGBTI' Confuses Desire, Behaviour and Identity—It's Time for a Rethink," *The Conversation*, January 18, 2018, https://theconversation.com/the-term-lgbti-confuses-desire-behaviour-and-identity-its-time-for-a-rethink-90175.

The acknowledgment of this state of affairs is most obvious in the way legislation regarding LGBTQ+ matters is now being framed. It is no longer being presented so much in terms of fixed identities that in some way track back to biology. Rather, it is being developed in terms of sexual orientation and gender identity.[56] These concepts deftly avoid any dependence on the old male-female binary and, in their legal manifestations, represent the legal recognition that human beings have fluid identities predicated on nothing more than psychological conviction. This is evident in the document that has set the terms of discussion for such legislation across the globe—*The Yogyakarta Principles*, the third matter of significance that I noted at the start of this chapter.

The Yogyakarta Principles

The Yogyakarta Principles, named after the Indonesian city where they were formulated in 2006, is a foundational text in connecting LGBTQ+ rights to the concept of human rights in general. The principles are presented as setting forth the bases for framing SOGI (sexual orientation and gender identity) laws around the world. The groups that formulated the original principles were the International Commission of Jurists and the International Service for Human Rights. Neither has any official governmental status. They are in essence independent bodies of self-appointed experts. But numerous countries around the world have adopted the principles of *Yogyakarta*, and it is fair to say that wherever sexual orientation or gender identity enjoys legal protections, there one can discern their underlying influence. Indeed, such has been the success of the

---

56. The obsession of critical theorists with refracting everything through the lens of power relations is central to this shift. In discussing the problems facing transgender children, Ann Travers (channeling and updating Wilhelm Reich) blithely declares that "to adequately empower trans kids, binary sex and gender systems need to be understood as part of a larger assemblage of power relations." *The Trans Generation: How Trans Kids (and Their Parents) Are Creating a Gender Revolution* (New York: New York University Press, 2018), 43. Cf. Heath Fogg Davis, *Beyond Trans: Does Gender Matter?* (New York: New York University Press, 2017), 142–43: "Sex-classification policies are material artifacts that were conceived and codified by people, and thus can be rewritten and overwritten by the same people or their successors. . . . [M]ore often than not the use of sex on bureaucratic forms or to physically segregate people is habitual rather than the product of strategic thinking about why and how sex is relevant to organizational aims, and why and how the use of sex is discriminatory." Davis's use of the language of segregation and discrimination is significant and belies the superficial objectivity of his observation.

document that a further ten principles were added at a second meeting in 2017. *The Yogyakarta Principles* both brilliantly summarizes the political implications of the LGBTQ+ movement and will also no doubt continue to influence political and legal attitudes toward the same.

The official website for *The Yogyakarta Principles* describes its origin and intentions in this way:

> In 2006, in response to well-documented patterns of abuse, a distinguished group of international human rights experts met in Yogyakarta, Indonesia to outline a set of international principles relating to sexual orientation and gender identity. The result was the Yogyakarta Principles: a universal guide to human rights which affirm binding international legal standards with which all States must comply. They promise a different future where all people born free and equal in dignity and rights can fulfil that precious birthright.[57]

Against the background of the narrative of parts 2 and 3 of this book, it is immediately obvious that *The Yogyakarta Principles* operates within the broad parameters of the expressive individualism that characterizes our age in general and not simply the world of sexual minorities. Victimhood is the presenting cause; freedom, equality, and dignity are the moral presuppositions that carry with them imperatives for action. This is clear from the opening paragraph of the introduction to the official text of *The Yogyakarta Principles*:

> All human beings are born free and equal in dignity and rights. All human rights are universal, interdependent, indivisible and interrelated. Sexual orientation and gender identity are integral to every person's dignity and humanity and must not be the basis for discrimination or abuse.[58]

This is a brilliant summary of the modern notion of the self, placing the accent on psychologized categories of sexual and gender identity,

---

57. *The Yogyakarta Principles: Principles on the Application of International Human Rights Law in Relation to Sexual Orientation and Gender Identity* (2007), accessed July 8, 2019, https://yogyakarta principles.org/.

58. *Yogyakarta Principles*, 6 .

set against the background of innate freedom and equal dignity. This is immediately followed by statements concerning the violence that is routinely experienced by those who deviate from the heterosexual norms in society. Indeed, *The Yogyakarta Principles* makes it clear that it is state imposition of sexual norms and the "policing of sexuality" by the state that is the source of "gender-based violence and gender inequality."[59] This is most definitely the view of the world formed by the likes of Wilhelm Reich, Herbert Marcuse, and their intellectual descendants, whereby sexual repression by the state is a primary means of political oppression. Innate freedom and a general background of sexual oppression are themes that underlie the entire document, and it is interesting to note (again in light of the earlier narrative of this book) that no significant distinction is made between the physical and the psychological in references to violence. This is again reflective of a world in which dignity is key to personal well-being and psychology is foundational to identity.[60]

This psychologized understanding of what it means to be human, to be a self, is explicit in the preamble:

> Understanding "sexual orientation" to refer to each person's capacity for profound emotional, affectional and sexual attraction to, and intimate and sexual relations with, individuals of a different gender or the same gender or more than one gender;
>
> Understanding "gender identity" to refer to each person's deeply felt internal and individual experience of gender, which may or may not correspond with the sex assigned at birth, including the personal sense of the body (which may involve, if freely chosen, modification of

---

59. *Yogyakarta Principles*, 6.

60. For example, a summary comment in the preamble describes the authors' collective feeling about the experience of sexual minorities: "Disturbed that violence, harassment, discrimination, exclusion, stigmatisation and prejudice are directed against persons in all regions of the world because of their sexual orientation or gender identity, that these experiences are compounded by discrimination on grounds including gender, race, age, religion, disability, health and economic status, and that such violence, harassment, discrimination, exclusion, stigmatisation and prejudice undermine the integrity and dignity of those subjected to these abuses, may weaken their sense of self-worth and belonging to their community, and lead many to conceal or suppress their identity and to live lives of fear and invisibility." *Yogyakarta Principles*, 8.

bodily appearance or function by medical, surgical or other means) and other expressions of gender, including dress, speech and mannerisms.[61]

Numerous points of importance stand out here. First, the definition of sexual orientation is essentially contentless and defined merely by desire. It could in theory include pedophilia or zoophilia. The previous paragraph refers to "consensual sexual conduct," which would implicitly exclude such sexual inclinations or acts, but the problem is that the consent of children or of animals is not a transcendental imperative recognized by law or custom around the world: adults routinely make children do things to which they do not consent, from eating their greens to going to school, and cows do not consent to being turned into hamburgers. This is not a robust foundation on which to build a comprehensive sexual ethic.

Second, gender is divided from sex, as is typical in the post–de Beauvoir world. More interesting, however, is the explicit way that psychology trumps biology: the personal "sense" of the body is important, and if that "sense" is out of step with the person's "deeply felt" identity, then the body can be modified. So the reality of the body is not as real as the convictions of the mind. And it is both irrelevant to identity such that it is no ultimate guide to who we are and is also vital to identity in that it may, if desired, be modified to fit the inner sense.

Third, gender is *assigned* at birth; it is not simply *recognized*. The language is fascinating and significant. Recognition would be an act of mimesis, of course, acknowledging an inherent authority in nature. Now the birth certificate involves merely a provisional and corrigible judgment based on empirical observation, presumably part of the oppressive state policing of sexuality that lies at the core of the problem that *The Yogyakarta Principles* seeks to address.[62]

The notion of self-definition that the preamble assumes is made explicit in principle 3, "The Right to Recognition before the Law":

---

61. *Yogyakarta Principles*, 8.

62. Cf. the language of gender "confirmation" surgery now used to refer to sex-change operations: "Gender Confirmation Surgeries," American Society of Plastic Surgeons, accessed July 8, 2019, https://www.plasticsurgery.org/reconstructive-procedures/gender-confirmation-surgeries.

Everyone has the right to recognition everywhere as a person before the law. Persons of diverse sexual orientations and gender identities shall enjoy legal capacity in all aspects of life. Each person's self-defined sexual orientation and gender identity is integral to their personality and is one of the most basic aspects of self-determination, dignity and freedom.[63]

This statement is both consistent with the modern notion of selfhood as a subjective psychological construct and also deeply problematic in several ways. First, while few if any would disagree that all persons should be equal before the law, the close connection of personhood with self-determined sexual identity renders personhood so subjective and plastic that the results in terms of formulating and applying the law would seem vulnerable to precisely the same subjectivity and plasticity.

Second, there are no limits set for what does and does not constitute acceptable sexual orientation. Here, of course, the issue of the dialogical nature of selfhood and of the *Sittlichkeit* of society is important. For all the principles' emphasis on self-determination, they operate with a tacit understanding of identity shaped by the wider world. This tacit understanding prioritizes sexuality and gender while at the same time setting limits for how these can be constructed.

In this area, *The Yogyakarta Principles* would seem vulnerable to Camille Paglia's criticism of liberal Christian approaches to sexuality. In 1991, a study committee of the Presbyterian Church (USA) produced a report on human sexuality titled *Keeping Body and Soul Together*.[64] Paglia, a lesbian feminist, subjected the report to withering, hilarious, and devastating critique, in the course of which she raised the pointed question of what limits of social acceptability were presupposed in the report's argument:

We can move tender, safe, clean, hand-holding gays and lesbians to the center—but not, of course, pederasts, prostitutes, strippers, pornographers, or sadomasochists. And if we're going to learn from the marginalized, what

---

63. *Yogyakarta Principles*, 11.

64. Presbyterian Church (USA), *Keeping Body and Soul Together* (Louisville, 1991), https://www.pcusa.org/site_media/media/uploads/_resolutions/human-sexuality1991.pdf. The General Assembly did not adopt the report, and so it has no official status within the denomination.

about drug dealers, moonshiners, Elvis impersonators, string collectors, Mafiosi, foot fetishists, serial murderers, cannibals, Satanists, and the Ku Klux Klan? I'm sure they'll all have a lot to say. The committee gets real prudish real fast when it has to deal with sexuality outside its feminist frame of reference: "Incest is abhorrent and abhorred," it flatly declares. I wrote in the margin, "No lobbyists, I guess!"[65]

Times have changed since 1991. Pornography is today mainstream, and sadomasochism would seem to be moving in that direction. Prostitution is now routinely called sex work. But Paglia's underlying point is still valid: the limits of acceptable sexual identity—even the prioritizing of sex as identity over other things, such as religion—is intrinsically arbitrary, even if historically explicable. As I have argued, there is a road that goes from the psychologizing of the self that Rousseau advocates to the sexual revolution of Reich and Marcuse and others. Yet the road traveled is not a necessary one. Psychologized identity could have taken other forms, and politics could have adopted other priorities. Further, as Freud indicated, the limits of sexual tolerance are really the limits of cultural taste. And *The Yogyakarta Principles* is no exception to this. It operates within the sexual tastes of our day and clearly assumes the stability of the legitimate limits of sexual identity even as it provides no foundation on which such stability can be based. It uncritically reflects and reinforces the intuitions of the modern social imaginary.

Perhaps the most fascinating of *The Yogyakarta Principles*, however, is principle 24, "The Right to Found a Family":

> Everyone has the right to found a family, regardless of sexual orientation or gender identity. Families exist in diverse forms. No family may be subjected to discrimination on the basis of the sexual orientation or gender identity of any of its members.[66]

Here a number of factors come together. First, the whole notion of a "right" to found a family is interesting. No rationale for this right is

---

65. Camille Paglia, "The Joy of Presbyterian Sex," in *Sex, Art, and American Culture: Essays* (New York: Vintage, 1992), 31.

66. *Yogyakarta Principles*, 27.

given, but it seems safe to assume that the authors regard having a family as a key step in normalizing nonheterosexual sexual identities because presumably having a family is a key means of being recognized within society. This in turn points to the function of the family as being primarily therapeutic: it is about the sense of psychological well-being of the parents rather than any broader necessary social function that such marriages would fulfill.

Second, we see the connection between the emerging moral imperatives of the sexual revolution and the possibilities created by science. In the proposal contained in principle 24, the authors assert that states will take all necessary measures to ensure access to adoption and "assisted procreation."[67] What nature has declared impossible—that two men or two women might conceive a child together—technology has made possible, and the sexual revolution has then made imperative.

Third, we see the logical sleight of hand that has become standard in debates about sexual identity and a normative concept of family. Families, we are told, exist in diverse forms. True, but that diversity has always been somewhat limited because of its deep connections to biology and to a basic binary distinction between male and female. On the basis of the highly subjective notion of selfhood and identity with which *The Yogyakarta Principles* operates, it is hard to see any limits to the use of the term "family" and therefore any limits to the claims of rights made by any social grouping whatsoever that one day decides that it constitutes a legitimate family.

With *The Yogyakarta Principles*, therefore, the basic ideology of transgenderism finds an influential political codification. The LGBTQ+ community may have celebrated the fiftieth anniversary of the Stonewall Riots in 2019, but it is very clear that the world in which we now operate is well beyond—and even at points inimical to—the rather traditional sexual categories of 1969.

---

67. *Yogyakarta Principles*, 27.

Concluding Thoughts

As even this brief chapter makes clear, the LGBTQ+ movement is complicated in terms of its origins, its internal dynamics, and its public ambitions. What might seem to be a unified community to those on the outside is actually a phenomenon that is the product more of its various constituent elements sharing common ideological and political enemies than of any strong internal coherence. It is also clear that its drive to inclusion ironically involves significant elements of exclusion—for example, those who affirm the normative nature of heterosexuality and those feminists who consider the female body to be decisive for their identity. But how does the LGBTQ+ movement fit into the broader categories that inform my narrative?

It is noteworthy that the lack of internal coherence of the LGBTQ+ movement makes it a poster child for the current age. As a political entity, it is truly an anticulture: it is defined negatively, by its rejection of past norms and the destruction and erasure of the same. Given the past hostility of the L and the G toward each other, it even involves a significant act of cultural amnesia relative to its own history. And it is a deathwork because it uses the idioms of past cultures based on sacred order (most obviously the language of marriage, love, and family) to undermine and destabilize those past orders by profaning their content and shattering their meaning. To separate gender from sex or to define marriage as a union between two (or more) people of the same sex is not to expand the traditional definitions of these things; it is to abolish them in their entirety. And the most honest advocates of LGBTQ+ thought are very clear about this.[68]

It is also clear that the alliance between the L and the G in the 1980s was central to how the movement has subsequently developed. By accepting a common cause with male homosexuals, lesbians effectively relativized the elements of feminism that had previously led them to see

---

68. See, for example, the debate within the LGBTQ+ community about the inclusion of BDSM (bondage, discipline/domination, sadism/submission, masochism) in Pride marches: Chingy L, "Why Kink, BDSM, and Leather Should Be Included at Pride," *Them*, June 17, 2019, https://www.them.us /story/kink-bdsm-leather-pride.

gays as just one more function of male-dominated culture. That meant that the relationship between the bodily experience of being female and the psychological experience of being female was decidedly attenuated. Viewed through the narrative of this book, psychological categories effectively trumped any notion of some kind of innate, physical nature. The way was thus open for the addition of the T, even though the very presuppositions of the T—a denial of the male-female binary and an assertion of gender as a fluid concept detached from physiology—ran directly counter to the assumptions of the L and the G. Victimhood and destabilizing the heterosexual norms of Western society provided sufficiently strong glue to bind the alliance together.

In uniting such disparate movements as the L, the G, and the T, the LGBTQ+ community repudiates the significance of the body for selfhood. To make room for the T, female experience tied specifically to the female body has to be set aside as an irrelevance to what it means to be a woman. The main casualty in this is traditional feminism, as the violent rhetoric surrounding TERFs and the fall from grace of once-revered figures such as Germaine Greer now indicate. But using Rieff's categories, this is also arguably another aspect of what makes the LGBTQ+ movement an anticulture. For Rieff, repudiation of the past as an authority is the decisive element here. And what more dramatic act of such repudiation can the individual attain than the rejection of the significance of one's own body for one's identity? When Caitlyn Jenner speaks of Bruce today, it is as if she is speaking of someone else, someone disconnected from who she is. Yes, she was Bruce—but Bruce was simply a mask, an act, a way of concealing who she really was from the public. Only in eliminating Bruce could Caitlyn be who she truly always has been.

Janice Raymond makes precisely this point about history and biology in the preface to the 1994 edition of *Transsexual Empire*:

> My view is that . . . the male-to-female transsexual is a "fantastic woman," the incarnation of a male fantasy of feeling like a woman trapped in a man's body, the fantasy rendered flesh by a further male medical fantasy

of surgically fashioning a male body into a female one. It is this female reality that the surgically-constructed woman does not possess, not because women innately carry some essence of femininity but *because these men have not had to live in a female body with all the history that entails. It is that history that is basic to female reality, and yes, history is based to a certain extent on female biology.*[69]

Raymond's use of the language of history here is telling: transgenderism is the repudiation of the significance of history, an intentional act of cultural—and personal—amnesia. In a passage reminiscent of Rieff, Germaine Greer makes the same point in more specific terms:

> There is a witness to the transsexual's script, a witness who is never consulted. She is the person who built the transsexual's body of her own flesh and brought it up as her son or daughter, the transsexual's worst enemy, his/her mother. Whatever else it is gender reassignment is an exorcism of the mother.[70]

One could expand Greer's point to include both parents: transgenderism involves the exorcism, or erasure, of parents in general, for they play no role in the identity of the transgender person at his or her most fundamental level of being beyond actualizing his or her mere existence.

Then there is the fact that the movement claims to be able to bend reality to its will, or, perhaps more accurately, denies the existence of a natural authority and thereby arrogates to itself the right to create that reality. Again, transgenderism is the most radical form of this mentality: my identity is entirely my own creation; to quote from the Boston Women's Health Book Collective in 2011, "I claim the right to choose my ultimate gender."[71] Here the move that Charles Taylor notes as characteristic of one major current of modernity—that which makes the world a place of poiesis rather than mimesis—seems to find its most extreme expression to date. Even the chromosomal coding of every single cell of a person's body has no final significance for those who, to repeat,

---

69. Raymond, *Transsexual Empire*, xx; emphasis mine.
70. Greer, *Whole Woman*, 80.
71. Health Book Collective, *Our Bodies, Ourselves*, 78.

claim the right to choose their ultimate gender. Yet transgenderism is only the latest and most extreme form of this move; it stands in obvious continuity with the antimetaphysical thought of the nineteenth century, most notably Friedrich Nietzsche. Transgenderism is a symptom, not a cause. It is not the reason why gender categories are now so confused; it is rather a function of a world in which the collapse of metaphysics and of stable discourse has created such chaos that not even the most basic of binaries, that between male and female, can any longer lay claim to meaningful objective status. And the roots of this pathology lie deep within the intellectual traditions of the West.

The contemporary debates surrounding LGBTQ+ also offer evidence of Alasdair MacIntyre's contention that ethical debate today is not about reasoning from commonly accepted premises but rather about the expression of emotional preferences. It is striking, for example, how much the Boston Women's Health Book Collective depends in their standard text, *Our Bodies, Ourselves*, on personal anecdotes and narratives for establishing particular points. Not discursive reasoning but individual stories of suffering and of affirmation carry the book's overall arguments. And the real poker tell here is the violence of the language applied to those feminists like Raymond and Greer who reject the idea that men can become women—as if merely throwing the words *essentialism* and *metaphysics* at opponents is now considered enough in a post-Nietzsche world to expose them as manipulative frauds motivated simply by hate.

For example, in the article on Raymond at the (ironically named?) website RationalWiki, she is variously accused of "virulent transphobia," "attacks on transsexual people," "hate speech," and being a "bigot."[72] The author provides no actual argument or evidence for these serious claims against a substantial intellectual. And perhaps more significant than the routine nastiness of web discourse is the gradual entry into scholarly works of the derogatory term TERF as a legitimate means of describing feminists who argue for the significance of biological sex in the oppression and liberation of women. For example, two articles in

---

72. "Janice Raymond," RationalWiki, accessed July 19, 2019, https://rationalwiki.org/wiki/Janice _Raymond.

Philosophy and Phenomenological Research use the term to describe individuals being critiqued, an act that elicited an outcry from a number of feminist academics who claimed that the term was "at worst a slur and at best derogatory."[73] The journal editor's response was that

> [the] consensus view [among the journal editors] was that though the term in question might evolve to become a slur, the denigrating uses that you have exhibited are on a par with denigrating uses of "Jew" and many other terms, and quite compatible with its having a descriptive meaning.[74]

One can only respond by saying that this consensus is not one shared by vast tracts of the internet. And unlike the term Jew, TERF is not used as a form of self-designation by feminists who reject transgenderism. Nor is it an argument that would find any favor if the debate was about a term that some regarded as a racial slur. What is clear is that those feminists (and others) who deny the claims of transgenderism will find that they will be dismissed on the basis of alleged animus, not on the basis of argument. The agreed rational basis for debate is gone. All that is left is emotional preference.

Finally, perhaps the most significant social aspect of transgenderism is the way it provides the latest and most potent reason for the dissolution of the traditional family. By the beginning of the twenty-first century, the psychologizing of the self, the sexualizing of psychology, and the politicizing of sex had all played significant roles in the abolition of the prepolitical. If sex is politics and children are sexual, then children's sexuality is political too. And transgenderism adds a dimension to that reality that goes far beyond that created by lesbianism, homosexuality, and bisexuality. With transgenderism, identity is almost entirely internalized, so that in theory a parent does not necessarily know whether a particular child is a son or a daughter. Such thinking not only places huge responsibility

---

73. Sophie Allen, Elizabeth Finneron-Burns, Jane Clare Jones, Holly Lawford-Smith, Mary Leng, Rebecca Reilly-Cooper, and Rebecca Simpson, "Derogatory Language in Philosophy Journal Risks Increased Hostility and Diminished Discussion," *Daily Nous*, August 27, 2018, http://dailynous.com /2018/08/27/derogatory-language-philosophy-journal-hostility-discussion/.

74. Allen et al., "Derogatory Language."

on the shoulders of the child ("Only you can decide who you are; not your father, not your mother, nor even your own body can give you any help here . . ."), it also places potentially huge power in the hands of the government, of the medical profession, and of the various lobby groups to whose tune they tend to dance. Transgenderism is not just a personal matter for those involved; it is not an example of something that, as Thomas Jefferson said, "neither picks my pocket nor breaks my leg"; it is also a political matter of far-reaching consequence for society in general. *The Yogyakarta Principles* makes that much patently obvious.

Reflections on the Triumphs
of the Revolution

In my vain life I have seen everything.

ECCLESIASTES 7:15

There are many aspects of modern society that I could have chosen to make the basic point of part 4. I could have looked at art and architecture, how the former now delights in the mockery and repudiation of the hallowed forms of the past and traditional canons of beauty and how the latter seems to specialize in buildings whose aesthetic appeal is as short lived as the materials from which they are constructed—perfect metaphors for, and products of, an age in which the satisfactions of the present moment are of overriding importance. I might have highlighted the crisis in confidence in the nation-state as a unit of political organization in a world in which individualism corrodes older notions of national identity from within and globalization makes national governments increasingly impotent to address the most pressing economic problems of the day. I could have discussed the way that Twitter, Instagram, and You-Tube have created a world in which life is performance art or the manner in which reality television projects the idea that outward expression of inward thoughts and feelings, however crude, is a sign of authenticity. Had I done so, I might have traced its influence even on our cultural elites, among whom, for example, politicians speaking with profanity is now considered evidence of integrity, a performance of authenticity, and openness about sexual preferences (at least those lionized by the *Sittlichkeit* of our culture) is an electoral asset. The days when the ideal politician was someone of reserve and outward discipline—when, for example, the mere existence of the phrase "expletive deleted" in transcripts of confidential discussions provoked public dismay—are long gone. Life in the world of the expressive individual now involves the public performance of what were once considered the more shameful elements of private character.

But in the interest of brevity, I focused on the triumph of the erotic in art and pop culture, on the triumph of expressive individualism and related therapeutic concerns in law, ethics, and education, and on the triumph of transgenderism as the latest logical move in the politics of the sexual revolution. And my central point is this: each of these phenomena is a symptomatic part of a larger cultural whole that is made up of the numerous pathologies I outlined in part 1 and for which I provided a selective history in parts 2 and 3. The individualism, the psychologized view of reality, the therapeutic ideals, the cultural amnesia, and the pansexuality of our present age are closely intertwined, and each can be properly understood only when set in the larger context of which the others are a significant part. One cannot, for example, address the issue of gay marriage without understanding the legal judgments that preceded *Obergefell.* And one cannot understand those without some knowledge of the wider impact of expressive individualism and therapeutic concerns on American society. Nor can one do so without reckoning with the way that sex and psychology have played a role in the framing of political issues since the 1960s. And to do any of these things properly, one must go back to the earlier influence of men such as Rousseau and the Romantics, Marx and Freud.

To address these questions from a Rieffian perspective, what this present age represents is an anticulture, a repudiation of the various regulations and regulative practices that characterized Western society until recently—particularly, though not exclusively, in the realm of sexual ethics. Behind this repudiation lies a deeper rejection, that of any and every sacred order on which they might be grounded, whether it be that provided by a formal religion, such as Christianity, or a commitment to some broader philosophical metaphysics, such as that found in Immanuel Kant. The result is a world that has accepted the challenge of Nietzsche's madman, to remake value and meaning in the wake of the death—indeed, the killing—of the Christian God, or, indeed, of any god. The repudiation not only of history but of any authority that might pose a challenge to the present—even the authority of physically determined sex in favor of the fluid concepts of sexual orientation and gender identity—is something that marks all the areas on which I have touched in this last section. And this is not simply a game for intellectuals and artists. Supreme Court judgments affect everybody. Pornography is easily available to all and communicates a powerful philosophy not only of sex but also therefore of relationships and even of what human beings are actually intended for. Peter Singer's ethics both reflect and shape the wider *Sittlichkeit*. Only a world that already imagines human beings to be nothing more than just another kind of animal would find his basic premises plausible. And such a world is then open in turn to being influenced with regard to its health care policies for both the very young and the very old. And transgenderism is set to change everything, from notions of privacy to the very language that ordinary people use in their day-to-day lives. The revolution of the self is now the revolution of us all. The modern social imaginary ensures that.

The long-term implications of this revolution are significant, for no culture or society that has had to justify itself by itself has ever maintained itself for any length of time. Such always involves cultural entropy, a degeneration of the culture, because, of course, there really is nothing worth communicating from one generation to the next. And with serious challenges to the idea that Western society is the intended goal of history—from Russia, from China, from Islam, and from the myriad political ideologies that have taken root on the internet—the anticultural nature of the contemporary West looks unstable and unconvincing.[1]

But as I noted in the introduction, this book is neither a lament nor a polemic. It is rather an attempt to explain how the revolution of the self came to take the form it has in the West and why that is so culturally significant. All that remains now is to offer some reflections on possible futures and possible responses to the cultural condition in which we find ourselves and in which we are all to some extent complicit.

---

1. In this context, the words of Leszek Kołakowski are sobering and akin to Philip Rieff's own melancholy judgment on our third-world culture: "To the extent that rationality and rationalization threaten the very presence of taboos of our civilization, they corrode its ability to survive. But it is quite improbable that taboos, which are barriers erected by instinct and not by conscious planning, could be saved, or selectively saved, by rational technique; in this area we can only rely on the uncertain hope that the social self-preservation drive will prove strong enough to react to their evaporation, and that this reaction will not come in barbarous form." *Modernity on Endless Trial* (Chicago: University of Chicago Press, 1990), 13.

Concluding Unscientific Prologue

A generation goes, and a generation comes,
but the earth remains forever.
The sun rises, and the sun goes down,
and hastens to the place where it rises.

ECCLESIASTES 1:4–5

I started this book by declaring that it was not to be read as either a lament or a polemic. Certainly, from the perspective of orthodox Christianity, there is no shortage of things about which I could lament or polemicize, from the casual pornification of the culture to the rampant fragmentation and crass worldliness of the church herself. And lamentation and polemic have their place: it is important to know that this world is not our home, that things are not as they should be, that we are strangers in a strange land, and that, to quote Gerard Manley Hopkins, "All life death does end."[1] It should be the Christian's natural state to feel that the times are out of joint and that we do not truly belong here. Yet lamentation can too often become just another form of worldliness, and polemic simply a means of making ourselves feel righteous. There is an odd masochistic pleasure to always decrying the times and the customs of the day, and in that sense, lamentation and polemic always run the risk of being less prophetic and more therapeutic in their motivation and their effect.

---

1. Gerard Manley Hopkins, "No Worst, There Is None. Pitched Past Pitch of Grief," Poetry Foundation, accessed March 11, 2020, https://www.poetryfoundation.org/poems/44398/no-worst-there-is-none-pitched-past-pitch-of-grief.

Yet it is a basic, practical truth that we live in this world at this time and are therefore required to respond to the problems we face in the context in which we find ourselves. In short, as any bridge or poker player knows, we have to play with the hand that we have been dealt. Simply lamenting that we are not holding better cards is of no practical value. In that spirit, I want to offer a few closing reflections on the significance of this book's narrative for the church today. Again, as I noted in the introduction, I am conscious that this book is (like all histories) a provisional, imperfect, and incomplete narrative. Particularly when it comes to our sense of selfhood, the intellectual narrative of the ideas that have given birth to our highly plastic view of human existence needs to be supplemented by a narrative of how the liquidity of our age intensifies this plasticity—the transient, temporary, and ephemeral nature of the institutions and the technology that shape our identity. I do believe that this age, while bearing so many analogies to those that have passed, represents a uniquely challenging time because of the coincidence of plastic people and a liquid world.

And thus I come finally to my concluding chapter, which, as is clear from its title, is intended not so much as the final word on the subjects discussed in this book—as if any word on the human self could ever be "final"—but rather as a prologue to future discussions. I have no privileged access to the shape of the future and therefore can offer only some preliminary suggestions as to how the arguments of this book might form a prolegomenon to addressing various matters as they manifest themselves in Western society in the coming years.[2]

This Secular Age

Central to my argument has been the notion that the LGBTQ+ issues that now dominate our culture and our politics are simply symptoms of a deeper revolution in what it means to be a self. The LGBTQ+ movement

---

2. Two books, by a Roman Catholic and an Eastern Orthodox, respectively, that offer extremely perceptive analyses of our current condition and that are also useful to Protestants are Charles J. Chaput, *Strangers in a Strange Land: Living the Catholic Faith in a Post-Christian World* (New York: Henry Holt, 2017), and Rod Dreher, *The Benedict Option: A Strategy for Christians in a Post-Christian Nation* (New York: Sentinel, 2018).

arises out of the sexual revolution, and the sexual revolution arises out of the kinds of philosophical ideas and trends that can be traced from Rousseau through the Romantics to Freud and then the New Left. Yet here is the rub: the LGBTQ+ community is only one example of that revolution in selfhood, albeit perhaps the most vocal and influential. The problem is that we are all part of that revolution, and there is no way to avoid it.

Charles Taylor has made this point at great length in his work *A Secular Age*, in which he notes that "belief in God isn't quite the same thing in 1500 and 2000."[3] There are numerous ideas underlying this statement, but the central issue is one of choice: we choose to be Christian today in a way that a Western European in 1500 did not. At that time, belief in God was the cultural default position, and being a member of the Catholic Church was the only option. In fact, it was not really an *option* at all: you were baptized a Catholic at birth, and there was no other church to which you could belong. It would have been impossible even to conceive of religious choice in today's sense in 1500.

Today, we do not simply choose to be Christians; we also choose what type of Christian we want to be: Presbyterian, Anglican, Methodist, Baptist. And within each of these subdivisions there are yet further sects—further choices—for which we can opt: Reformed, Arminian, charismatic. Then there are worship styles to consider, as well as a host of other subjective variables—where we feel comfortable, welcomed, supported. We can choose our churches as we choose a house or car. We may not have infinite choice and may still be subject to some material restrictions, but the likelihood is that we have more than one church option with which we can choose to identify.

Nor does this allow for any kind of Roman Catholic or Eastern Orthodox triumphalism, whereby the historical continuity and unity of the institutions can be presented as an antidote to Protestant fragmentation. To be a Roman Catholic today is to make a choice. Thoughtful Roman Catholics may object to this claim by pointing to the sacramental power that they ascribe to baptism. But that does not really address the

---

3. Charles Taylor, *A Secular Age* (Cambridge, MA: Belknap Press of Harvard University Press, 2007), 13.

matter of lived experience: every faithful cradle Catholic has still made a decision to live his or her Christian life as a Catholic amid a world of other possible options, from atheism to Islam to Bible churches and Pentecostalism. When it comes to how we think of ourselves, we are all expressive individualists now, and there is no way we can escape from this fact. It is the essence of the world in which we have to live and of which we are a part.

Acknowledging this reality is an important foundation for addressing those symptoms of this present age that we find to be more egregious. For example, it should immediately curtail any simplistic Pharisaic response that sees ourselves as somehow standing apart from the broader cultural context that has given us the LGBTQ+ movement. Their general culture of expressive individualism and of choice of identity is ours too. We cannot escape that fact, and numerous authors—Michael Horton, Christian Smith, and David Wells, to name but three—have chronicled the impact this has had on the church.[4]

It should also enable us to have a better understanding of why the sexual revolution has apparently moved so fast and, if anything, appears to be gaining speed, as transgenderism seems to be making such headway in the culture and as one after another sexual taboo collapses in the face of what often looks like an unstoppable tidal wave of sexual libertinism. The reason for this speed is that the underlying causes of these phenomena are deeply embedded within our culture and have been slowly but surely transforming how we think of ourselves and our world for many, many generations.

None of this is to argue that we should simply lament the situation, for expressive individualism is not an unmitigated evil. In some ways, it marks a significant improvement on that which it replaced. One of the aspects of the modern culture of expressive individualism is the emphasis it places on the inherent dignity of the individual. The more strictly hierarchical nature of honor-based societies, of the kind we find

---

4. Michael Horton, *Christless Christianity: The Alternative Gospel of the American Church* (Grand Rapids, MI: Baker, 2012); Christian Smith and Melinda Lundquist Denton, *Soul Searching: The Religious and Spiritual Lives of American Teenagers* (Oxford: Oxford University Press, 2009); David F. Wells, *No Place for Truth: Or, Whatever Happened to Evangelical Theology?* (Grand Rapids, MI: Eerdmans, 1992).

in feudal Japan or medieval Europe, contained much that a Christian might criticize, not least the notion that some human beings are worth more than others because of their position within the social hierarchy. With Rousseau's emphasis on the individual and the state of nature as the ideal, the shift to individual, intrinsic dignity is clear. And that is something with which Christians should sympathize. We are not supposed to regard the life of a poor person as of any less value than that of a wealthy or important public figure.

Yet it is here, in the idea of the equal dignity of all human beings, that one of the problems with the modern political project becomes clear. The idea that all human beings are of equal worth is rooted in the idea that all human beings are made in the image of God. The problem with expressive individualism is not its emphasis on the dignity or the individual value of every human being. That is what undergirded the fight against slavery in the nineteenth century and the civil rights movement of the 1950s and 1960s. Rather, it is the fact that expressive individualism has detached these concepts of individual dignity and value from any kind of grounding in a sacred order. This is what allowed Philip Rieff's grandfather, who spent time as a slave laborer in a Nazi concentration camp, to make his dramatic and counterintuitive claim that Hitler actually won in the West.[5] The West had become to him a decreated world, exemplified by its sexual chaos. It had come to reject the created, divine image as the basis for its morality, and there was nothing left but a morass of competing tastes. Whether it is the intellectual iconoclasm of critical theory or the more banal impact of consumerism, the untethering of what it means to be human from any kind of metaphysical framework has rendered the notion of universal individual dignity something that threatens to push the West into a kind of totalitarian anarchy, to use an oxymoron.[6]

---

5. Philip Rieff, *My Life among the Deathworks: Illustrations of the Aesthetics of Authority*, ed. Kenneth S. Piver, vol. 1 of *Sacred Order / Social Order* (Charlottesville: University of Virginia Press, 2006), 189.

6. The failure of liberalism and liberal democracy is the subject of Patrick J. Deneen's powerful book *Why Liberalism Failed* (New Haven, CT: Yale University Press, 2018).

Understanding the Anticulture

Closely connected to understanding the nature of our secular age as one in which expressivism and choice have triumphed and co-opted us all is understanding that we live in a Rieffian anticulture. The break with the past that modernity represents is decisive, for it cuts us off from any agreed-on transcendent metaphysical order by which our culture might justify itself. With no higher order to which we might look in order to understand human existence teleologically, we both are isolated from the past, where ends transcending the individual were assumed, and are left free floating in the present. Our world really is starting to look like the brave new world described by Aldous Huxley, a place where life is lived merely for the present, where the pleasures of the immediate moment—whether produced by artificial means (drugs, consumption, virtual reality) or by sterile sex—are the only things that truly matter.[7]

This is the world of emotivism and the world of deathworks. To take the former, the reason why ethical and political discussions are so acrimonious and futile today is that there is no commonly accepted foundation on which such discussions might constructively take place. That the key issues in American society are now decided by the law courts is a function of this disconnect: democratic processes are regarded as having less and less legitimacy, given that winning at the ballot box might simply indicate to the losing side that the majority of the electorate are hate-filled bigots of the kind from which law courts are designed to protect people. To this, one might add the way that political discourse is marked by the pathologies, and mirror-image counterpathologies, of critical theory: there is a deeply therapeutic aspect to forms of politics that operate on a simplistic them-and-us binary and find easy targets

---

7. A key moment in Huxley's novel is when Mustapha Mond, the "Controller," bans publication of an academic paper, "A New Theory of Biology," because it argues for teleology on the basis of biology: "It was a masterly piece of work. But once you began admitting explanations in terms of purpose—well, you didn't know what the result might be. It was the sort of idea that might easily decondition the more unsettled minds among the higher castes—make them lose their faith in happiness as the Sovereign Good and take to believing, instead, that the goal was somewhere beyond, somewhere outside the present human sphere; that the purpose of life was not the maintenance of well-being, but some intensification and refining of consciousness, some enlargement of knowledge." *Brave New World and Brave New World Revisited* (New York: Harper Perennial, 2005), 162. Mustapha Mond clearly spots the connection between the nature of teleology and the therapeutic society.

to blame for the ills of this world, whether they be white heterosexual males out to oppress everyone else or LGBTQ+ radicals committed to the overthrow of civilization.

Christians can be complicit in this thinking. Careers are made, right and left, in Christian circles through adopting stances on matters such as race and sexuality that ignore proper historical analysis for frameworks built on a simple zero-sum game operating with the binary categories of power and impotence. In such a context, each and every opponent is simply an irrational hate-monger, seeking to present as natural a position that is simply a personal preference.

In this context, it is interesting to note how much of the debate about sexuality in Christian circles likewise tends to operate in terms of personal narratives isolated from any larger metaphysical or theological framework. Even in the church, personal stories have a powerful emotional impact that can easily transform the chief end of human beings into the personal happiness that stands at the heart of the therapeutic culture.

There are other aspects of the anticulture in which Christians are complicit. The routine use of sarcasm and insult in polemic may not be a monopoly of the present age, but given that such is now profoundly associated with a deeper cultural iconoclasm and cynicism than in the past, we might do well as Christians to think critically about how frequently we resort to it—especially when debating with other Christians.

At a very practical level, the way Protestantism has often failed to reflect the historical concerns of the church in its liturgy and practice, most obviously in the megachurch movement and the manner in which it has frequently adopted the aesthetics of the present moment in its worship is arguably a sign of the penetration of the anticulture into the sanctuary of historic Christianity. Christians today are not opponents of the anticulture. Too often we are a symptom of it.

In short, our response to the major issues of our day—particularly those associated with the LGBTQ+ movement and its demands—cannot be isolated from the wider framework of the anticulture in which we live. We cannot blithely accept no-fault divorce (in which we are too often willing participants), for example, and then complain that *Obergefell* redefined marriage. To address the symptoms adequately, we need to think long and hard about the causes, their wider ramifications, and our relationship as Christians to them.

Understanding the Debate about LGBTQ+ Issues

The argument of this book has two immediate implications for Christian discussion of LGBTQ+ issues in terms of the wider social and political context in which they occur.

The first is that these debates are not primarily about sexual behavior. Certainly, sexual behavior is something about which Christians should be concerned. The Bible does teach that the body has a proper and appropriate sexual use, and it does teach that sex has a particular significance. To use the body sexually in ways inconsistent with its purpose and to engage in sexual activity that does not reflect the biblical purpose of sex is wrong and to be clearly confronted as such by the church in her teaching and in her application of that teaching. But the LGBTQ+ discussion is much deeper than that because it connects to matters of identity, of who we think we are at the most basic level. And the problem is that expressive individualism, manifested as sexual identity, is the way the world shapes us all.

The second implication is that the reality and power of this shaping should not be underestimated, and we need to understand ourselves as profoundly subject to it. Our social imaginaries as Christians are often too little different from that of the culture around us. We can easily slip into using categories that are actually misleading and that militate against clarity on key issues.

An Irish teacher at my grammar school used to tell this joke: A rabbi was wandering the streets of Belfast late one night and was confronted by an armed member of one of the local paramilitary organizations. "Are you a Catholic or a Protestant?" the armed man demanded. "I'm a Jew," the rabbi replied. "Well, are you a Catholic Jew or a Protestant Jew?" came the response. Now, this may not be that amusing as a joke, but it makes an important point: societies have categories for thinking about people and identity, and a real problem occurs when those categories are simply not adequate or appropriate. That is the question that the church needs to ask about sexual identity: Are the categories that society now prioritizes actually ones that are appropriate? If the post-Freud taxonomy represented by the acronym LGBTQ+ rests on a basic category mistake (that sex is identity), should Christians not engage in a thoroughgoing critique of such and refuse to define themselves within its framework? Indeed, there is evidence to suggest that conceding the categories leads to unfortunate confusion.

For example, in June 2019, Christian publisher Zondervan released a book with the title *Costly Obedience: What We Can Learn from the Celibate Gay Community*.[8] Setting aside the questions that currently cluster around the legitimacy or otherwise of the notion of "celibate gay Christian," what is most interesting is the language of "cost" that is being used. Only in a world in which selves are typically recognized or validated by their sexuality and their sexual fulfillment—in which these things define who people are at a deep level—can celibacy really be considered costly. Further, only in a world in which sexual identities—and specifically nonheterosexual sexual identities—enjoy particular cultural cachet will the celibacy of one particular group be designated as somehow especially hard or sacrificial. Traditional Christian sexual morality calls for celibacy for all who are not married and chastity for those who are. It is, strictly speaking, no more costly or sacrificial for a single person not to have sex with someone than it is for a married person to be faithful or not to visit strip clubs and prostitutes—or, for that matter, for a person not to steal another's property or slander someone's good name. But that does not appear to be the case precisely because of how the *Sittlichkeit*, the moral framework, of our culture has been so shaped by the triumph of the erotic and the correlative overturning of traditional sexual mores. To abstain from sex in today's world is to sacrifice true selfhood as the world around understands it. It is to pay the price of not being able to be who one really is. And that is therefore costly—but only from a perspective

---

8. Mark Yarhouse and Olya Zaporozhets, *Costly Obedience: What We Can Learn from the Celibate Gay Christian Community* (Grand Rapids, MI: Zondervan, 2019).

shaped by an uncritical and unreflective acceptance of the categories of sexualized identity stemming from Freud.

Now, to be clear, the fact that the sexual revolution is historically unique in the way it presses sexuality as foundational to identity in a manner unprecedented in the past does not make the questions of identity and of desire that it raises somehow less real. In part 1, I noted Taylor's important insight, drawn from G. W. F. Hegel, that who we are is a dialogue between our self-consciousness and the world around us. The desire human beings have to belong, to be recognized, to be authentic is informed by the *Sittlichkeit* of the society in which we live. External environment is critical, and the desires that this environment creates can be both novel and very real. The person who is never parted from her iPhone might well line up outside the store at some early hour to obtain the latest model on the day it is launched. The same person no doubt experiences distress and frustration if her phone breaks down or if the network is unavailable for some reason. Both the desire for an iPhone and the feeling of frustration when deprived of the same, are real, even though they would have been unknown to someone in the 1960s, let alone the 1460s. Human nature may not change in the sense that we are always made in the image of God, but our desires and our deep sense of self are, in fact, shaped in profound ways by the specific conditions of the society in which we actually live. That iPhones were not available to Shakespeare does not make the desires associated with them somehow imaginary.

When we apply this to the sexual revolution, it should be clear that in the age in which we live, we are taught to be authentic in such a way that identity, recognition, and belonging are now deeply connected to the sexual desires we have and the manner in which we express them. It is, for example, not a surprise that the number of children and adolescents reporting gender dysphoria has grown rapidly in the last few years.[9] This does not necessarily mean that for centuries there have been significant

---

9. See Riittakerttu Kaltiala-Heino, Hannah Bergman, Marja Työläjärvi, and Louise Frisén, "Gender Dysphoria in Adolescence: Current Perspectives," *Adolescent Health, Medicine and Therapeutics* 9 (2018): 31–41, https://dx.doi.org/10.2147%2FAHMT.S135432.

numbers of transgender people who have been unable to express themselves, any more than the rapid increase of sales in smartphones in the last decade indicates that vast numbers of people in previous generations lived lives of inauthenticity because they were unable to post trivia about their lives onto the web while traveling to work or sitting in the waiting room at the doctor's office. But it does not allow us to dismiss these feelings as unreal in the way they exist today.

This all makes the task of the church extremely difficult at this point in time because the framework for identity in wider society is deep rooted, powerful, and fundamentally antithetical to the kind of identity promoted as basic in the Bible. It will not be a sufficient or effective response to the challenges of the day simply to pass resolutions or adopt statements on isolated symptoms. The church has to address the matters that the sexual revolution and expressive individualism raise in a far more thoroughgoing fashion, a point to which I will return. First, however, I want to offer some thoughts on the possible shape of the future.

Possible Futures

The deep-seated nature of our culture of expressive individualism implies that it is unlikely to be radically transformed or overthrown in the near future. Too many factors, from the consumer-based nature of the modern economy to the prevalence of internet pornography to the chimerical promises of technology, are likely to keep pressing our culture in the same basic direction that it has been moving for the past few centuries. In addition, the collapse of the authority of traditional institutions, most notably the church in all its various forms, would suggest that any return to a society built on a broad religious, or even a mere metaphysical, consensus is extremely unlikely. If sacred or metaphysical order is necessary for cultures to remain stable and coherent, then we currently face an indefinite future of flux, instability, and incoherence. This makes any predictions about the future extremely provisional, but there are four areas about which I want to offer some speculative thought: sexual morality, gay marriage, transgenderism, and religious freedom. Each of these topics is something the Western church has an interest in.

SEXUAL MORALITY

It is clear that the morality of the sexual revolution is itself in trouble at the present moment. It was built on the notion that sex was recreational fun and that, as long as the parties involved had consented, everything was permissible. That philosophy is now in deep difficulties. First, as the Boston Women's Health Book Collective pointed out in 1970, the kind of promiscuity promoted by the sexual revolution tended to favor men and actually turn women into playthings under the guise of liberating them. On the expectations of constant sexual availability and promiscuity promoted by the sexual revolution, and drawing an analogy between the revolution's impact on women's liberation and that of Reconstruction on former slaves in post–Civil War America, the authors of *Women and Their Bodies* declared,

> These alienating, inhuman expectations are no less destructing or degrading than the Victorian puritanism we all so proudly rejected. . . . We must destroy the myth that we all have to be groovy, free chicks.[10]

The pill and access to abortion may have freed women from the consequences of promiscuity, but even feminists realized that the overall situation was far more complicated than that.

Of course, most of us intuitively know that sex is more than mere recreation, however casually we might pretend to treat it. This is why sexual assault, even in today's society where almost all sexual taboos have been abandoned, is still regarded as heinous. As I noted earlier, if I slap a person in the face, I have behaved egregiously and may even be prosecuted for assault. But we all know that if I sexually assault someone, I have done something much more terrible. A slap violates the body; a rape violates the person in the deepest way possible. That point does not need to be argued; we all intuitively know that to be the case.

Second, the #MeToo movement has both pinpointed the difficulty of defining consent when there are disparities of power between the parties involved and also highlighted the fact that sex is more than mere recreation.

---

10. Boston Women's Health Book Collective, *Women and Their Bodies* (Boston: New England Free Press, 1970), 16.

Indeed, the ironies of the #MeToo movement are all too painfully obvious. It is spearheaded by Hollywood actresses, many of whom have made careers out of representing sexual activity on the screen as nothing more than a fun, recreational activity. And its very existence points to the fact that sexual activity is far more than that. Soap operas and movies may portray individuals hopping from one partner to another or recovering from infidelity in a moment, but reality has a way of catching up with us all. Further, #MeToo clearly cries out for setting sex within a moral context, and yet the only moral context its advocates seem able to countenance is one involving an increasingly complex and confusing approach to what is and is not consent. The notion of personal sexual virtue has been abandoned, to be replaced by heteronomous cultural dictates.

Where this will move in the future is hard to predict. Consent is not only a highly complicated notion, it also has equivocal status as a guiding moral and legal principle. As noted earlier, in our society, children are made to do all kinds of things to which they do not consent, from eating vegetables to attending school. Is the principle of consent, therefore, enough to prevent the advent of pedophilia as an acceptable form of sexual activity? And it would seem hard to argue against incestuous relationships between consenting adults using appropriate methods of birth control, if consent or the risk of congenital birth defects are the only bases on which one might object to them.

In short, the sexual revolution is in some difficulty at the moment, but there is little evidence that its contradictions will be resolved by a return to traditional moral codes. If the AIDS crisis demonstrated anything, it is that the discussion of problems generated by sexual behavior has been moved decisively from the realm of personal morality to the realm of technical solutions and civil legislation. When sex is identity, then sexual morality is a function of expressive individualism, not some greater theological or metaphysical reality.

GAY MARRIAGE

It seems likely that gay marriage as an institution is here to stay. Whether it has opened the door to a general collapse in marriage as a two-person arrangement remains to be seen. Certainly, in terms of its underlying philosophy, there is nothing to stop such an eventuality, but as I noted in chapter 8, the basic redefinition of marriage did not take place with *Obergefell v. Hodges* in 2015 but when Governor Ronald Reagan signed no-fault divorce into law in California in 1970.

Gay marriage also has in favor of its longevity as a social phenomenon the fact that our culture of psychological man and expressive individualism places great emphasis on aesthetics in determining what is and is not acceptable. Strange to tell, changing attitudes to abortion provide evidence of this. The general cultural tide has been turning against the most radical pro-abortion policies, and this is not the result of abstract philosophical pro-life reasoning winning the day but rather the effect of sonograms showing that the baby in the womb looks like a small person. Such images pull at the heartstrings and elicit an intuitive, emotional reaction.

If aesthetics and emotions work in favor of conservatives and Christians on the abortion issue, however, I would argue that the opposite is the case when it comes to gay marriage. Gay marriage has all the potent therapeutic rhetoric and images on its side. It is about love. It is about happiness. It is about allowing two people to commit to each other. It is about acceptance. It is about inclusivity. And to oppose it is to be against all those things. Given the premises of expressive individualism, to be an opponent of gay marriage is to be more than just a sour-faced killjoy; it is to act out of irrational bigotry akin to that which motivates racists. No less august a body than the Supreme Court of the United States made that point when it overturned the Defense of Marriage Act. Further, the Jeffersonian principle of toleration, that it "neither picks my pocket nor breaks my leg" and therefore I have no interest in opposing it, carries huge weight in a society that prizes individual freedom. I argue below that the way sex has been politicized means that, in reality, this principle is far from an accurate way of viewing gay marriage, but again, it is the rhetoric and the aesthetic impact of the rhetoric that makes the argument a powerful one. In a world in which emotivism rules, those whose language tracks most closely with the emotional temper of the time inevitably present the most persuasive arguments, even if they are not really presenting arguments at all.

TRANSGENDERISM

The transgender issue is, however, potentially quite different from that of gay marriage. I noted in chapter 10 that transgender people were not obvious candidates for membership of the alliance formed by lesbians and gays because of some basic philosophical differences between the groups. I also noted that some members of the lesbian and gay community object to the inclusion of transgender people in the LGBTQ+ acronym. In short, the LGBTQ+ alliance is not an inherently stable one. When and if the unifying enemy—heteronormativity—has been defeated, the coalition is unlikely to continue to exist in its current form. What shape it will take only time will tell.

Further, there are powerful countercurrents that press against the long-term normalization of transgenderism. Transgenderism is tearing feminism apart from the inside, again as I noted in chapter 10. As I argued there, this is in part the outworking of compromises required by lesbians when they formed an alliance with gay men in the 1980s. In the phenomenon of TERFs, in the attacks on traditional feminists such as Germaine Greer, and in the strange alliance emerging between radical feminists and conservative Christians opposed to transgender rights legislation, it is clear that traditional party lines will not hold in this matter.

Transgenderism also strikes at matters of personal privacy and rights in a way that more narrowly gay and lesbian ideology does not. School, workplace, and public-bathroom policy will affect everyone. More acutely, the issue of parental rights relative to a child claiming to be transgender is likely to prove very serious, bringing into sharp focus the relative status of the family and the state. The abolition of the prepolitical reaches its total completion with the transgender question, as even the physical body relative to individual identity becomes a highly contested political area—and, one might add, a highly psychologized and therefore subjective one.

This points in turn to the basic problem of biology. It is hard for non-scientists to tell which side is most driven by ideological commitments in its approach to the evidence of the connection between biology and gender, but nobody has to be an expert in chromosomal science to see the statistics relative to male and female sports. As of February 2020, the world record for the men's mile is held by Hicham El Guerrouj, with a time of 3'43.13". The women's record is held by Sifan Hassan, with a time of 4'12.33". In other words, no woman has ever come anywhere near to breaking the four-minute barrier for the mile, something achieved by the legendary amateur middle-distance runner Sir Roger Bannister in 1953. To put it more pointedly, no male student running only as fast as the fastest woman in history would be remotely competitive at the Division 1 college level over that distance. Indeed, had my own son identified as a woman in college, he would currently hold the world record.

The other factor in biology is the medical treatment that is now being deployed to allow transgender people to realize their identities. The long-term impact of hormone treatment and surgery is unknown, but the current state of the evidence suggests that such will not prove to be simple cures for the underlying problem.[11] In addition, the question of when and how to administer such treatment is vexed even within the medical profession. And it is here that the real Achilles' heel of the movement is likely to be found. It is easy to imagine that, in thirty or forty years' time, adults who were used as, in effect, experimental subjects for their parents' trendy gender ideology and subsequently had their minds, bodies, and lives traumatized by medical treatment, will sue their parents, the doctors, and the insurance companies who financed the whole mess. Without wishing to sound too much like a Marxist, it is quite likely at that point that capital will determine the future shape of the morality of gender ideology, and transgenderism will become a minority interest once again.

---

11. See the Williams Institute report by Ann Haas, Philip L. Rodgers, and Jody L. Herman, "Suicide Attempts among Transgender and Gender Non-Conforming Adults: Findings of the National Transgender Discrimination Survey" (Los Angeles: Williams Institute, 2014), https://williamsinstitute.law.ucla.edu/wp-content/uploads/AFSP-Williams-Suicide-Report-Final.pdf. Ryan T. Anderson offers a number of testimonies to the failure of transitioning in *When Harry Became Sally: Responding to the Transgender Movement* (New York: Encounter Books, 2018), 49–76.

RELIGIOUS FREEDOM

At a superficial level, the world of expressive individualism might seem to be a world that would inevitably be marked by religious freedom. Charles Taylor and others have argued at great length that the Reformation was the watershed that unleashed the notion of religious choice in the West and therefore laid the foundations for the rise of the expressive individual as the normative self. Before the Reformation, religious identity in the West was a given: one was a member of the Catholic Church from birth (or, to be precise, from baptism shortly thereafter). There were, of course, Jews and Muslims in Europe, and in theory, one could have chosen to leave the church and join these groups, but such was only ever a minority interest and impossible even in theory for the vast majority of the population. Only with the Reformation does religious choice become a possibility and then a distinct marker of identity.[12] The history of expressive individualism is therefore intimately connected to the history of religious freedom. Alexis de Tocqueville's own observations of the role of religion in the early American republic confirms precisely this point, that religious choice predicated on religious freedom is historically foundational to the American experience.

It is, however, increasingly clear that the idea of religious freedom is coming under hostile pressure in Western society and no longer enjoys the status of an unequivocal good in the broader social imaginary. There are a number of obvious examples indicating that this is the case. The opposition to the state of Indiana's Religious Freedom Restoration Act in 2015 was eloquent testimony to the fact that where traditional religious freedom collided with the perceived rights of the LGBTQ+ community, the latter was more likely to have the sympathy of big business and the media. So-called "woke capitalism" has changed the relationship between social and religious conservatism and commercial corporations. In the United States, court cases involving the contraceptive mandate in the Affordable Care Act and involving the provision of

---

12. On the relationship between religious liberty and the rise of modern notions of freedom, see Robert Louis Wilken, *Liberty in the Things of God: The Christian Origins of Religious Freedom* (New Haven, CT: Yale University Press, 2019).

cakes and flowers for gay weddings also indicate that religious freedom might well be understood far more restrictively in the future. Religious freedom and expressive individualism would now appear to be increasingly antithetical to each other.[13]

Why is this? First, there is a general decline in religious commitment in the West, which is particularly marked in western Europe but is also now a striking feature of American society. It would seem reasonable to assume that as fewer and fewer people care about their own religious commitments, so they will care less and less about religious freedom as an important commitment for society as a whole.[14]

Second, the *Sittlichkeit* of the West has come to see sexual identity as the key to the expression of personal identity. Therefore, any religion that maintains a traditional view of sexual activity and refuses to recognize identities built on desires and activities that they regard as wrong is by definition engaged in oppressing those who claim such identities. Furthermore, if the Supreme Court's judgment in *United States v. Windsor* is representative of wider social attitudes, then traditionalists only maintain their beliefs about sex and sexual mores on the grounds of irrational bigotry. In short, they are either stupid or immoral or both. In such a world, the idea that religious freedom is a social good is not simply increasingly implausible, it is also increasingly distasteful, disturbing, and undesirable. To put it differently, the social imaginary of the West is no longer that of the American founders, for whom religious freedom was regarded as a good that actually helped social cohesion; it is now regarded as something that poses a potentially lethal threat to that cohesion.

One might object that stories of religious persecution still strike a deep chord in the West. Tales of the persecution of Christians and Uighur Muslims in China and the very existence of the term Islamophobia

---

13. The ruling in Masterpiece Cakeshop, Ltd. v. Colorado Civil Rights Commission, 584 U.S. ____ (2018) is particularly interesting in this regard. Yes, the Supreme Court decided that the proprietor was not required to bake a cake for a gay wedding, but this was on the grounds that it infringed on his right to freedom of artistic expression. It was thus a victory for religious freedom but not a particularly strong one.

14. See Nathaniel Peters, "The Rise of the Nones," *Public Discourse*, August 18, 2019, https://www.thepublicdiscourse.com/2019/08/53246/.

seem to indicate some concern for the right to religious expression. Yet the actual situation is more complicated. In each of these cases, the perception is that a weak and powerless minority is being mistreated by a larger, more powerful group. It is not so much that Chinese Christians and Uighurs are religious as that they are a minority. The same applies even more clearly with talk of Islamophobia. It is very doubtful that many of the politicians in America and Europe would be sympathetic to Muslim views on women or homosexuality, but the deployment of the term Islamophobia is not intended to address the freedom of the Islamic community in these areas; rather, it is meant to highlight irrational and often racial prejudice against Muslims.

Neither of these issues—powerlessness and ethnic minority status— feature as part of the mainstream social imaginary with reference to the Christian religion in the West. There, Christianity is overwhelmingly white, has enjoyed huge cultural and political power, and is generally regarded (sometimes accurately, sometimes unfairly) as having misused that power, from the Crusades to more recent child abuse scandals. The truthfulness of such perceptions is irrelevant: these are the things that inform the social imaginary, as shown by a glance at the portrayal of religious conservatives in cultural products, from sophisticated literature, such as Nathaniel Hawthorne's *The Scarlet Letter*, to moronic cheap shots, such as the music video for Taylor Swift's "You Need to Calm Down."

With the *Sittlichkeit* and the modern social imaginary as they currently exist in the West, the prospects for religious freedom in the broadest terms of *free exercise* seem bleak. Indeed, the question of what exactly free exercise means is likely to be determined by the wider question of the nature and legitimacy of sexual identity. In Rieffian terms, the conflict between traditional religion and modern sexual identities is a clash—perhaps the quintessential clash—between the second-world culture and the anticulture of the third, so completely opposed are they at the most fundamental level. There is no compromise that can really be reached here because there is no way that the one can be assimilated to the other. They rest on completely different premises and are aimed at antithetical outcomes. Given this, it is hard to conceptualize a culture in which the rights of religious conservatives and the rights of those who identify as sexual minorities can both be accommodated. It is precisely because matters of basic identity, and therefore of what constitutes dignity and appropriate recognition, are at stake that makes a negotiated settlement impossible. To allow religious conservatives to be religious conservatives is to deny that people are defined by their sexual orientation, and to allow that people are defined by their sexual orientation is to assert that religious conservatism is irrational bigotry and dangerous to the unity of the commonwealth. That would seem to make the free exercise of religion, in terms of the individual's right to apply his beliefs to life outside the Sunday worship service, something that can no longer be assumed.

Whether the psychological and subjective categories that are embodied in *The Yogyakarta Principles* and that inform sexual orientation and gender identity laws will provide as sound and long-lasting of a foundation for American society as the freedom of religious exercise guaranteed in the First Amendment remains to be seen. Given the civil war among feminists over the transgender issue, the prospects do not look good—though history would seem to indicate that a high risk of disaster has rarely deterred enthusiasts from pressing ahead with their schemes. The possible future for religious freedom is one that looks far less robust than its past.

Whither the Church?

Given the rather bleak analysis above, what should the church be doing at this present moment? Briefly, I would suggest three things that should mark the church as she moves into the future.

The first is that the church should reflect long and hard on *the connection between aesthetics and her core beliefs and practices*. I noted above that one of the hallmarks of ethical discussion today is its dependence on personal narratives. *Our Bodies, Ourselves*, the feminist bible, is full of personal testimonies presented as incontrovertible precisely because they are personal testimonies—the highest form of authority in an age of expressive individualism. And this aesthetic concern reflects the perennial power of sympathy and empathy in shaping morality. I noted this characteristic in Rousseau and the Romantics in part 2, especially the way Thomas De Quincey reveals how mischievous aesthetics can be when detached from any broader frame of reference. We live today in a world that embodies the culmination of this tendency. As Mario Vargas Llosa expresses it, a central characteristic of our contemporary culture is

> the impoverishment of ideas as a driving force of cultural life. Today images have primacy over ideas. For that reason, cinema, television and now the Internet have left books to one side.[15]

The evidence of this upending of traditional discourse and thought is all around us. From the massive shift in popular opinion in favor of gay marriage to the simplistic bromides on both sides of the political aisle that now characterize views on complicated issues such as immigration and nationhood, the role of aesthetics through images created by camera angles and plotlines in movies, sitcoms, and soap operas is powerful.

The church needs to respond to this aesthetic-based logic, but first of all she needs to be consciously aware of it. And that means that she herself must forgo indulging in, and thereby legitimating, the kind of aesthetic strategy of the wider culture. The debate on LGBTQ+ issues within the church must be decided on the basis of moral principles, not on the attractiveness and appeal of the narratives of the people involved. If sex-as-identity is itself a category mistake, then the narratives of suffering, exclusion, and refusals of recognition based on that category mistake are really of no significance in determining what the church's position on homosexuality should be. That is not to say that pastoral strategies aimed at individuals should not be compassionate, but what is and is not compassionate must always rest on deeper, transcendent commitments. Christianity, as both Martin Luther and John Henry Newman knew, is dogmatic, doctrinal, assertive. The biblical narrative rests on (and only

---

15. Mario Vargas Llosa, *Notes on the Death of Culture: Essays on Spectacle and Society*, trans. John King (New York: Picador, 2012), 37.

makes sense in light of) a deeper metaphysical reality: the being of God and his act of creation.

If the church is to avoid the absolutizing of aesthetics by an appropriate commitment to Christianity as first and foremost doctrinal, then second, *she must also be a community*. If the struggle for Christianity is the struggle for the nature of human selfhood, then it is worth noting that Hegel's basic insight, so compellingly elaborated by Taylor, that selves are socially constructed and only come to full self-consciousness in dialogue with other self-consciousnesses, is of great importance. Each of us is, in a sense, the sum total of the network of relationships we have with others and with our environment. Yes, we possess a common human nature, but that nature has expressed—and does express—itself differently in different eras and cultures.[16]

This makes Christianity look highly implausible at the current time. If the message about the self is that of expressive individualism or psychological man, and if that message is being preached from every commercial, every website, every newscast, and every billboard to which people are exposed on a daily basis, the task of the church in cultivating a different understanding of the self is, humanly speaking, likely to provoke despair. Yet there is hope: the world in which we live is now witness to communities in flux. The nation-state no longer provides identity, as the globalized world makes it seem impotent and ineffective and as decades of being told in the West that patriotism is bad have taken their toll on the social imaginary. Many cities are anonymous places, and suburbs function as giant commuter motels. The loss of commercial town centers and the rise of the internet have detached people from real communities. Now bizarre phrases such as "online community" and "he pledged allegiance to ISIS online" actually make sense because we know

---

16. In this context, it is important to resist falling into the opposite error to that of the free-floating historicist relativism that underpins the radical understanding of selfhood pressed most obviously by the sexual revolutionaries. This is particularly important in the current debates over sexuality and gender. The temptation that transgenderism raises is to assert a hard essentialism whereby we absolutize a particular cultural form of masculinity and femininity (say, that of 1950s white middle-class America) out of fear of conceding too much to the transgender lobby. The answer to free-floating relativism is not the arbitrary decision to make the distinct preferences of our culture as a whole normative for all times, places, and people.

how the very idea of community has been evacuated of the notion of bodily proximity and presence.

One might indeed be tempted to despair at this point if it were not for the fact that human beings still need to belong, to be recognized, and to have community. Perhaps this is where the church can learn from the LGBTQ+ community, for, whatever moral disapproval we must have toward it, it was—is—a real community where real people look after each other in terms of meeting very real needs. And communities shape consciousness. There is a reason why Paul comments in 1 Corinthians 15:33 that bad company corrupts morals. Our moral consciousness is very much shaped by our community. And for this reason, the church needs to be a strong community. Yes, this may be hard in an era when the proliferation of denominations and churches has made ecclesiastical commitment potentially just one more form of consumer choice. But we have no power to change that general context, and we cannot allow it to excuse us from behaving as a community.

That brings me to my third point: *Protestants need to recover both natural law and a high view of the physical body.* Some will immediately object that natural law will not persuade the wider world to change its opinions about anything. I would concede that. My concern here is not primarily for the outside world but for the church herself. She needs to be able to teach her people coherently about moral principles. It is unlikely that an individual pastor is going to be able to shape a Supreme Court ruling on abortion (though he should certainly try as he is able), but he is very likely to be confronted with congregants asking questions about matters from surrogacy to transgenderism. And in such circumstances, a good grasp of the biblical position on natural law and the order of the created world will prove invaluable.

Connected to this, of course, is the importance of the body. Protestantism, with its emphasis on the preached word grasped by faith, is perhaps peculiarly vulnerable to downplaying the importance of the physical. But to tear identity away from physical embodiment and to root it entirely in the psychological would be to operate along the same trajectory as transgenderism. A recovery of a biblical understanding of embodiment is vital.[17] And closely allied with this is the fact that the church must maintain its commitment to biblical sexual morality, whatever the social cost might be. If, as Rieff claims, sexual codes are definitive of cultures, then an abandonment of Christian sexual morality by the church can be done only on the basis of a rejection of the sacred framework of Christianity and at the cost of the loss of Christianity as a meaningful phenomenon.[18]

One last comment relates to the issue of historical precedent. It is appropriate that Christians who acknowledge that they have a religion that is both rooted in historical events and transmitted through history via the church ask whether there is an age that provides precedent for the one in which we live. Nostalgic Roman Catholics might point to the high medieval period, when the papacy was powerful and Thomas Aquinas's thought offered a comprehensive synthesis of Christian doctrine. Protestants might look back to the Reformation, when the Scripture principle galvanized reform of the church. But neither period is truly a plausible model for the present. The pope is not about to become the unquestioned head of some united world church to whom secular princes all look for spiritual authority; Thomism is not about to unify the field of knowledge; and the Reformation unleashed religious choice on the world in a manner that meant the Reformation itself could never again occur in such a form. If there is a precedent, it is earlier: the second century.

In the second century, the church was a marginal sect within a dominant, pluralist society. She was under suspicion not because her central dogmas were supernatural but rather because she appeared subversive in claiming Jesus as King and was viewed as immoral in her talk of

---

17. The best work on the body from a Christian perspective is John Paul II, *Man and Woman He Created Them: A Theology of the Body* (Boston: Pauline Books and Media, 2006). A useful introduction is Christopher West, *Theology of the Body for Beginners: A Basic Introduction to Pope John Paul II's Sexual Revolution* (West Chester, PA: Ascension, 2004). A fine Protestant approach to the issues is Nancy R. Pearcey, *Love Thy Body: Answering Hard Questions about Life and Sexuality* (Grand Rapids, MI: Baker, 2018).

18. On this topic, the statistics regarding the sexual habits of Christian teenagers and young people are very discouraging; see David J. Ayers, "Sex and the Single Evangelical," Institute for Family Studies, August 14, 2019, https://ifstudies.org/blog/sex-and-the-single-evangelical.

eating and drinking human flesh and blood and expressing incestuous-sounding love between brothers and sisters.

This is where we are today. The story told in parts 2 through 4 of this book indicates how a pluralist society has slowly but surely adopted beliefs, particularly beliefs about sexuality and identity, that render Christianity immoral and inimical to the civic stability of society as now understood. The second-century world is, in a sense, our world, where Christianity is a choice—and a choice likely at some point to run afoul of the authorities.

It was that second-century world, of course, that laid down the foundations for the later successes of the third and fourth centuries. And she did it by what means? By existing as a close-knit, doctrinally bounded community that required her members to act consistently with their faith and to be good citizens of the earthly city as far as good citizenship was compatible with faithfulness to Christ. How we do that today and where the limits are—these are the pressing questions of this present moment and beyond the scope of this volume. But it is a discussion to which I hope the narratives and analyses I have offered here might form a helpful prolegomenon.

Index

essentialism, 174, 358–59, 376
ethical discourse, as expressions of
    emotional preference, 26
"ethically sourced pornography," 286,
    293
ethical subjectivism, 122
ethics
    as emotional preference, 161
    exists within a tradition, 83
    rooted in sentiment, 119–21
euthanasia, Singer on, 316
evolution, 185–86, 188–89
existence precedes essence, 176,
    254–55
existentialism, 254, 257, 278
expressive individualism, 24–25, 46,
    50, 52, 64, 70, 79, 88, 96, 122,
    194
    and dignity, 331
    not unmitigated evil, 386
    and pornography, 287, 294
    precondition for sexual revolution,
        150
    in public performance, 282
    and religious choice, 386
    and religious freedom, 399–400
    roots in Rousseau, 125–26
    sexual component, 267
    as sexually expressive, 268
    and the therapeutic, 330, 380
expressivism, 86, 130, 388
external authority, 50, 154, 259, 333,
    337, 351
extramarital sex, 21

false consciousness, 250–53
family, therapeutic function of, 372.
    See also traditional family
Fascism, 229
fashion, and creation of markets, 94
fate, 75
feelings, 23, 330
female identity
    depoliticized by transgenderism, 360

and female bodily experience, 358,
    359, 361, 363, 374
and female psychological experience,
    374
feminism
    on body and personhood, 374
    civil war among, 397, 402
    and pornography, 285–88
    psychological transformation of,
        254–63
Feuerbach, Ludwig, 181–82, 215
Firestone, Shulamith, 51, 226,
    260–63, 354
first worlds, as pagan, 75
forgetfulness, 100–101
formation, by performing, 49, 50
40-Year-Old Virgin (film), 22, 299
Foucault, Michel, 36, 274n7
Foundation for Responsible Robotics,
    291–92
Frankfurt School, 229–30, 231,
    246n40, 267
freedom of religion, 399–402
freedom of speech, 55, 250–51, 252,
    325–28, 332, 337
free market of ideas, as illusion, 329, 330
French Revolution, 107, 132, 137,
    144, 147, 277
Freud, Sigmund, 12, 28, 42, 74, 107,
    201–23
    on children as sexual beings, 295
    on civilization, 127, 218–21
    on community as a good, 48
    on ego and superego, 170
    on female identity as incomplete
        man, 345
    on happiness, 203–5, 213, 222
    influence of, 202, 265–67
    pessimistic view of the world, 218,
        231
    on Reich, 243
    on religion as an illusion, 74–75,
        220